WEALTH, VIRTUE, *and* MORAL LUCK

WEALTH, VIRTUE, and MORAL LUCK

Christian Ethics in an Age of Inequality

Kate Ward

GEORGETOWN UNIVERSITY PRESS / WASHINGTON, DC

The publisher is not responsible for third-party websites or their content. URL links were active at time of publication.

Library of Congress Cataloging-in-Publication Data

Names: Ward, Kate 1983– author.
Title: Wealth, virtue, and moral luck : Christian ethics in an age of inequality / Kate Ward.
Other titles: Moral traditions series.
Description: Washington, DC : Georgetown University Press, 2021. | Series: Moral traditions | Includes bibliographical references and index.
Identifiers: LCCN 2021001962 (print) | LCCN 2021001963 (ebook) | ISBN 9781647121372 (hardcover) | ISBN 9781647121389 (paperback) | ISBN 9781647121396 (ebook)
Subjects: LCSH: Christian ethics. | Equality—Moral and ethical aspects. | Wealth—Moral and ethical aspects. | Poverty—Moral and ethical aspects.
Classification: LCC BJ1275 .W36 2021 (print) | LCC BJ1275 (ebook) | DDC 170—dc23
LC record available at https://lccn.loc.gov/2021001962
LC ebook record available at https://lccn.loc.gov/2021001963

22 21   9 8 7 6 5 4 3 2   First printing

Printed in the United States of America

Cover design by Jeremy John Parker
Cover art by James B. Janknegt, *Lazarus and the Rich Man*, 2011, oil on canvas, 40 × 30"
Interior design by BookComp, Inc.

For Matt
"What we would like to do is change the world . . ."

CONTENTS

ACKNOWLEDGMENTS

To finish a book—to fully think a thought about something that matters and get it down on paper—is a great joy. It takes time, space, emotional and material support, and education—privileges I do not take for granted, and which many people worked very hard to help me attain. Many of those people are not known to me, but many more are, and I want to thank them.

PhDs call our most important teachers "doctor-parents." I could not be prouder that my work carries the intellectual genes of James F. Keenan, SJ, Lisa Sowle Cahill, and Kenneth R. Himes, OFM, my dissertation committee at Boston College. Jim Keenan, as my director, made it his mission to shepherd a project that was mine and none other. Through his leadership of Catholic Theological Ethics in the World Church, Jim's students are part of a global community of scholars concerned with concreteness, mercy, and flourishing, just as he is. Lisa Cahill has a map of the entire theological enterprise in her head, and invites her students into the scholarly community by helping us fumble our way from inchoate starting points into the known world. Ken Himes is a fount of practical advice on navigating academia and has sponsored me in many wonderful opportunities to think about inequality with others. Each of these dear mentors shows through their lives how the work of theological ethics can be a vocation of joy.

I am grateful for the support and encouragement of so many current and former members of the Boston College faculty, and would particularly like to thank M. Shawn Copeland, Catherine Cornille, John Darr, Richard Gaillardetz, Yonder Gillihan, Kristin Heyer, Mary Ann Hinsdale, David Hollenbach, SJ, Mary Jo Iozzio, M. Cathleen Kaveny, Stephen Pope, and Andrea Vicini, SJ. Thanks to the members of the Boston College ethics doctoral seminar, which includes faculty and students from the Boston College School of Theology and Ministry, for helping me think through this book's work early on. My fellow BC students Meghan Clark, Jessica Coblentz, Marianne Tierney FitzGerald, Nichole Flores, Kate Jackson-Meyer, Chris Jones, Conor Kelly, Megan McCabe, James O'Sullivan, and Sarah Thomas were (and are) the most generous and enjoyable dialogue partners and friends. My work at Boston College was supported financially by the Margaret O'Brien Flatley Fellowship and the Clough Center for Constitutional Democracy. I am grateful to the Clough Fellows and the Center's director, Vlad Perju, for interdisciplinary feedback on this project.

I have been fortunate to think through the ideas that make up this book with many wonderful conversation partners. Thanks to the Theologian in Residence Program in Fort Collins, Colorado, for the invitation to discuss economic inequality in 2015, and to the members of the interdisciplinary faculty seminar on inequality at Boston College in 2015–16. I presented an earlier version of chapter 3 at the Society of Christian Ethics in 2017 and published it as "Toward a Christian Virtue Account of Moral Luck" in the *Journal of the Society of Christian Ethics* 38, no. 1, Spring–Summer 2018, 131–45. Thanks to all who offered feedback, particularly the Society's two anonymous reviewers. Thanks to Mark Doorley and members of the Villanova Ethics Program, particularly Mary Hirschfeld, for an enriching discussion of chapter 7. I thank Christine Firer Hinze for many opportunities, including an invitation to Fordham's Good Economies Conference in 2016. Thanks to Dan Finn for generative conversations about ethics and economic life.

My employer, Marquette University, supported my work on this book with a Summer Faculty Fellowship and a research leave funded by the Way Klingler Young Scholar Award. I am lucky to be part of a department whose members fully encourage one another in pursuing the truth. Bob Masson, Susan Wood, and Danielle Nussberger have provided invaluable leadership as Theology Department chairs. I was grateful for the invitation to explore economic inequality with the members of the Marquette Lonergan Project, led by Joseph Ogbonnaya and our dearly missed colleague, the late Robert M. Doran, SJ. Thanks as well to Marcus Plested and members of the department for the generous and helpful discussion at our department research colloquium. Josh Burns, Mark Johnson, Irfan Omar, Sharon Pace, and Jame Schaefer have been generous with advice and support. Deirdre Dempsey is a dear and wise colleague and friend. My fellow (relatively) junior faculty—Michael Cover, Ryan Duns, SJ, Conor Kelly, Drew Kim, Alex Martins, Jeanne-Nicole Mellon St. Laurent, and Aaron Pidel, SJ—so often remind me of the solidarity and fun to be found in our shared vocation as teachers and scholars. As Conor rightly points out, the research work of tenure-track faculty like us is possible because of the labor of many contingent faculty who do not have the privilege of supported time to write. During my time at Marquette, these colleagues have included Brian Bajzek, Gretchen Baumgardt, Mark Chapman, Nick Elder, Chris Gooding, Jen Henery, Sean Larsen, Jonathan Metz, Matt Neujahr, Karen Ross, Krista

Stevens, and Lee Sytsma. They have been unstintingly generous in enriching our department through their colleagueship, service, and scholarship as well as their teaching, and I am lucky to call many of them friends.

At Catholic Theological Union, I discerned my dream of being a theologian. I am grateful to so many wonderful faculty from my years there, including Laurie Brink, OP, Dawn Nothwehr, OSF, Robin Ryan, CP, C. Vanessa White, and Regina Wentzel Wolfe; Dan Lunney of the National Catholic AIDS Network; and the late Mary Elsbernd, OSF, who taught at Loyola University Chicago. At Harvard, I would like to thank Erin Driver-Linn, my undergraduate adviser, for teaching me so much about being a scholar. Warmest thanks to Jacqui Landry, then chaplain at the Harvard Catholic Student Center, for nurturing my dreams of theological scholarship. Thanks to all my dear siblings at Call to Action for introducing me to so many theologians doing such important work.

I am deeply grateful to Richard Brown, Hope LeGro, and Al Bertrand for the opportunity to publish with Georgetown University Press. Thanks to Kristin Heyer, who generously encouraged me in developing this book while on the Moral Traditions Series editorial team, and to the current editorial team members, David Cloutier, Andrea Vicini, SJ, and Darlene Fozard Weaver. Elizabeth Crowley Webber and Alfred Imhoff professionally shepherded my work to a finished product. I am especially grateful to the Press's two anonymous reviewers, and to David Cloutier for helping me incorporate their feedback. Humbling experiences are not usually thought to be pleasant, but the Moral Traditions editorial process has been an exercise in humility in its best sense of encountering reality, helping me better appreciate what I have been trying to say, and improving my ability to communicate it. This is all thanks to the generosity and charity of my editors and reviewers.

Most of all, thank you to my parents, Deborah Hormell Ward and Robert Ward, for their unconditional love and support, for helping me get the best possible education, and for showing me how to love God in the needy neighbor. Editors, if I nail word counts and deadlines, credit goes to my parents for those daily newspaper skills. Thanks to Dave Ward and Erica Van De Wal-Ward for camping trips, vacations in Queens, and delightful Zoom calls. Few people can say they have read a loved one's entire dissertation, but my aunt Mary Ellen (Moe) Ward shows up in this way and so many more. My dear in-laws, Chris and Bob Filipowicz, are an endless well of love and encouragement, not to mention dinners out and childcare help. Audrey, Anjali, Christie, Abbe, Andrew, Phil, Karen, Ian, Molly W., Molly M., and Lindsay: I am beyond lucky to have you as friends. Most of all, I thank my husband,

Matt Filipowicz, my first reader and thinking partner, who constantly inspires me to do the ethicist's work of envisioning the world as it should be. As well as a source of humor and wise counsel, he is a daily exemplar of the virtues of humility, fidelity, and justice. This book is dedicated to him. And now there's Malcolm, our beam of light.

WEALTH, VIRTUE, and MORAL LUCK

INTRODUCTION

Reframing the Problem of Inequality

We who are living through the unsettled twenty-first century increasingly recognize economic inequality as a political, social, and even moral problem. We might see inequality as a question of individual greed, as advocates imply when they point out that Jeff Bezos, the founder of Amazon, could single-handedly end world hunger. This observation is not just a quantitative assessment of Bezos as the world's wealthiest individual; it is a moral critique that seeks to blame the need of those living in global poverty at least in part on the vice of the wealthy who could meet their needs without suffering personal hardship.[1] In a different vein, when the hunger charity Oxfam reports that eight men own the same amount of wealth as the poorest half of the world, it does not intend primarily to critique those individuals' morals. Rather, Oxfam acknowledges that today's extreme inequality is shaped by national and international policies, and suggests that adequate moral will from many stakeholders could change the situation.[2] Both perspectives acknowledge that inequality is not simply a matter of statistics; it correlates with and causes many social ills for those at a variety of income levels. Because of these types of harm, which demand our moral concern, and because we often see it as rooted in moral failings, whether individual greed or societal indifference, it is common today to view inequality as a moral problem.

This book argues that our understanding of inequality as a moral problem is incomplete. It is not enough to say that inequality is caused by moral failings. We must also see that influence runs in both directions: inequality harms persons' moral development. In unequal societies, wealthy and poor people experience vastly different treatment by others and opportunities for action. These different life circumstances shape our growth in the moral life. Many people view inequality as a moral problem without, perhaps, considering its impact on their own ordinary lives. This book aims to make this impact visible.

From its very inception, Christian ethics saw a moral problem in unequal relationships between the wealthy and the poor. As Jesus's first followers began to remember him by sharing the Lord's Supper, the Apostle Paul charged them

3

with "doing more harm than good" when they followed the common social practice of treating the rich and the poor differently (1 Corinthians 11:17–34, NAB). Paul's forceful denouncement of economic inequality as "contempt for the church of God" immediately precedes his recounting of Jesus's institution of the Eucharist. Today, these words are proclaimed in Catholic churches the world over as part of the Eucharistic Prayer. A few centuries later, the early Christian thinkers called the Church Fathers took clear positions on the relationship of wealth and poverty, finding that wealth threatened its possessor's virtue and that the rich were better off helping the poor by divesting.

More recent Christian ethical perspectives have adopted the term "inequality," which labels, often to criticize, the relationship between persistent poverty and extreme wealth. Papal Catholic social teaching has evolved from viewing inequality as natural in the late 1800s, to recent popes Benedict XVI and Francis diagnosing inequality as a moral problem harmful to the common good. One common theological analysis of inequality is called the relational or theft model.[3] This view proposes that there is a relationship between the poverty of many and the wealth of a few—that is, extreme inequality exists because the wealthy steal their prosperity from others. Joerg Rieger sees this relationship in action when he focuses on the moral responsibility of the richest 1 percent. Other theologians offer practical solutions, such as Kathryn Tanner's call to challenge finance-dominated capitalism, or theological solutions, like Amaryah Shaye Armstrong's theology of dispossession. Elizabeth Hinson-Hasty, C. Melissa Snarr, and Rieger urge the potential of faith-based organizing to overcome inequality's harm to the common good.

This book shares the widespread conviction that inequality is a moral problem, but it takes a different approach. I agree with many concerned observers that inequality's harm to the common good impose moral duties on those who benefit within unequal systems. But in this book, I show that not only does inequality make moral claims on us; it also shapes us morally as we live within it.

If we pursue the intuition that inequality harms persons morally, we can identify a potential mechanism in the fact that inequality shapes nearly every sphere of human interaction, from political life to residential choice, even marriage and family patterns. Because we know that wealth and poverty result in differential treatment from others, we might hypothesize that inequality, too, affects us morally by shaping our encounters with others in unequal societies, and thus each person's sense of self. Philosophy offers the term "moral luck" to describe when a person's development of virtue is influenced by factors outside her control. This book argues that wealth and poverty function as moral luck to hinder virtue pursuit, and that inequality makes their impact worse.

Chapter 1 sets the stage by describing the face of inequality within nations and around the globe and its broad implications for communities, nations, and the world. Observers including the Economic Policy Institute, the World Bank, and UNICEF agree that inequality of both wealth and income is higher now than it has been in the past century, both globally and within many nations, including the United States. Inequality is not a natural phenomenon; it can be increased or decreased by choices made by societies and enacted through their governments. And economic inequality is a problem distinct from poverty, for three reasons. It correlates with and causes many social ills for those at a variety of income levels, with effects not reducible to poverty alone; it self-perpetuates; and—as this book shows—inequality functions as moral luck to harm virtue.

To further explore the premise that inequality affects morality, we first need a clear, precise account of what the moral life looks like. For many Christian ethicists (and others), virtue offers a language for this account. Virtues are persistent qualities of persons that enable them to live well with others and take action in pursuit of good goals. The theologian Lisa Fullam says that virtues are "anthropological truth claims," describing the human life well lived.

Chapter 2 describes the moral life through the lens of virtue ethics, beginning with a brief introduction to the renascence of virtue thought in Christian theology and philosophy over the past thirty years. Inspired by Fullam, I present a Christian anthropology of the person as constituted in community, capable of reason, persistently striving, seeking the flourishing of self and others, and sustained by God's grace. This anthropology suggests a list of key virtues that the Christian tradition urges persons to pursue. I draw on Thomas Aquinas and contemporary virtue theorists to provide rich descriptions of the eight virtues I consider throughout: prudence, justice, solidarity, fidelity, humility, self-care, temperance, and fortitude. Each virtue is illustrated with one or two exemplars from the Christian tradition and the contemporary United States. These virtues describe the well-lived human life in terms of relationships with others and with our selves—precisely the places where wealth or poverty inflects our experience of virtue pursuit. Virtue ethicists have long lauded their approach for offering the possibility of moral conversations that are attentive to particular circumstances, but only recently have they begun to explore the impact of differing life circumstances on virtue pursuit.

The impact of differing life circumstances on virtue pursuit is the next link in the book's argument. I am trying to show that inequality affects persons morally—but surely it does not affect us all in the same way? Inequality, by definition, means that some people have very different experiences from others. Because virtue is pursued in communities and through concrete actions, different experiences can translate into a different moral path. Moral luck is the tool we need to describe this reality.

Chapter 3 makes the case for a Christian account of moral luck and demonstrates how moral luck can accord with a Christian anthropology of moral existence in light of God. Amid rising attention to privilege and its impact on individual lives, many people question the idea that life circumstances fundamentally shape who we are and what we are able to become. Yet many of these same people debate whether to give or deny their children privileges that may "spoil" them, or display great respect for someone who remains hopeful despite hardship. Thus, there is indeed a broad consensus that life circumstances shape our moral lives, for better or worse, and indeed in complex ways.

Christian ethics does not have a traditional term for the impact of life circumstances on the pursuit of virtue, although some recent work comes close, but philosophers have developed a detailed account of this reality using the term "moral luck." In chapter 3 I detail the development of this term in philosophy since the 1970s, focusing on its feminist proponents, including Martha Nussbaum, Claudia Card, and Lisa Tessman. Tessman explains that virtues become "burdened"—that is, they do not contribute to flourishing as virtues are usually thought to do—when we cannot pursue the virtues without risking harm to ourselves. The chapter includes a detailed explanation of how moral luck functions in actual lives: through the social judgments of others encountered in our communities; through our own internalization of others' judgments; and through the ability to pursue practices, or the inability to do so. These three mechanisms—self-regard, practices, and communities—reappear when I explain how wealth and poverty function as moral luck, with inequality exacerbating the problem.

Although Christian theological ethics cannot adopt the philosophical approach to moral luck uncritically, a Christian virtue account of moral luck can be rooted in the theological tradition and can help express Christian virtue ethics' deepest concerns for the recognition of all persons' humanity and desire for their integral flourishing. Scripture and Thomas Aquinas bequeath inchoate accounts of moral luck to Christian ethics. Contemporary womanist theologians, such as Melanie L. Harris and Rosita deAnn Mathews, develop an implicit Christian account of moral luck that insists on oppressed persons' moral agency and integrity. This Christian ethical account of moral luck provides a tool to describe the impact of life circumstances on virtue pursuit while acknowledging both the pervasiveness of sin and the Christian hope for God's promised redemption. Indeed, moral luck occupies a crucial place in Christian virtue ethics.

So, moral luck describes how differing life circumstances affect virtue pursuit. It is clear that wealth and poverty are life circumstances that differ from one another—but how do we describe wealth and poverty? In chapter 4, I begin by exploring three definitions of wealth and poverty: quantitative, positional, and basic goods. Quantitative definitions, which define wealth and poverty by amounts in currency, reign in the social sciences. Positional definitions trade on our human tendency to social comparison. As an example of a positional definition, the Occupy Wall Street movement pointed at the richest 1 percent of people as those with the most outsize power, suggesting that the remaining 99 percent had more in common with one another than with those at the top. When it comes to moral experience, that a "1 percenter" leads a different life than someone in the poorest half is clear; less clear is that her experience differs markedly from that of someone in the richest 2, 5, or even 10 percent. I conclude that basic goods definitions, which focus on whether persons have meaningful access to what they need to survive, best capture Christian ethical concerns with human flourishing. Thus, in this book, I define wealth as *having more than we need*, and poverty as *lacking the basic goods of life*, or being able to meet one's needs only through constant and precarious *struggle*.

These definitions of wealth and poverty capture several morally significant dynamics. In contemporary economies, where most people gain their basic needs through work for wages, those with more than they need exercise control over those who struggle to survive. When I started reflecting on this, I realized that my own economic status, with a household income close to the US median, allows me to control others every day, and to take that control for granted.[4] I thought of the philosopher Peter Singer, who points out that the funds spent on nonessentials by middle-class, rich-world consumers could literally save the lives of the global poor, so that our thoughtless consumption condemns others to death. I found in this an echo of the Church Fathers, whose moral critique of wealth emphasizes that the surplus of the wealthy could meet the legitimate needs of the poor.

Wealth as "having more than we need" and poverty as "struggling to survive" are qualitative definitions that can apply in multiple contexts while still containing enough real content to serve a morally hortatory purpose. They reflect the dynamics of basic security and inclusion or exclusion from social life that are at the heart of Scripture and the Christian tradition's concern with wealth and poverty. These mutually exclusive definitions allow everyone who reads this book to identify their social location in terms familiar from the Christian Scriptures.

From here, it remains to interrogate how having more than we need, or struggling to survive, affects the pursuit of virtue. There is no neutral or default experience of economic inequality; it affects our life circumstances and pursuit of virtue differently depending on our place in the economic hierarchy. To understand how inequality functions as moral luck, we must first understand how wealth and poverty affect our pursuit of virtue. Two constructive chapters draw together resources from theology, the quantitative and qualitative social sciences, journalism, and memoir to give an account of how economic status can affect virtue pursuit for the wealthy and the poor. First, chapter 5 offers a detailed description of how wealth, understood as having more than we need, affects the pursuit of virtue. Drawing on a broad array of interdisciplinary sources, I proceed through the virtues described in chapter 2 one by one, assembling information to explain how wealth affects the pursuit of these virtues.

There are two major ways wealth affects the pursuit of virtue: it can become an end in itself, and it can endow a wealthy person with hyperagency. "Hyperagency" is the term that the sociologist Paul Schervish uses to describe how wealthy people experience greater power over their environment and the people in it than others do. Although inspired by Schervish's work, I use the term differently than he does. Here, hyperagency highlights the ways consumers with nontrivial discretionary income exercise control over poor workers and other participants in global markets. Those with more than we need also exercise hyperagency in comparison with the poor who do not have discretionary income. Though a third of US families cannot meet their basic needs on their incomes, more than 40 percent control tens of thousands of dollars or more in discretionary spending per year. And though many people in this group would likely not identify as wealthy, the discretionary income they control could literally save poorer people's lives, a key point in the Christian tradition's long-standing suspicion of wealth. My primary goal here is not to argue that those with discretionary income should use it to save poor people's lives—a case already well made by Singer and others—but rather, to examine the virtue impact on those who wield such power, no matter how they use it.

In addition to hyperagency, wealth also shapes virtue when it becomes an end in itself. Because wealth tends to improve access to practices, whether virtuous or vicious, it can also support the pursuit of certain virtues, such as the virtue of self-care. If I am right about wealth's impact on virtue, Christians can no longer claim that the proper attitude to wealth can make its possession morally neutral—or, in Augustine's phrasing, that it is possible to "have wealth as not having it." Those of us with more than we need must face and acknowledge the ways that our wealth affects our virtue and recommit to practices that cultivate virtue in spite of this.

In chapter 6, using the same interdisciplinary method, I assess how poverty, defined as being unable to meet one's needs or meeting them only through constant and precarious struggle, functions as moral luck. Although it is important to acknowledge the risk of stigma in investigating poor people's virtue pursuit, to avoid the question would be exhorting poor people to "pull themselves up by their bootstraps," morally speaking, without asking whether they are realistically able to pursue virtue and what, if anything, wealthy people can do to help. Caring for the bodily needs of those living in poverty is important, but so is concern for their moral lives, just as Christians are rightly concerned about the virtue pursuit of the wealthy. The voices of poor people discussing their own lives are key sources in this chapter, and I hope it is clear that the concern with poverty's impact on virtue originates with them.

As with wealth, poverty does not have a uniformly positive or negative effect on the virtuous life; it encourages the pursuit of some virtues and burdens the pursuit of others. I show that there are four major ways poverty affects the pursuit of virtue: through the cognitive impact of scarcity, which makes many ordinary tasks more difficult than they would otherwise be; by hindering access to certain practices; and by diminishing the self-regard of poor persons as societal disregard is internalized. Also, virtues are burdened when placed in conflict with the pursuit of other virtues, which is more likely to happen in contexts of scarcity.

The final chapter shows how inequality exacerbates the impact of wealth and poverty on virtue. Here I rely on all the work of the preceding chapters. I have argued that wealth affects virtue through hyperagency and becoming an end in itself, and that poverty affects virtue through scarcity, internalized negative self-regard, burdening virtues, and limiting access to practices. In this chapter, I draw on social scientific data and other sources to show how inequality increases the impact of these realities. I offer responses to the impact of economic inequality on virtue. These include practical economic solutions and theological solutions, including encounter, conversion, satisfaction with contentment, and renewed dependence on God.

Practical solutions can reduce inequality by redistributing wealth to the poor and can provide the space for theological approaches to work. For example, reducing economic segregation in communities can improve the possibility of encounter, the meeting of genuine selves that changes our view of the world and our own place in it. Structural economic solutions are vital to improve the situation of poor people in unequal economies and reduce practical barriers to their virtue pursuit, such as the burdened cognitive processing that comes from scarcity. Ultimately, virtue pursuit calls for dispositions such as conversion and recognition of our own dependence, spiritual solutions that no structural change can guarantee.

Reversing the segregation that often occurs when people with more than they need withdraw their lives from the poor is an example of a practice with significant potential to support virtue pursuit for both the wealthy and the poor. Deliberate integration is a practice that public economic proposals can encourage and one that Christian organizations—including schools, universities, and parishes—should certainly lead. When evaluating practical solutions from a virtue perspective, we should take account of their animating logic as well as their projected impact on inequality. I briefly discuss the proposal of a universal basic income, which Pope Francis advocates as much for its logic of unconditional human worth as for its promise for reducing inequality.

It is worth restating that discussing the virtue effects of wealth and poverty does not deny that people in both groups retain moral freedom. Christian believers already know that the world where we pursue virtue is tainted by sin, which affects each one of us, despite our best efforts. What I have tried to do is show concretely how this can manifest for rich and poor people in today's unequal societies. Acknowledging obstacles to our virtue pursuit might invite some to despair. Instead, I hope that this morally hortatory account of wealth's and poverty's impact on the moral life helps readers understand, with particularity, the challenges they are likely to face in their own lives and the necessity to depend on God for growth in virtue. Once we have understood our own moral luck and the shape it gives our virtue pursuit, we can see as never before the urgency of building a world, as Dorothy Day has said, where it is easier to be good.

NOTES

1. The Twitter account @HasBezosDecided tweets "Jeff Bezos has decided not to end world hunger today" every day. The account joined Twitter in July 2019 and had more than 103,000 followers in December 2020. @HasBezosDecided cites research by two international nongovernmental organizations suggesting that ending world hunger would require $11 billion per year over a period of fourteen years. Bezos' wealth is estimated at $200 billion. Laborde et al., "Ending Hunger." The critique makes the reasonable assumption that Bezos would continue to earn money through work and investments were he to donate a yearly amount that would end world hunger.

2. Oxfam International, "Just 8 Men."

3. Naudé and du Plessis use the term "relational"; Naudé and du Plessis, "Economic Inequality." Cloutier notes that some relational models envision inequality as theft; Cloutier, "Exclusion."

4. My family has more than we need on this income, thanks in part to a low local cost of living and the privilege of having no debt. I do not intend to imply that anyone with an income near the US median would necessarily have more than they need. See chapter 4 for more on basic goods definitions of wealth and poverty.

CHAPTER I

GROUNDWORK

Inequality is not a neutral phenomenon but is rightly viewed as a problem. It correlates with many social ills, including poor health and early death. Inequality self-perpetuates; absent significant intervention, inequality changes economic and social systems to make it progressively less likely that an unequal society will return to being more egalitarian. Finally, inequality harms morality.

Previous theological work on inequality has been relatively rare and diffuse. This chapter points out a lacuna in that work: theologians have yet to address inequality's documented effects on moral formation. Proposing a mechanism for this harmful effect, I conclude the chapter by pointing out that wealth and poverty carry powerful societal messages about persons' intrinsic worth.

THE FACE OF CONTEMPORARY ECONOMIC INEQUALITY

Today's extreme levels of economic inequality, observable within and across national boundaries, are clearly cause for concern.[1] An Oxfam International study recently reported that twenty-six billionaires own the same amount of wealth as the poorest half of the world's population.[2] In the United States today, as much as 50 percent of national yearly income is captured by the top 10 percent of earners, with as much as 20 percent going to the richest 1 percent. In periods that are now synonymous with extreme inequity, France's Ancien Régime and Britain's Gilded Age saw similar levels of inequality.[3] The economist Thomas Piketty suggests that the United States could set a record for inequality by 2030, with the richest 10 percent of earners capturing 60 percent of national income and less than 15 percent going to the lowest-earning half.[4] Within nations, economic inequality increases along lines of historical exclusion, such as gender and race. For example, in the United States, Black households earn less income and hold less wealth than white households, and racialized wealth inequality is much higher than that of income.[5]

Many countries, wealthy and poor alike, have seen inequality increase in recent decades. Since 2007, inequality has risen in the United States, the United Kingdom, and most Western European countries, as well as in the rapidly growing economies of China, India, and Indonesia.[6] "The world clearly seems to have entered a phase in which rich and poor countries are converging in income," says Piketty, with growth slowing in postindustrial regions—the United States and Western Europe—and increasing in countries like China and India.[7] In the United States, this has been touted as a positive corrective force, which could ultimately bring the majority of Indian and Chinese workers to lifestyle parity with Americans.[8] But the reality is not so encouraging. In those poorer nations for which Piketty was able to obtain data, patterns of inequality appear to mimic those in the United States, with the wealthiest 1 percent taking home about 15 percent of national income, compared with about 20 percent of national income going to the highest-earning centile in the United States.[9] This suggests that the profits being made in poor but rapidly growing nations like China and India are primarily benefiting a few rich individuals, leaving the majority of workers who contribute to the growth behind.

Among wealthy nations, the United States consistently ranks as one of the most unequal in the world.[10] For this reason and because I am a US citizen, in this book I pay particular attention to US patterns of inequality. Although inequality is sometimes understood as the natural outgrowth of freely functioning markets, economists detail numerous ways that government policies promote today's high levels of inequality. This view, shared by experts across the political spectrum, is paradoxically reassuring. It means that today's extreme inequality is not inevitable; nations have intensified it through their policies, which citizens of democracies can change.

According to Piketty, unique economic factors that significantly exacerbate today's rising inequality are the rising incomes of a small group of extremely well-paid managers; lower tax rates on the highest incomes; and government funding itself through debt instead of taxes. Piketty attributes an unprecedented increase in inequality in the United States and other rich nations since 1980 in part to the staggeringly high incomes earned by high-level managers at large companies, who were often able to set their own compensation without any clear correlation to their own productivity.[11] Changes in law that lowered the top marginal tax rate encouraged workers at this level to demand astronomically high wages and benefits.[12] Under midcentury tax rates, for example, a significant amount of today's extreme executive pay would have gone to taxes, leaving only a small incentive for companies to pay such high managerial salaries.[13] Similar increases in the number of highly salaried "supermanagers" took place in Great Britain, Canada, and Australia over the same period.[14] Piketty concludes, "The history of the distribution of wealth has always been deeply political, and it cannot be reduced to purely economic mechanisms; . . . the resurgence of inequality after 1980 is due largely to the political shifts of the past several decades, especially in regard to taxation and finance."[15]

Another political choice that amplifies inequality is the decision to fund the state through debt rather than taxation. For Piketty, following Marx, public debt is in some ways "a tool of private capital."[16] Instead of paying higher taxes to provide needed revenues for government, wealthy citizens who loan government money by purchasing bonds come to hold power over all the taxpayers, rich and poor, who are expected to pay it back. In practice, government debt is usually held by a minority of wealthy citizens and thus constitutes an inequality in power.[17]

Governments also exacerbate inequality through regulations that favor the wealthy at the expense of those who are worse off. Subsidies for sports arenas prop up professional athletes' salaries; taxpayer-funded bank bailouts provide vast compensation packages for some bank managers; and despite their important role in encouraging creative research, patent protections can enable usurious price hikes on prescription drugs. In fact, "it is difficult to identify any general category of the extremely rich that does not benefit substantially from government interventions," summarizes the economist Jeffrey Miron.[18] The economists Brink Lindsey and Steven Michael Teles, who identify as liberal and libertarian, respectively, call this "regulatory capture" and detail its scope in their 2017 book *The Captured Economy*.[19] As Miron mentions, "regulatory capture" is visible in government subsidies for financial institutions that incentivize risky investments and sky-high salaries for a privileged few.[20] Occupational licensing inflates the salaries of highly paid professionals, even as it functions as a barrier for lower-wage workers who want to improve their earning power.[21] Restrictive zoning protects the property values of "incumbents," people who already own, while keeping others from becoming property owners and accessing the many economic benefits of living and working in desirable, population-dense areas.[22]

All these examples of regulatory capture have regressive effects: they benefit those who are already wealthy at the expense of those who are not. For example, "the direct effect of zoning within any given city is to transfer wealth from renters to homeowners," Lindsey and Teles write.[23] Moreover, regressive regulations have a self-perpetuating effect: concentrating more wealth in the hands of those who are already wealthy enables them to continue to shape regulation to their advantage. But Lindsey and Teles hold out hope that increasing the conflictual, deliberative practice of US politics, even incrementally, can help limit regulatory capture and foster increased economic equality.[24]

The economist Dean Baker concurs with Lindsey and Teles that government policies play a substantial and poorly understood role in levels of inequality. Like them, he warns about the impact of policies that strengthen patent protection and support the growth of the financial services industry. Baker also notes that governments influence inequality when they set monetary and fiscal policy. Those policies shape employment rates, and low unemployment, by tightening competition for even low-paid jobs, reduces inequality.[25] Another factor in lower real wages, reduced public-sector unionization in recent decades, "can be explained both by direct changes in government policy and also a failure of the government to respond to changes in practices by private employers that have the purpose of making it more difficult for workers to organize."[26]

Governments also affect global and intranational inequality when they report income and wealth data transparently—or fail to do so. Piketty shares the disturbing finding that some governments of poorer countries, including India's, have recently limited the transparency of their income data, possibly attempting to conceal growing inequality.[27] However, even countries where transparency is official policy, like the United States, can fail to give a full picture of national inequality. For example, some reporting agencies group the top 10 percent of earners together, so that no more is known about their income than that it is above a certain figure. "The decision to ignore the top end is hardly neutral," says Piketty; "the official reports of national and international agencies are supposed to inform public debate about the distribution of income and wealth, but in practice they often give an artificially rosy picture of inequality."[28] Similarly, while the poverty rate itself has remained relatively stable in the United States since the 1960s, many families who were already below the poverty line have become poorer. This fact is obscured if one only looks at the official federal poverty level.[29]

A Harvard Business School researcher found that most Americans underestimate the true extent of national inequality: they think the United States is significantly more egalitarian than it really is. Furthermore, if they were able to influence the economy, most people in the United States would prefer that it be more egalitarian than they believe it is—in other words, they would prefer an economy that is far more egalitarian than the present reality.[30] This finding supports Piketty's claim that true transparency about inequality is an important first step in addressing it.

That so many would prefer a more egalitarian economy demonstrates the popular understanding that extreme inequality is unjust, and even harmful. Recent decades have seen increasing attempts across many disciplines to ask whether that is so. Should economic inequality be treated as a problem distinct from poverty? Experts increasingly say yes, for several reasons. Inequality correlates with and causes many social ills, with effects that are not reducible to poverty alone. It self-perpetuates, making unequal societies even more so. Finally, it interferes with the development of moral virtue.

INEQUALITY, AS DISTINCT FROM POVERTY, CAUSES MANY SOCIAL ILLS

Whether inequality should be regarded as a problem that is distinct from poverty depends on whether it is harmful in the ways poverty is widely understood to be. Poverty is viewed as a problem to be eliminated because so many other social ills tend to accompany poverty: poor educational outcomes, substandard living conditions, sickness, and early death. Many still ask whether, if a society were able to meaningfully address poverty—to raise the living standards of even the poorest people to a dignified level—a high level of societal inequality would still be a problem.[31] Recent research has answered this question conclusively: many of the social ills long thought to be linked with poverty are better predicted by economic inequality. Inequality correlates to or even causes many significant social problems, including poor health outcomes and early death. It increases competitive consumption, which harms those who spend without increasing their happiness as well as those who cannot afford to do so. And inequality constrains economic growth, which causes suffering in and of itself and reduces the odds that societies will be able to raise the living standards of the poor through economic growth alone. Notably, wealthy, middle-class, and poor people are all affected by increased rates of these social evils in unequal societies, although poor people are affected the most.

In his provocatively titled 2013 book *The Killing Fields of Inequality*, the sociologist Göran Therborn wrote: "[Inequality] has many effects: premature death, ill-health, humiliation, subjection, discrimination, exclusion from knowledge or from mainstream social life, poverty, powerlessness, stress, insecurity, anxiety, lack of self-confidence and of pride in oneself, and exclusion from opportunities and life-chances. . . . Inequality kills."[32]

Indeed, extreme inequality's negative effect on life expectancy is well documented. Many groups of poorer people in the United States have suffered declining life expectancy in recent years, even as economic growth has continued, leading Therborn to conclude that "only AIDS in southern Africa and the restoration of capitalism in Russia have had a more lethal impact than the US social polarization in the boom years of Clinton and Bush."[33] A 2016 study reported that the poorest 1 percent of men in the United States have life expectancies similar to same-age men in much poorer Sudan and Pakistan.[34] In Western Europe in recent decades, as inequality increased, poorer people gained life expectancy more slowly than richer ones. People in every class could expect to live longer than those born earlier, but the effect was stronger for wealthier people. More troublingly—in the United States, Russia, and Ukraine—poorer people actually *lost* life expectancy over a period of recent decades. In those countries, the average life span for poor people in times of higher inequality was shorter than it had been in decades when society was more equal.[35]

A 2013 study suggests the cause of inequality's harmful impact on life expectancy. Researchers found that white women in the United States without high school diplomas had lost five years of life expectancy: they could expect to live, on average, five years less than the generation before them could. People of color overall still have shorter life expectancies than white people, but such a rapid decline for poor, uneducated white women means that many in this group are dying very early in life—in their twenties, thirties, and forties. One theory is that the decline in employment opportunity for the least-educated people harms health, diminishing social opportunities and worsening early mortality. In one observer's view, these women die early not simply because of poverty but also because of the "desperation" born of diminished opportunity.[36] Therborn concurs with this view, saying that the reduced life span of poorer people in unequal societies likely ties to "psychosomatic consequences of different class or status situations. Lack of respect and lack of control of your life and work situation are bad for your health and increase your risk of premature death."[37] He cites longitudinal studies suggesting that unemployment produces extra deaths, even when researchers control for the use of unhealthy stress relievers such as alcohol and tobacco.[38]

In unequal societies, poor health and early death disproportionately affect poor people, creating what researchers call a "health gradient." Inequality is more salient for public health than poverty; a country's overall wealth does not reliably predict its citizens' health. For example, the United States has an average life expectancy a few years lower than that of Norway, which has similar average income to the United States. Meanwhile, Japan has the highest average life expectancy of any wealthy country, but its average national income is only in the middle of wealthy countries.[39] Disparate life spans accompany economic inequality within societies, as well as between nations. For example, in Sweden in 2010, the discrepancy in life expectancy between men in a middle-class area and men in a poor rural area was higher than the gap in average life expectancies between Sweden and much-poorer Egypt.[40]

Even more remarkable is that while inequality increases poor health and early death *disproportionately* among the poor, it also sickens and shortens the lives of those who are better off. Middle-class and well-off people in highly unequal societies can expect more health problems than they would in more egalitarian contexts. They, too, can expect better health and longer lives if their society manages to reduce inequality and its attendant social dysfunctions. In unequal societies, according to researchers, "the effects of inequality are not confined just to the least well-off: instead, they affect the vast majority of the population.... [In the presence of a socioeconomic health gradient, you] could take away all the health problems of the poor and leave most of the problem of health inequalities untouched."[41]

A comprehensive source on the relationship of inequality to social problems is the 2009 book *The Spirit Level*, by the epidemiologists Richard Wilkinson and Kate Pickett. They show that many social evils—including poor health and early death, mental illness and drug addiction, teen pregnancy, early dropping out from education, violence, imprisonment, and a lack of social mobility—are all positively correlated with economic inequality. Pickett and Wilkinson write,

> Among the rich developed countries and among the fifty states of the United States, most of the important health and social problems of the rich world are more common in more unequal societies. In both settings the relationships are too strong to be dismissed as chance findings.... If—for instance—a country does badly on health, you can predict with some confidence that it will also imprison a larger proportion of its population, have more teenage pregnancies, lower literacy scores, more obesity, worse mental health, and so on. Inequality seems to make countries socially dysfunctional across a wide range of outcomes.[42]

Wilkinson and Pickett note that the effects of inequality on these social realities are too strong to be the result of one anomalous country, like the United States, as an outlier. The social problems described above have traditionally been viewed as problems of poverty, but inequality of wealth or income predicted these evils *better* than poverty rates in every case Wilkinson and Pickett examined, in societies as large as countries and as small as US zip codes.[43]

Research suggests several mechanisms for inequality's social harm. Inequality degrades quality of life by promoting conspicuous consumption, by impeding growth and distributing it regressively, and through what the physician and public health advocate Jonathan Mann calls "dignity-denying events."

Mann notes that while the existence of a socioeconomic health gradient has long been recognized, few researchers have bothered to ask *why* one exists. Although it seems self-evident that desperate poverty would have negative effects on health, it is less intuitive that one rung of the middle class can expect slightly better health than the next-poorest rung. Mann finds much for public health to do in understanding this gradient. He suggests, among other things, developing language to describe and quantify the "dignity-denying events" that likely play a major role in harming well-being up and down the economically unequal social ladder.[44] As we will see, socioeconomic gradients exist with regard to many other goods, including education, in unequal societies, and a better understanding of dignity-denying events could help improve outcomes in these areas as well.

Inequality also harms quality of life when it increases competitive consumption. Status competition drives consumption, making demands on people's time and resources without increasing their overall happiness or well-being. One economist has suggested that consumption by the rich, which lowers everyone else's status in comparison, imposes a cost on society that the rich should pay for through their taxes.[45] The theologian David Cloutier suggests that the impulse to consume for competitive purposes roots in the vice of luxury, and he recommends that societies create social norms against such a vicious practice.[46] When inequality rises, people tend to consume more by increasing their working hours and their rates of spending on credit, without increasing their savings. Thus attempting to compete with their neighbors on living standards, "people in more unequal countries do the equivalent of two or three months' extra work a year," with clear negative effects for health and participation in public life.[47] Because inequality increases competitive consumption, reducing inequality could have a positive environmental impact. Indeed, "governments may be unable to make big enough cuts in carbon emissions without also reducing inequality."[48]

Economic growth, or increase in gross domestic product (GDP), has rightly been called a problematic measure of prosperity.[49] Many governments trumpet increased GDP as indicative of more widespread well-being among their citizens, or argue that measures designed to increase GDP will automatically translate into better lives for many. But the theologian and economist Daniel Finn notes that increasing GDP does not map neatly onto an increased quality of life: "Many of the expenditures measured in GDP are actually unfortunate necessities and do not represent any increase in well-being."[50] For example, rising housing prices in a given metropolitan area might force a family to spend more money on housing, on commuting farther to work from an affordable neighborhood, and on takeout food because they do not have time to cook after a long commute. All these expenditures would contribute to growth in GDP, but none necessarily means that the family is enjoying a better quality of life.

Furthermore, Piketty notes that "there is no fundamental reason why we should believe that growth is automatically balanced."[51] GDP can increase even as inequality rises, in which case many individuals in that society would experience little to no increased income at all. However, times of slowed growth and contracting economies are often accompanied by layoffs, increased unemployment, and higher prices, all of which lead to suffering, especially for the poorest people in an economy. So though growth in itself should not be considered automatically equivalent to widespread flourishing, its absence can add to human suffering and is cause for concern. Thus it is noteworthy that extreme inequality is widely believed to hinder growth.

Two International Monetary Fund economists found that though economic growth can occur in societies with high inequality, *sustained* growth is more likely to take place in societies with less inequality.[52] Contrary to persistent messaging that a rising tide lifts all boats, even when growth does take place, inequality can keep the poorest in society from enjoying its benefits. A World Bank report on economies in Africa found that "the region's high inequality . . . hinders the conversion of growth into poverty reduction. Faster reduction in poverty is possible, but it will require a decline in inequality— [of] both outcomes and opportunities."[53] In highly unequal societies, the poor lack access to goods such as education, transportation, and credit that would help them take advantage of available economic opportunities. The study's authors call for "more inclusive growth processes and, where possible, even redistribution" to help growth in African economies benefit the poorest people there.[54] The United Nations Development Program has similarly warned that inequality can keep the benefits of growth from going to those who need it, saying that "about a quarter of human development in the world is lost due to unequal distributions."[55]

Inequality narrows the reach of growth's benefits even in wealthy countries. In the United States since 1980, the poorest 90 percent of people have given up 15 percent of *total national income*, which has been transferred to the richest 10 percent. As this happened while the economy was growing rather slowly, the effect was for incomes at the middle and lower end to essentially stagnate. Meanwhile, the wealthiest 10 percent of people in the United States appropriated three-quarters of such growth as did take place, and "the richest 1 percent alone absorbed nearly 60 percent of the total increase of US national income in this period."[56]

The evidence that inequality harms key aspects of functioning more directly than poverty reminds us that income does not translate directly into capabilities, or what a person is able to be and to achieve. The economist Amartya Sen notes that as a country becomes richer, the income needed to achieve certain minimal functioning usually rises. For example, in the United States, though not in some poorer nations, many people need a car and a phone to hold employment and to socialize with friends and loved ones. Those at the poorer end of the spectrum may face a choice between social interaction and other basic aspects of human life, such as a nutritious diet, while poorer people living in economies less geared toward the consumption standards of the rich are not forced to choose.[57]

"Reducing inequality strikes a double blow against poverty," notes the economist Rolph van der Hoeven. Because countries with relatively greater equality of assets and income tend to grow faster than more unequal countries, "on the one hand, a growth path characterized by greater equality at the margin directly benefits the poor in the short run. On the other hand, the resulting decrease in inequality creates in each period an 'initial condition' for a future that is growth-enhancing."[58] Van der Hoeven proposes government redistribution to improve equality within countries, but warns that such policies must be appropriate to local economies. For example, taxation works best in nations where most of the economy is in the formal sector.[59] However, he notes that "to achieve poverty reduction, it might be preferable to redistribute growth imperfectly than to maintain the status quo imperfectly."[60]

INEQUALITY SELF-PERPETUATES

The argument that inequality is simply a natural outcome of freely functioning economic processes presumes that just as inequality "naturally" increases, it is just as likely to "naturally" decrease, so that those who are concerned with inequality need do nothing but wait. However, mounting evidence suggests that economic inequality is not equally likely to decrease as it is to increase; instead, it self-perpetuates. As it increases, inequality changes economies to reduce the chances that it will decrease again without substantial intervention. This evidence suggests that those who are concerned with the present level of inequality are right to urge intervention today, because

due to inequality's self-perpetuating characteristics, it most likely will continue to increase. And we can expect this increasing economic inequality to
be accompanied by increasing levels of the social evils, like poor health and
early death, that are discussed above.

This section of the chapter details four mechanisms through which
inequality self-perpetuates. Inequality stifles the political voice of the poor
and the middle class; decreases social mobility; and harms child development and educational outcomes. Finally, the rate of return on investments
outpaces growth.

Inequality Affects Political Voice

One powerful way economic inequality self-perpetuates is by increasing the
political voice and power of wealthy people relative to poor and middle-class
ones. This makes it difficult for lower-income people to exercise agency in the
public square when their interests conflict with those of the wealthy. I began
this chapter citing a report by Oxfam International describing the tiny number of wealthy individuals who control half the world's wealth. Oxfam uses
this statistic to warn against the link between extreme inequality and "political capture," when government begins to serve not the whole population but
only the minority of wealthy elites. Oxfam cautions that this phenomenon
can result in widespread "opportunity capture," when wealthy elites receive
high-quality education and health care and pay lower tax rates, while the
poorer majority are excluded from such benefits. The conservative law professor Patrick Garry shares Oxfam's concern that inequality unfairly tilts the
playing field, noting that "the elite ... increasingly occupy an almost completely different economy than that in which the middle class is struggling."[61]

Inequality also threatens equitable governance when it enables what the
economist Robert Reich calls "the secession of the successful." Wealthy
citizens, who can afford to pay privately for goods such as education and
security, may withdraw their use of and support for public versions of these
goods, harming those who cannot afford to pay for them.[62] Although many
value the individual freedom that allows those who can afford it to opt out
of public goods, others worry, with the historian Benjamin Carp, that "if we
allow schools, libraries, policing, and firefighting to become a two-tiered system (with one tier for the elite and another tier for everyone else), then that
threatens the democratic-republican ideal of everyone contributing their fair
share for the greater needs of the commonwealth."[63]

The political scientists Kay Schlozman, Henry Brady, and Sidney Verba
study the relationship between income and political voice in the United States.

Their 2012 book *The Unheavenly Chorus* reports that political involvement is significantly affected by income: "with the single exception of attending a protest, political activity rises with socio-economic status."[64] Although people in the highest income percentiles were only slightly more likely than poorer people to attend a campaign meeting or work for a campaign, they were much more likely to make a donation, with more than 30 percent of people in the top 10 percent of income having done so.[65] Wealthier people are also more likely than lower-income ones to be "persistently" politically active.[66]

This disparity of involvement has a significant policy impact, limiting poorer voters' ability to promote their own economic interests through the democratic process. Anthony Downs is an influential American political economist who explored the relationships between voters' political positions and their economic interests. According to his understanding of political participation, democratic governments can gain wide support by redistributing the incomes of the wealthy few to the poorer majority, thus losing the support of the wealthy but gaining favor with many lower-income voters. However, the "Downsian model" does not hold true in the United States.[67] Schlozman, Verba, and Brady find that US inequality explains this apparent inconsistency clearly: "Within the electorate as a whole, as well as within each of the major parties, the median voter, campaign worker, and campaign contributor are more affluent than and less inclined to support income redistribution than is the median citizen. What is more, the donor of the median dollar is even further, often much further, from the median citizen."[68] Wealthy individuals' tendency to donate more frequently than poorer ones has increased over time and is likely related to increasing economic inequality.[69]

Politically active organizations misrepresent the average American in similar ways. Many are really business or trade associations rather than membership organizations: "less than one-eighth of the organizations active in national politics are membership associations of individuals."[70] Many politically active organizations represent the interests of wealthy people, but "with the exception of unions, those who do unskilled work have no occupationally based membership groups at all to represent them."[71] To put it another way, 80 percent of US adults—"a group that includes lower-level white-collar, blue-collar, and service workers as well as those who are unemployed, in school, at home, disabled, or retired—are represented by a mere 9 percent of the economic organizations" active in US politics."[72]

Schlozman, Verba, and Brady note that inequality of political voice challenges the American ideal of participatory democracy: "Americans are more likely to accept economic than political inequalities; they expect not only that citizens should possess the equal right to be active but also that citizens should express equal political voice on the level playing field of democracy and that public officials should respond equally to all. Thus the transmission of political inequality from one generation to the next would present a double challenge to American ideals."[73]

Unhappily, inequality of voice is, in fact, transmitted from generation to generation. Parents' education and political involvement strongly predict the political involvement of their children, and racial disparities similar to those in educational attainment exist in political participation.[74] Furthering persistent racial, educational, and class-based gaps in political voice, laws banning those convicted of felonies from voting—even after their sentences are served—disproportionately silence the political voices of young, poor men of color.[75]

Schlozman, Verba, and Brady note that equality of political voice is valuable for many reasons besides its important role in the United States' self-understanding. Equal political voice promises to develop individual capacities for democracy, encourage full participation in public life, foster social trust, and convey that government projects are just and legitimate.[76] The threat that economic inequality poses to all these good goals is extremely troubling. Stifling the political voice of the poor and the middle class is just one more way that economic inequality perpetuates itself. If political voice were equally heard, poor and middle-class people could address inequality through their votes. The fact that this does not happen in the United States indicts the US political system, and helps keep economic inequality entrenched.

Inequality Decreases Social Mobility

Some might be willing to accept high inequality if society retained significant mobility across generations. Class mobility does not necessarily help reduce inequality, but it does suggest a certain fairness in a society's resource distribution, where hard work and talent lead to higher incomes while feckless people born well off suffer the consequence of diminished wealth. However, even if we would accept a high degree of inequality in society given a commensurately high degree of class mobility, this is not the case in most societies today.

High inequality, in fact, reduces class mobility. The more unequal a society, the less likely a poor person is to meaningfully improve their lot in terms of income, occupation, education, and health, or a wealthy person is to significantly decrease their own.[77] In a cross-cultural study, a multinational group of researchers found that "inequalities in economic status are quite persistent across generations, especially among children of low-income parents and, most especially, in the United States."[78] Norway and Sweden, among the most equal of wealthy countries, have relatively high degrees of social mobility. The very wealthy, highly unequal United States is often ranked at the very bottom among wealthy countries in terms of mobility.[79]

Economic segregation—rich and poor people living separately—also increases with inequality and contributes to decreased mobility, as one is less likely to make connections with those outside one's class. Pickett and Wilkinson write that in addition to its consequences for mobility, economic segregation harms quality of life in other ways: "The concentration of poor people in poor areas increases all kinds of stress, deprivation and difficulty—from increased commuting times for those who have to leave deprived communities to find work elsewhere, to increased risk of traffic accidents, worse schools, poor levels of services, exposure to gang violence, pollution and so on."[80] Reducing inequality in the United States could contribute to increased social mobility.

Inequality Harms Childhood Development and Life Prospects

Education is a commonly touted engine of class mobility, and another potential justification for inequality. That is, if educational quality and attainment were more or less equal across income in economically unequal societies, we might accept inequality on the grounds that children in that society had fair prospects for improving their income, wealth, and quality of life. Unfortunately, this is another potential justification for extreme inequality that does not hold true in reality.

Inequality correlates with poor educational outcomes, displaying gradient patterns similar to those for health. Contrary to notions that high inequality encourages those near the bottom to work harder to rise, rates of inequality correlate with dropout rates for high school.[81] Across the US states, inequality predicts high school dropout rates better than poverty. Pickett and Wilkinson write that "it looks as if the achievement of higher national standards of educational performance may actually depend on reducing the social gradient in educational achievement in each country."[82] In wealthy countries with higher equality, whether a child has poor parents or rich ones has less of an effect on her educational outcome. In the United States, unfortunately, this is less the case. Although disparities in school funding exist in the United States and are increasingly recognized as unfair, parental socioeconomic status—a composite of income and education—continues to be the single factor with the most impact on a child's educational outcome.[83] And Schlozman, Verba, and Brady caution that parental income's impact on educational achievement is actually increasing: "Over the last generation, the well off have increased their capacity to bequeath educational advantage to their offspring.... [There is] a growing advantage of affluent students in access to higher education."[84]

Inequality affects parenting in ways that shape the development of a child's capabilities even before she enters school. Pickett and Wilkinson write: "Social inequalities in early childhood development are entrenched long before the start of formal education.... Babies and young children need to be in caring, responsive environments.... They need opportunities to play, talk and explore their world, and they need to be encouraged within safe limits, rather than restricted in their activities or punished. All of these things are harder for parents and other caregivers to provide when they are poor, or stressed, or unsupported."[85]

Because of the many stresses of being low income, poverty in childhood has especially pernicious effects on brain development and success in adult life, including earning potential.[86] However, a strong social safety net can help. A group of researchers compared the United States, which has high child poverty and a relatively weak safety net, with Norway, which guarantees all citizens adequate income, health care, and education. They found that Norway has higher mobility than the United States across all income quintiles. That is, though childhood income still predicts adult income, the effect is not as strong as it is in the United States, likely due to the Norwegian safety net. A particularly strong effect was found in early childhood, suggesting that social benefits should be focused on very young children.[87]

Several researchers have called upon the United States to guarantee universal, high-quality prekindergarten education to improve equality of educational achievement. This is an expensive proposal with the potential for a significant impact.[88] Thomas Piketty concurs that significant investment in education could decrease both poverty and inequality by raising the earning power of those in the lower and middle classes, "decreasing the upper decile's share of both wages and total income."[89] The suggestion that significant redistribution can help offset the educational gradient caused by inequality helps refute the claim that inequality is a neutral, "natural" process requiring no intervention.

Inequality Self-Perpetuates through r > g

Plenty of evidence challenges the assumption that inequality may fall as "naturally" as it once rose without intervention. We have explored three ways that inequality self-perpetuates by changing social systems. Inequality keeps rich people rich and poor people poor by creating disparities in political voice; by limiting social mobility; and by causing educational gradients that limit the prospects of those born poor. Another way inequality self-perpetuates is through economic forces that ensure investments grow more quickly than economies as a whole. Thus, those who begin with wealth will always remain wealthier, over time, than those without. This is the argument made by the economist Thomas Piketty in his influential 2014 book *Capital in the Twenty-First Century.* Analyzing prodigious amounts of data from varying, though mostly wealthy, countries, Piketty finds that under capitalism, the rate r of return on investments over time always outpaces economic growth g—or, over time, $r > g$.[90] Without major economic shocks or significant governmental intervention in markets, the distance between rich and poor will not only persist but will continue to grow. (The period after World War II, much vaunted in the United States and Europe for widespread prosperity, featured both the shock of two world wars and significant government intervention.) This, Piketty says, "has clearly been true throughout most of human history, right up to the eve of World War I, and it will probably be true again in the twenty-first century,"[91] but it is "a historical fact, not a logical necessity."[92] Compounding the problem, the largest wealth-holdings grow fastest of all, further distancing the wealthiest from the rest.[93]

Many economists, and some theologians, argue that *some* level of inequality should be maintained, to encourage economic growth or worker innovation, but $r > g$ strikes a cautionary note. Even beginning from a low level of inequality, Piketty believes that $r > g$ will inevitably work to concentrate wealth in the hands of the few at the expense of the rest,[94] potentially eroding the peace and stability of society.[95] For example, Piketty believes that the particularly high inequality of the United States "absolutely" contributed to the 2008 financial crisis by encouraging lower-income people in the United States to rely on cheap credit.[96]

Furthermore, "inequality of wealth is always and everywhere greater than inequality of income from labor," says Piketty, with outsize consequences for social stability and justice.[97] Although the wealthy rentiers of two hundred years ago lived off their capital without working, today many rich people are both workers—often with very high incomes—and rentiers, or investors. And larger investments grow quickly, so, Piketty says, "the entrepreneur always tends to turn into a rentier."[98] Piketty says that throughout most of history, there was no profession in which one could earn a lifestyle as comfortable as that afforded by inherited wealth.[99] One of the most disturbing claims in *Capital* is Piketty's insistence that if inequality is not addressed, this will soon be the case again.[100]

Piketty believes the tendency of $r > g$ to increase inequality can be addressed by a modest global tax on capital.[101] A global tax on capital would increase transparency and public understanding of the extent of the world's largest fortunes. It would deter corruption, a particular scourge in many poorer countries, and would help restore public revenues lost when the wealthy conceal assets from taxation.[102]

INEQUALITY FUNCTIONS AS MORAL
LUCK TO HARM VIRTUE

I have argued that inequality is a problem distinct from poverty because it correlates with many social evils and self-perpetuates by changing social structures. Less examined, but extremely important for grasping inequality's work in societies, is its harm to personal morality. This book details how inequality functions as moral luck by affecting the ability of both wealthy and poor people to pursue virtue. The next section of this chapter presents social science evidence that links inequality to moral failure. Inequality reduces empathy for others' suffering; is driven by a failure to perceive the humanity of others; and increases violence, fear, and the desire to punish.

Shocking anecdotes from wealthy countries suggest that today's economic inequality accompanies a disturbing lack of empathy for those living in poverty. Soaring unemployment in Spain led to an increase in hungry people "dumpster diving" for food in trash bins. Diagnosing such practices as offensive to human dignity, officials in one city responded by installing locks on municipal trash cans.[103] A management company in London installed metal spikes on sheltered areas of its property, treating needy people looking for a respite from the elements like animal pests. After a national outcry in 2015, the cathedral of the Roman Catholic Archdiocese of San Francisco removed a deterrent system that intermittently drenched its doorways—and anyone sleeping under them—with water.[104] Spikes and artificial downpours are particularly blatant manifestations of "hostile architecture," which discourages people from spending time in public places. The architectural historian Ian Borden said hostile architecture sends the message that "we are only republic citizens to the degree that we are either working or consuming goods directly."[105] I myself observed this practice in Boston, where public benches and sculpture platforms have been retrofitted with metal bars, dividing them into sections that accommodate sitting but not lying down to sleep. The public environment increasingly refuses desperate people the utterly minimal comfort of sleeping exposed to the elements on a marble plinth.

The US nonprofit National Coalition for the Homeless reports that at least 187 US cities criminalize homelessness with bans on such "fundamental human activities" as sleeping, sitting down, or sharing food.[106]

Anecdotes of punitive attitudes toward the needy during the first decades of the new millennium, when economic inequality soared, evoke how inequality can erode social empathy. Large-scale studies prove the point. Among wealthy nations, more unequal societies imprison more people and do so for longer periods of time, despite scanty evidence that either measure reduces crime or recidivism. Pickett and Wilkinson write,

> In societies with greater inequality, where the social distances between people are greater, where attitudes of "us and them" are more entrenched and where lack of trust and fear of crime are rife, public and policy makers alike are more willing to imprison people and adopt punitive attitudes towards the "criminal elements" of society.... And as prison is not particularly effective for either deterrence or rehabilitation, then a society must only be willing to maintain a high rate (and high cost) of imprisonment for reasons unrelated to effectiveness.[107]

Pickett and Wilkinson suggest that high inequality indicates those with power display a punitive mind-set toward those without it.

In addition to diminishing empathy, inequality is responsible for increasing violence, sensitivity to shame, and fear of others in society. People in more unequal societies commit more acts of violence.[108] Summarizing a variety of sociological findings to explain why this might be, Pickett and Wilkinson write,

> Violence is most often a response to disrespect, humiliation and loss of face ... Even within the most violent of societies, most people don't react violently to these triggers because they have ways of achieving and maintaining their self-respect and sense of status in other ways.... As a result, although everybody experiences disrespect and humiliation at times, they don't all become violent; we all experience loss of face but we don't turn round and shoot somebody. In more unequal societies more people lack these protections and buffers. Shame and humiliation become more sensitive issues in more hierarchical societies; status becomes more important, status competition increases and more people are deprived of access to markers of status and social success.[109]

Even children experience inequality's effects on violence. Children in more unequal societies are at greater risk for bullying and physical fights and are more likely to feel that their peers are not "kind and helpful."[110]

Although increasing economic inequality can promote vices like violence and insensitivity to others' suffering, inequality can also result from preexisting moral blind spots, including the failure to recognize others as human. Piketty explores the role of racism in describing and understanding inequality in the United States. A pervasive myth depicts the United States as much more egalitarian than the "Old World," Western Europe. By some accounts, even in the US Gilded Age described by Henry James and Edith Wharton, the United States had almost half the capital/income ratio of Europe; that is, the ratio of the total wealth owned to national income earned in one year was less, and inequality was correspondingly lower.[111] However, as Piketty shows, the antebellum US capital/income ratio resembles that of the Old World when the market value of enslaved people in the US South is included in the assessment of capital.[112] Thus, if Americans want to portray their history as more egalitarian than Europe's, they can only do so by erasing the painful history of chattel slavery and its ramifications for US national life today. For Piketty, the United States' failure to incorporate slavery into its evaluation of its own relative egalitarianism helps explain twentieth-century racial segregation and the present-day failure to develop the US welfare state.[113]

As a converse to these sobering accounts, it is possible that reducing inequality within a nation may encourage empathy within that nation toward poorer societies. Pickett and Wilkinson found that more equal wealthy nations took positions that were more favorable to poorer nations in international trade agreements and climate compacts. They wrote, "It looks as if the inequalities which affect the way people treat each other within their own societies also affect the norms and expectations they bring to bear on international issues. Growing up and living in a more unequal society affects people's assumptions about human nature. . . . If we put our own houses in order, we may look more sympathetically on developing countries."[114]

When we review the many social problems that increase simultaneously with inequality, it comes as no surprise that inequality reduces empathy and increases fear and distrust. We have seen that inequality stifles the political voice of low-income people, limits economic growth, and brings severe consequences for health and life span—for the poor especially, but ultimately for everyone, in unequal societies. Inequality hampers child development and education and decreases social mobility. All these social evils are attributable to inequality itself, not simply to poverty alone. It is no surprise that such serious challenges could erode social cohesion and feelings of common humanity.

CHRISTIAN ETHICAL WORK ON INEQUALITY

Despite long-standing Christian concern for wealth and poverty as moral issues, scholars inspired by Christian thought have only lately turned their attention to economic inequality. Both theologians and social scientists who work in dialogue with Christian theology have moved beyond their starting points of asking whether inequality is a problem in its own right. Although few go so far as to call for a norm of absolute equality, most conclude that contemporary levels of economic inequality are problematic and proceed to ask how the tools of their respective disciplines can help shape a response. This section examines their work.

Is Inequality a Problem?

Theologians have pursued collaborations with quantitative scientists inspired by the Christian faith to investigate the question of whether inequality is a problem. In one such project, the economists Geoffrey Brennan and Anthony M. C. Waterman note that perspectives on scarcity present one of many inevitable clashes between theology and economics: though many economists view scarcity and inequality as essentially neutral phenomena, contemporary Christian theologians see them as evidence of moral failing.[115] It is true that until relatively recently, many theologians who urged societal attention to inequality tended to assume, rather than demonstrate, that inequality reflects injustice. Works along these lines came from John Mohan Razu and Clement Campos in India, Vimal Tirimanna in Sri Lanka, the late John Mary Waliggo in Uganda, and John Sniegocki in the United States.[116] Among this group, the UK scholar Sebastian Kim rightly notes that the Church's missionary expansion is inextricably bound up with the colonial history that laid the groundwork for today's global inequality. He says the Church "shares the responsibility for [today's] inequality when it is either silent on the issue, or when it accumulates wealth at the expense of others."[117] Noting that many Christian scholars remained focused on the problem of poverty and its alleviation, the Chilean theologian Tony Mifsud suggested in 2007 that the issue of inequality more accurately captures the concerns of the faithful and carries scope for real social improvement.[118]

It is also easy, as Brennan and Waterman imply, to find economists, even theologically conversant ones, who accept inequality to a certain degree. Albino Barrera presents a theodicy of economic scarcity, arguing that though scarcity is not part of the divine plan, we can act as co-creators with God when we redistribute goods in situations of economic scarcity.[119] Waterman himself entertains the idea that inequality may be beneficial in a utilitarian sense, although he raises the moral objection of its potential to foster "deadly sins," including avarice and envy.[120] Andrew Yuengert acknowledges that participation in society can often depend on the possession of certain goods, but, inspired by Amartya Sen's Capabilities Approach, holds that "inequality in itself is not morally offensive, as long as those at the bottom of the distribution have a dignified standard of living."[121] Charles M. A. Clark, an economist working in the Catholic social thought tradition, suggests that inequality can be viewed as unjust depending on its cause: "wealth that is created for the individual at the expense of the community is repugnant to human dignity and the common good due to its promotion of poverty."[122] Clark's example of unjust wealth creation is the practice of creating profits for shareholders by passing costs of doing business onto employees or consumers.

The economist Clive Beed and the sociologist Cara Beed argue that regardless of the causes of inequality, a biblical perspective demands that those who have more share with those who have less. In their view, the Bible supports a relative definition of poverty: "the Bible calls someone poor if he is unable to live adequately in terms of the standards of the time."[123] This relative definition of poverty does not allow Christians to dismiss the concerns of those who are poor in wealthy countries with the claim that they are better off than the poor in poorer nations, and it treats both inequality and poverty as issues of concern.

Ultimately, both theologians and quantitative scientists express a range of views on whether and how inequality becomes problematic. For example, the theologian Dennis McCann argues that inequality becomes immoral "if, and only if, it . . . marginalizes persons and communities, . . . denying them access to appropriate levels of social participation."[124] Stefano Zamagni breaks with many of his economist colleagues when he warns that inequality is unquestionably a problem, and one that redistribution alone cannot solve. He warns that the constant growth presumed by modern democracies inevitably results in destabilizing inequalities that redistribution will not fix, demanding systemic change: "The endurance and reputation of democratic governments are determined much more by their ability to increase total wealth than to redistribute it fairly among citizens. . . . So if we want to combat the endemic increase in inequality as a threat to peace and democracy, we must act primarily on the production of wealth and income, not only its redistribution."[125]

The political scientist Mary Jo Bane believes that Catholics of all political persuasions can agree that today's extreme levels of inequality are problematic, and can agree on certain moral positions for responding, such as the belief that extreme wealth is not a worthy goal for humans to pursue. She cautions that Christians may legitimately disagree on policy developments most likely to help respond to inequality and discourages religious leaders from preaching a "'Catholic position' on specific issues, like the minimum wage, levels of government spending, or the tax code."[126]

There are very few book-length works on inequality from theologians, and none from Catholic scholars as of this writing. Douglas Hicks, a Presbyterian, and Joerg Rieger, a Methodist, offer books reflecting very different answers to the question of whether and how inequality becomes a problem.

Hicks's 2000 monograph *Inequality and Christian Ethics* uses Amartya Sen's Capabilities Approach to argue for Christian attention to the issue of inequality, particularly the question of "how much inequality is too much."[127] Hicks draws on Reinhold Niebuhr and Gustavo Gutiérrez to argue that "inequalities that obstruct the conditions for equality and solidarity—and thus the basic sense of stake or participation on the part of all people—should be transformed."[128] Trained as an economist as well as a theologian, Hicks argues that economists should aim to foster equality and solidarity when they design programs for public use. More recently, Hicks has commented that economic inequality remains a concern for Christians because "human well-being is always relational."[129] For Hicks, economic inequality imposes relative hardship on poorer members of society.

Rieger is far more pessimistic than Hicks with regard to the economic status quo, and would find "how much inequality is too much" an inadequate question. In his 2009 book *No Rising Tide*, Rieger declares that inequality is clearly immoral when we look at wealth or poverty in terms of the relative power they afford.[130] In a recent article on inequality, he argues that middle-class Western Christians do not benefit from modern neoliberal capitalism, and do not wield power within it, to the extent that many believe. He says the power wielded by those at the high end of unequal societies—the richest 1 percent or even one-thousandth of people—dwarfs the ability of middle-class people to act within unequal societies. He calls for middle-class Christians to focus on what they have in common with the poor in their own societies and globally, to create solidarity and work for more justice within unequal systems.[131] He continues the argument in a 2016 book coauthored with Rosemarie Henkel-Rieger, where they write that "deep solidarity is possible when the 99 percent realize that most of us benefit less and less from the current economic situation. . . . In terms of simple math, someone who earns $150,000 a year is closer to someone who earns $15,000 a year than to someone who earns $500,000 a year— the realm where membership in the 1 percent barely begins."[132]

Although I appreciate the challenge of Rieger's vision and its applications for political strategy, it is a plain fact that many middle-class Western

Christians live at the high end of the global income and wealth spectrums. Piketty points out that "the average global fortune [accumulated wealth] is barely €60,000 (~$75,700) per adult, so that many people in the developed countries ... seem quite wealthy in terms of the global wealth hierarchy."[133] Global income, if equally divided, would be about €760 (~$960) per month, again placing many US and European workers among the globally wealthy.[134] And though it is true that the same income may translate into radically different levels of functioning depending on the society, the middle-class Westerners Rieger addresses have presumably achieved a high level of functioning on their income.

Official Catholic social teaching has evolved from accepting inequality to viewing it as materially and morally harmful. Although *Rerum novarum* (1891) expresses deep empathy for economically generated suffering, Leo XIII accepted economic inequality, writing that "unequal fortune is a necessary result of unequal condition [meaning talent and capacity]; such inequality is far from being disadvantageous either to individuals or to the community."[135] Leo did not see inequality as a sign of injustice, but forty years later, Pius XI did, doubting that "so enormous and unjust an inequality in the distribution of this world's goods truly conforms to the designs of the all-wise Creator."[136] Drew Christiansen notes a positive evolution in Catholic social thought near the middle of the twentieth century, with an increased emphasis on relative economic equality. This evolution, Christiansen says, owed much to the emphasis on solidarity in Vatican II documents and Pope Paul VI's work.[137] Current exponents of Catholic social thought, including popes and scholars, have continued this concern with economic inequality and the recourse to solidarity in response.

Pope Benedict XVI and Pope Francis have clearly named inequality as a problem and proposed specific solutions to it. Benedict XVI links inequality to wasteful consumerism and corruption in his encyclical *Caritas in veritate* (2009), calling inequality a "scandal" opposed to human dignity. He called for states to promote participation in society through welfare programs that reduce inequality.[138] Daniel Finn notes that *Caritas in veritate* echoes many concerns with inequality raised by social scientists—including those covered earlier in this chapter—and concludes that "income inequality itself, and not simply unmet needs, ought to increase in importance in any moral evaluation of economic life."[139]

Pope Francis's 2013 apostolic exhortation *Evangelii gaudium* gives sustained and specific attention to the problems of inequality. Francis asserts that inequality is created, not inevitable, and that it can be changed; that it impedes social participation for all; and that it tends to generate violence.

Francis depicts inequality as both a justice problem and a virtue problem. For him, inequality is both a symptom and a cause of culpable indifference to the poor that harms the indifferent in their relationships with others and with God.[140]

Although theologians have generally welcomed the recent papal emphasis on a concrete response to inequality, they also raise concerns. The Nigerian theologian Agbonkhianmeghe Orobator welcomes *Caritas in veritate*'s emphasis on inequality, but he criticizes the document for focusing on Western problems to the exclusion of African concerns. For example, Pope Benedict's encyclical assumes "the decline of opposing blocs [of nation-states]" as global forces, but Orobator points out that such blocs still exist, and cause conflict and economic decline, in Africa.[141] In the United States, Alex Mikulich critiques Catholic social thought, including the US bishops' 1986 pastoral *Economic Justice for All*, for failing to pay sufficient attention to racism and its role in shaping economic inequalities along racial lines.[142]

Categorizing Views of Inequality

David Cloutier identifies three theological approaches to inequality. The "inequality as exclusion" model finds inequality problematic when the poor are shut out from dignified human life, including social and democratic participation. Cloutier identifies this model more with "less-developed countries" in contrast with the United States, which "mostly avoids these problems."[143] Willis Jenkins, also noting that inequality violates justice by excluding poor persons from participation in economic and political life, criticizes responses that seem to deify participation in economic life. Although it is genuinely important to help those in need participate in society and achieve the basic goods that can derive from economic participation, Christians should avoid uncritically equating economic participation with human well-being and purpose. Jenkins trenchantly remarks that "while biblical figures constantly want to get the poor out of debt, many Christian microcredit organizations think that getting the poor into debt is the best way to liberate them."[144]

For Cloutier, the "inequality as fragmentation" model locates inequality's harm in its destruction of a sense of common purpose, trust in others, or shared destiny.[145] Even though the poor may not be completely excluded in unequal societies—and the rich may enjoy great power within them—members of both groups lack the sense so central to Christian ethics that their well-being is bound up with that of others.

Cloutier comments on a third model, inequality as theft, through which theologians make both moral and empirical claims. Early Church theologians portrayed the wealthy as literal thieves, hoarding goods that rightly belong to the poor. Modern economists who portray any economic activity as benefiting all have branded this view naive. However, Cloutier's own work draws on contemporary economic views that understand that certain economic goods, in fact, have zero-sum characteristics, and do not tend to common benefit. Cloutier urges theologians to continue to work with economics to better specify which sectors of the economy can be rightly described, with the terms and moral fervor of early Church theologians, as "theft" from those in need.[146] Although the ability of highly paid financiers to hoard wealth by controlling their own compensation is certainly a concern, Cloutier rightly notes that middle-class, financially comfortable people similarly engage in "opportunity hoarding" and are not innocent with respect to "inequality as fragmentation."[147]

The theologian Piet Naudé and the economist Stan du Plessis offer a different taxonomy, contrasting what they call "relational" and "achievement" perspectives on inequality. The first sees the riches of some as generated by the exploitation of many, whereas in the latter "the social process that generates high income for one person is thought to be largely independent from the process that generates incomes elsewhere," and the extremely high incomes of some must be due to unusual hard work and merit.[148] Both these models explain part of the nature of contemporary inequality, the scholars suggest, and there is a moral difference between them. Because God's intent for humanity is justice, "theology cannot endorse the instrumental arguments for unjust inequality" that suggest inequality is necessary to foster, for example, improved technology or specialization.[149] Inequality also contradicts the theological values of reconciliation and preference for the poor.[150]

Theological Solutions to Economic Inequality

As a consensus has grown that inequality is harmful, theologians have turned their focus to proposing religious responses. The Dutch theologian Jurjen Pieter de Vries dissents from proposals such as complete equality of incomes or "income ceiling" taxation of all incomes over a certain level. Still troubled by extreme contemporary levels of inequality, he suggested maintaining a relationship between the highest and lowest salaries of particular companies, which governing boards and workers' unions would have the duty to enforce. Governments could enforce this as well as providing for minimum incomes, and churches retain the duty to challenge their own members when they appear to succumb to greed.[151]

Recent special issues of journals offered diverse theological solutions to the problem of inequality. A 2016 issue of the *Anglican Theological Review*, focused on theology and economics, included several essays discussing inequality.[152] For example, Kathryn Tanner reviews the literature on "finance-dominated capitalism" to urge religious attention to the systemic roots of inequality: "If interlocking structural forces like these are at the root of wage stagnation and increasing inequality, castigating individuals for their greed or lack of charity loses much of its point and force as the focus for religious concern."[153] Willis Jenkins determines that though conversations about sin are unlikely to meaningfully change acceptance of great wealth and economic inequality, Christian practices may: "Christianity cultivates selves different from and out of joint with the sort of self that is required to maintain extreme inequality."[154] And Amaryah Shaye Armstrong calls for a theology of dispossession in light of racialized inequalities of property and power.[155] Elsewhere, Myriam Renaud urged mainline Protestant congregations to respond to the ways income inequality shapes congregants' experiences, such as the "meaning versus help" divide—wealthy people may look to religious communities for a source of meaning in daily life while working-class and poor people expect material or spiritual support.[156]

In 2017, Kenneth Himes and I coedited a special issue of the journal *Religions* that brought together responses to the problem of inequality from disciplines including theology, philosophy, law, political science, history, and education.[157] Amid the theological contributions were James O'Sullivan's evaluation of the United Nations' Millennium Development Goals and Sustainable Development Goals through the lens of Catholic social thought. Although the goals have the potential to address inequality, O'Sullivan finds they are also beset by inadequacies, particularly in terms of accountability and commitment to structural change.[158] Shaji George Kochuthara shows that neoliberalism and globalization have increased the impact of economic inequality already present in his native India, and points to ethical solutions in Catholic social thought, particularly the virtue of solidarity and the limits on the right to private property.[159] Joyce Ann Konigsburg uses Catholic social thought to argue for a living wage as a tool to promote economic equality.[160] I detail how Pope Francis's vision of hospitality as response to inequality is particularly Jesuit and echoes the concerns of feminist theological ethicists.[161] And Himes criticizes John A. Ryan, an early-twentieth-century Catholic economic thinker, for failing to recognize the need for "ceilings" as well as "floors" in the ethical distribution of economic goods.[162]

The *Journal of Religious Ethics* offered five essays as part of a special "focus on inequality" in its June 2019 issue. The authors, many with academic credentials in both theology and economics, evaluate inequality at the level of economic systems, criticizing widespread assumptions about people and markets that enable inequality's harm to the common good. For example, Mary Hirschfeld explains that theology views persons as constituted by social relationships, not "atomistic individuals," as a common secular view has it. Widespread cultural understandings of human nature and worth must change for inequality's harm to be addressed.[163] Christina McRorie shows how heterodox approaches to economics challenge the view that redistributive policies intended to enhance equality are interventions imposed from outside onto a market sphere imagined as autonomous.[164] In a similar vein, Douglas Hicks argues against understandings of market transactions that depict parties to exchanges as separate from their social contexts, ignoring "third parties" such as government and future generations.[165] Both Kenneth Himes and the focus section's editor, Paul Weithman, discuss the virtue of solidarity in the context of economic inequality, with Himes outlining the ways economic inequality translates into exclusion of the poor from common life in the contemporary United States.[166] Weithman notes that posttax inequalities are little studied compared with pretax inequalities of income, and speculates about economic segregation's potential effect on solidarity.[167]

Several recent works focus on the potential of faith-based organizing to oppose economic inequality and defend a view of interdependent human life through a wise use of common resources. C. Melissa Snarr finds that US interfaith organizations rarely include the perspectives of working poor people, unless they are organizing movements that incorporate labor unions. Collaboration between organized labor and interfaith outreach groups is, for Snarr, a hope-filled sign of the potential of religious resistance to inequality.[168] For Elizabeth Hinson-Hasty, hope comes in the potential, rather than the present, of organizing: "In the United States, one reason for a less than robust engagement of middle-class people of faith in resistance movements is the broad perception that an undifferentiated group of people known as 'the middle class' still exists. . . . The reality is that now even most middle-class people in the United States are one tragedy away from living in poverty."[169] Hinson-Hasty's 2017 book *The Problem of Wealth* concludes with original parables inspiring readers to meditate on concrete ways to share economic resources more equitably.[170]

Inequality Shaping Morality

Relatively few theological works address inequality's moral impact; this is the primary lacuna this book fills. However, there are enough suggestions and allusions in existing works to give hope that this is a fruitful line of inquiry.

In her 2013 book *Global Justice, Christology, and Christian Ethics,* Lisa Sowle Cahill suggests that economic inequality erodes civic virtue and calls for the development of the virtues in response: "The key to recognizing equality [of all human persons] lies in the practical intensification and extension of the human capacities for empathy and compassion."[171] Laurenti Magesa compares an indigenous African communitarian ethic with Catholic social thought, arguing that both perspectives correctly demand approaches of solidarity in response to inequality.[172] Another rare work on the connections between economic inequality and virtue is Christine Firer Hinze's 2004 book chapter on John A. Ryan's economic thought. Ryan urged economic redistribution, not only to help the poor live better lives, but also because he thought overconsumption by the wealthy could harm their development of virtue, particularly temperance.[173] Firer Hinze suggests that Christian communities today should consider Ryan's advocacy for a ceiling on living standards, as well as a floor that meets baseline needs. Julie Hanlon Rubio echoes Ryan's concern in her 2010 book on shaping virtues in a family setting, pointing out that tithing not only helps the poor but also encourages the development of virtues within the family.[174] Kenneth R. Himes and I have called on moral theologians to pay attention to inequality as an issue distinct from poverty, upholding the virtue of solidarity in response to the unique moral challenges posed by inequality.[175]

Olubiyi Adeniyi Adewale comments on the moral impact of inequality from his Nigerian context with an essay on the Gospel parable of Lazarus and the rich man (Luke 16:19–31). Adewale shows that people in Jesus's ancient Palestinian context believed that dogs contribute to healing when they lick sores, an understanding that continues today in African belief. This parable teaches us that we reveal ourselves as less than human—less human even than dogs—when we are able to help the poor yet fail to do so.[176] For Adewale, inequality holds up a mirror to our moral capacities and failures.

Some theologians suggest that economic inequality both causes, and is caused by certain moral failings. Paulinus Odozor, a theologian from Nigeria working in the United States, finds that both external pressures and internal moral struggles contribute to the high levels of inequality in many African societies. Destructive trade and development policies imposed by Western nations are among the external factors. Internal cultural tendencies suggesting moral deficits include governmental misallocation of resources and widespread failure to recognize the humanity of outsiders or others.[177] Similarly, the US theologian Mary Elizabeth Hobgood argues that failure to recognize the humanity of others also feeds economic inequality when systemic racism allows white Americans to ignore the extent and root causes of their own "economic disempowerment."[178] And Bryan Massingale diagnoses a uniquely US "cultured indifference to the poor" shaped by racism, individualism, and consumerism.[179]

CONCLUSION: A MECHANISM FOR INEQUALITY'S MORAL IMPACT

Until relatively recently in many societies, inequality attached to caste or rank more directly than to money, and being poor was not associated with personal moral failure. Thomas Piketty notes that even the highly unequal patrimonial societies known to Balzac and Austen did not claim that to be poor was to be less virtuous: "Modern meritocratic society, especially in the United States, is much harder on the losers, because it seeks to justify domination on the grounds of justice, virtue, and merit, to say nothing of the insufficient productivity of those at the bottom."[180] And he notes that often, even middle-class people subscribe to such a distorted interpretation of meritocracy as an explanation for why they are not themselves among the poor.[181]

In modern capitalist societies, wealth is not just a useful commodity that makes life easier. Rather, it has become viewed as evidence of many valuable and desirable personal qualities, including intelligence, diligence, moral rectitude, trustworthiness, creativity, and good skills in relationships, including parenting. Wealth is in fact nearly convertible into various other valuable qualities, including education, meaningful work, and romantic desirability. All this inevitably influences the sense of one's own worth, qualities, and prospects, whether one is well off or poor.

Contemporary capitalist meritocracy promotes the belief that the wealthy are more deserving of intangible goods like safety, power, and long lives, because they must have achieved their wealth through remarkable personal merit. On the heels of this belief comes the inference that poor people, because they lack the work ethic needed to achieve comfort and stability, deserve their suffering in life. In meritocratic capitalist societies, our income and wealth form a convenient proxy for society's valuation of us. A few minutes of one person's time can be "equivalently worth" another's full workweek. Linguistic phrases like "he's worth billions" or "she could buy and sell us if she wanted to" link wealth to inherent worth and to power.

The fact that money is changeable for so many other goods in society heightens the power of its messaging about what we are worth and what we deserve. In the United States and most other societies, the wealthy live longer than the poor; they are safer where they live; and consumer industries multiply to offer them amusement, comfort, and status. Capitalism conveys that wealthy people deserve to be safe and happy; that others should spend their time meeting the whims and ensuring the comfort of the rich; and that it is important for rich people to pursue fulfillment.

In unequal societies, like the United States, the poor live shorter lives and suffer worse illness than the wealthy. They do not enjoy the same range of opportunities to pursue education or personal development or to gain a voice in politics. The message is loud and clear: they do not deserve to live safe and healthy lives; their lives are not as valuable as those of the rich; and their pursuit of fulfillment does not benefit society and is of no use to them. In addition to these implicit systemic messages about individual worth, members of society treat others differently based on their perceived income level.

Psychologists and sociologists have contributed greatly to our understanding of societal messages to individuals based on wealth and poverty. The sociologist Göran Therborn wrote that though poverty may look different in such different countries as the United States and India, poverty "has a universal social meaning. To be poor means that you do not have sufficient resources to participate fully in the everyday life of the bulk of your fellow citizens."[182] The psychologist Bernice Lott explains that low-income people carry both material and psychological burdens due to class-based interpersonal discrimination and structural barriers to accessing social institutions.[183] Discrimination based on actual or perceived poverty appears in private social life and in public contexts, including doctors' offices, schools, and accessing social services. Health care providers treat patients on Medicaid differently, prescribe psychoactive drugs more often for low-income children, and are more likely to advise poor mothers to limit their childbearing. Consciousness of income difference can cause shame and anxiety to low-income people.[184] In light of the potential for low-income people to internalize such negative messages about their own worth, the Latin American Episcopal Conference (CELAM) wrote of the need for "conscientization" among the Latin American poor, a raising of awareness of their own rights, worth, and God-given dignity.[185]

"Rather than adopting an attitude of gratitude toward the rich," Pickett and Wilkinson note, "we need to recognize what a damaging effect they have on the social fabric" in light of the material and psychological harms inequality deals to the poor.[186] Mary Elizabeth Hobgood aptly describes the flip side of negative stereotypes and discrimination against poor persons: middle-class and wealthy people can come to view themselves as inherently superior beings. She writes:

It becomes easy to justify our positions and the unearned privileges we enjoy, as well as the suffering of the lazy or unlucky 'unfortunate' others. We learn that self-discipline and hard work usually pay off, and due to our own hard work and individual merit, we are entitled to things that other people do not have. . . . [T]he ideology protecting our privileges in the upper tiers of the working class conditions us to deny attention and feeling to those we have learned are unworthy.[187]

Hobgood warns that middle-class people who accept the belief that the rich are better and more worthy people might spend their lives attempting to grow wealthy, rather than working to grow in virtue.

This brief survey of the ways wealth and poverty affect self-understanding through social status suggest a mechanism for their impact on the moral life. Inequality, a serious and growing problem both within and between nations and one distinct from poverty, raises the volume on the persistent messages our wealth or poverty send us about our own goodness, potential, and ability to shape the world around us. Now that we have explored what inequality is, the next chapter defines and details virtue, taking the next step in my project to show how inequality shapes virtue's pursuit.

NOTES

1. Throughout this book, "economic inequality" refers to inequality of both income and wealth.
2. Elliott, "World's 26 Richest People."
3. Piketty, *Capital*, 263.
4. Piketty, 264.
5. Schlozman, Verba, and Brady, *Unheavenly Chorus*, 76.
6. Olinto and Saavedra, "Overview," 3; Morcroft, "Global Income Inequality."
7. Piketty, *Capital*, 67.
8. Cowen, "Income Inequality."
9. Piketty, *Capital*, 326.
10. OECD, "Crisis Squeezes Income"; OECD, *In It Together*, 248.
11. Piketty, *Capital*, 24.
12. Piketty, 335.
13. Piketty, 509–10.
14. Piketty, 315.
15. Piketty, 20.
16. Piketty, 131.
17. Piketty, 135.
18. Miron, "The Role of Government in Creating Inequality," in *Anti-Piketty*, ed. Delsol and Martin.

19. Lindsey and Teles, *Captured Economy*.
20. Lindsey and Teles, 62–63.
21. Lindsey and Teles, 108.
22. Lindsey and Teles, chap. 6.
23. Lindsey and Teles, 121.
24. Lindsey and Teles, chap. 7.
25. Baker, "Rising Inequality," 9–10.
26. Baker, 12.
27. Piketty, *Capital*, 328–29.
28. Piketty, 267–68.
29. Schlozman, Verba, and Brady, *Unheavenly Chorus*, 73.
30. Norton and Ariely, "Building a Better America"; Gudrais, "Loaded Perceptions."
31. Presenting a conservative perspective on inequality, James Nuechterlein answered this question in the negative in *First Things*: "Not many Americans would lose sleep over inequality if no Americans lacked economic necessities." Nuechterlein, "Living with Inequality," 3–4.
32. Therborn, *Killing Fields*, 7.
33. Therborn, 7.
34. Chetty et al., "Association."
35. Therborn, *Killing Fields*, 9.
36. Potts, "What's Killing Poor White Women?"
37. Therborn, *Killing Fields*, 82–83.
38. Therborn, 10; for a recent example, see Dwyer-Lindgren et al., "Inequalities."
39. Pickett and Wilkinson, *Spirit Level*, 12 (chart 1.3).
40. Therborn, *Killing Fields*, 110.
41. Pickett and Wilkinson, *Spirit Level*, 181.
42. Pickett and Wilkinson, 174.
43. Pickett and Wilkinson.
44. Mann, "Medicine."
45. Pickett and Wilkinson, *Spirit Level*, 222–23.
46. David Cloutier, *Vice*, 167–69.
47. Pickett and Wilkinson, *Spirit Level*, 223.
48. Pickett and Wilkinson, 215.
49. Nussbaum, "Poverty," in *Poverty*, ed. Grusky and Kanbur, 47.
50. Finn, *Moral Ecology*, 63.
51. Piketty, *Capital*, 16.
52. Berg and Ostry, "Inequality."
53. Chuhan-Pole et al., "Africa's Pulse," 14.
54. Chuhan-Pole et al., 26.
55. Therborn, *Killing Fields*, 103.
56. Piketty, *Capital*, 297.
57. Sen, "Conceptualizing and Measuring Poverty," in *Poverty*, ed. Grusky and Kanbur, 30–46.
58. van der Hoeven, "Income Distribution," 255.
59. van der Hoeven, 257–59.
60. van der Hoeven, 259.
61. Garry, "Conservatism."
62. Reich, "Secession."

63. Carp was responding to the California wildfires of 2018, when the use of private firefighting services by wealthy celebrities inspired a national debate about whether the existence and use of private services ultimately harms widespread access to a formerly public good. Madrigal, "Kim Kardashian's Private Firefighters."

64. Schlozman, Verba, and Brady, *Unheavenly Chorus*, 123.

65. Schlozman, Verba, and Brady, 126.

66. Schlozman, Verba, and Brady, 170.

67. Schlozman, Verba, and Brady, 235–37. Making a similar point, Thomas Piketty notes that in United States, "It was war that gave rise to progressive taxation, not the natural consequences of universal suffrage"; Piketty, *Capital*, 514.

68. Schlozman, Verba, and Brady, *Unheavenly Chorus*, 261.

69. Schlozman, Verba, and Brady, 174–75.

70. Schlozman, Verba, and Brady, 267.

71. Schlozman, Verba, and Brady, 326.

72. Schlozman, Verba, and Brady, 331.

73. Schlozman, Verba, and Brady, 178.

74. Schlozman, Verba, and Brady, 197.

75. Schlozman, Verba, and Brady, 554.

76. Schlozman, Verba, and Brady, 113–14.

77. OECD, *Broken Social Elevator?*

78. Smeeding, Jäntti, and Erikson, "Introduction," 2.

79. Pickett and Wilkinson, *Spirit Level*, 160; OECD, *Broken Social Elevator?* 70.

80. Pickett and Wilkinson, *Spirit Level*, 163.

81. Kearney and Levine, "Income Inequality."

82. Pickett and Wilkinson, *Spirit Level*, 108.

83. Garcia and Weiss, "Education Inequalities"; Gamoran, "What Will Decrease Educational Inequality?"

84. Schlozman, Verba, and Brady, *Unheavenly Chorus*, 86; Reardon, "Income Inequality."

85. Pickett and Wilkinson, *Spirit Level*, 110–11.

86. Heckman, "Lifelines."

87. Duncan et al., "Economic Deprivation."

88. Heckman, "Lifelines"; Noah, *Great Divergence*, 184–85.

89. Piketty, *Capital*, 306–7.

90. A group of Piketty's critics, mostly economists, took issue with aspects of his application of this formula, including the time frame over which Piketty believes it to be true and Piketty's failure to acknowledge that capital must be productively invested for the formula to be true. Still, it is worth noting that even Piketty's critics agreed with his basic premise, writing that $r > g$ "is not controversial in itself." Martin, Lecaussin, and Delsol, "Anti-Piketty," chaps. 19–22.

91. Piketty, *Capital*, 358.

92. Piketty, 353.

93. Piketty, 431.

94. Piketty, 443.

95. Piketty, 10.

96. Piketty, 297.

97. Piketty, 245.

98. Piketty, 395.

99. The exception is the period between and just after the two world wars, thanks to the massive economic shocks of those wars and the fact that many *rentiers* drew down their capital by maintaining their prewar standard of living. Piketty, 369.

100. Piketty, 408.

101. Piketty, 471.

102. Piketty, 522, 539.

103. Daley, "Hunger."

104. Ohlheiser, "San Francisco Cathedral."

105. Quinn, "Anti-Homeless Spikes."

106. National Law Center on Homelessness and Poverty, "No Safe Place."

107. Pickett and Wilkinson, *Spirit Level*, 155.

108. Pickett and Wilkinson, 140–41.

109. Pickett and Wilkinson.

110. Pickett and Wilkinson, 139.

111. Piketty, *Capital*, 152.

112. Piketty acknowledges that this is a disturbing calculation to make, but he believes that it serves the cause of justice today to understand the historical US economy, and modern US duplicity about our own history, as accurately as possible. I agree on all counts.

113. Piketty, *Capital*, 160–62.

114. Pickett and Wilkinson, *Spirit Level*, 231.

115. Waterman and Brennan, "Christian Theology."

116. Waliggo, "Call"; Tirimanna, "Globalization"; Campos, "Doing Christian Ethics"; Sniegocki, *Catholic Social Teaching*; Razu, "India Unleashed."

117. Sebastian Kim, "Editorial."

118. Mifsud, "Moral Reflection."

119. Barrera, *God*.

120. Waterman, "Inequality."

121. Yuengert, "What Is 'Sustainable Prosperity'?"

122. Clark, "Wealth."

123. Beed and Beed, "Recent Christian Interpretations," 412.

124. McCann, "Inequality."

125. Zamagni, "Catholic Social Thought," 81.

126. Bane, "Catholic Social Teachings," 404.

127. Hicks, *Inequality*, 236.

128. Hicks, 232.

129. Hicks, "How Economic Inequality Is a Theological and Moral Issue," 443.

130. Rieger, *No Rising Tide*.

131. Rieger, "Ethics."

132. Rieger and Henkel-Rieger, *Unified*, 60–61.

133. Piketty, *Capital*, 438.

134. Piketty, 62.

135. Pope Leo XIII, "Rerum novarum," 17.

136. Pope Pius XI, "Quadrigesimo anno," 5.

137. Christiansen, "On Relative Equality."

138. Benedict XVI, "Caritas in veritate."

139. Finn, *Christian Economic Ethics*, 313.

140. Francis, "Evangelii gaudium"; Ward, "Jesuit and Feminist Hospitality," 71.

141. Orobator, "Caritas in veritate."
142. Mikulich, "Where Y'At Race?"
143. Cloutier, "Exclusion," 150–51.
144. Jenkins, "Is Plutocracy Sinful?" 46.
145. Cloutier, "Exclusion," 153–54.
146. Cloutier, 154–55.
147. Cloutier, 160, 163.
148. Naudé and du Plessis, "Economic Inequality," 78.
149. Naudé and du Plessis, 91.
150. Naudé and du Plessis, 91–92.
151. de Vries, "Moral Considerations."
152. Schor, "What Can We Do?"; Welby, "Does Inequality Really Matter?"; Bretherton, "Soteriology"; Bader-Saye, "Closing the Gap."
153. Tanner, "Inequality," 173; Tanner also discusses inequality in *Christianity*, chap. 7.
154. Jenkins, "Is Plutocracy Sinful?" 42.
155. Armstrong, "Spirit."
156. Renaud, "Call."
157. Ward and Himes, *Growing Apart.*
158. O'Sullivan, "Twenty-First-Century Global Goal-Setting."
159. Kochuthara, "Economic Inequality," 141.
160. Konigsburg, "Economic and Ethical Implications," 74. For an economic analysis of approaches to helping families achieve living wages, see Quinn and Cahill, "Relative Effectiveness," 69.
161. Ward, "Jesuit and Feminist Hospitality."
162. Himes, "Catholic Social Teaching," 49.
163. Hirschfeld, "Rethinking Economic Inequality."
164. McRorie, "Heterodox Economics."
165. Hicks, "Inequality, Justice."
166. Himes, "Catholic Social Teaching, Economic Inequality."
167. Weithman, "Religious Ethics."
168. Snarr, "*Elaborating* Faith."
169. Hinson-Hasty, *Problem*, 190.
170. Hinson-Hasty, chap. 8.
171. Cahill, *Global Justice*, 264.
172. Magesa, "African Indigenous Spirituality."
173. Hinze, "What Is Enough?"
174. Rubio, *Family Ethics.*
175. Ward and Himes, *Growing Apart.*
176. Adewale, "Afro-Sociological Application."
177. Odozor, "Truly Africa!"
178. Hobgood, "White Economic and Erotic Disempowerment," 48.
179. Massingale, "Ethical Reflection."
180. Piketty, *Capital*, 416.
181. Piketty, 417.
182. Therborn, *Killing Fields*, 21. This definition of poverty echoes those used by many theologians of liberation. E.g., Gustavo Gutiérrez defines poverty as "the lack of economic goods necessary for a human life worthy of the name"; Gutiérrez, *Theology*, 288.

183. Lott, "Social Psychology."
184. Lott.
185. CELAM, "Medellín Document: Peace."
186. Pickett and Wilkinson, *Spirit Level*, 262.
187. Hobgood, *Dismantling Privilege*, 82.

CHAPTER 2

CHRISTIAN VIRTUE ETHICS

This chapter begins with a brief introduction to the renewed flourishing of virtue thought in Christian theology and philosophy in recent decades. Virtue helps us live well; the virtuous person is on her way to achieving the human good. Christian theology gives a particular account of that human good, which is explored in a brief anthropological account of "the human person fully alive." The chapter continues by describing a constellation of virtues that will later serve to illuminate the impact of wealth and poverty in the moral life. I draw on the work of Augustine, Thomas Aquinas, John Paul II, and James Keenan and other contemporary virtue theorists, to provide rich accounts of the virtues of prudence, justice, temperance, fortitude, self-care, solidarity, and humility. Each virtue is illustrated with one or more exemplars who embody virtue in their particular lives.

VIRTUE ETHICS

Christian virtue theory is rooted in the theological conviction that God desires human flourishing. Virtue theory describes what human flourishing—human excellence—looks like in light of the Christian belief that humans are created by and in relationship with God.[1] As Lisa Fullam says, "Virtues are anthropological truth claims," describing the person or community that lives the human life well.[2] Augustine defined a virtue as "a habit that cannot be misused," that cannot be directed to the harm of the human person.[3] Virtues do not simply help us meet some external moral standard. Rather, virtue theorists believe the virtuous person is happier, more flourishing, and more fully alive than the one who lacks virtue.[4] Virtue theory offers a vision of the human good as well as a path to achieving it.

Virtue ethics asks, "Who or what kind of person am I? What kind of person should I be? How should I act in order to become that kind of person?"

As Maureen O'Connell notes, "Virtues integrate internal dispositions into external actions."[5] That is, having a virtue makes it easier to discern and to do the virtuous thing, and vice versa: virtuous actions help form virtuous habits.

Virtue theorists use the term "practices" to describe behaviors or patterns of action that originate out of, or would tend to help develop, virtuous qualities in persons.[6] Practices are patterns of action; they have a consistent quality. And they are reflected upon; at some level, the person understands that consistently acting in this way will promote a particular virtue.

The virtuous person does not live in a constant state of tension, policing her own thoughts and grudgingly forcing herself to do virtuous deeds. Rather, her desires are so well ordered that she wants to do the virtuous thing, and does it easily. To have the virtue of justice, for example, means something different from simply making a firm commitment to act in a just way, praiseworthy though such a commitment may be.

After significant attention to virtue ethics by Christians in the ancient and medieval periods, the approach receded in popularity until recent decades.[7] The retrieval of virtue theory from a Christian standpoint was inspired by dissatisfaction with other available ethics methods, including proportionalism and a variety of interpretations of normative or act-based ethics.[8] Virtue ethicists argue that act-based ethics is lacking for several reasons. A focus on acts can lead to an obsession with avoiding bad deeds or accumulating good ones—what Catholics have called scrupulosity. Act-based ethics can also lead to an impoverished view of the moral life: "Well, at least I'm not a murderer." In contrast to this, virtue ethics demands a mature, complex view of a person's moral life. Virtue ethics acknowledges that each person is on a journey toward the good, and though we will never attain perfection, we can act to shape our own progress toward the good as we move through life in our particular communities.

We can assess others' acts, but much more rarely can we assess their virtues. Lisa Fullam takes the extreme view that we can never declare another person virtuous: "Acts, in a sense, may be symptoms of virtues: a pattern of acts consistent with a given virtue raises the index of suspicion that a certain virtue is at work, but no act, nor even a collection of acts, is adequate to establish that 'so-and-so is humble.'"[9] Fullam is making a point about epistemological humility; ultimately, the totality of a person's character is between that person and God. But her rigorous stance seems at odds with the fact that we often do assess others' virtue: when we evaluate someone as a partner in business or in love, when we admire or distrust others for their consistent patterns of action, when we strive to imitate the ordinary saints in our lives. The exemplars who appear later in this chapter performed remarkable acts that clearly demonstrated particular virtues. We who seek to learn from such lives can indeed extrapolate from actions to character.

That said, virtue ethics reminds us that we are more than our actions and that we always carry within us the potential for improvement. Andrew Michael Flescher has argued that in fact, virtue ethics seems to demand that we continually push ourselves to go above and beyond the call of duty on behalf of others: "Living altruistically is the kernel of living virtuously."[10] Virtue ethics directs us to attend to a lifelong moral journey rather than obsessing over individual actions, but though virtue ethics has been criticized for encouraging a navel-gazing focus on one's own self, this is a misunderstanding. Virtue is always pursued in daily interactions with others, in navigating the competing demands life makes on us to nurture relationships with others, pursue justice, and care for ourselves.[11] This relational aspect of virtue ethics has particularly endeared it to Christian moralists.

Virtue is particularly hailed for its usefulness in pluralistic contexts that are attentive to cultural particularity. Maureen O'Connell praises virtue ethics for its historical consciousness and ability to attend to the specificities of individuals and situations.[12] Christina Astorga notes that our cultural standpoints—such as gender, class, and power—also influence the virtues we esteem and how we develop them.[13] Monica Jalandoni suggests that when a local culture has a tendency to value a particular virtue, this does not rise to the level of a social virtue, but may be considered "what Thomas [Aquinas] calls inchoate virtue or the beginning of virtue." In her example, Filipino society displays the virtue of fortitude inchoately, because Filipino people believe it is good to display endurance and have done so in response to economic hardships, tyrannical governments, and natural disasters.[14] James Bretzke has argued that virtues are especially helpful in cross-cultural ethical conversations, because they furnish a shared language that every local community will "thicken" in order to describe a virtue in its own particular way.[15]

Virtue's proponents in theology observe its deep affinities with a Christian worldview. For example, it helps believers derive ethics from Scripture; stories are an effective way to discern and think about the virtues; and narratives, like virtue frameworks, tend to build toward a goal.[16] Virtue ethics do not present easy instructions about how to act in particular situations; rather, like stories, they invite us to moral deliberation. In a sense, this is both a benefit and a drawback of virtue ethics. For Paulinus Odozor, "the virtues make our pondering easier [but] being virtuous does not remove the pain of having to make hard decisions in this life."[17]

Odozor's evocation of "hard decisions" points to an ongoing debate in virtue ethics: whether the "unity thesis," that a virtuous person must possess

every virtue in equal degrees, can be sustained. This view, which is best associated with Thomas Aquinas, presents a high bar that makes it difficult to
envision who could be considered virtuous. Andrew Kim defends Aquinas
on the grounds that "virtue in the conditions of this world is possessed by
degrees in stages of time," so Aquinas can still insist on the unity of virtue
without also implying a binary between virtue and its absence.[18] James
Keenan proposes cardinal virtues that govern how we act in relationships,
rather than governing individual "powers" of the human person, as in Aquinas's virtue framework. Because relationships sometimes place competing
claims on persons, Keenan believes his virtues system improves on Aquinas's,
which fails to acknowledge that life presents us with situations in which the
virtues may conflict.[19]

Responding to Keenan, Lisa Fullam argues that "unless we are created
absurdly, virtues cannot conflict with one another, but clearly *acts* of a particular virtue often conflict."[20] Fullam finds a good reason for preserving
the ideal of virtue's unity: it forces us to confront how life circumstances
throw attempted acts of virtue into conflict in different, potentially unfair
ways. Because the effects of social sin endow particular people with unequal
experiences, members of oppressed groups are more likely to face conflicts
between acts of virtue, such as when women are socialized to neglect their
own self-care while prioritizing care for others.[21] If we simply accept that
everyone faces conflicts of virtue, we might miss the fact that some, due to
life circumstances, are more likely to be forced into tragic choices.

WHAT MAKES CHRISTIAN VIRTUE ETHICS CHRISTIAN?

"Christian virtue ethics" is not monolithic. In fact, scholars of Christian religious ethics or moral theology disagree significantly about what, exactly, constitutes a Christian virtue ethic. Some moralists reject the notion of Christian
virtue ethics entirely—alleging, among other things, that it is narcissistic,
elitist, or too withdrawn from the Christian community.[22] Another influential
view is that laid out by Stanley Hauerwas and Charles Pinches in *Christians
Among the Virtues* (1997). Hauerwas and Pinches take the exceptional stance
that Christian virtues are unintelligible outside Christian lives and communities: "The courage of a Christian is different from that of a Buddhist. No
appeal to human nature is sufficient to insure the commonality of all human
virtue; . . . an account of growth in Christian virtue cannot be generic."[23]
I agree with these scholars that virtue becomes particular because it is formed
in particular communities with particular ends, and that virtue for Christians

is shaped by Christian communities and narratives.[24] On that, few if any Christian virtue theorists would disagree. Certainly no one is arguing that a Christian's path to virtue is going to look exactly the same as the path taken by someone of a different faith, or of none. But for many scholars, Hauerwas and Pinches insist too strongly on the unique *character* of Christian virtues.

Most Christian virtue theorists occupy a middle view between that of virtue ethics as unChristian and Christian virtue ethics as exclusionary. In this view, universally intelligible virtues attain particular cultural resonance as persons live out the virtues in their local communities. This makes virtue useful for cross-cultural dialogue and ethical dialogue with other disciplines.[25] Lúcás Chan explained this middle approach this way: "Though virtues are context sensitive, they are not ultimately confined to a limited context but remain open to revision."[26]

In fact, this middle approach is not confined to Christian ethics. The philosopher Martha Nussbaum advances it with her nonrelative virtues. She argues that though virtues will always be understood and lived out in light of particular cultural, context-dependent values, certain goods of human life, lived out and experienced through the virtues, are universal.[27]

That said, Christian virtue theorists, and Catholics in particular, have eagerly adopted this middle way because it shares considerable resonance with the Catholic concept of the natural law. Natural law theory states that certain basic human goods are self-evidently intelligible to anyone, universally across cultural differences.[28] Christians who adopt this middle perspective often argue that what makes Christian virtue ethics unique is the context in which virtue is pursued and formed—in Christian communities and by Christian Scripture.[29] The virtues that are pursued and formed are not unique, but the context that shapes them is.[30]

I appreciate Lisa Sowle Cahill's impatience with some Christians' insistence that the goods Christians value are unintelligible outside the Church:

> We only distract ourselves from the most crucial issues of social ethics, religious ethics, and Christian ethics, when we argue as though the basic necessities of human well-being for other groups or cultures are alien to us, as are our goods to them. . . . Certain basic goods are humanly self-evident. . . . The biggest moral challenge Jesus presents is not to uphold a unique vision of the good, but to reach across class, race, gender, and culture to create greater solidarity around goods. Practical solidarity, which is the same thing as action, can then yield dialectical and dialogical understandings of what will further human well-being on particular occasions, and in particular relations.[31]

Cahill is right to say that certain basic goods are universally intelligible.[32] Because virtue pursues the good, many virtues also have universal relevance, even as particular cultures will always interpret virtues within their own context. Christian virtue ethics are Christian, not because the virtues pursued lack meaning for non-Christians but because Christians pursue these virtues in Christian communities and in light of Christian Scripture and tradition.

"ANTHROPOLOGICAL TRUTH CLAIMS": WHO IS THE VIRTUOUS PERSON IN CHRISTIAN LIFE?

Lisa Fullam memorably defines virtues as "anthropological truth claims"; the virtues describe the fully realized, flourishing human person. The virtues described in this chapter have particular relevance for economic life, but they are also foundational to gaining a picture of what it means to be a flourishing human being on the path to God. I briefly sketch a Christian understanding of the human person to contextualize the constellation of virtues this chapter describes.

Anthropology—giving an account of the human person—is fundamental to Christian theology because the human person is first and foremost God's creature. Understanding the character of the human person sheds light on God's creative activity and God's intent for ongoing relationship with humanity. Christian theological anthropology takes many forms, but its practitioners would broadly agree that the human person possesses these attributes: constituted in community, capable of reason, persistently striving, seeking the flourishing of self and others, and sustained by God's grace.

Recent anthropological accounts take the communal or social human nature as foundational to the meaning of human life, dethroning reason from its earlier role as the sole key to human uniqueness. From a scriptural perspective, this insight is justified by God's creation of human companionship in Genesis; God's offer of the covenant to the Israelite community rather than to particular individuals; and Jesus calling followers into community with him and one another—among other resources.[33] Social science confirms that human beings cannot survive without the support and companionship of others. This understanding of our social nature as foundational to the human person comports well with virtue theory, which observes that we learn how to be virtuous in community, and cannot do so alone.

Reason has a troubled history as a definitive human anthropological attribute. For many centuries, Christian thinkers viewed it as axiomatic that the capacity for abstract thought granted humans a unique status among God's creatures. More recently, however, theologians have pointed out that elevat-ing reason in this way runs the risk of labeling many groups of human beings as subhuman, including born and unborn children and persons with men-tal disabilities.[34] Reason as anthropological constant has also been deployed against nonwhite or non-European groups of persons who were wrongly depicted as having inferior reasoning capacity.[35] This harmful history cau-tions against claims that reason *is* what makes a life human. However, we can say that in the experience of many, reasoned reflection is a significant *part* of human life with and for others.[36] Unfortunately, the moral life is not always self-evident or "common sense."[37] Those of us granted the use of reason must remain prepared to exercise it as we discern and pursue the virtuous life.

A classical theological view depicts the human person as persistently striving toward goals, an anthropology that lends itself to a teleological ethics such as virtue. This anthropological constant can operate more inclusively than an account of reason; for example, Miguel Romero defends the ability of persons with profound mental disabilities to perform virtuous acts in pur-suit of the divine plan.[38] Many Christian theologians observe that humans will always strive toward goals, though particular goals may or may not con-tribute to human flourishing. Our striving must be rightly ordered to prox-imate, or more immediate, ends that will help us journey to our final end of unity with God.

A visible outgrowth of our striving, communal nature is that humans tend to seek the flourishing of ourselves and others. Christian theology does not abide social-Darwinist or classical economic understandings of humans as competing for survival.[39] Divine revelation and human experi-ence together reveal the insight that humans naturally desire the flourishing of others around them and strive to balance fostering others' flourishing with their own. Human nature desires the good for self and others; sin limits but does not totally erase this reality.

A final and fundamental observation of Christian anthropology is that human nature is created and remains sustained by God's grace.[40] Pertinent to virtue ethics, this observation reminds us that though we may experience our life's journey as responding to our own volition and actions, God's agency enables every achievement we might view ourselves as making.

The remainder of this chapter describes a constellation of virtues that present a fuller picture of this anthropology, the good human life as Chris-tian tradition understands it. Although the remainder of this book examines these virtues through the lenses of wealth and poverty, they are not only relevant to economic life but also function as anthropological truth claims, helping to enflesh human life's full potential.

PRUDENCE

Prudence is the virtue that helps us determine the actions needed to pursue the good in our concrete situation.[41] In the words of Josef Pieper, prudence "signifies the directing of volition and action toward objective reality."[42] The philosopher George Klubertanz points out that prudence by definition pursues truly human goods and cannot be used to pursue evil; the common use of the word to mean pragmatic calculation is inaccurate in the context of virtue theory.[43] Similarly, Pieper cautions us against accepting the popular reading of prudence as a sort of crabbed timidity or crass practicality.[44] Rather, it denotes a clear-eyed read of reality: "He alone can do good who knows what things are like and what their situation is. The pre-eminence of prudence means that so-called 'good intention' and so-called 'meaning well' by no means suffice. Realization of the good presupposes that our actions are appropriate to the real situation, that is, to the concrete realities which form the 'environment' of a concrete human action; and that we therefore take this concrete reality seriously."[45]

For Aquinas, prudence is the only virtue that governs the intellect. This is because prudence has to do with our knowledge of reality and our assessment of the past, present, and future.[46] When we use our reason for vicious ends, Aquinas says we engage in covetousness, the source of several vices opposed to prudence.[47] Reason enables us to detect the truth, but prudence needs to guide our reason to respond to concrete reality rather than our own, potentially vicious desires.

Pieper emphasizes how completely prudence relies on "real concreteness"—that is, experience of the real situation at hand.[48] Virtues are true insofar as they respond to reality. Pieper emphasizes: "The precedence of prudence [in Aquinas's taxonomy] indicates that the realization of goodness presumes knowledge of reality. Whatever is good is ascertained by prudence; in turn, whatever is prudent is established by the 'thing itself.'"[49] This is why "everyone who sins is imprudent"; they are failing to respond appropriately to reality, that is, to the good.[50] Far from dictating a preordained set of rules or duties, prudence helps us respond to the world around us in accordance with reason. Reason is a God-given quality, which is why aligning with reason is virtuous.

Most virtue ethicists see prudence as occupying a chief place among the virtues, but they vary in how they describe this. In Aquinas's virtue system, prudence appoints the end to the other moral virtues and perceives the actions necessary to pursue the good, but the virtue of prudence does not perceive the good. That is the job of *synderesis*, a sort of natural inclination to do good and avoid evil.[51] For Aquinas, we apprehend the good through synderesis, and prudence helps us apply it to specific situations.[52] This allows him to take the consoling view that even persons who do not have virtue are able to perceive and pursue the good, however imperfectly. In the words of Dennis Billy, prudence "appoints" and "personalizes" the proximate goals along the way to pursuing the human good, and the moral virtues (temperance, justice, and fortitude) help us to focus on these goods.[53] In James Keenan's words, prudence *perfects* and *directs*. It *perfects* our pursuit of the good by guiding us in what to do, and it *directs* the other virtues in helping us do what prudence prescribes.[54]

For Aquinas, prudence governs the other virtues by helping us choose according to reason. He says behavior according to reason takes the form of a mean between two extremes. Prudence inspires us to deliberate before taking action. It helps us assess the good for individuals as well as the common good.[55] Paul Wadell writes that "truly prudent persons . . . are able to think things out well, not just for today, but for the whole of the good life. They are truly prudent because they are able to judge wisely, in everything they do, about what helps and hinders their striving for God."[56] However, as Pieper notes, even the prudent person is never assured of total certainty about the rightness of her action.[57]

Aquinas describes prudence as composed of multiple good qualities. Memory of the truth of things is an important part of prudence. Pieper says that falsification of memory through error can be fatal to prudence, so we need to apply rigor to maintaining our knowledge of things to remain consonant with the truth.[58] "*Docilitas*," translated as "teachability" or intellectual humility, is a part of prudence that Pieper equates with open-mindedness. A closed mind and the conviction that one knows all there is to know on a certain subject can be fatal to prudence.[59] Other component parts of prudence include understanding or intuition; readiness to do the prudent act, which Aquinas calls shrewdness; the ability to use reason; foresight (discerning the end for humans and orienting present activities to it); the ability to assess circumstances when deciding how to act, which Aquinas calls circumspection; and caution, which accounts for the reality that even seemingly good choices can have bad aspects.[60]

A clear picture of the prudent person thus emerges. Graced with a clear understanding of the good, she easily chooses actions to pursue it. She has a sense of the context of her actions in history, thanks to memory. She can reason and respond with intuition but is also able to discern when her criteria for judging situations may be flawed. When deciding to act, she remains aware of the potentially negative consequences of even seemingly positive choices.

Exemplar of Prudence: Malcolm X

Malcolm X (1925–65) was a Black civil rights activist and lay religious leader in the United States. His childhood was profoundly shaped by white racist violence, which his family believed responsible for his father's suspicious death.[61] While serving time in jail as a young man for a series of robberies, then–Malcolm Little converted to the Nation of Islam (NOI), a sectarian movement that blended orthodox Islamic views with calls for Black secession, hatred of white people, and violent resistance to racist oppression.[62] Malcolm X threw himself into organizing for the NOI, traveling widely to promote its views. Much admired for his steady leadership style and skill as a communicator, he rose to a top position within the NOI. His social connections, income, and, eventually, housing for his wife and family all derived from his status within the religious organization.[63]

Troubled by immoral behavior on the part of NOI leader Elijah Muhammad, Malcolm X began his shift away from advocating violence with his famous 1964 speech "The Ballot or the Bullet."[64] He began to develop a theological justification for his evolving views during a pilgrimage to Mecca and subsequent travel through several majority-Muslim nations. There he saw Muslims of all races and backgrounds praying to God in the orthodox Islamic tradition he had come to revere.[65] He experienced a proud, diverse, and global Islam, a religion of peace, which was easily distinguishable from the separatist violence preached by the NOI. When he returned to the United States, he publicly broke with the NOI, attempting to correct the record on the discrepancy between mainstream Islam and NOI teachings.[66] He denounced separatism and racial hatred, and he sought an alliance with the nonviolent civil rights movement.[67] After his tragic assassination by vengeful NOI members in 1965, his posthumous autobiography continued the public analysis and recantation of many of his earlier violent and misinformed views.[68]

From a US standpoint, it is difficult to think of any twentieth-century public figure who made a more radical public recommitment of life than Malcolm X, and who was able to so profoundly change in response to learning that previous views were wrong.[69] Malcolm's transformation was not occasioned by any public exposure of wrongdoing, like other famous recantations that may come to mind. Rather, it was simply his exposure to the truth— Islam is a nonviolent religion that invites people of all races into relationship with God—and his prudent ability to discern the truth and respond to it, that occasioned this dramatic shift. His right judgment, intellectual humility, and ready response to the truth he discerned demonstrate that he is an exemplar of prudence par excellence.

Malcolm X's conversion and public recantation were not uninformed or naive. He was aware of the real possibility of the consequences that did, tragically, follow. His commitment to the truth, and to rectifying the spread of untruth he had done so effectively as a skilled leader and communicator, ultimately made him a martyr to the truth he had found, and to his own estimable prudence.

JUSTICE

Although common usage often speaks of "justice" as an ideal that exists outside ourselves, virtue thought reminds us that it can also be a personal characteristic. The virtue of justice is a persistent quality that helps us pursue the ideal of justice; Paul Wadell writes that "a person of justice is *habitually* disposed to take the needs and well-being of others into account because he or she recognizes there is never a moment in which the claims of others, including God and other species, do not impinge on us."[70] We can define justice as the virtue that helps us give others what is due to them, to help them achieve the human good.

In the views of Western philosophers including Adam Smith and David Hume, justice is a negative virtue, through which we simply avoid harming others.[71] But a Christian understanding of justice demands more; the just person actively responds to the claims others' needs make on her. Rather than simple avoidance of harm, which would often result in maintaining the status quo, a Christian understanding of justice "works to return to others what was rightfully theirs in the first place."[72]

For Aquinas, justice is always toward other humans, not including oneself.[73] "Legal" justice orients us toward the common good, whereas particular justice directs us to be just in our interactions with particular individuals.[74] Jean Porter points out that for Aquinas, justice is the only moral virtue that governs the will, rather than the passions. Aquinas relies on this distinction when he describes how we act unjustly. Unjust actions result from the intellect's failure to understand the relationship between two people and what is due to another person. Thus justice is the virtue that helps us grasp the truth about what is due to others. We could add that justice is the virtue that helps us see other people *as human*—that is, as individuals who deserve to attain full human flourishing. Members of oppressed groups often argue that they are seen as less than human by those in power. This indicates a failure of the virtue of justice with those who act this way.

James Keenan notes that justice is the only one of Aquinas's cardinal virtues that bespeaks an understanding of the human person as relational.[75] Thus Wadell calls it "the virtue of human togetherness," which deals with our relationships with others that always already exist, whether we realize it or not.[76] In Keenan's virtue system, justice is the virtue that governs general, rather than particular, human relationships. It inspires us to treat all others equally in light of the common good. For Keenan, justice is "a forward-looking virtue [that] prudently anticipates a way of seeing society more respectful of persons."[77]

The just person, first and foremost, sees other people as fully human and in relationship with herself. She understands the common good and the claims that all humans make on her. She is able to judge what is due to other humans as humans, and she willingly acts on those judgments. She desires for all people the same human flourishing that she wants for herself and those she loves, even though finite human ability may force her to direct her efforts more narrowly.

Exemplar of Justice: Dan Price

With different relationships to wealth, we experience different opportunities to perform acts of justice. Two contemporary exemplars of this basic truth are Dan Price, CEO of Gravity Payments, and a group of then-graduate students known as the Duke Collective.

Dan Price gained worldwide attention in 2015 when he announced plans to raise the salaries of every employee at Gravity Payments, his small financial processing company, to $70,000 or more. He chose this figure because it is close to the threshold where studies suggest the relationship of income and happiness "maxes out"; that is, an increase in income no longer reliably increases happiness.[78] To achieve this, Price increased spending on employee pay while lowering his own $1.2 million salary to $70,000. In addition to the wave of mostly favorable publicity, he says today that the move brought enormous benefits in company productivity, largely due to reduced anxiety on the part of lower-paid employees.[79] More importantly, however, he connects the decision to his own flourishing, the flourishing of Gravity employees, and that of the broader society.

Price has frequently acknowledged a claim of justice, as well as a social anthropology, in discussing his decision. For example, he spoke about how moved he was that the wage increase enabled many Gravity employees to buy homes, save for retirement, and start families. The potential embodied in his employees' children brought home to Price that his actions spread benefit beyond the original employees, perhaps even beyond his own lifetime.[80] He expressed that though life certainly requires the meeting of basic needs, the happy life develops when we place a "relatively modest" threshold on our own needs, which allows us to focus on contributing to society and building relationships with others.[81] The simple realization that his employees had the same right as he himself did to an income that could grant them family stability and maximize the relationship of income to happiness led to Price's decision to pay them all a salary of at least $70,000. A well-articulated understanding of the good life led Price to take bold action in pursuit of justice, realizing that financial comfort would encourage his employees' flourishing and expand outward to the flourishing of society in the present day and years to come. He made a bold sacrifice of his own income and consequent financial power to honor his conviction about what is due to others.

Exemplar of Justice: The Duke Collective

A group of graduate students at Duke University in Durham, North Carolina, embarked on a radical practice of justice in 2012 when they began to pool their incomes into a common fund.[82] PhD student stipends are often too low to support a family or even an individual without resorting to work outside the graduate program, which can interfere with studies. Graduate student funding is also marked by disparity between individual students and across academic disciplines. (In 2014, some relatively fortunate students received stipends of $27,000 a year, while one member of the group earned $15,200 and one had no income for the year.[83]) Sharing all their resources, from graduate stipends to cash gifts, allowed all these students to manage financially without worrying about interruptions in income. Participants in the collective, which was open to anyone who wished to join, explicitly connected their sharing of funds to their own flourishing. They spoke of "solidarity" among the group, and one said simply "It's a better way to live your life."[84]

The students of the Duke Collective demonstrated a rich practice of the virtue of justice. They understood implicitly that the basic wherewithal to live is part of what is due to all people, simply by virtue of their human nature. And they acted on this conviction to enable their friends and colleagues to receive the basic needs that are due to them as human beings. Their radical action demonstrates that one need not be in a position of financial power, like Dan Price, to practice the virtue of justice in relationship with others who are struggling to survive.

SOLIDARITY

The word "solidarity" is used variously to describe the theological-anthropological reality of the unity of the human family; an ethical principle or norm of being guided by that reality; a practice in response to that reality; and a virtue.[85] This reflection focuses on the virtue of solidarity, the consistent personal quality of unity with and commitment to others' good.

Pope John Paul II, a leading promoter of the virtue of solidarity, explains that it helps us see others as persons like ourselves rather than tools for our use.[86] However, it is not a vaguely felt sense of sympathy but a consistent orientation: "a firm and persevering determination to commit oneself to the common good; that is to say to the good of all and of each individual, because we are all really responsible for all, . . . a commitment to the good of one's neighbor with the readiness, in the gospel sense, to 'lose oneself' for the sake of the other instead of exploiting him, and to 'serve him' instead of oppressing him for one's own advantage."[87] Similarly, M. Shawn Copeland warns that solidarity does not emerge automatically from similarity of life circumstance, including race, class, or gender identity.[88] It is rooted in something more fundamental to human nature than these categories: the free, responsible choice to attend to another's concrete reality and commit to pursuing her good.[89]

John Paul II emphasizes that we may express the virtue of solidarity differently depending on our own social power and privilege:

> Those who are more influential, because they have a greater share of goods and common services, should feel responsible for the weaker and be ready to share with them all they possess. Those who are weaker, for their part, in the same spirit of solidarity, should not adopt a purely passive attitude or one that is destructive of the social fabric, but, while claiming their legitimate rights, should do what they can for the good of all. The intermediate groups, in their turn, should not selfishly insist on their particular interests, but respect the interests of others.[90]

He approvingly notes that poor people express solidarity when they recognize common cause with one another and advocate for their own good to the rest of society. Communities and nations can also express solidarity with one another. In fact, without impinging on the free self-determination of states, "solidarity demands a readiness to accept the sacrifices necessary for the good of the whole world community."[91]

John Paul II, and others including Bryan Massingale, recommend solidarity to those in power as well as those who have been excluded from power.[92]

Other theologians highlight the particular need for solidarity on the part of those with significant privilege. Rebecca Todd Peters develops an ethic for privileged "first-world Christians," viewing solidarity for such people as accountability to less advantaged people and willingness to be transformed by encounter with them. Her theology of solidarity calls First World Christians to begin with a starting point of mutuality, recognizing that privileged people do not solve the problems of the less privileged for them, but both groups may work together to address injustice.[93] In a response to Peters, Traci West cautions that solidarity for privileged people demands recognition that systems of oppression affect the lives of the privileged even as they cause the oppressed to suffer.[94] In the same vein, the cultural critic bell hooks says that "genuine solidarity with the poor . . . includes the recognition that the fate of the poor both locally and globally will to a grave extent determine the quality of life for those who are lucky enough to have class privilege."[95] Privileged and oppressed persons are always already linked in systems of power and domination, so a standpoint of solidarity does not create bonds so much as it acknowledges their prior existence and declares a commitment to transforming their nature.

Ethicists present different views of what solidarity looks like for the poor and excluded. A notable, though unusual, take comes from Miguel De La Torre, who envisions poor outcasts extending solidarity to the rich and influential. De La Torre imagines that the parable of Lazarus and the rich man (Luke 16:19–31) might have ended differently if Lazarus had advocated for himself. Perhaps Lazarus could have shown the rich man the error of his selfish ways; and the rich man, converted, would not have ended the story suffering in Hades. De La Torre writes:

> Even though the rich man forfeited salvation by refusing to fulfill his ethical responsibility to the poor man, the poor are still responsible for acting as moral agents to create a just society. Those who are privileged by the way society is constructed are in need of liberation and salvation because they too are created in the image of God. . . . When the marginalized seek out the liberation of the oppressors, they verify the humanity of both the privileged and themselves.[96]

De La Torre seems to suggest that Lazarus had an ethical responsibility to promote the rich man's liberation and salvation, but it is hard to detect this message in the Scripture passage. The parable itself contends that the rich man had the witness of "Moses and the prophets" to teach him his responsibility to the poor (Luke 16:29). Surely Lazarus was under no obligation to provide the rich man with more moral guidance than he should already have gotten from his knowledge of "Moses and the prophets" and from Lazarus's presence at his gate, a form of witness in and of itself. De La Torre is right to assert that the poor are able to act as moral agents for greater justice in society, and in fact have a responsibility to do so, just as every person does. However, a more usual Christian interpretation of solidarity would focus on the ability of the poor to practice solidarity with other oppressed persons when they work for change, rather than insisting on their duties to the rich.[97]

Working for social change together with others may be an example of what Kristin Heyer, following Massingale, calls conflictual solidarity. Although institutional solidarity transforms structures and incarnational solidarity is lived out in practice, conflictual solidarity acknowledges that widening the circle of justice involves struggle. Restoring dignity to those who have been stripped of it means that those who enjoy outsize privileges will have to give some up. Privileged people may resist this change, so conflictual solidarity prepares advocates to meet with such resistance.[98]

The person who has solidarity knows at a very basic level that the flourishing of all humanity is bound up with her own, and—just as important—she acts on this conviction. If she is marginalized, solidarity may suggest that the best way to encourage the well-being of all humanity together is to work for the flourishing of those in her own and other marginalized groups. If she is privileged, solidarity will require her to work for the full humanity of those who are marginalized. It is clear that the person who has solidarity works for those on the margins. But she does not do this from a standpoint that regards one group over and against the other—one that positions the privileged as benevolent helpers, or envisions the well-being of those on the margins as requiring the degradation of the fortunate. With the virtue of solidarity, we work for the flourishing of those on the margins from a standpoint that says none are fully human until all are fully human. We shape ourselves in line with God's own preferential option for the poor.

Exemplars of Solidarity: The Four
Churchwomen of El Salvador

Maura Clarke, MM; Ita Ford, MM; Dorothy Kazel, OSU; and Jean Donovan, a Catholic laywoman, were murdered by militants in El Salvador on December 1, 1980. Inspired by their faith, they had lived and worked for and with the poor of El Salvador under a US-backed military regime that wanted to keep poor people impoverished, isolated, and afraid. For their work attempting to help poor people survive under a violent military regime, they paid with their lives.

In their own ways, each of the four churchwomen left lives of privilege, with good educations and safe livelihoods, to come to El Salvador.[99] The brutal military-led government, supported by the United States, treated all poor people like insurgents, kidnapping and killing to impose a reign of terror. The churchwomen transported people to safety, offered medical help, distributed food to the poor, and documented human rights violations to create a historical record. Although they believed that resistance to the military regime was just, their efforts went to all people in need.[100] To the military regime, which even opposed offering medical treatment to wounded people, the churchwomen posed an unacceptable threat.[101] On the minister of defense's tacit orders, security forces kidnapped, raped, and murdered Maura, Ita, Dorothy, and Jean, leaving their bodies in a field.[102]

The four churchwomen had understood clearly that their lives were in danger. They remained in El Salvador because of their love for the poor and their deep conviction that the Gospel called them to serve there. Jean Donovan wrote to a friend: "Several times I have decided to leave El Salvador. I almost could, except for the children, the poor, bruised victims of this insanity. Who would care for them?"[103] And Maura Clarke connected their work to Christian witness: "If we abandon [people] when they are suffering the cross, how can we speak credibly about the resurrection?"[104] Making the concerns of others their own to the end of their lives, the four churchwomen died as martyrs to Christ's love and exemplars of solidarity.

FIDELITY

For James Keenan, who calls fidelity a cardinal virtue, fidelity "is the virtue that nurtures and sustains the bonds of those special relationships that humans enjoy—whether by blood, marriage, love, citizenship, or sacrament."[105] Fidelity presumes that we are able to recognize which committed relationships make special claims on us. Margaret Farley notes that "if all our commitments are absolutely binding, then we shall expect to be overwhelmed by their competing claims, with no way to resolve them or, ironically, to live them faithfully in peace."[106] Keenan says, "Fidelity requires us not only not to end or walk out of loving relationships but more importantly to defend and sustain them."[107] It demands embracing the loved one in all their particularity, acknowledging that loving relationships can be messy and at times chaotic.

Fidelity is a contemporary term for an ancient understanding. Augustine gave the Christian tradition the concept of ordered loves, where humans owe love first to God, next to ourselves, then to others in close relationships with us, and then on to all humans and all creatures.[108] In Aquinas's exploration of the order of love, he takes on fraught questions such as whether we should love our parents or children more, or our spouse more than our parents. Though Aquinas does not call it this, Question 26 of the *Secunda secundae* is a series of careful attempts to define the contours of the virtue of fidelity.

Aquinas leads us toward the concept of fidelity with his ideas of particular justice, the justice due to a specific individual (contrasted with general justice), as well as domestic justice, or justice within the family. He acknowledges that right relationships between individuals can be described differently depending on the context, whether in a particular situation, between family members, or generally. For example, we do not have a duty to support every child or elderly person, but we do have duties to our own children or aging parents.[109]

Margaret Farley is another leading exponent of fidelity with her 1986 book *Personal Commitments: Beginning, Keeping, Changing.* She notes that fidelity is different than constancy, a distinction Farley takes from the philosopher Gabriel Marcel. In constancy, acts of love are performed out of a sense of duty; in fidelity, we are emotionally present in doing our acts of love. Constancy can help sustain a commitment at a time when we may feel fidelity to be lacking, but if fidelity never returns and only constancy remains, something in the commitment is lost.[110] So as with every virtue, there is an element of fidelity that involves the self's affective experience. Fidelity is not just about the performance of actions, but also involves a circular continuity between actions and feelings.

Farley says that "fidelity entails decisions to look and to receive what is seen."[111] Like prudence and humility, it is a virtue that has to do with encountering the truth—in this case, the truth about another with whom we are in close relationship. Farley says that in fidelity we hold together our memories of the past and our hopes for the future. We connect our present self and the relationship as it is now with the self who made this commitment and the relationship as it was then.[112] Fidelity for Farley also demands what she calls "relaxation of heart," an alert and receptive patience.[113] Mutuality, mutual presence, and community support for commitments also aid fidelity, underscoring the social nature of the virtues.[114] Lisa Fullam subdivides fidelity into three "subsidiary virtues": those that cultivate freedom, create security, and foster mutuality.[115]

The faithful person can accurately recognize which committed relationships make special claims on her, and she acts to honor these commitments. She sees the beloved other as they truly are and desires their flourishing, rather than regarding the other as an extension or accessory of herself. Although the faithful person is attuned to the positive and negative feelings that arise while living out close relationships, she honors a commitment that goes beyond the feeling of the present.

Exemplar of Fidelity: Dorothy Day

Dorothy Day (1897–1980), a writer and convert to Catholicism, is both an exponent and exemplar of fidelity through her witness as cofounder of the Catholic Worker (CW) movement, whose members foster deep relationships with the poor out of love for Jesus. Formed as a young woman in the socialist and peace movements of the early twentieth century, Day connected her desire for social change with her emerging Catholic faith when she met Peter Maurin, who propounded a personalist, small-scale vision of Catholic social action. The CW began life as a newspaper publishing Maurin's ideas, but quickly developed into a program of direct social action when workers unemployed at the height of the Depression showed up at the newspaper's office asking for food.[116] Although Day is often remembered as a social activist who carried out civil disobedience for peace and worker justice, what set her apart from many activists was her deep spirituality of personal love for the needy person, a commitment to extend the type of close relationship governed by fidelity to all who are in need and seeking help.

Day beautifully detailed the CW philosophy of personal relationship with the poor in her decades of voluminous writing for the CW paper and elsewhere. She consistently taught that the way to love and serve Jesus is to love the neighbor in specific by encountering her face-to-face. "All our life is bound up with other people," she wrote in a meditation on the Gospel figures who served and lived with Jesus. "What a simplification of life it would be if we forced ourselves to see that everywhere we go is Christ, wearing out socks we have to darn, eating the food we have to cook."[117]

Throughout Day's life, from the days of the CW's founding, she conducted her work of writing, speaking, and leadership while living in "houses of hospitality," in community with the needy who came seeking help, affected by the mental illnesses, addictions, personal dramas, and other chaos surrounding the needy guests and the "workers" who came to help.[118] Although she wrote frankly about the challenges this closeness could bring, fidelity to the poor, for her, was the way to grow in virtue as a Christian. "How do we know we believe [in Christ?]" she wrote. "Because we have seen His hands and His feet in the poor around us. . . . We start by loving them for Him, and we soon love them for themselves, each one a unique person, most special!"[119]

Day's life has been portrayed as emblematic of the potential conflict between the virtues of fidelity and justice.[120] It is true that both she and her daughter spoke frankly about the strains Dorothy's dual vocation as single mother and the CW's leader could place on their time together. If Dorothy's life strikes us as unusual, and indeed it is, it is not because she is a parent who failed at loving her daughter, but because she is a human who succeeded at love of neighbor beyond what many humans believe is possible. "We cannot love God unless we love each other, and to love we must know each other," she wrote in the conclusion to her autobiography, *The Long Loneliness*.[121] Day shows Christians how community with the poor and outcast can be seen, and lived out, not simply as a matter of justice but as a matter of loving relationship, of fidelity.

HUMILITY

Humility is frequently misunderstood as self-abasement, but a truthful Christian account of humility includes awareness of one's own God-given gifts and goodness as well as one's struggles and limitations. Certain Christian thinkers overemphasize the focus on limits that can lead to a twisted notion of humility as self-degradation, whereas Aquinas presents the balanced view that this account will follow—one in which true humility admits of, and may even encourage, a positive self-evaluation.

Saint Augustine (354–430) is sometimes credited with a self-abasing view of humanity, but Deborah Wallace Ruddy expertly shows the nuance in his virtue of humility. For Augustine, God exhibits humility by coming to earth in the person of Jesus. Thus, we imitate God when we are humble.[122] Christ's humility heals us from the sin of pride; mediates between God and humankind, as Christ takes part in the lowliness of humanity; and shows us how suffering and self-emptying can be redemptive.[123] Such an emphasis on Christ's sacrifice means that humility for Augustine emphasizes awareness of one's own lowly nature. Unlike Aquinas, Augustine has no interest in dialogue with pagan views that saw positive self-estimation as virtuous magnanimity. Even given that, however, Augustine's humility is far from rank self-abasement. Because Christ's humility brings about human redemption for Augustine, it promotes, instead of detracting from, intrinsic human worth. "You were first loved to become worth loving," Augustine said. Ruddy explains that "the humbling of the Word simultaneously reveals the desperate state of humanity and the immense worth of humanity."[124] For Augustine, humility helps us resist worldly powers and their false values.[125]

Views of humility like Augustine's can be misused when those in power want the oppressed to remain aware of their lowly human nature, without practicing such humility themselves. This has inspired some to reject humility altogether. Michelle Voss Roberts defends a feminist retrieval of the virtue of humility as portrayed by the medieval writer Mechthild of Madgeburg. Although Roberts acknowledges that Mechthild's account of humility betrays a self-abasement that modern feminists rightly reject, she retrieves its positive aspects. Mechthild's humility invites realism about bodily finitude, and the soul conforms itself to the divine nature by being willing to descend as God descended by becoming human in the person of Jesus.[126] Roberts concludes that "genuine humility is an attitude that cultivates a space to meet the divine in ourselves, others, and the world around us. It leads not to the negation but the empowerment of the self. . . . Humility, then, cannot be conflated with characteristically 'feminine' sins."[127]

Thomas Aquinas's account of humility allows, and in some cases insists on, positive self-evaluation and is most appreciated by contemporary virtue ethicists. Humility helps us moderate our desires for "high things" and form a truthful view of our own capacities.[128] It is coupled with magnanimity, which encourages us in "the pursuit of great things according to right reason."[129] Magnanimity and humility are two sides of the same coin; we fall prey to the vice of pride by thinking too much of ourselves, but expecting too little of ourselves is the vice of pusillanimity, or small-souledness.[130] As Elizabeth Lee puts it, "whereas humility entails being honest about one's weaknesses [for example, by accepting needed help graciously,] magnanimity encourages being honest about one's strengths."[131]

With both humility and magnanimity, we can act and move through the world with a reasonable amount of ambition (in Aquinas's words, hope) for what we might accomplish—neither too much nor too little. Fullam catches the proper balance by noting that "if you have really done something noteworthy, denying so is a lie," so that to always prioritize self-abasement either requires one to lie or to avoid striving to achieve anything impressive.[132] Aquinas explicitly says that humility does not entail regarding oneself as a worse sinner than everyone else. Rather, humility requires that we realistically assess the qualities we have that are "of God" and the qualities of our neighbor that are of God. In humility, we can acknowledge superior qualities of our neighbor when we find them.[133] Humility forbids the moral despair that can result from seeing only the excellences of others and urges us to imagine that others have God-given gifts, even if we ourselves are unable to see anything at all praiseworthy in them.[134] For Fullam, humility reminds us to compare our gifts with others' gifts and our faults with their faults, avoiding the common tendency to compare our gifts with others' weaknesses.[135]

Fullam reminds us that for Augustine, humility meant knowing the truth of ourselves as sinful; there was no such thing as excessive self-abasement for Augustine. Aquinas changed this, drawing on Aristotle's sense of humility as a mean between the extremes of self-abasement and self-exaltation. Thomistic humility means knowing the truth of ourselves both as good and as limited.[136] A robust Christian account of humility is like what Kathryn Tanner calls "non-idolatrous self-esteem," through which we recognize ourselves as limited and finite, as not God, while acknowledging our own worth as God's creature.[137]

The destructive practices sometimes misattributed to humility—for example, an abused woman accepting her own mistreatment—do not display true Thomistic humility. Without blaming women who do this, we can see that it is not virtuous behavior and should not be promoted within Christian ethics.[138] We demonstrate a failure of humility when we view our own mistreatment by others as something other than a violation, or when we react excessively to our own mistreatment. Humility helps us sort out these reactions in accordance with reason.

The humble person regards herself as good and rejects assaults against her human dignity. At the same time, she accepts her bodily frailty and her own personal failings, without obsessing over either. She can appreciate both her own good qualities and those of her neighbor, without jealousy. She regards herself as subordinate to God and as equal in dignity to other human beings. At the same time, she does not equate her own dignity with any marker of social status. This means that she does not react in anger when others question her social status or the power structures that support it. If she is lacking in social power, she does not accept a vision of herself as less worthy than others.

Exemplar of Humility: Dolores Huerta

When Dolores Huerta began her life's work in farmworker organizing in the late 1950s, she encountered resistance from white and Latino men who did not think a woman was qualified to lead in the labor movement.[139] Throughout her life, she achieved impressive victories as an organizer and activist due to her palpable passion for justice, her skill in helping others believe in their own power, and her willingness to work tirelessly at great personal sacrifice. In 1962, she and César Chávez cofounded the United Farmworkers union, whose accomplishments include winning farmworkers the right to organize; union contract benefits such as better wages and unemployment and medical insurance; the abolition in California of the backbreaking *cortito* hoe; and the national ban of DDT, one of many pesticides that endanger farmworkers' lives.[140]

The historian Richard A. Garcia holds that Huerta's work as organizer and activist embodies her four "philosophical axioms," which he characterizes this way: "first, to establish a strong sense of identity; second, to develop a sense of pride; third, to maintain always the value of service to others; and fourth, to be self-reflective and true to oneself."[141] These qualities clearly track with humility correctly understood as a true sense of one's own goodness, worth, and limitations. Huerta correctly values her extraordinary ability as an organizer and activist, once commenting "I know that the history of our union would have been quite different had it not been for my involvement."[142] She also readily acknowledges her own temper and recalls how she and Chávez, who died in 1993, were prone to fighting.[143] Throughout their decades as coleaders of the movement, she willingly allowed Chávez to be the focus of public acclaim when that seemed the best way to help their movement succeed in a sexist world.[144] Aware that women are frequently expected to defer and self-efface, Huerta in recent decades has explicitly worked to empower women to reject mistreatment, to honor their own voices, and to lead.[145]

Huerta epitomizes humility in the truest sense. Her actions and writings express a person who acknowledges her own limitations as well as her innate human dignity and her unique gifts and achievements; who celebrates others' achievements rather than feeling threatened by them; and who supports others in realizing their own worth and potential. "The more people feel that power that they have in themselves, that they are the ones responsible to make these changes, then the changes happen," she says.[146] Huerta expressed humility in its truest sense in this statement in 2005: "I've always been comfortable in a leadership role. . . . I had a great deal of respect from the workers and the public. This still applies to this day."[147] Her example of humility must be counted among her many revolutionary accomplishments.

SELF-CARE

James Keenan proposes self-care, which "addresses the unique relationship that I as a moral agent have with myself" as a cardinal virtue. Common parlance treats self-care as a practice, but as a virtue it combines the orientation or stance that allows us to value our selves enough to care for them, and the practice that reinforces this caring stance toward ourselves. Keenan prefers "self-care" to the often-used "self-love" to avoid confusion with the transcendental virtue of charity or love of God. He notes that love of God, friends, humanity, and self often conflict in painful ways, as we see expressed in Jesus's agony in the Garden of Gethsemane.[148] Self-care "calls for a recognition of knowing one's own capabilities" and "prompts us to attend to our own personal histories where areas of need or particular vulnerability need to be recognized." In addition to our vulnerabilities, self-care invites us to recognize our own good qualities.[149] Self-care is often given negative connotations—including navel-gazing, self-preoccupation, and selfishness—but the philosopher Robert Merrihew Adams notes that these negative behaviors are not necessarily true exaggerations of virtuous traits: "Selfishness is clearly possible without any degree of self-love at all."[150]

Ethicists who do use the term "self-love" assist us in developing a complete picture of self-care as a virtue. Darlene Fozard Weaver says that "right self love consists in a self-determining response to God which is actualized in but not exhausted by neighbor love."[151] We learn how to love ourselves when we love God, because right relationship with God defines our flourishing. Because humans are social beings, our flourishing also requires right relations with other people, so self-love is related to the love of others.[152]

Emilie Townes illustrates communal self-love with the beautiful speech given by Baby Suggs, holy, in Toni Morrison's *Beloved*. Suggs exhorts free Black persons bearing the scars of slavery and ongoing racial violence to love themselves and one another. Townes emphasizes that self-love, or loving one's heart, "is not an exercise in individualistic nihilism. It is a radical, and often communal, response to cultural, social, religious, economic, and political hegemony."[153] Self-love for members of oppressed groups demands learning to love one's embodied self and the embodied fellow members of one's own group, as Baby Suggs, holy, instructs Black children, men, and women to do.[154]

"Contrary to popular beliefs about the human being's 'natural' survival instincts," notes Emily Reimer-Barry, "self-care requires an enormous amount of determined action and cannot be assumed."[155] In her study of women living with HIV/AIDS, Reimer-Barry found that the women had often struggled with self-care before their diagnosis and that for some, dealing with illness encouraged them to pursue self-care. She argues that self-care is as much a part of Christian tradition as self-sacrifice, and that both need to be held in tension within healthy relationships.[156]

Self-care and self-love sound like contemporary concepts spawned from modern individualism and therapeutic culture; but in fact, Thomas Aquinas offers a robust vision of ethical self-care in the *Summa Theologiae*. Indeed, contrary to stereotypes of self-debasing medieval spirituality, Aquinas asserts that we should love ourselves more than we love our neighbor. He argues that we are created to love God, so our love for people responds to the other's union with God. But our own union with God is more present to us, and more important for our eternal happiness, than that of others, so we naturally experience self-love as greater than love of others. Aquinas also notes that Scripture suggests self-love as an appropriate model for love of others, when Jesus asks us to love our neighbor as our selves.[157]

Aquinas's understanding of self-love as love for my own share in the divine good reminds us that attention to one's own virtue development is a crucial part of the practice of self-care. We must also care for ourselves physically, mentally, spiritually, and in our moral development. The more virtuous I become with God's help, the greater my own share in the divine good, and the more self-love I have and can practice.

The self-caring person, like the humble person, must see the truth about herself, about what she needs to care for herself physically, spiritually, mentally, and as a moral being. To the extent that circumstances permit, she must practice self-care by acting on her understanding of what she needs. It goes without saying that this may at times require accepting hardship or challenge—self-care can demand forgoing, rather than indulging in, immediate comfort. Self-care calls for maintaining a balance between the challenge that develops our faculties and the comfort and protection that restore them.

Exemplar of Self-Care: Saint Ignatius Loyola

Saint Ignatius Loyola (1491–1556) was born into a well-off Spanish family and educated for a life of military and courtly distinction. After a conversion experience during recovery from a battle wound, Ignatius gave up a life of material comfort and status-seeking to commit more fully to his Christian faith. Early in his spiritual journey, Ignatius practiced rigorous bodily penances, including extreme fasting and sleep restriction, and even stopped grooming his hair and nails. He believed these practices would help him demonstrate his love for God and feel closer to the Divine presence. While living in such extreme asceticism, Ignatius became sick and so depressed that he thought about death nearly continually.[158] However, later in life, as the founder of the Jesuit order, he taught his followers about the importance of balanced self-care for the body and spirit.

The *Constitutions* of the Jesuit order, where Ignatius laid out the guidelines for the community's life together, dictate the importance of self-care when they call for wise use of food, rest, and other healthy goods. Although

Jesuits can pursue more stringent ascetic practices if they feel it helps their spiritual growth, Ignatius did not require extreme deprivation: "In what pertains to food, clothing, and other external things, they will follow the common and approved usage of reputable priests."[159] In general, members of the Society of Jesus were to pursue "moderation in spiritual and bodily labors . . . which do not lean toward an extreme of rigor or toward excessive laxity."[160] Ignatius thought moderation was easier to consistently achieve and would help the community maintain its collective well-being.

Ignatius's early experience with extreme self-deprivation clearly informed his views on the importance of self-care in the spiritual life. He could have ordered the Jesuits to follow the extreme rigor of his early disciplines, but instead he counseled healthy moderation in food and clothing, even urging Jesuits to reside "in healthy locations with pure air."[161] Contemporary research confirms what Ignatius experienced, that extreme food deprivation can lead to depressed mood.[162] In contrast, a reasonably moderate practice of self-care would allow Ignatius's followers to remain healthy and well in body, mind, and spirit, and thus able to pursue their vocation and serve God.

TEMPERANCE

Temperance is the virtue that enables us to moderate our physical desires in accordance with good goals. For Thomas Aquinas, temperance is a broad "umbrella" virtue that includes other virtues like humility, studiousness, reasonable use of anger and sexual desire, and chastity (moderation of sexual behavior, whether one is married or celibate).[163] Many treatments of this virtue that draw on Aristotle, Aquinas, or both authors interpret it fairly narrowly, as moderating one's desires for and use of goods, particularly food and drink.[164] Aquinas himself says that temperance is about the pleasures of touch, in which he includes food, drink, and sex.[165] He says that temperance suggests attending to a person's own bodily needs, health, and—following Augustine and Aristotle—to their station in life: "Temperance regards need according to the requirements of life, and this depends not only on the requirements of the body, but also on the requirements of external things, such as riches and station, and more still on the requirements of good conduct."[166] Elsewhere, he says that temperance moderates the pleasures "most natural to us," which explains why Aquinas's temperance includes humility, which moderates the pleasure of experiencing hope for the future.[167]

An important part of temperance for Aquinas is honesty, which means correctly assessing what is pleasing to reason, what is naturally right for humans and part of God's plan.[168] Josef Pieper describes temperance as "self-less self-preservation" and notes that Aquinas also describes it as "serenity of the spirit," not a surface calm but a well-balanced inner order.[169] Pieper explains that temperance is a tool to help us achieve the good but is not the good in itself: "Discipline and moderation and chastity are not in themselves the fulfillment of [humanity]."[170] Rather, by helping us keep our own being in order, temperance helps us achieve our own good and progress toward higher goals.

Temperance is about shaping right desires rather than repressing wrong ones. Jean Porter writes: "The truly temperate person need not repress her desires, because she spontaneously desires that which is in accord with her genuine good, comprehensively understood, and does not desire what is inconsistent with that good."[171] Continence, which for Aquinas falls short of being a virtue, is when we desire things that appeal to the senses in immoderate and unreasonable ways, but forcibly restrain those urges.[172] In Aquinas's view, desire is not bad—it can be good as long as it receives its right orientation from temperance. Nicholas Austin explains that true temperance "does not repress desire, but forms and redirects it, placing it at the service of right relationship to oneself, others, the Earth, and God."[173]

Diana Fritz Cates writes that though Aquinas does not state this specifically, his view of temperance suggests that neither poor or wealthy people who are temperate indulge their resources in expensive food and drink. Somewhat obviously, it would not be prudent for people with limited resources to spend them this way. Even for people who can afford to indulge, money spent on costly food could be better used to promote the common good and help the poor.[174] This reasonable inference highlights the fact that a discussion of temperance tends to presume a moral agent who has plenty of access to goods and must learn to use them wisely, rather than someone struggling to fulfill her desires in an environment of scarcity.

The virtue of temperance is not frequently discussed today under just that name, but a wide literature on consumerism, consumption, and the spiritual power of advertising indicates that the virtue that moderates our desires for goods is highly relevant to today's theological concerns.[175] David Cloutier calls for a Christian revival of the morally disapproving term "luxury" to denote excessive, exploitative, and morally damaging consumption practices. He suggests that we can avoid luxury by "acquiring necessities justly," by avoiding products made under exploitative conditions, and by enjoying and supporting goods that benefit everyone, like public parks and radio stations.[176] Julie Hanlon Rubio invites Christian families to retrieve the practice of tithing. By giving 10 percent of their after-tax income to programs that genuinely assist the poor, Rubio finds, Christian families could make a significant impact on problems like poverty and inequality while inculcating virtue in their own members.[177] We can easily imagine that such temperate practices would encourage the development of more temperate desires for goods.

Laura Hartman takes up similar concerns in her Christian ethic of consumption. Consumption is not equivalent to the vice of "consumerism" but is a life practice all humans must do. Hartman suggests that ethical consumption avoids sin, including the self-regarding sin of gluttony and the participation in social sin of consuming products made in exploitative ways. (She acknowledges that consumers today will likely fail to avoid all participation in social sin but urges they try.) She also insists that ethical consumption honors creation when we enjoy and share the goods we consume. Ethical consumption honors the neighbor who may share our table or work to make the goods we consume, and it is eschatological—we consume ethically when we consume with an eye toward God's planned future for creation.[178] For Hartman, the ethical consumer—read, the temperate person—is well informed about the consequences of her consumption, especially as it affects other human lives, and she acts on this information when she consumes. Her consumption is other-directed. In other words, temperance for Hartman is linked with both fidelity and justice.

Cloutier, Rubio, and Hartman are right to note that temperance gains in importance when we consider the impact of consumption by wealthy and privileged people on poor people and the natural environment. Today it is most helpful to move beyond understanding temperance as the virtue that helps us moderate our consumption of food and drink, or even the virtue that helps us moderate our desires for all sensory pleasure. Temperance does these things, but also, and importantly, it helps us moderate our exercise of power. Temperance is thus particularly crucial for those who wield disproportionate power in the world due to unjust power dynamics such as racism, sexism, and extreme economic inequality.

Ancient Greek philosophers described a virtue called *sophrosyne*, which Alasdair MacIntyre says is "the virtue of the man who could but does not abuse his power."[179] *Sophrosyne* is often translated "temperance," and one aspect of it is indeed moderating desire for sensory pleasure; although, as MacIntyre goes on to show, the concept is more complex.[180] Still, the ancient understanding of a virtue that helps moderate one's use of power provides firm footing to suggest that we expand our understanding of temperance today. M. Shawn Copeland has suggested virtues of "resolve and sacrifice or relinquishment" as a path to solidarity for white women who wish to avoid abusing their power to silence the voices of racially marginalized women.[181] "Relinquishment" is an evocative contemporary description of *sophrosyne*. It acknowledges that in order to allow others to claim their rightful power, those with power must give it up, must listen rather than speaking, and must follow rather than lead.

The temperate person experiences right desires for goods—that is, she desires them insofar as they help her to function and to pursue greater goods, like earthly justice and union with God. She does not reject the pleasure that can accompany a good meal, even as she does not obsess over luxurious delicacies; and she does not derive pleasure from the sheer act of acquiring more things. In situations where she exercises power, she refrains from abusing it, and in fact she does not habitually experience the intemperate desire to abuse her power. She can act more readily to pursue other virtues—for example, to pursue justice by giving others what is due to them—because she is not distracted by immoderate obsession with goods, pleasures, and power.

Exemplars of Temperance: Saint Katharine Drexel

Katharine Drexel (1858–1955), one of the first North Americans to be canonized, embodies temperance in its expression as "sacrifice or relinquishment," in M. Shawn Copeland's terms. Drexel was born into a wealthy, privileged family that inculcated her in Catholic piety. Called to religious life, Drexel donated her inheritance, millions of dollars at the time, to promote Catholic evangelism, primarily to the religious order she founded to serve Native American and African American people.[182] The Sisters of the Blessed Sacrament founded schools and universities, including Xavier University in New Orleans, to address the routine denial of educational opportunities to Black and Native American people. As these institutions gained stability, the order practiced temperance as relinquishment by turning them over to the communities the institutions served.[183]

Drexel's total divestment of fortune, autonomy, and social status is a superlative exemplar of temperance for those with power or resources. Her biographer, Cheryl C. D. Hughes, describes how the feminist theologian Rosemary Radford Ruether retrieves the Christian spiritual concept of *kenosis* or self-emptying, which has been maligned as encouraging self-hatred. In Ruether's view, *kenosis* demands "the self-emptying of power as domination."[184] It is this kenotic spirituality, divesting from destructive power in order to leave room for Christ to enter, that Hughes sees in Drexel's life and witness.[185]

Exemplars of Temperance: Oseola McCarty

Oseola McCarty (1908–99) saved hundreds of thousands of dollars from the modest income she earned washing clothes by hand over a wood fire, and donated the majority of her hard-earned fortune to the University of Southern Mississippi so needy students could achieve the education she never had. McCarty began working as a child and left school in the sixth grade to support ill family members through her work washing clothes. Until retiring from work at the age of eighty-six years, she maintained a modest lifestyle, living simply, traveling little, and saving her income in the bank. Her extraordinary generosity to future generations of students brought her late-in-life fame, but this national and international attention did not change her temperate habits.[186] Like many of these exemplars, McCarty was recognized as a paradigm of virtue during her life. Her gift inspired many others to philanthropy, most of whom were much wealthier than McCarty and sacrificed much less in their own giving.[187]

The witness of McCarty's life reminds us that temperance is not stinginess or the inability to take pleasure in the goods of this world. More generous with others than she was with herself, McCarty had a deep understanding of the usefulness and goodness of money. Her own temperate desire—never wanting to spend more—enabled her lifelong support of her church community and her life-changing gifts to so many students.

FORTITUDE

The virtue of fortitude is classically defined as combining courage and perseverance. For Aquinas, fortitude helps us overcome our tendency to depart from reason when we encounter difficulty.[188] Thus it encompasses not only bravery in the face of danger but also persistence, even steadfastness, demonstrating constancy in one's own mind.[189] Aquinas gives a martial flavor to fortitude by saying that it has to do with courage in the face of the danger of death, especially death in battle, but he goes on to say that "the principal act of fortitude is endurance, that is to stand immovable in the midst of dangers rather than to attack them."[190] This suggests a broader interpretation of fortitude as enduring many of life's dangers, pains, and disappointments. Endurance of difficulty is far from passive, but it represents "an action of the soul cleaving most resolutely to good."[191] Aquinas also suggests that we demonstrate fortitude when we think about upcoming dangers and how to withstand them, which again applies fortitude far beyond the battlefield.[192]

Fortitude also encourages action; moderate anger can assist fortitude in "strik[ing] at the cause of sorrow," taking action for a just cause.[193]

Josef Pieper notes that "fortitude presupposes vulnerability."[194] It requires first knowing what the good is, in order to be able to persevere in its pursuit.[195] Thus fortitude is bound up with prudence, which helps us choose a path to persevere in, and humility, which helps us recognize our own vulnerability. Stanley Hauerwas and Charles Pinches argue that Christians are called to oppose war and cannot support a view of fortitude with death in battle as its highest act. They show that Aquinas transforms Aristotle's warlike view of fortitude by including charity, so that the highest act of fortitude becomes martyrdom, a death that is courageously accepted when and as it comes. "[The martyr's courage] is none other than an extension of the daily courage we need to carry on as faithful servants of God,"[196] they write, "a courage that will make us patient enough to fight a just war."[197] For Hauerwas and Pinches, Christian courage or fortitude requires persevering in the pursuit of God's plan, even when this means opposing the dominant political order.[198]

Karen Lebacqz and Shirley Macemon note that "fortitude—the strength to work for the good no matter the cost—encompasses both attack and endurance. When evil can be eradicated, it is to be attacked; when it cannot be eradicated, it is to be endured."[199] This provides an important qualification to a common interpretation of patience, which Lebacqz and Macemon, following Aquinas, deem a part of fortitude. They note that patience is often understood to mean bearing suffering for as long as required—which often means as long as the one recommending patience thinks best! This distorted view of patience is often prescribed by those who have power to those who do not, including women, people of color, and members of other oppressed groups.[200]

An interpretation of patience focused on justice regards patience as "strengthening the spirit precisely to sustain the struggle for good or for justice."[201] Patient endurance of oppression is the right response only when fighting back is not an option, for whatever reason, and only in a context that understands defending one's own good as the ultimate goal. Katie Geneva Cannon catches this sense of fortitude when she describes the communal virtue of "unshouted courage," which "is the quality of steadfastness, akin to fortitude, in the face of formidable oppression. The communal attitude is far more than 'grin and bear it.' Rather, it involves the ability to 'hold on to life' against major oppositions."[202]

Long before today's womanist and feminist interpreters, Josef Pieper described patience in a similar way, writing that it is "not the indiscriminate acceptance of any sort of evil, ... not the tear-streaked mirror of a 'broken' life (as one might almost think, to judge from what is frequently shown and praised under this term) but rather is the radiant essence of final freedom from harm."[203] As a virtue, fortitude, and patience as a part of it, must always serve the person's flourishing, whether this means resisting oppression through action or by refusing to be defined by oppression.

Barbara Hilkert Andolsen finds fortitude sorely needed in the US Church's response to racism. In responding to such a systemic, intractable problem, Andolsen says, fortitude in its sense of perseverance is called for.[204] Andolsen's call to persevere in response to racism is directed particularly at white people, who may wrongly feel that racism is not a problem for them to deal with. Another reflection on fortitude's role in situations of unequal power comes from Samuel K. Roberts, who identifies fortitude or courage as the virtue that helps restrain clergy members and others in positions of power from misusing their power in ways that violate justice.[205]

A person who has fortitude understands the costs of courageous acts and does them anyway. She perseveres when acting virtuously is difficult, frustrating, disheartening, or boring. She may not be afraid of things that would terrify a person lacking fortitude, but she is not foolhardy. She understands the connection between the costliness of certain acts and their value. This was true of the religious martyrs Aquinas thought of as he was writing, and it is true today for people who demonstrate courage by standing up to entrenched systems of injustice. The virtue of fortitude is clearly necessary to persevere in the development of the other virtues and to choose the brave acts each virtue may demand.

Exemplar of Fortitude: Helen Prejean

Sister Helen Prejean, CSJ, has lived out her Catholic faith for decades as an activist against the death penalty and spiritual adviser to men on death row. This ministry demands that Sister Prejean confront many of the most painful realities of broken human life: the details of horrific capital crimes, the anguish of victims' families, the ghoulish desire of some for revenge, and the graphic brutality of state execution methods including the electric chair.[206] Other injustices are more apparently banal, such as the shameful failure of the United States to provide adequate legal counsel to the prisoners it kills; the anonymous professionalism of the respectable citizens who carry out executions; and efforts by elected and appointed leaders to disavow their own responsibility in state-sanctioned death.[207] From confronting these horrific truths through her personal ministry to those sentenced to death and victims' families, Prejean has broadened her focus to join with many others to fight against the legal practice of capital punishment in the United States.[208]

Sister Prejean embodies fortitude in both its senses: bravery and patient endurance. In her ministry, she goes where many Department of Corrections leaders are unwilling to enter: all the way to the execution chamber with the convicted men she serves as spiritual adviser. She describes the courage it takes to witness the horror of a violent, grisly state-sanctioned death, as well as her conviction that her strength originates outside herself as a gift from God. "I know that it will terrify me. How could it not terrify me?" she mused when preparing to witness the execution of Patrick Sonnier, the first man she would accompany to his death. "But . . . I tell him it won't break me, that I have plenty of love and support in my life. 'God will give me the grace,' I tell him."[209]

Sister Prejean's endurance in her difficult work has borne fruit in her own lifetime, resulting in many changed hearts and minds and altered Catholic teaching. When Sister Prejean was just beginning her anti-death-penalty work, the then–archbishop of New Orleans, Phillip Hannan, wrote a letter assuring Catholics "that they can in good conscience endorse capital punishment," despite an earlier communication from the US Conference of Catholic Bishops opposing it.[210] In 2018, Pope Francis revised the *Catechism of the Catholic Church* to unambiguously declare the death penalty "inadmissible," a welcome development in teaching in which Sister Prejean's longtime witness, including as an adviser to Francis and John Paul II, played an undeniable role.[211] With the bravery to witness the worst ways humans can brutalize one another and the endurance to fight passionately for justice throughout a long lifetime of seeing it violated, Sister Helen Prejean embodies fortitude in its fullest understanding.

CONCLUSION

This chapter has described several virtues that help shape persons for the well-lived human life as Christians understand it. I share with many other virtue ethicists a middle view of virtue's universality and uniqueness: though virtues gain a distinct character in particular communities, such as the Church, ultimately the goods virtues seek and the virtues themselves are intelligible across human experience. Prudence, justice, humility, solidarity, self-care, temperance, and fortitude describe in detail the well-lived human life as Christians see it, although, certainly, those of other or no faiths might agree with much or all of this account of flourishing human life.

This chapter has gestured to ways that life circumstances shape the pursuit of virtue. For example, both Saint Katharine Drexel and Oseola McCarty are exemplars of temperance, but their lives as a wealthy, white religious leader and a poor, Black manual laborer offered them very different opportunities for practicing that virtue. It is easy to see that different life circumstances offer distinct opportunities for pursuing, practicing, and developing virtue, but Christian virtue ethics needs a more sustained investigation of this phenomenon. The next chapter offers this by developing a Christian virtue account of moral luck, a concept that names and describes the impact of life circumstances on virtue pursuit.

NOTES

1. Pope, "Virtue," 397.
2. Fullam, "Humility," 255.
3. Klubertanz, *Habits*, 177.
4. Lisa Tessman's theory of the burdened virtues provides an important caveat to this view.
5. O'Connell, *Compassion*, 51.
6. The use of "practice" in virtue acquisition is often credited to Alasdair C. MacIntyre, *After Virtue*, chap. 14, despite the fact that MacIntyre's definition of "practice" is highly technical, tailor-made for the essential role it plays in his argument. When Christian virtue theorists use the term "practice," they usually mean it in a sense more like the definition I give above.
7. Keenan, "Fundamental Moral Theology."
8. Keenan, *History*, 76–77.
9. Fullam, "Humility," 256.
10. Flescher, *Heroes*, 11.
11. Keenan, "Seven Reasons."
12. O'Connell, *Compassion*, 46–47.
13. Astorga, *Catholic Moral Theology*, 428.
14. Jalandoni, "Fortitude," 207.
15. Bretzke, "Human Rights."
16. Kotva, *Christian Case*; Hauerwas and Pinches, *Christians*; Keenan, *Moral Wisdom*, 96–97; Porter, "Virtue Ethics"; Chan, *Ten Commandments*.
17. Odozor, *Moral Theology*, 260–61.
18. Kim, "Progress," 148.
19. Keenan, "Proposing."
20. Fullam, "Joan of Arc," 76.
21. Fullam, 76–77.
22. Kotva, *Christian Case*.
23. Hauerwas and Pinches, *Christians*, 117.
24. Hauerwas and Pinches.
25. See Keenan, *History*, 217.
26. Chan, *Ten Commandments*, 14.
27. Nussbaum, "Non-Relative Virtues."

28. Cahill, "Justice."
29. Cahill. In another example, Christopher P. Vogt avers that non-Christians could form the overlapping virtues he describes as essential to living out Catholic social thought, but notes that living the values of Catholic social thought is incumbent upon Catholics in a particular way and that virtues can help support the link between personal faith life and public action. Vogt, "Fostering," 417n79.
30. Hauerwas and Pinches assert that particular virtues, such as hope and obedience, take on unique significance for Christians due to their presence in the Christian Scriptures and tradition; Hauerwas and Pinches, Christians, chaps. 7–8. I do not disagree, but this does not mean that, e.g., non-Christians simply cannot develop the virtue of obedience in ways Christians can recognize.
31. Cahill, "Community," 10.
32. This is a view shared by secular philosophers, such as Nussbaum and Amartya Sen, who promote capabilities theory. Nussbaum, Creating Capabilities; Sen, Development.
33. Doak, Divine Harmony, chaps. 1–3.
34. Berkman, "Are Persons with Profound Intellectual Disabilities Sacramental Icons?"; Romero, "Happiness."
35. Copeland, Enfleshing Freedom, 10.
36. Copeland, "Toward a Critical Christian Feminist Theology," 28–29.
37. Lonergan, Insight, 198–202, 250–51.
38. Romero, "Profound Cognitive Impairment."
39. As Christine Firer Hinze says, the person in Christian anthropology is not the selfish, competitive "homo economicus" but the community-oriented, vulnerable "homo solidaritus." Hinze, Glass Ceilings, 105–6.
40. Alison, Joy.
41. Fullam, "From Discord to Virtues," 102.
42. Pieper, Prudence, 22.
43. Klubertanz, Habits, 187.
44. Pieper, Prudence, 14–16.
45. Pieper, 25.
46. Thomas Aquinas, Summa Theologica (herafter ST), II-II, 47.1.
47. Aquinas, II-II, 55.8.
48. Pieper, Prudence, 54.
49. Pieper, Brief Reader, 11–12.
50. Pieper, Prudence, 20.
51. Keenan, "Virtue," 261.
52. Pieper, Prudence, 26–27.
53. Quoted by Keenan, "Virtue," 261.
54. Keenan, 262–63.
55. Aquinas, ST, II-II, q. 47 art. 10.
56. Wadell, Happiness, 190.
57. Pieper, Prudence, 36–37.
58. Pieper, 32–33.
59. Pieper, 34.
60. Aquinas, ST, II-II, q. 49.
61. Marable, Malcolm X, 30–31.
62. Marable, 67–68.
63. Marable, 145–50.

64. Cone, *Martin*, 188–90.

65. Marable, *Malcolm X*, 309; Cone, *Martin*, 304–5.

66. Marable, *Malcolm X*, 334.

67. Marable, 332–33.

68. Marable, *Malcolm X*, chaps. 14, 15.

69. Cone writes that Malcolm regarded his time in the Nation of Islam as well as his earlier phase as a petty criminal as "great mistakes." Cone, *Martin*, 301.

70. Wadell, *Happiness*, 228.

71. Schmidtz and Thrasher, "Virtues."

72. Wadell, *Happiness*, 223.

73. Aquinas, *ST*, II-II, q. 58 art. 2. His rather limited framing of the virtue of justice does not hinder convincing attempts to develop an environmental ethic from Aquinas's thought, even extending to accounts of "justice towards the environment." See, e.g., Jenkins, "Biodiversity."

74. Aquinas, *ST*, II-II, 58.6–7. I discuss particular justice more fully later in this chapter, in the section on fidelity.

75. Keenan, "Proposing."

76. Wadell, *Happiness*, 221.

77. Keenan, "Virtue Ethics," 130.

78. Kahneman and Deaton, "High Income."

79. Davidson, "Does a $70,000 Minimum Wage Work?"

80. Ludema and Johnson, "Gravity Payment's."

81. Ludema and Johnson.

82. Student Union of Michigan, "Graduate Student Workers."

83. Patel, "To Make Do."

84. Student Union of Michigan, "Graduate Student Workers"; Patel, "To Make Do."

85. For the theological reality, see Massingale, *Racial Justice*, 127–28. For the norm, see O'Connell, *Compassion*, 86–87. The bishops of Latin America evoke the feeling and the practice of solidarity when they call their brother clergy to solidarity with the poor; see CELAM, "Medellín Document: Poverty." For the virtue of solidarity, see Clark, *Vision*, chap. 4.

86. John Paul II, "Sollicitudo rei socialis."

87. John Paul II, 38.

88. Copeland, "Toward a Critical Christian Feminist Theology," 14.

89. Copeland, 22–23.

90. John Paul II, "Sollicitudo rei socialis," 39.

91. John Paul II, 45.

92. Massingale, *Racial Justice*, 117.

93. Peters, "Conflict."

94. West, "Response," 80–81.

95. bell hooks, *Where We Stand*, 130.

96. De La Torre, *Doing Christian Ethics*, 179.

97. E.g., John Paul II, "Sollicitudo rei socialis," 39.

98. Heyer, "Social Sin."

99. Sr. Joan Roccasalvo, CSJ, "Remembering."

100. Markey, *Radical Faith*, 232–33, 236.

101. Markey, 238–40.

102. Markey, 245; Bonner, "Diplomat."
103. Roccasalvo, "Remembering."
104. Markey, *Radical Faith*, 241.
105. Keenan, "Virtue Ethics," 127.
106. Farley, *Personal Commitments*, 20.
107. Keenan, "Virtue Ethics."
108. Today, theologians add the created natural world as a rightful recipient of our love. Wadell, *Happiness*, 212–13.
109. Aquinas, *ST*, II-II, 58 art. 7.
110. Farley, *Personal Commitments*, 46.
111. Farley, 54.
112. Farley, 56–58.
113. Farley, 58–60.
114. Farley, 60–65.
115. Fullam, "From Discord to Virtues."
116. Day, "Foreword."
117. Day, "Room."
118. Day, "Mystery."
119. Day.
120. Yohe, "Dorothy Day."
121. Day, *Long Loneliness*.
122. Ruddy, "Humble God."
123. Ruddy.
124. Ruddy, 91.
125. Augustine, *Trinity*, VIII.11.
126. Roberts, "Retrieving Humility."
127. Roberts, 70.
128. Aquinas, *ST*, II-II, Q. 161, art. 1-2.
129. Aquinas, *ST*, II-II, Q. 161, art. 1; Craig A. Boyd shows how Aquinas corrects Aristotle's definition of magnanimity, which relied too much on self-sufficiency for a Christian view that insists life is lived, and virtue formed, in community. Boyd, "Pride."
130. Pieper, *Virtues*, 37.
131. Lee, "Virtues," 36.
132. Fullam, *Virtue*, 5; Keenan taught this truth to high school students with the example of pitching a shut-out baseball game. Keenan, *Virtues*, 70.
133. Aquinas, *ST*, II-II, Q. 161, art. 3.
134. Fullam, "Humility," 258. Fullam, *Virtue*, 40–44.
135. Fullam, *Virtue*, 40.
136. Fullam, 98–99.
137. Tanner, *Politics*.
138. Fullam, *Virtue*, 44.
139. Schiff, *Lighting the Way*, 310–11.
140. Schiff.
141. Garcia, "Dolores Huerta," 66.
142. Huerta, "Reflections," 4.
143. Schiff, *Lighting the Way*, 318–19.
144. Schiff, 316–17.

145. Huerta and Rosenbloom, "Ask a Feminist."

146. Breslow, "Dolores Huerta."

147. Schiff, *Lighting the Way*, 338.

148. Keenan, "Proposing Cardinal Virtues," 728. In a popular work, he wrote about the virtue of self-esteem, which shares resonances with self-care and what I have described as the virtue of humility. Keenan, *Virtues*, chap. 11.

149. Keenan, "Virtue Ethics," 132.

150. Adams, "Self-Love," 502.

151. Weaver, *Self Love*, 166.

152. Weaver, 86.

153. Townes, "To Be Called," 195.

154. Morrison, *Beloved*, 88–89, quoted by Townes, "To Be Called."

155. Reimer-Barry, "In Sickness," 136. Reimer-Barry does not explicitly portray self-care as a virtue but more as a practice that is evident in a person's behavior. She also uses it interchangeably with "self-love."

156. Reimer-Barry.

157. Aquinas, *ST*, II-II, 26.4.

158. Saint Ignatius, Olin, and O'Callaghan, *Autobiography*, 40–41.

159. Padberg, *Constitutions*, 12.

160. Padberg, 415.

161. Padberg, 416.

162. Baker and Keramidas, "Psychology."

163. Jean Porter suggests a flexible and personal sexual ethic based on Aquinas's inclusion of chastity as a part of temperance. If temperance in food and drink suggests moderate, reasonable behavior that meets the unique needs of each individual, she envisions the same for a sexual ethic, while noting that this conflicts with Aquinas's explicit deontological norms for sexual behavior. Porter, "Chastity."

164. See, e.g., Roberts, "Temperance."

165. Aquinas, *ST*, II-II, Q. 141 4–5.

166. Aquinas, II-II, Q. 141, art. 7.

167. Aquinas, II-II, Q. 141, art. 7

168. Aquinas, II-II, Q. 145, art. 3.

169. Pieper, *Fortitude*, 48–49.

170. Pieper, 33–34.

171. Porter, "Chastity," 287.

172. Aquinas, *ST*, II-II, Q. 155.

173. Austin, "Thomas Aquinas."

174. Cates, "Virtue," 326. Certainly Augustine took this view of virtuous eating practices for the wealthy. See Ward, "Porters," 216–42, 228.

175. Hartman, *Christian Consumer*; Himes, "Consumerism"; Kavanaugh, *Following Christ*; Cavanaugh, *Being Consumed*.

176. Cloutier, "Problem."

177. Rubio, *Family Ethics*, chap. 7.

178. Hartman, *Christian Consumer*.

179. MacIntyre, *After Virtue*, 136. MacIntyre goes on to make it clear, despite his gender-exclusive language, that both men and women were believed capable of *sophrosyne*—not the case for all of the ancient virtues.

180. Curzer, "Aristotle's Account."
181. Copeland, "Toward a Critical Christian Feminist Theology," 25.
182. Hughes, *Katharine Drexel*, 108–9, 134–36.
183. Hughes, 133.
184. Hughes, 170, quoting Ruether, *Sexism*, 137–38.
185. Hughes, 170, quoting Ruether, *Sexism*, 137–38.
186. Zinsmeister, "Oseola McCarty"; Bragg, "All She Has."
187. Bragg, "She Opened World."
188. Aquinas, *ST*, Q. 123, art. 1.
189. Aquinas, Q. 123, art. 2, 11.
190. Aquinas, Q. 123, art. 4-6.
191. Aquinas, Q. 123, art. 6.
192. Aquinas, Q. 123, art. 9. Aquinas would not have enjoined anxious perseverating over potential threats, which is clearly inimical to flourishing. What he is suggesting would probably look more like practical assessment of and preparation for the risks one might reasonably encounter in one's life, not anxious avoidance of any potential threat. Klubertanz describes two other false interpretations of fortitude. Overactivity, so common in today's capitalist society, is not a reasonable interpretation of perseverance. Neither is stubborn adherence to a predetermined mode of life which prioritizes details of activity over goals. Klubertanz, *Habits*.
193. Aquinas, *ST*, Q. 123, art. 10.
194. Pieper, *Fortitude*, 13.
195. Pieper, 18.
196. Hauerwas and Pinches, *Christians*, 162.
197. Hauerwas and Pinches, 164.
198. Hauerwas and Pinches.
199. Lebacqz and Macemon, "Vicious Virtue?" 284.
200. King, "Letter," 5; Jalandoni, "Fortitude," 211–12. For a womanist theology of suffering that repudiates the caricatures of Christian virtues such as patience used against enslaved Black women, see Copeland, "'Wading.'"
201. Lebacqz and Macemon, "Vicious Virtue?" 284.
202. Quoted by Harris, *Gifts*, 120.
203. Pieper, *Virtues*, 28.
204. Andolsen, "Grace."
205. Roberts, "Virtue Ethics."
206. Prejean, *Dead Man*, 19–20, 64–65, 118, 217.
207. Prejean, 32, 101, 170–74.
208. Prejean, *Death*.
209. Prejean, *Dead Man*, 38.
210. Prejean, 54–55.
211. Prejean, "Regarding the Evolution"; Clarke, "Sister Helen Prejean's 'Happy Day.'"

CHAPTER 3

TOWARD A CHRISTIAN VIRTUE ACCOUNT OF MORAL LUCK

Christians extol moral agency.[1] They refer to the moral life as a "journey" accomplished through sustained effort, and they venerate persons who display heroic moral goodness. Such high esteem for moral agency might lead us to doubt that life circumstances beyond our own control could fundamentally shape our efforts to attain moral goodness. Yet commonsense examples show that they do. We all understand parents' worries that giving children certain privileges might "spoil" them, encouraging vices like selfishness or impatience. We admire people who remain hopeful throughout serious hardship. Few would assert that someone who hopes through a life of comfort and ease displays the same kind and degree of virtue as the person who hopes while enduring war, famine, or captivity. To insist that there is no distinction between the hopeful tycoon and the hopeful refugee erases the personal dimension that virtue ethics takes for granted, and misses something essential about human experience.

Life circumstances do indeed shape our moral lives, for better or worse, and in complex overlapping ways. Life circumstances such as gender, sexual or racial identity, and wealth and poverty affect moral development as they influence one's self-image, treatment by others, and opportunities for action within society.[2] Philosophers refer to this reality as moral luck, and they often explore it in the context of virtue ethics, with its ingrained attention to growth, context, and community. Feminist philosophers have given the most sustained attention to moral luck, explaining conclusively how life circumstances such as privilege and oppression function as moral luck. This chapter outlines a detailed picture of moral luck based on their work.

Yet, as I show here, Christian virtue theorists cannot uncritically adopt the account of moral luck that feminist philosophers propose. Just as

Christians contextualize universally intelligible virtues by describing them in light of theological narratives and envisioning their pursuit in religious contexts, the concept of moral luck needs its own development in light of Christian sources. Happily, the theological tradition provides ample material. Thomas Aquinas, the most influential Christian virtue theorist, acknowledged the reality of moral luck as today's feminist philosophers describe it. For Aquinas, understanding moral luck should remind us that our ability to pursue virtue at all depends on God. Contemporary woman-ist theologians also engage moral luck, bringing a proactive focus to how persons shaped by moral luck should respond. They recommend that persons harmed by moral luck work for moral improvement within the Christian community.

As with the virtues, accounts of moral luck may differ among communities while remaining, fundamentally, mutually intelligible. As in philosophy, moral luck in a Christian virtue context attempts to realistically confront and understand the way life circumstances, including privilege or lack thereof, can affect persons' pursuit of virtue. What is unique in a Christian concept of moral luck is its use: to recall agents' dependence on God for their pursuit of virtue and to hold out hope for redressing moral luck's fragmentation of selves with the help of God and community.

All persons share the common experience of being thwarted by moral luck in our pursuit of virtue, and depending on God to grow in the virtuous life. Still, it is crucial to understand the particular and different ways life circumstances can affect virtue pursuit. This task is so important because virtue is necessary for human flourishing. Moral luck offers a tool to assess whether communities are truly offering all their members the opportunity to flourish as full human beings with moral agency, or whether some members of the community are expected to pull themselves up by their own bootstraps, morally speaking. Moral luck warns of the difficulties and pitfalls we will most likely face in the pursuit of virtue, and has the potential to change how we evaluate the virtue of others, including whether we regard their virtues as morally heroic. Perhaps most importantly, understanding moral luck helps persons gain a more accurate picture of what the pursuit of virtue will require of us, in each of our particular lives. For Christians, this includes an awareness of our dependence on God for moral growth, and a commitment to moral action. This Christian account of moral luck addresses those suffering under structures of oppression and also those who benefit from inequalities; emphasizes both dependence on God and persons' moral agency; and is rooted firmly in the Christian tradition.

STRUCTURES, INJURY, AND LUCK: APPROACHES TO THE IMPACT OF CIRCUMSTANCE ON MORALITY

The renascent Christian virtue tradition has offered approaches to virtue in general, virtues for particular professions,[3] and virtues for responding to specific aspects of human life, such as childhood,[4] sexuality,[5] parenting,[6] sickness,[7] and death.[8] Still, although numerous promising attempts have been made, there is no generally accepted Christian virtue explanation of how particular life situations can affect our ability to pursue and acquire the virtues. Here, I briefly detail previous attempts to capture this reality.

First, it is important to emphasize that life circumstances only tell part of the story of a person's virtue development. Virtue is neither entirely under our own volition nor something that can be summarily inculcated in us or stripped from us by life events.[9] Rather, life circumstances present us with a certain array of arenas for action and our own choices affect how we acquire or fail to acquire virtue within those arenas. One person's acquisition of virtue may differ from that of another not only because their life circumstances differ but also because they may make different choices, persist or fail to persist in the pursuit of those choices, and respond differently to changing circumstances and events along the way.[10]

EARLIER APPROACHES TO LIFE CIRCUMSTANCES AND VIRTUE

Daniel Daly offers the concepts of *structures of virtue and structures of vice* to describe how social or cultural institutions take part in shaping virtuous or vicious persons.[11] Daly's structures describe the moral contexts that contribute to shaping persons, within which persons make choices that lead to them becoming more or less virtuous. He finds this framework more satisfactory than a term with some history in magisterial and theological statements, the structures of sin. When society negatively affects moral persons, the result is often persistent problems of character that are better described as vices than as sins.[12]

The structures of virtue and vice are clearly described, helpful frameworks that do real and necessary work in Christian virtue theory. However, like the "structures of sin" theorists he improves upon, Daly does not explore how value differences ingrained in structures can affect people within the same society in different ways related to their social positioning.

For example, racism is a structure of vice (or sin) that clearly creates different sorts of morally salient experiences for white people and people of color.

Moral injury is a fairly new concept with a highly particular use in religious ethical discourse. It was coined in 2009 by a group of psychologists who observed that agents of harmful acts sustain moral injury when they suffer morally because of what they have done. The authors describe moral injury as the result of "perpetrating, failing to prevent, or bearing witness to acts that transgress deeply held moral beliefs and expectations [which] may be deleterious in the long-term, emotionally, psychologically, behaviorally, spiritually, and socially."[13] These psychologists, and recently, some theologians, examine the moral injury sustained by soldiers in war, although the concept has also been used to explore bullying, incarceration, and racialization.[14]

Moral injury could be a helpful concept in virtue ethics, because it describes harms to self-image and moral reflection. As the psychologist Brett Litz and his colleagues argue, moral injury interferes with flourishing by presenting overwhelming impressions that the subject is bad, immoral, and irremediable. Furthermore, the acts that have caused moral injury can acquire outsize significance in the subject's mind, making reflection on sustained patterns of behavior difficult.[15] Moral injury fragments the agent's sense of self, perhaps into prewar and postwar selves.[16] The theologian Mark Wilson explicitly situates moral injury in a virtue context when he suggests that the morally injured pursue virtues of humility, fidelity, and availability.[17]

Conversely, moral injury's usefulness is limited by its relatively narrow scope of reference to acts committed by an agent. As Wilson clarifies, "individuals suffering moral injury take themselves to have *done* or *not done* something," under tragic conditions (emphasis in the original).[18] Unlike moral luck, moral injury does not provide a framework for reflection on the moral impact of life circumstances such as privilege and oppression, beyond the impact of the specific actions those circumstances might occasion. In fact, scholars engaged in studying moral injury in religious contexts have argued against its use in this way.[19] Because of its specificity, moral injury might helpfully be understood as a subtype of moral luck, as will become clear just below. Moral luck can cover the ground these approaches do not, offering another, more comprehensive tool in the virtue ethicist's toolbox. I now introduce the understanding of moral luck in philosophy before moving on to its distinct presence in the Christian tradition.

MORAL LUCK IN PHILOSOPHY

Philosophers introduced moral luck in the context of deontological ethics, but virtue theorists have adopted it as a crucial term for understanding the impact of context, particularly privilege and power dynamics, on the virtues.[20] This section details a philosophical account of moral luck in virtue ethics, focusing on the philosophers Martha Nussbaum, Margaret Urban Walker, Claudia Card, and Lisa Tessman.[21] As they show, moral luck helps understand and describe the impact of life circumstances on the virtues—on who we are able to become, morally speaking, and ultimately whether we are able to flourish. In particular, moral luck allows us to conceive and explain the impact of oppression or privilege on virtue formation.

Moral luck is "luck that impacts either on character development or on one's ability to do morally good or right things in particular contexts," as Claudia Card describes it.[22] Bernard Williams and Thomas Nagel introduced the term.[23] Williams argues that Kantian morality, with its focus on the will, has not adequately dealt with the fact that not every consequence of our actions is within our control.[24] Nagel shows that people take moral luck into account in their everyday moral assessments: "We may admit that if certain antecedent circumstances had been different, the agent would never have developed into the sort of person who would do such a thing, but since he did [develop into that sort of person and then do something blameworthy] *that* is what he is blamable for."[25] This 1979 treatment forecasts the application of moral luck to virtue ethics.

Philosophers distinguish between incident moral luck—circumstances beyond our control that affect the moral implications of singular actions or situations—and constitutive moral luck, in which circumstances beyond our control affect who we are able to become.[26] An example of incident moral luck is that two people may recklessly drive drunk, both incurring the guilt of needlessly risking their own and others' lives. However, if a pedestrian is present in only one case, only one drunk driver will bear the additional culpability of actually *causing* the death of an innocent person. Although both drivers took the same irresponsible risk, most observers would assign additional guilt to the driver whose recklessness had a fatal result, although the source of the harm caused is effectively random.

The term "moral luck" does not imply any assessment of whether the luck in question is positive or negative. In common usage, "luck" usually means something positive has happened by chance, as in "She has all the luck." If we want to be clear that negative things have happened by chance, we specify "bad luck." In contrast, "moral luck" simply calls our attention to factors beyond the agent's control that have an impact on her moral life. The term does not specify, in and of itself, whether those chance factors have positive or negative results.

Martha Nussbaum's 1986 book *The Fragility of Goodness* introduced moral luck into discussions of virtue ethics. For Nussbaum, acknowledging moral luck invites us to reflect on activities and relationships that are widely viewed as integral to a characteristically human life and yet are inherently "vulnerable to reversal." These activities and relationships, including "friendship, love, political activity, [and] attachments to property or possessions" are particularly likely to invite uncontrollable instances of moral luck into our lives.[27] This becomes a particular risk if our conception of the good life involves multiple relationships and attachments, as we may then find that moral luck brings them into conflict and presents us with difficult choices. Then again, if we admit that emotions, appetites, and other unpredictable aspects of human experience can provide us with moral insight, we are likely to find that our path through the moral life is equally unpredictable.[28] If we agree that a characteristically human life involves the pursuit of valuable activities and practices, such as love, that are inherently vulnerable to reversal, then our concepts of the good, moral life must acknowledge moral luck.

Nussbaum shows that Aristotle gave an account of moral luck. He believed experiences shape virtues and that serious hardships can erode even virtues constructed during a long life. Circumstances can prevent us from virtuous activity by depriving our activity of a key means or resource, or by removing the intended object of the activity, as when the death of a friend removes the activity of friendship. And circumstances can impede the performance of virtuous activity, or even exclude it completely.[29]

Nussbaum reflects on the fragility of goodness through Aristotle's description of the myth of Priam, the virtuous king of Troy who suffers the tragic death of his son. Aristotle believed certain "external goods"—such as friendship, wealth, political skill, and good family relationships—are needed for *eudaimonia*, the full human flourishing that accompanies virtue attainment. He acknowledged that suffering "the luck of Priam" might not thoroughly destroy virtue; a good person could find ways to pursue the good even in tragic circumstances. But even a person as virtuous as Priam, if subjected to such tragic luck as Priam was, could not enjoy true *eudaimonia* in Aristotle's view.[30] Full human flourishing, *eudaimonia*, demands not only virtue— although it does require that—but also certain external goods, which life's luck does not guarantee even to the virtuous.

Nussbaum insists that Aristotle believed luck not only can change our ability to enjoy happiness and express our virtues once acquired; luck also can change our ability to develop or keep the virtues. In his *Rhetoric*, for example, Aristotle reflects on the virtues that older and younger people tend to develop. He believes younger people are more trusting, more courageous, and more capable of "greatness of soul" because they have not yet become beaten down by life. In contrast, the elderly are more humble, suspicious, and attached to property, because life has taught them that these qualities are necessary for survival.[31] Nussbaum writes,

> These remarkable observations show us clearly to what extent Aristotle is willing to acknowledge that circumstances of life can impede character itself, making even acquired virtues difficult to retain. Especially at risk are those virtues that require openness or guilelessness rather than self-defensiveness, trust in other people and in the world rather than self-protecting suspiciousness.... The virtues require a stance of openness toward the world and its possibilities.... Virtue contains in this way (in a world where most people's experience is that "things go badly") the seeds of its own disaster.[32]

For Aristotle, Nussbaum finds, virtue requires activity. We would not consider a person virtuous who had acquired virtue over the course of a long life and now survived in a coma. But our activity, within spheres of life most humans deem important—such as relationships, political action, and using possessions—inevitably exposes us to moral luck. This in turn runs the risk of challenging our virtuous responses and even ending *eudaimonia*. This is why Nussbaum calls goodness fragile: "Virtuous condition is not, itself, something hard and invulnerable."[33] Virtuous living is always and by definition subject to reversal from moral luck.

For Margaret Urban Walker, acknowledging virtue's vulnerability to circumstance helps us rightly evaluate the moral qualities of others. Walker says that moral luck helps us evaluate an agent's integrity when we see how the agent understands and responds to the moral situation in which her life circumstances have placed her.[34] For example, Walker believes we would rightly censure an agent for "shrugging off" blame that fell to her because of moral luck—such as a drunk driver who killed a pedestrian but who might have escaped blame if no pedestrian had been present. "Given the nature of the case," an unmoved response from the blameworthy agent "could be disappointing or irritating, shameful or indecent, shocking or outrageous."[35]

Walker is, of course, correct that communities *should* rightly censure those who shrug off blame in these situations. Unfortunately, it is far from clear that communities always *do*. In the case of the negligent driver, many communities would expect affective remorse and redressive action, even though the driver's responsibility for the harm fell to her because of moral luck. And yet it is hotly contested whether either response is appropriate on the part of those who experience unearned privilege at the expense of others, which is another way moral luck doles out benefits and harm. In the United States, for example, white people enjoy relative prosperity and safety at the cost of historical and contemporary violence against people of color, and particularly because of the historical plunder of the labor, wealth, and lives of African-descended people.[36] Those who enjoy economic privilege engage in another shrugging off of responsibility when they refuse to acknowledge that all members of society are not given an equal chance to enjoy the comfort and prosperity they themselves enjoy.[37] Moral luck indeed presents communities with a tool for evaluating the integrity of agents, but it must be used in concert with thorough evaluation of the morally relevant circumstances of their actions, including historical realities of privilege and oppression.

Recognizing this need, Walker proposes the "virtues of impure agency," integrity, grace, and lucidity, to help us navigate responsibility in a world where virtue is fragile to moral luck. Integrity helps each of us protect our moral self as consistent and unitary, particularly when moral luck bestows trying situations that present unexpected moral challenges.[38] Making redress is an important act of expressing integrity in situations where one has caused harm, even inadvertently. However, Walker says, "acceptance, non-aggrandized daily 'living with' unsupported by fantasies of overcoming or restitution, may in its quiet way be as profoundly admirable as integrity in those situations which permit no reconstructive address. I would call this, simply, *grace*."[39] Integrity and grace are supported by "*lucidity*, a reasonable grasp of the nature and seriousness of one's morally unlucky plight and a cogent and sensitive estimate of repairs and self-correction in point."[40] Walker's virtues of impure agency "are constituted in important part by a reliable capacity to see things clearly, to take the proper moral measure of situations, so that a fitting response may be fashioned."[41] In this regard, they all seem to fall under the classical definition of prudence, which helps us assess situations and determine our response to them.

Walker says that agents must recognize their own vulnerability to moral luck, and prepare themselves to take responsibility for harm they may not have intended, for others to recognize them as dependable. "To the extent that we ourselves are such agents and possess integrity, we can depend, morally, on ourselves even in such a bad spot."[42] The previous chapter discussed how the virtue of self-care is demonstrated in part by taking responsibility for one's own moral development. Understanding moral luck helps create the conditions for virtue pursuit, allowing agents to take responsibility for the types of harm to which they may add in a world where they do not exercise complete control.

Claudia Card explains how persistent aspects of identity function as moral luck. Although much of Card's reflection focuses on gender, her thought is broadly applicable to identities that may become connected with "politically disadvantageous starting points or early positionings in life."[43] The presence of moral luck in identity means "not that certain virtues are more appropriate to certain people but that different combinations of circumstances in fact provide opportunities for, stimulate, nurture, or discourage the development of different virtues and vices, strengths and weaknesses of character."[44]

Card acknowledges that any individual may be at once disadvantaged and privileged in various ways, and that all these complexities contribute to shaping character. Although it may not be possible or helpful to declare persons unilaterally privileged or disadvantaged, "still, the dimensions of powerlessness take their toll. They impact the way we develop, as do our 'closets' if we choose to 'pass.'"[45] Luck is best understood not simply as circumstances external to us but also as circumstances that are "contingent to our moral agency" and that may also be internal to selves.[46] For example, one person's actions may be another's luck, because how others respond to us can obviously shape our moral agency—think of how a parent's confidence or fearfulness can encourage a child to become more brave or more cowardly.[47] Significant relationships, such as those with partners or family members, are obvious sources of constitutive moral luck, as are "relationships structured by basic social institutions (educational, economic)."[48] Pushing beyond earlier work, Card envisions moral luck not simply as a matter of assigning or reserving praise or blame but also an approach to understanding moral agents as interlinked and shaped by circumstances, particularly privilege and oppression.[49]

For Card, the primary way oppression can damage moral agents is by making it more difficult to function as integrated selves: "Oppression splinters us (both within ourselves, as individuals, and from each other, within a group) by putting us constantly into double binds."[50] The self must be integrated in order to fully take responsibility for its desires and actions, but the splintering effect of oppression complicates this: "Responsible agency [dissolves when] internal connections are broken or inadequately developed. . . . Nor is the importance of morally responsible agency diminished by differences among us in the ease or difficulty of developing it. For the importance of morality does not rest simply on the extent to which it enables us to take credit for self-manufacture. Its importance lies, in part, in grounding the will to resist such things as abuse, exploitation, and oppression."[51]

In addition to splintering selves, oppression can shape them in further harmful ways, eliciting isolation, impotence, and pain.[52] It can result in selves "being deprived of, or prevented from developing, Rawls' primary good, self-respect."[53] We begin to see how the moral luck of identity interferes with virtue formation, inhibiting positive qualities that lead to flourishing, such as self-respect, and promoting others that impede flourishing, like isolation.

Understanding moral luck challenges views that persons' moral behavior may differ for reasons that are simple, innate, or purely volitional. Card argues that views of women's morality as more focused on care than justice overlook the moral luck of gendered power imbalances in shaping agents' virtues and vices.[54] Differences in moral decision-making between women and men are likely not "innate" but reflect the moral luck of social expectation: "the responsibilities of the different kinds of relationships that have been the focus of the choices of women and men in sexist societies yield different ethical preoccupations, methods, priorities, even concepts."[55] Card notes that Mary Wollstonecraft came to this insight already in 1792, when she argued that those qualities praised in women in sexist society are really vices that help men control women.[56] The theologian M. Shawn Copeland relays the same insight on the part of Ruth Shays, the daughter of an African American slave: "The mind of the man and the mind of the woman is the same. But this business of living makes women use their minds in ways that men don't have to think about; . . . it is life that makes all these differences, not nature."[57]

Card suggests that the moral luck of gender can predispose persons to different vices, such as domination and aggression for men, and passivity and trickery for women.[58] She writes, "Feminist thinkers are understandably reluctant to address publicly women's reputation for lying, cunning, deceit, and manipulation. But, are these vices, one may ask, if they are needed for self-defense? They are surely not virtues, . . . even if . . . needed for survival under oppressive conditions. Human good may be unrealizable under such conditions."[59]

Card broadens her view out from gender to discuss how systems of oppression generally affect the moral luck of those privileged and oppressed within them: "The privileged are liable to arrogance with its blindness to others' perspectives. The oppressed are liable to low self-esteem, ingratiation, . . . as well as to a tendency to dissemble, fear of being conspicuous, and chameleonism—taking on the colors of our environment as protection against assault. . . . It may also be our moral luck to develop special insights and sensitivities, even under oppressive institutions."[60]

At times, those who are oppressed may have no possible course of action that does not involve a "moral remainder," a negative consequence that could not be avoided. A moral remainder, which is always negative in Card's understanding, can indicate that harm was done to someone who did not deserve it. It can also describe a negative impact on the moral formation of the agent.[61] This is one reason why, in Card's words, "human good may be unrealizable" under particular conditions of oppression—moral remainders that damage agents or others will inevitably result.

Racial identity, too, is an example of moral luck, as Card explains: "By profiting in various ways, willingly or not, from ethnic privilege, I may now have acquired moral responsibilities. [My assigned ethnic identity] may be part of my moral luck, something to be taken into account if I am to appreciate the political meanings of my relationships and interactions with others."[62] Societies impose particular meanings and values on particular racial and ethnic identities, demonstrating how moral luck can impose duties on us, even though we do not choose it.

For Card, one particular duty imposed on those in societies with racial privilege systems is developing a "higher order race consciousness." This requires that we strive to understand how racism and racialization, the assignment of people to racial groups, shape our perceptions of our own self-worth as well as society's systems and institutions.[63] For example, those of us who are socialized into white racial consciousness are taught to be "color blind," not to look too closely at the history of racism in our particular context and the ways in which it grants us privilege. Moral awareness, consciousness-raising, is required: "Uncovering particular histories, such as those underlying our racial and ethnic social identities, can help us to appreciate who it is our moral luck to have become, to determine what responsibilities we now have, how we are related to one another, the meanings of the institutions in which we now participate and by which we have been formed, and what kinds of choices we now have."[64]

We should not assume that our identities, their meaning, and the duties they do or do not impose on us are "transparent." Instead, we should interrogate our social location and its contingent duties while remaining open to accessing difficult social memories.[65] We can see how Card, like Walker, implicitly calls for prudence in response to moral luck. Though moral luck is chance beyond our control, it does not leave us devoid of agency. It calls for wise evaluation of morally significant realities and proper responses, exactly what the virtue of prudence helps us achieve.

Building on Card's work, Lisa Tessman provides the most sustained investigation into how experiences of privilege and oppression can serve as moral luck. She notes that some experiences of moral luck are systemic, due to pervasive social forces, while others might be idiosyncratic and limited to particular instances. Systemic luck, she believes, is more likely to be constitutive of character.[66]

Moral damage, a category Tessman takes from Card, results when a person fails to develop the virtues as fully as she might have, due to systemic, constitutive moral (bad) luck.[67] For oppressed people, evidence of moral damage might include identifying with one's oppressors or failing to appreciate one's own human dignity. Such traits can help oppressed persons survive oppression, but they do not ultimately contribute to the person's true flourishing.[68]

An agent can be morally damaged by simply trying to survive as an oppressed person or by attempting to resist oppression. Developing virtue under oppression carries a burden, in that unequal societies are not set up to help oppressed persons flourish. That is, "resistance, while politically necessary, does not automatically release the self from the burdens or the damages that oppressive conditions evoke."[69] Being oppressed in a way that seems to demand resistance is a particular type of systemic moral luck that poses particular risks to one's development of virtue.[70]

For example, displaying the courage and self-sacrifice that resisting oppression may demand can invite danger for the activist or her loved ones. Resisters may develop insensitivity to any type of danger or vulnerability, which might compromise the flourishing of their relationships.[71] Some resistance movements may demand that members cultivate traits that oppose the self's flourishing, such as anger or extreme self-sacrifice, or may punish members who criticize the group's actions.[72] And group loyalty is a burdened virtue, in that justice may demand criticism of a group's actions or even its self-understanding, an action that can draw accusations of disloyalty from fellow group members.[73] Tessman summarizes: "Oppression creates communities that are precarious as good objects of loyalty, and thereby tends to make loyalty either burdened . . . or unavailable."[74] Oppressed communities in resistance are not reliable sites to develop virtue.[75]

Tessman follows Card in noting that systems of oppression damage the virtues of both those with privilege and oppressed persons. The privileged who are morally affected by their social positioning risk developing what Tessman calls "the ordinary vices of domination." She calls these vices ordinary to distinguish them from the types of vices that lead to acts of extreme hatred, but that are almost never believed to contribute to the agent's flourishing.[76] Although investigating the vices oppressed people may exhibit can feel like victim blaming, understanding the vices of those who benefit from oppression is all the more important because they are not usually understood as vices. In fact, Tessman believes that the majority of those occupying dominant roles in oppressive societies will come to exhibit the vices of domination.[77] She writes: "Those enjoying economic advantage are popularly believed to be living the good life, regardless of the moral flaws that lead them to accept, develop, or maintain their unjust position. . . . Thus many groups of people thought to be living well clearly exhibit moral vices (e.g., callousness, greed, self-centeredness, dishonesty, and cowardice, in addition to injustice) or at least the absence of certain specific moral virtues (perhaps compassion, generosity, cooperativeness, and openness to appreciating others)."[78]

Tessman acknowledges the possibility that members of privileged groups who actively resist oppressive structures may be able to change their characters and resist the "ordinary vices of domination," but she reminds us that the point of moral luck is that moral development is not entirely subject to our own wills.[79] She complains that too many virtue theorists speak as if the average reader were assumed to be virtuous. Instead, emphasizing the "ordinary vices of domination" invites readers to explore the impact of their privileges on their own moral development.[80] Virtue ethics approaches are sometimes accused of presenting an overly reassuring portrait of moral goodness and exaggerating the extent of individual moral agency.[81] Although Tessman believes this criticism at times is valid, her work shows how effective virtue ethics can be in a morally hortatory, less reassuring mode that reminds persons of their limitations, likely failures, and ensuing responsibilities.

Tessman concludes that analyzing the burdened virtues helps us develop a realistic eudaimonistic ethics—one focused on flourishing—in an imperfect world. Oppressed persons' actions within constrained circumstances may lead them to develop traits that do not contribute to their flourishing; that may actively harm their own flourishing or that of others; or that may simply enable them to survive for the time being. To acknowledge this is not to reject all hope for a world where flourishing is possible for everyone, but simply to recognize that the burdens placed on oppressed people by systemic inequalities include moral burdens.[82] Oppression harms oppressed people by denying them the external conditions for flourishing and by harming their ability to flourish morally. Importantly, however, systems of oppression also morally harm those advantaged by oppression, predisposing them to acquire particular vices. Thus, Tessman shows, systems of oppression affect advantaged and disadvantaged similarly in just this way: by imposing moral luck.[83]

By now it has become clear that moral luck helps describe broad and pervasive realities related to the virtuous life. Yet moral luck is not the ultimate arbiter of a person's moral destiny. It simply acknowledges that life circumstances—including gender, race, and socioeconomic status—present us with a certain set of arenas for action. It does not deny that our own choices affect how we acquire or fail to acquire virtue within these arenas. Despite the pervasive reality of moral luck, moral agency always remains present. Because virtue is necessary for flourishing, moral luck helps us ask who is being helped and who denied the opportunity to flourish.

I believe that Nussbaum, Walker, Card, and Tessman would agree that "the luck of Priam"—moral luck so tragic that it completely obliterates a person's virtue—is relatively rare.[84] In most circumstances, moral agency still matters, and persons can pursue virtue even in situations of incredibly tragic moral luck. However, it seems fair to note that these philosophers tend to emphasize the harm of moral luck rather than the persistence of individual agency. Card and Tessman, in particular, are pessimistic about the moral agency of persons harmed by systems of oppression and domination; recall Tessman's lament that the average reader is too often wrongly assumed to be virtuous. Their emphasis on moral luck is a needed corrective to optimistic approaches that seem to promise virtue acquisition as the reward for individual effort.

By now it should be clear that moral luck has the potential to do necessary work in Christian virtue ethics, but also that Christian virtue theorists cannot adopt the concept without significant inculturation. I proceed to investigate preliminary Christian accounts of moral luck, showing what they accomplish and how they differ from the account advanced by feminist philosophers.

MORAL LUCK IN CHRISTIAN ETHICS

Christian virtue ethics has given little attention to moral luck, but Christian ethicists are well aware that life circumstances can shape who we are able to become.[85] I focus on precursory descriptions of moral luck from just three sources: Scripture, Thomas Aquinas (d. 1274), and the writings of contemporary womanist theologians. The Christian virtue account of moral luck I develop from these sources retains philosophers' attention to the prevalent moral impact of unjust social structures and the difficulty of pursuing the virtuous life. Distinct from the philosophical view, it retains Christian hope for moral improvement. A Christian account of moral luck suggests that despite the fragmentation of moral luck, wholeness of self is possible through dependence on God and right relationship in community.

Moral Luck in Scripture: Preliminary Gestures

Although a complete investigation into moral luck in Scripture merits its own book, a few gestures show that Scripture is rich in understandings of how life circumstances shape who we become, and that moral development is not always entirely volitional. For example, the Book of Job reflects on Job's moral response to great suffering. When Job is visited with the staggering bad fortune Nussbaum would call "the luck of Priam," he ceases to display the virtue of patience that had originally sustained him. Yet by the end of his story, he acknowledges his dependence on God and asks God's forgiveness. For the biblical scholar Daniel Harrington, the Old Testament invites us to lament our suffering in solidarity with others and to remember that God can triumph over suffering.[86] Moral luck such as Job's is real, it affects our virtue, and it is lamentable, but it does not have the last word on our relationship with God.

In the Gospels, one recurrent example of moral luck is a personal call by Jesus, an opportunity not given to everyone. Gerhard Lohfink argues that there are "a variety of callings" for Jesus's followers in the Gospels.[87] Not everyone is called to leave all they have and follow Jesus, but those who are so called incur blame if they reject the invitation. Lohfink finds this reading more satisfactory than one often assigned to the story about the rich young man who rejected Jesus (Mark 10:17–22), that only a "more perfect" way of life involves renunciation of possessions.[88] Everyone is called to wholeness or integrity, Lohfink says, but this integrity looks different for different characters in the Gospels. Receiving a particular call, to follow or to remain, may indicate an example of moral luck, but agents are still responsible for accepting the call they receive.

The developing field of biblical virtue ethics demonstrates ongoing reflection on moral luck in Scripture. For example, Lúcás Chan explores hospitality in the Book of Ruth, drawing attention to Ruth's constrained options as a Moabite widow and Boaz's self-understanding as the descendant of strangers.[89] The Israelite community's self-understanding as descendants of strangers is, of course, foundational to a great deal of Hebrew Bible ethical discourse. This tradition acknowledges the moral luck of inhabiting a particular status (you are the descendants of strangers) and the responsibility of moral agents for their response (welcome the stranger among you).[90]

Moral Luck in Thomas Aquinas

Without using the term "moral luck," Thomas Aquinas gives accounts of both incident and constitutive moral luck. As in the example given above of drunk driving, incident moral luck refers to circumstances affecting the morally significant outcomes of particular acts. Aquinas considers this type of situation in his discussion of whether circumstances increase the gravity of a sin. The example of the drunk driver fits Aquinas's discussion of harm that follows directly from a sinful act (not drinking per se, but callously risking harm to others), even though it is neither foreseen nor intended by the agent. Such harm, for Aquinas, increases the consequences of a sin.

Unforeseen harm, in fact, is integral to evaluating sin. It is part of what makes a certain sin the type of sin it is, and not another—what it means to be part of the sin's "species" for Aquinas.[91] Even an action that is good according to its species can become bad according to its circumstances. For example, we might help others, which is a good type of act, for a bad reason, such as to win public praise.[92]

Circumstances can aggravate sin even when connected with the sin only accidentally. An example might be that someone steals a car with a medical inhaler inside it, and the asthmatic who needed the inhaler dies. Stealing is a sin, but causing the asthmatic's death is related only by accident. Still, in this case Aquinas says the sinner is culpable for having failed to consider the harm they caused.[93] Other, more obvious examples of harm caused through sin include harm that is foreseen and intended in doing the sin, and harm that is foreseen but not intended, which the agent in a sense writes off as the cost of sinning. For both these types of harm, Aquinas says, the agent is culpable. This is Aquinas's clear and detailed treatment of incident moral luck. Addressing the many ways the moral significance of particular acts can be changed by circumstances, it parallels the views of contemporary philosophers.

Like Card and Tessman, Aquinas also addresses constitutive moral luck, luck that shapes the kind of persons we are. One example is in his discussion of "whether the excellence of the person sinning aggravates the sin."[94] He believes that sin is more strongly "imputed" to three groups of people: those who have enjoyed many blessings and should have more reason to be grateful to God; those who violate a specific charge, like the duty of a prince to defend justice; and those who are much admired and thus cause scandal by their sin.[95] In Aquinas's view, each of these privileged life circumstances can exacerbate the gravity of a sin.

Aquinas specifically mentions that one life circumstance that can increase the seriousness of sin is "any excellence, even in temporal goods." Sin is imputed more strongly to us if we sin despite personal talents or wealth; the blessing itself does not cause the disadvantage, but the fact that we abuse it.[96] Taken together with the cautions to those with specific duties and those in power, this entire discussion recalls the Gospel challenge "From the one to whom much is given, much will be expected" (Luke 12:48).

Aquinas identifies threats to virtue in experiences of privilege and oppression. Excellence in temporal goods exacerbates sin, and the stress of a difficult life can lead to blameworthy moral ignorance. Attempting to explain how Aquinas can, on one hand, acknowledge that temporal goods often play a role in virtue formation, and on the other hand, assert that God gives everyone the temporal goods they need to pursue virtue, the philosopher John Bowlin suggests that "Aquinas considers the relation between external goods and virtuous action thoroughly ambiguous."[97] Any external good, such as wealth, may be used either virtuously or viciously, as may the absence of an external good.[98] Life circumstances do not fully determine morality, but they present us with particular circumstances for action, by which we are shaped and for which we are responsible.

Aquinas's understanding of vincible and invincible ignorance contributes to our Christian account of moral luck in important ways, particularly as we approach privilege and oppression. In general, ignorance does not excuse us from sin if we are ignorant about something we should have known, whether that means basic human goods or part of our specific duty. Ignorance does excuse us from sin if we are incapable of knowing, and therefore doing, better.[99]

Aquinas describes two types of voluntary or vincible ignorance, neither of which excuses us from sin. The first is direct, voluntary ignorance, wherein we intentionally prolong our ignorance in order to "sin the more freely." Voluntary ignorance is often cited today describing privileged persons who choose to remain ignorant of the effect of their privilege on others, though they could easily know better.[100]

Another type of voluntary ignorance may be harder to accept. Aquinas says that even ignorance caused by "stress of work or other occupations," which keeps us from knowing what we should have known, does not excuse us from sin.[101] There is something pitiable about the person so consumed with work and stress that she neglects her moral duty, and we may wish to avoid blaming such a person. But Aquinas, probably thinking of the impact on those such a person wounds through her ignorance, charges her with "negligence." Such ignorance is "itself voluntary and sinful, provided it be about matters one is bound and able to know."[102]

Judith Kay explains how Aquinas's distinction between "nature" and "second nature" allows him to criticize harmful habits that may be developed, at least in part, in response to pernicious cultural factors—another example of constitutive moral luck. Human nature, of course, is inherently good and seeks the good. The vices we acquire limit our freedom and may appear so innate to our being that they attain the status of a "quasi" or "second nature."[103] Kay's example of internalized oppression is a good example of moral luck that is constitutive, yet not entirely determinative. Oppressed persons, who live with the understanding that their society does not value their personhood, will be more liable to develop the harmful habit of internalized oppression than others who are not similarly marginalized. Aquinas's account of "second nature" allows virtue ethicists to understand the pervasive impact of such a harmful habit while understanding how oppressed persons retain moral agency and the potential for goodness.

Constitutive moral luck can also be found in "natural disposition," which can enable certain persons to develop virtue more perfectly than others.[104] In his *Disputed Questions on the Virtues*, Aquinas acknowledges that virtue can exist to different degrees in different people: "With respect to the perfection or quantity of virtue from the point of view of *its being in* its subject, there can be inequality even within one type of virtue, in that one of those who possess it can be better disposed than someone else to whatever comes under that virtue; this might be through a better natural tendency, or more practice, or a better rational judgment, or the gift of grace."[105]

This "natural disposition" to a virtue or a virtuous practice is clearly an example of constitutive moral luck. We can all think of people who seem to have innate gifts for temperance, patience, or bravery, while others could work toward those virtues for a long time without achieving the same perfection as one who tends to them naturally.

Even grace can explain why persons develop virtue to different degrees—a difficult idea to accept, perhaps, but a reminder that for Aquinas, no one can form even the acquired virtues without God's help.[106] Bowlin finds that for Aquinas, God's charity "effectively eliminat[es] fortune's authority over virtuous habits and actions," affording the possibility of perfect virtue to those struggling with no matter what life circumstances.[107] Even those who have acquired virtue need God's grace in order to persevere.[108] As Jean Porter points out, Aquinas was much more comfortable acknowledging limitations on human freedom than modern thinkers tend to be, and God's predestination is a preeminent example of grace functioning as a limitation on human freedom.[109] Aquinas thus acknowledges many examples of moral luck related to the acquisition of virtue, including personal inclination, greater opportunity to practice a virtue, harmful "second nature" habits, and even God's will.

Life circumstances can constitute moral luck when our lives do not afford us the chance to practice virtuous habits. Another occasion of moral luck is when life circumstances prevent us from developing virtue, even when we have the chance to practice certain habits. Aquinas's example is that drunkenness can prevent us from improving in the habit of science (deductive reasoning), even if we practice the habit.[110] Tessman's burdened virtues provide another appropriate example. Someone who practices self-advocacy under a situation of oppression might fail to acquire the virtue of fortitude, because her dangerous circumstances mean that to advocate for herself is less a brave than a foolhardy act.

Some Christians suppose that Christian belief is constitutive moral luck, in that they think only Christians can behave morally and acquire virtue. Because Aquinas's virtues system is explicitly Christian and has union with God as its end, it is worthwhile to investigate whether he agrees. In a recent book, David Decosimo has convincingly shown that Aquinas did believe that non-Christians, or "pagans," could acquire the moral virtues.[111] "Pagan virtue" (not Aquinas's term, but useful shorthand) is imperfect with regard to the beatific end; but it *is* perfect with respect to "orienting a person well to the true good of common life."[112] Pagans can attain the political virtues, which are connected because they share the goal of the common good.[113] True virtue for Aquinas must be unified, but some scholars who disagree that Aquinas accepts pagan virtue have argued that only charity can unify the virtues. Decosimo shows that pagans can possess the political virtues, which are unified by having the common good as their end, and so in this sense pagan virtue is true. More broadly, he reminds us that Aquinas thought true virtue was rare, whether we are Christian or not. Christian belief is no guarantee of virtue, just as pagan belief does not eliminate virtue's possibility.[114] So for Aquinas, Christian religious belief or the lack thereof is not constitutive moral luck.

Similarly, some might suggest that Aquinas's infused virtues, which God works "in us without us," are a preeminent form of moral luck.[115] This is not wrong so much as it is immaterial. Moral luck, according to both philosophers and theologians, has to do with the virtues we are able to pursue ourselves—in Aquinas's language, the acquired virtues. Conversely, Aquinas says that humans are not even capable of pursuing the theological virtues—only God can give them to humans. It is not worth the time to speculate about whether particular circumstances of a human life or structures of human society make God more or less likely to infuse the theological virtues in a person.[116] Some theologians currently hold that all virtue is infused, while Florence Caffrey Bourg points out that Catholic understandings of the family as a school of virtue suggest an acquired aspect to the theological virtue of faith. Although discussion of the meaning of infused virtue continues in lively fashion, few would disagree that the ultimate import of Aquinas's teaching is to remind us of our dependence on God to achieve God as end. His use of the acquired virtues points out our own ability and responsibility to shape our characters, and it is here that moral luck plays a role.

Aquinas clearly gives accounts of incident and constitutive moral luck. He acknowledges that privilege can be a source of moral luck, affecting our ability to acquire the virtues. In this, he shares the concerns of contemporary feminist philosophers whose work raises up historically marginalized perspectives. For him, moral luck reminds us about the difficulty of pursuing virtue in this life and of our dependence on God for all we are able to become.

Womanist Theologians and Moral Luck

Moral luck is a useful category for Christian virtue ethics, not only because it enables dialogue with philosophical virtue ethics but also because the category does real work that Christian ethics deeply needs. Our reading of feminist philosophers and Aquinas clearly shows how privilege can function as moral luck, but Christian ethics will also want to know whether moral luck describes something real about the moral experiences of those who are pushed to the margins of society. Womanist theology shows that it does. Womanist theologians, who work out of the dual contexts of "the oppressed Black community's concerns and struggles and the context of women's struggle for liberation and well-being," as Delores Williams says, have done some of the most sustained and incisive work on how inhabiting oppressed identities shapes moral selves.[117]

Certainly, the groups womanist theologians and feminist philosophers are not univocal; each field is diverse and home to its own differences. Yet it is possible to discern commonalities of approach to moral luck in both cases, to note that womanist theologians differ significantly from feminist philosophers precisely in ways that are critical for Christian virtue ethics and that help us see how a Christian ethical account of moral luck can be distinctly Christian. I show this here by comparing womanist sources with Tessman where appropriate. The areas to which I attend are the persistence of moral agency; the prospects of integrity for selves; the role of communities in moral formation; and the possibility of hope.

Katie Geneva Cannon's field-defining 1988 book *Black Womanist Ethics* acknowledged the reality that moral luck affects virtue. Life circumstances shape the use of moral agency, Cannon says, as "Blacks and whites, women and men are forced to live with very different ranges of freedom."[118] Cannon judges as inadequate ethical traditions that locate moral agency in a pure, voluntaristic freedom that every moral agent is assumed to share. She sheds light on the moral wisdom found in the Black woman's literary tradition and the male-led Black Church to show that women and men constrained by multiple oppressions "develop virtues that allow them to live with dignity on their own terms."[119] The personal disposition of "unctuousness," a smooth response to ill treatment, and the virtues of "quiet grace" and "unshouted courage" emerge among Black women exercising moral agency in a racist world that fights against their flourishing.[120] Oppressed persons exercise moral agency when they recognize their own dignity as created in God's image and work toward a world acknowledging this dignity.[121] Although Cannon freely acknowledges the reality of moral luck, she maintains a hopeful assessment of the exercise of moral agency, even amid intersectional oppression.

Following Cannon, womanist theologians consistently acknowledge the moral burdens laid on African American people by racism while urging a broader focus on the genuine moral agency of those oppressed by race, gender, and other divisive social forces. For example, M. Shawn Copeland affirms James Baldwin's insight that white supremacist societies teach Black people to despise themselves.[122] She recounts how under slavery, Black women's bodies were made sites of violence, where sexist and racist hatred was forcibly visited on them. To heal and grow toward self-love, Black women had to learn to love their own bodies—the "enfleshing freedom" of her book's title.[123] Cheryl Townsend Gilkes reinforces the importance of loving one's own despised body with her meditation on body size and its intersection with racist and sexist erasures of Black women's bodies. In her own fond recounting of her experience as a larger-bodied African American woman, she models love of one's own body despite oppression and offers hope for developing self-love despite damaging moral luck.[124] Copeland and Gilkes realistically face—they do not discount—the material reality of physical and psychic violence against Black women's bodies. But their Christian stance allows them to claim that this violence does not strike the final blow that ineluctably shatters victims' selves and strips them entirely of their moral agency.

Emilie Townes notes that the history of slavery and lynching and the present-day realities of economic and environmental racism can threaten to shatter selves and to cleave selves from their communities. For Townes, the pervasiveness of these oppressive structures means that African Americans "have learned to hate ourselves without even realizing the level of our self-contempt."[125] There is an urgent need for self-love among African Americans, which necessitates what Townes calls "an ontology of wholeness." Rejecting such dualisms as self/other, body/mind, and victim/success, an "ontology of wholeness" prioritizes the relationship between self and other. Townes's ontology of wholeness takes the integrity of selves as its goal, recognizing that this will come in unity with one's community; no one can fully flourish while many in her community remain in pain.[126] Townes's work parallels Tessman's ordinary vices of domination, which show how privileged life circumstances both undermine an ontology of wholeness and demonstrate its necessity for human flourishing. The agent who does not realize her own complicity with structures of oppression has a fragmented self precisely because she fails to be in community with those her silence oppresses.

Although Townes offers an insight that Tessman would share, that "resistance is not synonymous with self-actualization," her Christian stance provides an important corrective to the views of Card and Tessman.[127] Acknowledging the moral luck of social positioning or the way resisting oppression burdens virtue are important tasks for examining who we are and who we can become. Yet it is not sufficient, particularly from a Christian perspective, to understand oneself solely as oppressed and broken—or solely as an oppressor, rent by inevitable complicity. Townes's Christian womanist view invites agents to see themselves accurately, asking "What would it look like if we actually believed that we are washed in God's grace?"[128] God's grace offers the real possibility of wholeness, even for selves vulnerable to the moral luck of racism, sexism, and physical and environmental violence.

Hope for wholeness in a world that shatters us is also found in Melanie Harris's womanist virtue ethics, drawn from the nonfiction writings of Alice Walker. Harris shows how Walker's work "names the injustice of racism and proposes a value of wholeness to counteract the fragmenting effects of racism."[129] Walker calls attention to the sin of dehumanization and the imperative of self-love to combat it.[130] Harris gleans seven virtues for a womanist virtue ethic from Walker's work: generosity, graciousness, compassion, spiritual wisdom, audacious courage, justice, and good community.[131]

Harris's description of the virtue of good community highlights another difference between womanist theologians and feminist philosophers like Tessman, who voices strong reservations about the burdened virtue of group loyalty for justice activists. For Harris, in contrast, a virtuous community does not hold members accountable to the community at the cost of the broader world. Rather, the local community holds members accountable for their own individual good, the good of the community and the good of the world at large. Harris writes:

> Being accountable means taking responsibility for one's failings, as well as one's contributions to mutual relationality, and finding ways to achieve a greater sense of balance between one's individual wants, needs, and desires and the wants, needs, and desires of others living into relationship with the Earth. . . . For communities, being accountable means holding one another and ourselves responsible to the interdependent web of life that holds us and connects us all together.

The African proverb "I am because We Are" connotes the idea of good community and accountability in that it underscores the interconnectedness that we all share with each other.[132]

Like many of her womanist colleagues, and unlike Tessman, Harris focuses on the potential for moral improvement in community, rather than on its potential moral dangers. She shares Walker's conviction that women can withstand the moral luck of oppression by racism and sexism to pursue virtue in community. As Jamie Phelps notes while evaluating the Black experience in the US Catholic Church, communities, including communities of faith, can embody social sin and can indeed be sites of fragmentation and moral luck. Yet faith communities at their best enable mature discipleship, the pursuit of holiness and virtue.[133] A Christian virtue ethic must follow Harris and Walker in viewing communities—preeminently the Christian community itself—as fertile grounds where virtue can grow.

An essay by Rosita deAnn Mathews invites an extended comparison with Tessman's views, one that highlights the ways womanist thought helps a Christian virtue account of moral luck be distinctly Christian. Mathews finds hope in the possibility of resisting evil by "using power from the periphery," neither completely standing outside of a system nor adopting its preexisting methods and values. Using power from the periphery means "using one's power to resist a threat by maintaining or establishing ethical principles and moral standards, and refusing to employ the aggressor's methods, . . . avoiding the use of practices utilized by those in power."[134] This practice, which Mathews recommends especially to African American women who must operate within hierarchical, patriarchal, and racist systems, holds out the hope of allowing agents to "maintain our soul," to retain their own ethical standards while working against oppression.[135]

Mathews acknowledges many of the same obstacles to exercising power from the periphery that Tessman lists in her description of the burdened virtues for social justice activists, but responds with a distinct emphasis on Christian hope and moral agency. For Mathews, those who exercise power from the periphery must maintain personal integrity and Christian commitment, resist any desire for power and status, remain accountable to and strengthened by the community, and endure through heavy opposition.[136] For Tessman, oppression's fragmenting effect threatens personal integrity; resisting "the ordinary vices of domination" is not fully under our control; community loyalty can erode the agent's capacity to criticize injustice within the community; and endurance can require developing anger to a degree that damages the self.[137]

The difference between Mathews and Tessman—and between woman-ist theologians' and feminist philosophers' understanding of moral luck—cannot be reduced to optimism and pessimism. Clearly, Mathews's Christian stance contributes to the hopeful nature of her diagnosis and solutions. More significant, however, are these scholars' different primary audiences. Mathews addresses African American women, who, she states clearly, know all too well the burdens of struggling for justice within systems that are designed not to hear them. Her primary audience does not need to be reminded of the personal moral burdens of working for justice; instead, Mathews offers clear prescriptions for how to do this and a word of hope that moral self-preservation is possible.

Tessman, by contrast, addresses two groups of people who might be surprised at the very idea of the burdened virtues of resistance. With her "ordinary vices of domination," she cautions those who wield power in oppressive systems that their willed ignorance of inequity may harm them morally. And with her warning of the burdened virtues, she reaches out to activists whose focus on social change might have led them to ignore the impact of activism on their own moral integrity. Although Mathews's perspective is valuable to those who struggle to maintain their own moral integrity despite occupying oppressed social locations, Tessman's message deserves to be heard by those in positions of power in unjust systems, including white people in racist societies and those with economic privilege.

Tessman might ask Christian virtue ethicists whether it is really appropriate to offer a word of hope to oppressors, as she describes those who benefit from unjust privilege. Perhaps her strong pessimism regarding moral agency is rhetorically required to break through the casual ignorance of the "ordinary vices of domination." But a Christian perspective does not allow ethicists to place any group of persons beyond the reach of God's grace. "It is easier for a camel to go through the eye of a needle than for a rich man to enter the kingdom of God, . . . but with God all things are possible" (Matthew 19:23–26). This teaching of Jesus trenchantly and humorously acknowledges the reality of moral luck and the simultaneous divine insistence that moral luck never has the last word.

Acknowledging moral luck means addressing the truth that life circumstances shape the way we move through, experience, and are formed by our communities. For the philosopher Margaret Urban Walker, agents shaped by moral luck need "a reliable capacity to see things clearly, to take the proper moral measure of situations."[138] This is constituted in part by the virtue of "*lucidity*, a reasonable grasp of the nature and seriousness of one's morally unlucky plight."[139] When womanist theologians take the moral measure of situations, they often invoke lament, which M. Shawn Copeland says allows theologians to "name and grieve" injustice, oppression, and abuse and their effects on persons.[140] While lucidly examining and lamenting the damaging effects of moral luck, womanist theologians express confidence in moral agents' ability to pursue and maintain virtue, even in situations of severe oppression.[141]

Although the burdens of our moral luck may fragment us, womanist theology insists that such fragmentation need not be the last word. Womanist theology adds a rich interplay between personal integrity and reliance on community to the searing lament of the personal fragmentation that can indeed result from moral luck. Mathews insists that Christians struggling under moral burdens can maintain integrity. Townes's "ontology of wholeness" insists that self and community pursue integrity together; I cannot be complete if my community is shattered. Womanist theologians move from lament of moral luck to proposing action in response, including practicing self-love; working for justice with others; naming oppressive structures; drawing on Christian theology; and remaining accountable to the Christian community.[142] Both feminist philosophers' strong caution about the moral luck of privilege, and womanist theologians' insistence on the moral agency of oppressed persons, belong in a Christian account of moral luck. A Christian virtue account of moral luck needs to address both those whom unequal structures privilege and those whom they oppress.

HOW LIFE CIRCUMSTANCES FUNCTION AS MORAL LUCK

Moral luck is a useful tool for describing the impact of life circumstances on the pursuit of virtue. It should be clear by now that there are several ways life circumstances function as moral luck. First, life circumstances affect practices. Few if any virtues are acquired through only one possible type of practice, but a life circumstance that makes particular practices impossible or extremely difficult will naturally impede the pursuit of the virtue(s) associated with these practices.[143] For example, I argue here that poverty impedes the pursuit of self-care, because acts of self-care often demand resources of money and time.

Another way life circumstances function as moral luck is by affecting self-regard, integrating societal biases and expectations into our own sense of self. All human societies maintain beliefs about certain groups or types of people and assign particular roles to groups or types of people. For individuals belonging to one or another of these groups, this aspect of their life circumstance becomes a site of moral luck where expectations are formed about one's self, potential, and worth relative to others. Claudia Card explained this particularly well in her work on gender as moral luck.[144] For example, I argue that when societies value wealthy people's personhoods over those of poor people, they present obstacles for wealthy people in pursuing the virtue of justice, which depends on understanding all persons as equally precious and worthy.

Finally, life circumstances function as moral luck and affect the pursuit of virtue through communities, given that the nature of our communities is at least partly a matter of luck. When we occupy different communities by circumstance or by choice, we may find ourselves surrounded by people dedicated to the pursuit of virtue and ready to encourage others in doing it; people whose focus is elsewhere for whatever reason; or people who openly disdain virtue and practice vice. Thus life circumstances affecting communities are evident forms of moral luck. I illustrate this later in this book through a discussion of how poverty tends to encourage solidarity among the poor, because of their mutual need for survival.

This chapter has proposed a Christian virtue account of moral luck and mechanisms through which life circumstances function as moral luck. Plenty of work remains to fully enflesh the role of moral luck in Christian virtue ethics. Sustained attention to race, gender, and other life circumstances as moral luck in Christian virtue ethics could help push back against criticisms of virtue ethics as an individualistic system that imposes the values of the dominant culture.[145] Another question for future research to explore is the relationship of moral luck to heroism. Do circumstances that can impede the pursuit of virtue encourage the development of moral heroes?[146] Continued work in this line of inquiry will help us understand virtue ethics more fully. Those who do the future work will no doubt discover different ways that life circumstances can function as moral luck. I offer these three common features—practices, self-understanding, and community—as a first step on the path.

CONCLUSION: MORAL LUCK
IN CHRISTIAN VIRTUE ETHICS

Charles Curran notes that a "Christian stance" in ethics views reality "in terms of the Christian mysteries of creation, sin, incarnation, redemption, and resurrection destiny."[147] A Christian account of moral luck clarifies connections between virtue thought and all these Christian mysteries. By taking into account the concrete circumstances in which the moral agent finds herself, moral luck evokes the reality of humanity as God's creation, God who became incarnate in a particular human life. Moral luck draws our attention to the reality that we frequently fail in virtue. It alerts us to those temptations to sin that may be particularly relevant to our own life circumstances. As Aquinas knew, awareness of the ways we are likely to fail in virtue because of our own particular life circumstances simply reminds us of our dependence on God for redemption. As womanist theologians explain, naming and lamenting our sins helps us pursue an ontology of wholeness, confident that what God desires is new life for each person and for her community. A Christian virtue ethics attentive to moral luck effectively describes the complex reality of a world where persons living in particular and different circumstances are affected by the pervasive reality of sin and must rely on God for redemption, even as they themselves take action in the pursuit of virtue.

Now we can begin to trace the outline of an argument about inequality's effects on the pursuit of virtue. Inequality is a life circumstance that does not affect everyone the same way; it matters very much, in contexts of vast inequality, whether we are rich or poor. To understand how inequality functions as moral luck to harm virtue, we first need accounts of what it means to pursue virtue when we are wealthy or poor. The coming chapters propose clear descriptions of the life experiences that characterize wealth and poverty, and they continue on to describe virtue pursuit in these different circumstances of human life. Once we have understood the distinct obstacles that wealth and poverty can place in the way of virtue pursuit, we conclude by examining how extreme inequality heightens these challenges for both the rich and the poor in unequal societies.

NOTES

1. Portions of this chapter appeared in "Toward a Christian Virtue Account," by Ward.
2. In this work, I use "life circumstances" and "context" interchangeably when attempting to describe those aspects of ordinary experience that may affect our virtue development. Some examples of such morally significant life circumstances are gender, ethnic or racial identity, sexual identity, and wealth and poverty. These facets of life experience affect moral development insofar as they influence how one is valued and treated by others in society. Thomas Aquinas notes that circumstances such as "place and condition of persons" can impact the moral significance of an act even if they do not impact the act directly; *Summa Theologica* (hereafter *ST*), I-II, 7.1. This is the type of circumstance I mean; they are morally significant, not insignificant or merely accidental. For me, "circumstances" captures what I am discussing better than "context." A man and a woman in the United States may occupy more or less the same *context*, but because US culture has

been shaped by pervasive cultural sexism, the *circumstances* affecting their lives will not be the same, and this may affect how they develop virtue.

3. Keenan and Kotva, *Practice*; Pellegrino and Thomasma, *Christian Virtues*.

4. Roche, "Children."

5. Fullam, "From Discord to Virtues"; Keenan, "Virtue Ethics"; Murphy, "Revisiting Contraception."

6. Rubio, *Family Ethics*; Rubio, "Passing on the Faith."

7. Hauerwas and Pinches, "Practicing Patience."

8. Vogt, *Patience*.

9. For Aquinas, the infused virtues are subject to God's gift, and the virtue of charity can be lost through one mortal sin, though an acquired virtue is not lost so easily (*ST*, I-II, 62.12). It is interesting to think about grace as a type of moral luck, but in this book I am primarily discussing what Aquinas would call the acquired virtues, which are responsive to human effort.

10. Other factors not under a person's control, such as temperament and neurochemistry, may certainly play a role in how we pursue the virtues, although I do not explore those factors here.

11. Daly defines "structure" this way: "A structure is an institution, a practice, a value laden narrative, or a paradigmatic figure that people find already existing or which they create on the national and global level, and which orientates or organizes economic, social, and political life." Daly, "Structures," 354.

12. Daly.

13. Litz et al., "Moral Injury."

14. Brock and Lettini, *Soul Repair*; Kinghorn, "Combat Trauma"; Powers, "Moral Injury"; Wiinikka-Lydon, "Moral Injury." These papers were presented at the Moral Injury and Recovery section at the American Academy of Religion 2014 annual meeting: Rashid, "Where Am I From?"; Bounds, "Way Down in the Hole"; and Vazquez-Torres, "Does Moral Injury Have A Race?" At the annual meeting in 2015, I presented the paper "Moral Injury and Virtue Ethics: Understanding the Moral Impact of Poverty."

15. Litz et al., "Moral Injury."

16. Wilson, "Moral Grief," 57.

17. Wilson.

18. Wilson, 61.

19. American Academy of Religion, "Call."

20. A few decades' worth of philosophical perspectives on moral luck are collected by Statman, *Moral Luck*.

21. I have not intentionally selected scholars with explicitly feminist commitments or excluded others; it is simply the case that feminist philosophers are breaking ground and establishing the field on moral luck.

22. Card, *Unnatural Lottery*, ix.

23. Latus, "Moral Luck."

24. Williams, "Moral Luck."

25. Nagel, "Moral Luck."

26. For a variety of perspectives, see Statman, *Moral Luck*.

27. Nussbaum, *Fragility*, 6–7.

28. Nussbaum.

29. Nussbaum, 327.

30. Nussbaum, 330–33.
31. Nussbaum, 337–38. Nussbaum does not endorse Aristotle's representation of the virtues of youth and age, but she believes we can learn from his conviction that life circumstances affect virtue development and expression. The philosopher Sara Ruddick comments on virtues for aging and ageism; Ruddick, "Virtues."
32. Nussbaum, *Fragility*, 228–29.
33. Nussbaum, 340.
34. Walker, "Moral Luck," 24.
35. Walker, 25.
36. Coates, "Case for Reparations"; Kendi, *Stamped*; Massingale, *Racial Justice*.
37. Pickett and Wilkinson, *Spirit Level*.
38. Walker, "Moral Luck," 27.
39. Walker.
40. Walker, 28.
41. Walker, 26–27.
42. Walker, 32.
43. Card, *Unnatural Lottery*, ix.
44. Card.
45. Card, 4.
46. Card, 31.
47. Card, 40.
48. Card, 40–41.
49. Card, 40.
50. Card, 42.
51. Card, 48.
52. Card, 92–93.
53. Card, 93.
54. Card, "Gender," 79.
55. Card, *Unnatural Lottery*, 52.
56. Card, 61.
57. Quoted by Copeland, "'Wading,'" 154.
58. Card, "Gender." Card focuses on the socially constructed aspects of gendered behavior, but it is possible that certain vicious aspects of behavior such as aggression also have neurobiological components. This distinction is not significant in discussing moral luck; either socially constructed or purely physical impacts of gender on behavior can function as moral luck.
59. Card, *Unnatural Lottery*, 53.
60. Card, 53–54. I believe Card is using "our" to refer to the oppressed from her standpoint as one oppressed by gender.
61. Card, 87.
62. Card, 175.
63. Card, 176.
64. Card, 181–82.
65. Card, 182.
66. Tessman, *Burdened Virtues*, 14–15.
67. Tessman, 17.
68. Tessman, 19.

69. Tessman, 108.
70. Tessman, 112.
71. Tessman, 125–27.
72. Tessman, 115–16 and chap. 6.
73. Tessman, chap. 6.
74. Tessman, 157.
75. Tessman.
76. Tessman, 54.
77. Tessman, 57–59.
78. Tessman, 54.
79. Tessman, 55.
80. Tessman, 57–58.
81. See, e.g., Kotva, *Christian Case*, 49. Kotva, a proponent of virtue ethics, here refutes Gilbert Meilander's criticism along the lines mentioned above.
82. Tessman, *Burdened Virtues*, conclusion.
83. Tessman, 57.
84. Tessman does envision the potential loss of moral agency as among the horrors faced by Holocaust victims; Tessman, *Moral Failure*.
85. However, see Kotva, *Christian Case*, 29–30.
86. Harrington, "Old Testament Approaches."
87. Lohfink, *Jesus*, 87–99.
88. Lohfink, *Jesus*.
89. Chan, "Hebrew Bible."
90. Carroll, *Christians*; Heyer, *Kinship*, 142–43.
91. Aquinas, *ST*, I-II, 73.8.
92. Bowlin, *Contingency*, 62–63.
93. Aquinas, *ST*, I-II, 73.8.
94. Aquinas, I-II, 73.10.
95. Aquinas.
96. Aquinas, reply to objection 3.
97. Bowlin, *Contingency*, 178–80.
98. Bowlin, 183–4. I agree with Bowlin that Aquinas acknowledges the impact of fortune on the moral life, but ultimately we are discussing different questions. Bowlin takes Aquinas to be asking whether "the virtues can succeed against fortune" (p. 215) and to conclude that, with God's help, they can. Though I think Bowlin answers his question convincingly, his framing of it strikes me as susceptible to Tessman's critique that too many accounts of virtue assume the average agent to be virtuous. The question of how fortune may impede with our development of virtue appears to me far more urgent.
99. Aquinas, *ST*, 73.3, Respondeo.
100. O'Connell, "Viability"; McCluskey, *Thomas Aquinas*, 175–78.
101. Aquinas, *ST*, 73.3, Respondeo.
102. Aquinas.
103. Kay, "Getting Egypt Out," 29–33.
104. Aquinas, *Disputed Questions*, trans. McInerny, 5.3.
105. Aquinas, *Disputed Questions*, ed. Atkins and Williams, 266–67, "On the Cardinal Virtues," article 3, response.
106. Aquinas, *Disputed Questions*, 5.3; Aquinas, *ST*, I-II, 109.2.

107. Bowlin, *Contingency*, 216.
108. Aquinas, *ST*, I-II, 109.10.
109. Aquinas, I-II, 109.6.
110. Aquinas, *Disputed Questions*, trans. McInerny. 5.3, response.
111. Decosimo, *Ethics*.
112. Decosimo, 182.
113. Decosimo, 140.
114. This paragraph borrows from Ward, "Ethics," 219–21.
115. Aquinas, *ST*, I-II, 62. Likewise, original sin could be regarded as a type of moral luck, but because it affects all humans after the Fall, it is not particularly useful to individual persons contemplating their own pursuit of virtue. See Aquinas, *ST*, I-II, 81–83.
116. Aquinas, I-II, 62.1, Respondeo. There is robust debate about how Aquinas's infused virtues should be understood by Christians today. Hauerwas and Pinches, emphasizing human dependence on God for moral growth, believe that all virtue is correctly understood as infused, while Florence Caffrey Bourg notes that the role of families in forming faith argues for an expanded vision of the theological virtues as acquired to some degree. Hauerwas and Pinches, *Christians*; Bourg, *Where Two or Three Are Gathered*, 130–31.
117. Williams, "Womanist Perspective."
118. Cannon, *Black Womanist Ethics*, 3.
119. Cannon, 7.
120. Cannon, chaps. 3–5.
121. Cannon, 160–61, describing the thought of the theologian Howard Thurman.
122. Copeland, *Enfleshing Freedom*, 17.
123. Copeland, 50–51.
124. Gilkes, "The 'Loves.'"
125. Townes, "To Be Called Beloved," 198.
126. Townes, 201–2.
127. Townes, 201.
128. Townes, 183.
129. Harris, *Gifts*, 61–67.
130. Harris, 71–72.
131. Harris, chap. 5.
132. Harris, 122.
133. Phelps, "Joy."
134. Mathews, "Using Power," 93.
135. Mathews, 102.
136. Mathews, 103–5.
137. Tessman, *Burdened Virtues*, 18, 55, 115, 133–57.
138. Walker, "Moral Luck," 26–27.
139. Walker, 28.
140. Copeland, "Presidential Address," 81.
141. Given their emphasis on the potential negative impact of privilege on virtue, it is no coincidence that Card and Tessman both identify as white and explicitly address white supremacy as moral luck. Tessman also discusses her experience as a lesbian activist in communities of resistance to heterosexist society.
142. As I mentioned above, it is worth remembering that Christian communities are, themselves, fragmented. Though they can be sites of resistance and repair following moral

luck, they are also sites of encountering moral luck, places where some types of Christians are more valued than others and where the resulting structures of inequality shape the pursuit of virtue for Christians in Christian community. E.g., racism, sexism, and the demonization and/or erasure of LGBTQ Catholics are all ugly realities in the US Catholic Church today, as well as features of its past; see, e.g., Grimes, *Christ Divided*. Though the Church is a space where virtuous pursuit in community is possible, it is also a fragmented space; and it is also a place for moral luck.

143. One counterexample might be Aristotle's virtue of magnificence, which is acquired and demonstrated through making large gifts. A good case could be made that this virtue as Aristotle understands it is not possible for the poor.

144. Card, "Gender," 79.

145. See, e.g., De La Torre, *Latina/o Social Ethics*, 28–30.

146. See Flescher, *Heroes*.

147. Curran, *Directions*, 35.

CHAPTER 4

DEFINING WEALTH AND POVERTY FOR CHRISTIAN VIRTUE ETHICS

The preceding chapters described the urgent issue of extreme economic inequality and promoted Christian virtue ethics as a tool for responding to it. I first highlighted the impact of economic inequality on persons and societies, establishing inequality as a problem distinct from poverty. The next chapters described a constellation of virtues characteristic of the flourishing human person, indicating their particular relevance to economic life, and established a Christian virtue account of moral luck, arguing that life circumstances shape the ways persons are able to pursue and develop virtue. The remainder of this book demonstrates the ways wealth, poverty, and economic inequality function as moral luck to affect the pursuit of virtue. Before doing that, however, I need to explain how I define wealth and poverty, and why.

Throughout this book, I define wealth as "having more than we need," and poverty as lacking the goods necessary for a life worthy of human dignity, or being able to secure those goods only through constant and precarious struggle. In this chapter, I explore quantitative, positional, and lifestyle or basic goods definitions of wealth and poverty, and explain why I ultimately prefer the last one.

DEFINING POVERTY

In the public sphere, policymakers and advocates often choose straightforward, quantitative definitions of poverty. These precise definitions vary broadly, depending on the framers. For example, in 2020, the US federal government defined poverty as an income of $12,760 for a single person or $26,200 for a family of four.[1] Challenges to this definition are common. The conservative Heritage Foundation insists that this income level often does not indicate real deprivation or struggle, arguing that the majority of US families living in poverty can regularly meet their basic needs and even enjoy many material comforts.[2] Conversely, advocates for the poor regularly assert that people in the United States can still struggle to meet basic needs with incomes much higher than the federal poverty level.[3] Reflecting that view, some US assistance programs are available to people with incomes at multiples of the federal poverty level, which seems to acknowledge that the benchmark is indeed inadequate.[4] In the realm of global poverty, the United Nations proposed a different quantitative definition with a Millennium Development Goal that sought to halve the number of people worldwide living on less than $1 per day.[5]

Quantitative standards make it easy to assess the number of people living in poverty, however it is defined, and to measure its rise and fall. But they are less successful at capturing differences in the experiences of those who are poor and those who are not. For example, within a nation like the United States, the same cash income may produce quite different experiences in rural areas, with a lower cost of living but fewer social services, than in urban ones where the reverse might be true.[6] A particular income might translate into differing amounts of basic goods over time as prices shift. Furthermore, the deprivations of poverty do not vanish as soon as income edges over a particular line; they are best understood as lying along a gradient.[7]

The theologian James Bailey has noted that income-based definitions of poverty define consumption as the highest good. Such definitions presume that one escapes poverty by achieving a certain level of consumption.[8] Bailey warns that focusing only on income and consumption misses the important role of accumulated assets in gaining financial stability and escaping poverty in the long term.[9] He urges a focus on asset building for the poor out of concern with capabilities and human flourishing.

Bailey's work aptly points out limitations of income-based definitions of poverty and points to an innovative practical agenda. An asset-based understanding of poverty is worth exploring for many reasons, including the fact that wealth inequality significantly exceeds income inequality in many wealthy nations.[10] One simple reason for this, though far from the only reason, is that households can have negative wealth when debts exceed assets. In the United States, wealth inequality is racialized to an even greater degree than income disparity. Black and Latino families are far more likely than white families to have no or negative net worth, that is, nothing or less than nothing to fall back on in times of hardship.[11] Although the distinction between assets and income is important to understand, asset-based definitions of poverty are still quantitative definitions and share their limitations.

When discussing wealth and poverty in ordinary life, perhaps we most instinctively reach for positional definitions. We may not know each of our neighbors' income in dollars, but we can identify the wealthy families (their homes are larger than our own) and name the areas of town where poor people live. The Heritage Foundation relies on a positional understanding of poverty to criticize quantitative definitions of poverty that include people with cable TV and cell phones, noting that many people in the United States disagree that persons with such possessions should be considered poor.[12] Positional definitions of wealth and poverty are easy to reach for, because they rely on our human tendency as social animals to compare our own situation with those of others.

This inveterate tendency to compare ourselves with others means that positionality matters a great deal in economic life. David Cloutier calls theologians' attention to the economic category of positional goods, goods that gain at least a portion of their value from their scarcity.[13] "Expenditure cascades," which result from the desire to maintain relative position in a community, can result in a great deal of spending with no discernible increase in quality of life for those at any income level, because if everyone is consuming more, no one increases in status relative to others.[14] For Cloutier, understanding positional goods helps explain how economic growth does not necessarily translate into increased well-being.

As Cloutier points out, despite widespread belief to the contrary, economists increasingly acknowledge that economic growth or national wealth do not simply translate into happiness. The Easterlin Paradox names the complex reality that though individuals may experience increased happiness with income growth, national happiness does not increase along with national income.[15] Moreover, even for individuals, an increase in income does not invariably translate into greater happiness. Moving from struggle to sufficiency does increase happiness, but moving from sufficiency to abundance typically does not. Increased income does boost happiness up to a point, but the effect levels off at incomes of about $75,000 in the US context.[16] And here again, position relative to others plays a role. Given the same income, we are likelier to be happy if we make more than our neighbors than if we make less: "An increase in neighbors' earnings and a similarly sized decrease in own income each have roughly about the same negative effect on well-being."[17]

It is worth noting that social scientists who investigate wealth and poverty observe some similar effects, whether the state being measured is absolute or positional. For example, the effects of scarcity on cognitional processing are similar among subsistence farmers in India—who are clearly poor by global standards—and poor people in the United States, who struggle to survive in their own contexts despite incomes that are significantly higher than those of Indian farmers.[18] People with lower class status interpret others' emotions better than those with higher class status, according to psychologists, whether their class status is objective or is induced by experimenter suggestion.[19] Both positional and material experiences of wealth and poverty influence our mental and moral lives.

Positional understandings of wealth and poverty play an important social-scientific role in understanding particular individuals' experience. The discovery that income growth has a limited ability to increase happiness supports religious and philosophical understandings that a meaningful life does not require great wealth. Equally significant is the finding that until a sufficiency income is achieved, more money does lead to more happiness. Wealth and poverty do influence lives in material ways that have absolute, not merely positional, aspects. This urges a focus on basic goods understandings of poverty, to which we now turn.

Although they might use statistics that reflect quantitative definitions of poverty, when theologians define poverty themselves, they often do so qualitatively, describing poor people's experiences rather than identifying an income threshold.[20] Theologians most typically discuss poverty in relation to the goal of full human flourishing. So the Peruvian liberation theologian Gustavo Gutiérrez defines it as "the lack of economic goods necessary for a human life worthy of the name."[21] At the Medellín conference, the bishops of Latin America and the Caribbean described poverty as "a lack of the goods of this world necessary to live worthily as men."[22] If someone lacks these goods, of course she does not become less than human. When theologians discuss living conditions as unworthy of human dignity, they refer to the long understanding in Christian thought that human rights issue from that inherent human dignity.[23] The human good is not only spiritual, but is also realized through our bodies and in our relationships with others. "A genuinely human life" includes intangible goods, such as the respect of others and the ability to develop our own gifts through work and education; the material goods necessary to care for our bodies; and the ability to pursue relational goods like marriage and family.[24] Struggling for survival does not blemish or remove the dignity that is inherent to every human being, and people living in poverty may feel that they express their own dignity precisely when they continue their struggle against difficult odds.

Basic goods definitions can have clear, specific content without relying on a shared concept of human flourishing. The Ghanaian feminist theologian Mercy Amba Oduyoye provides an example: "The inability to feed, house, and clothe oneself from one's own resources is the stark face of poverty. Individuals, organizations, and governments that cannot meet these basic needs independently of donations, grants, and loans are poor."[25] And not only theologians advert to basic goods definitions. For example, the United Nations discusses "multidimensional poverty" as lacking access to certain basic goods of human life, such as education, adequate nourishment, and clean drinking water.[26]

Expanding upon qualitative definitions of material need, some theologians extend the biblical term "poor" to all persons who are excluded, marginalized, or deprived. For example, the Indian liberation theologian Aloysius Pieris uses "poor" as "shorthand for a variety of 'non-persons' such as those who are deprived of the freedom of access to the basic human needs owing to a sinful arrangement of the affairs of this world," in addition to people with mental and physical handicaps and "the spiritually fallen" who are excluded by those who regard themselves as righteous.[27] As another example, this broader definition of "poor" might apply to LGBTQ persons, however materially well off, who are ostracized from their local churches.[28] There are sound theological reasons for using this broad understanding of the biblical and theological term "poor." I believe it is true that God cares preferentially for all those who are excluded in the ways that Pieris describes.

However, this book hews to a more narrowly material definition of poverty. Both material circumstances of wealth or poverty and the dynamics of exclusion or inclusion are vitally important in Scripture and throughout the Christian theological tradition. Each dynamic of human life deserves to be examined seriously and not collapsed into another. In this book, poverty is not simply exclusion but also struggle for survival, and "the poor" are those who lack adequate material resources to live in their own society in a way that accords with their innate human dignity.

An income guideline is a minimalist definition for poverty, employed as a rough proxy for the metric that really matters to policymakers and other concerned parties—human flourishing and the basic goods that enable it. Qualitative metrics for poverty, with remarkable consistency across disciplines, reference these basic goods directly.

Like positional understandings of wealth and poverty, basic goods definitions take a portion of their meaning from context. For example, all humans need water and rest to lead a human life worthy of the name. Whether they need warm coats to achieve this, however, depends on the yearly weather patterns where they live. At the same time, basic goods definitions have real content; they are not purely subjective. Defining poverty as having less than one needs does not allow us to call people poor who have only one yacht while their neighbor has two, no matter how much they may feel this privation harms their quality of life.

I have defined poverty as lacking access to what one needs to survive or accessing those goods only through constant and precarious struggle. Inspired by Oduyoye's understanding of poverty as relying on outside help to meet basic needs, this facet of my definition also recognizes that inconsistent access to basic goods is not the same as secure and reliable access. Organizations addressing poverty increasingly talk of "food insecurity" or "housing insecurity" to recognize the reality that whether people are fed or housed at a particular moment in time is not the full story of their access to these goods.[29] If someone has housing, but must forgo medical care to afford it, or has food for her children, but must visit food pantries multiple times a month to secure it, she can fairly be said to achieve these basic goods through precarious struggle and to qualify, in my definition, as poor.

Liberation theologians often use the biblical language of "the poor," which I am loath to abandon for its religious resonance.[30] But some nongovernmental organizations and groups that work on behalf of those living in poverty prefer people-first language: "people in poverty." This language foregrounds the persons being discussed as well as subtly reminding us that one may be poor or not at particular times in her life; poverty is not necessarily a permanent characteristic of persons.

Both these linguistic approaches sidestep the question of whether a person sees herself as poor. Like the quantitative benchmarks used by nongovernmental organizations, the definition of poverty as struggle applies whether or not a person self-identifies as poor. We can explore the moral effects of the material privation that poverty describes while reserving the agency of self-definition to persons struggling to survive. Amy Barbour and Martin Wickware draw our attention to "the inability of identity categories (e.g., Black, woman, or transgender) to map precisely onto how people understand their own identities." Yet, they insist, "marginalization according to these socially constructed categories continues to condition how people are received in the world, regardless of how they themselves articulate the complexities of their identities. Because people are targeted for discrimination, exploitation, torture, and murder based on these categories, the question of the nonperson continues to arise."[31] Poverty has material consequences that affect persons' experience in the world, even though persons can never be fully defined by one simple category such as "poor" and may not claim such a label on their own behalf.

Moreover, Christian voluntary poverty—as practiced, for example, by people in vowed religious life— is not the same as struggling to achieve basic goods. As a choice made from a standpoint of control (usually by persons who are, in this book's terminology, wealthy), voluntary poverty does not invite the same struggle for survival as unchosen material poverty, and does not make the same impact on virtue.[32] As the legal scholar Robert Rodes succinctly says, "Voluntary poverty is not the condition of the poor. The poor are people who have things happen to them that they do not want to have happen."[33] Poverty's unchosen, agency-constraining reality is widely understood as integral to its moral effects, whether those are viewed as beneficial or harmful. Dorothy Day, who practiced voluntary poverty as the cofounder of the Catholic Worker movement, observed this and emphasized the relationship between precarious, unchosen poverty and true faith in God.[34] Voluntary poverty represents a free choice of (most often) materially comfortable persons to mitigate the impact of their wealth on their virtue. Although this choice is rightly prized in the Christian tradition, it is not the same as unchosen poverty.

Defining poverty by the material standard of basic goods does not deny that its impact on persons goes far beyond the material. To be poor means to be at the disposal of others and to be treated in society as disposable.[35] Poverty's material privation and its connection with a despised social status wreak harm on selves. Gutiérrez again captures it well: "Alienation and despoliation as well as the very struggle for liberation have ramifications on the personal and psychological planes which it would be dangerous to overlook."[36] A qualitative definition of poverty—lacking the goods necessary for a dignified human life, or attaining those goods only through constant and precarious struggle—keeps poverty's social context and personal impact at the forefront of our understanding.

DEFINING WEALTH

People who are poor are less likely to be present for academic or policy discussions of poverty than wealthy people are for discussions of wealth. Perhaps attempts to define wealth feel especially fraught as specialists confront the risk of self-implication. Thus it is no surprise that quantitative, positional, and lifestyle-based definitions of wealth among secular and theological writers vary, and describe a broad range of lifestyles.

As with poverty, quantitative definitions of wealth vary depending on the speaker. The nonprofit Resource Generation organizes "young people with wealth" to support social change through philanthropy and eventually divest. The group accepts applications from "high-income earners" beginning at incomes of $65,000 and from those with inherited wealth of any amount, beginning with $250,000 or less.[37] Another common quantitative definition would identify millionaires, those owning $1 million or more in wealth, as rich. But drawing on the work of the sociologist Paul Schervish, a writer for *National Review* recently tried to trouble that definition. Graeme Wood portrayed the iconic millionaire status as "not what it once was," insisting that those who control a million dollars in the form of a valuable home or a defined-benefit pension plan are "rich but not carefree; . . . certainly [not] top-hat-wearing Scrooges."[38] Wood's careworn millionaires might be among those Joerg Rieger calls "middle-class" when he urges Christians who are not part of the wealthiest 1 percent to organize with the poor against those plutocrats. Inspired by the Occupy Wall Street movement, Rieger urges middle-class Christians not to regard themselves as wealthy for the sake of political common cause with the truly needy.[39]

A common positional understanding of wealth holds that the wealthy are those who have more than me, whatever my own resources. These definitions are clearly in play in the broad resistance to self-defining as wealthy. In a finding oddly resonant with Rieger's dichotomy of the wealthy, powerful 1 percent and the 99 percent majority they oppress, only 1 percent of Americans are willing to describe themselves as "upper class."[40] The wealthiest 1 percent of Americans have family incomes of more than $443,000 a year; but globally speaking, one joins the richest 1 percent of all world citizens with an income of just $34,000.[41] Clearly, many people in the United States—and well-off persons elsewhere—compare themselves with their fellow citizens, not with the global human family, when asking themselves if they are wealthy.

Positional definitions might inform those who insist on distinctions among the sources of wealth or income. Some writers use "wealthy" to denote those who inherited money, in contrast to "rich" or "affluent" to identify those who have a lot of money now. Others use all these terms as more or less synonymous, as I do. To the limited extent that US culture expresses reservations about the moral impact of wealth, it does so for inherited wealth alone. "Being born with a silver spoon in the mouth," or being a "trust fund baby," are mildly derogatory terms aimed at a much smaller group than those I define as wealthy. In contrast, those whose wealth is the result of earned income are widely respected, even lionized, in the United States.[42] Perhaps this is why those who have inherited wealth often believe that they have achieved success through their own efforts, even when confronted with the paradox.[43]

The theologian Mary Elizabeth Hobgood finds moral and political significance in the source of one's wealth when she divides society into two classes: the working class and capitalists. For her, workers who enjoy substantial incomes and a certain degree of control over their working lives, who often call themselves "middle class" in the United States, have more than they realize in common with the poorer wage earners often referred to as "working class." Neither group can be called "capitalists" in the sense that they do not control the means of producing wealth.[44] However, Hobgood reminds the wealthier members of the working class that they also benefit from the exploitation of lower-wage workers and wield power over them by virtue of their relative economic privilege.[45]

From the standpoint of political organizing, Hobgood and Rieger may be right to define only a small group of "capitalists" or "1 percenters" as rich. As I show in chapter 1, economic inequality harms society by awarding disproportionate political, economic, and social power to its wealthiest members. Political organizing that seeks to unite all people who do not enjoy such outsize power is a wise response. However, Hobgood is equally correct to point out that high-income workers do indeed wield power over their lower-paid fellow workers. Although I concede Hobgood and Rieger's point that the political interests of all those who work for income, whether at minimum wage or at six-figure salaries, are properly understood as linked, the impact of these disparate circumstances on the pursuit of virtue seems to be quite distinct. Indeed, when it comes to the impact of material possessions on virtue pursuit, many members of "the 99 percent" could, with equal accuracy, count themselves among the wealthy. Turning to lifestyle understandings of wealth helps me demonstrate why.

As with quantitative definitions, lifestyle-based definitions of wealth can vary widely. For example, Jessie O'Neill, an inheritor of generational wealth and a therapist who works with wealthy individuals, describes "affluence" as maintaining a lifestyle that mainstream US culture regards as upper-class without needing to work.[46] Conversely, in the memoir-cum-social-satire *Primates of Park Avenue*, the sociologist Wednesday Martin observes wealth earned from extremely high-income work. Martin identifies wealth through such lifestyle signifiers as owning real estate in New York and having more than four children.[47]

Martin's examples clearly convey their meaning to a fairly limited audience, and all lifestyle-based definitions of wealth can diminish in usefulness when they are too context-dependent. (For example, some offhandedly use "the suburbs" as shorthand for a lifestyle of comfortable middle-class privilege, which obscures the present reality of growing poverty in US suburbs.[48]) My definition of wealth as "having more than we need" is a lifestyle definition that is broadly applicable enough to escape such limitations. It could also be considered a basic goods definition, because it uses basic goods as the benchmark to exceed. Let me explain why this definition is best for the purposes of Christian ethics.

When middle-class readers in wealthy societies hear scriptural warnings to "the rich," perhaps we imagine them directed at the richest 1 percent, nothing for us to worry about—and perhaps that is a mistake. Increasingly, theologians realize that any adequate framework for approaching the Christian tradition on wealth and poverty must address all of humanity. Sondra Ely Wheeler, in her classic text on the New Testament's ethics of wealth, uses words like "riches" and "possessions" fairly interchangeably. Discussing Luke's discourse on renunciation for the sake of the Kingdom of God, she says it "call[s] into question many of the assumptions of middle-class existence, including the fundamental assumption that there *is* such a thing as 'economic security' and that Christians are entitled to it."[49]

David Cloutier joins Wheeler in refusing to let the middle class in wealthy societies off the hook. Cloutier notes that focusing only on the extremely wealthy or the desperately poor tends to result in a "middle-class exemption," which conveniently absolves the majority of US Catholics from examining their own lives and choices.[50] Similarly, Miguel De La Torre warns that reading Scripture from a middle-class perspective can both ignore the perspective of poor Gospel characters and wrongly expect the wealthy—imagined as those richer than the reader—to solve the world's problems.[51] Ethical frameworks that consciously or unconsciously introduce a middle-class exemption into the Christian tradition on wealth and poverty ill serve the tradition, the poor, and most especially those who are left exempt, but who deserve to hear the message that the tradition holds for them, however challenging it may be.

Chapter 5 demonstrates that wealth—having more than we need—makes an impact on our moral life by endowing us with hyperagency and by becoming an end in itself. Wealth does this whether the power it gives us relative to others is moderate or nearly absolute. I suspect that many 1 percenters, those living on half a million dollars a year or more, give little thought to how their wealth affects their virtue, conscious though they may be of giving from that wealth to support the common good. Perhaps more controversially, I argue the same about most of the people who will read this book: relatively educated Westerners whose households live on income(s) from work, people who would agree that they have more than they need but who would likely never self-define as rich.[52] The next chapter demonstrates how such people wield hyperagency over and compared with the poor and how wealth affects virtue in their lives as well as those of the 1 percent.

Defining "wealth" as "having more than we need" inevitably raises the question of how to describe what we need. The sociologist Paul Schervish has found that even extraordinarily wealthy people, with fortunes in the tens of millions of dollars and above, often do not believe they have enough to feel secure.[53] Closer to the poorer end of the spectrum, some US families might gratefully proclaim that they have more than they need, even though they rent the place where they live, or even though two or more adults in the household must work full-time for pay to supply those needs.

Because this book is a work of virtue ethics, readers should assess their own needs for themselves. Useful guidelines might be drawn from the philosopher Martha Nussbaum's Capabilities Approach, a basic goods definition of human well-being and freedom.[54] Capabilities describe important aspects of human existence. If a person is able to exercise all her capabilities, even if she chooses not to, she has the potential to lead a flourishing human life. Guided by the Capabilities Approach, we might ask: Does our wealth allow us to live a human life of normal length and to preserve our health and bodily integrity? Are we able to exercise our senses, creativity, and reason? Can we develop and maintain relationships with other persons, other species, and with nature? Are we able to participate in politics and other aspects of public life, and to exercise control over our material environment and possessions? Is our material wealth enough—is it more than enough—to empower us to pursue every aspect of these capabilities, if we chose to do so?[55] Nussbaum's list of capabilities shares many items with the goods described as "necessary for leading a life truly human" by the Second Vatican Council.[56] Catholic theologians and Nussbaum, a secular philosopher, develop remarkably similar accounts of the goods undergirding the good life.

Obviously, many factors besides income affect access to the goods needed to flourish as human.[57] Still more obviously, the income needed to secure these basic aspects of human flourishing must, by any stretch of the imagination, be significantly less than the amounts Schervish's wealthy interviewees said they needed to "feel secure." In chapter 5, I suggest that any amount of discretionary income, money left to spend after basic needs are met, affords persons a degree of hyperagency. Depending on family size, many households reach this point on incomes of about $40,000 to $50,000 yearly. In other words, many, many people given the middle-class exemption by other ethical frameworks actually have enough wealth, and more than enough, to achieve their basic needs.

THE STRENGTHS OF THESE DEFINITIONS

The definitions of wealth as "having more than we need" and poverty as "having to struggle to survive" exhaust the range of potential circumstances. Under these definitions, a person or a family cannot be considered both wealthy and poor at the same time—we either have everything we need to live in a particular context, or we do not. However, it is equally clear that one may be wealthy or poor at different times throughout life. A loss or gain of a job, an illness of oneself or a family member, or even a joyous event like adding a child to the family can change the reality of whether one has all one needs.[58] It makes no sense for ethicists to operate with definitions that exclude significant sectors of the population from teachings as significant and recurrent throughout the Christian tradition as those on wealth and poverty. Doing so would allow a great majority of believers to opt out of hearing one profoundly significant message of the Gospel.

A broad definition of wealth, one that could include most citizens of a given zip code or even a particular nation, serves theology because it is morally hortatory. It helps believers recognize challenging messages addressed *to them* in Scripture and Christian tradition, and challenges them to pursue lives of holiness. This book's definitions of wealth and poverty participate in what Lisa Sowle Cahill calls a "neo-Franciscan" stream in contemporary Christian ethics, one concerned with personal holiness developed in community and lived out on a daily basis. Cahill contrasts this with the neo-Thomist stream of theological ethics, which aims at the reform of unjust structures.[59] Authors associated with the neo-Franciscan stream are concerned with encouraging all believers to pursue holiness, rather than preaching minimalist ethics to ordinary Christians. They tend to make greater demands of ordinary believers than might have been the case in the past. Ethicists such as David Cloutier, Julie Hanlon Rubio, Katie Grimes, and Eli Sasaran McCarthy insist that destructive social structures like consumerism, racism, and militaristic violence demand responses of both communal action and personal transformation.[60] They connect Christian belief to ordinary life and advocate practices that challenge many ordinary Christians to change their habits. Consistent with the concerns of the neo-Franciscan stream in ethics, defining wealth as "having more than we need" trusts believers to live up to the demands the Gospel places on relatively ordinary lives. It empowers ordinary believers to examine the impact of their wealth on their pursuit of virtue and of holiness.[61]

Although inequality is generally measured in quantitative terms, qualitative definitions of wealth and poverty provide crucial insight into inequality's impact on virtue. We saw in chapter 1 that inequality correlates with and even causes many of the social ills that have traditionally been blamed on poverty, including poor health, early death, and punitive policies such as hyperincarceration. Although many of these ills fall along a gradient—harming everyone in more unequal societies, not only the poor—the poor disproportionately suffer. Inequality heightens the challenges of poverty, including the obstacles that poverty can pose to the pursuit of virtue.

Although the very richest people in unequal societies enjoy high levels of security and privilege, inequality also harms those who have more than they need, including many with lavish lifestyles. We have already seen evidence of the "health gradient," which shows that wealthier people in more unequal societies fare worse on many determinants of health than their counterparts in more egalitarian contexts. This is a clue that in unequal societies, wealth versus poverty is not simply a question of disposable income, of having more toys or trendy home decor. Poor people in unequal societies lack access to goods crucial to the enjoyment of a fully human life, while wealthy people enjoy full and easy access to these same goods. The awareness that their wealth conveys not just property but also goods such as education, leisure, and power over others encourages wealthy people to engage in behaviors intended to secure their position, such as self-segregation and conspicuous consumption. These behaviors further increase inequality, harm the poor, and challenge wealthy people's pursuit of virtue. This will become clear from what follows.

Qualitative definitions of wealth and poverty suit projects in theology. Because they are broadly useful across cultures, regions, and years, this book's definitions of wealth and poverty invite reflection on one's own situation and convey real content that is not reducible to feelings of positional disadvantage. Understanding poverty as struggle to survive reveals similarities between the global poor and those barely making it in wealthy countries. Quantitative definitions can obscure these real connections. Wealth as having more than we need is a morally hortatory definition, calling attention to the ways in which wealth, while bestowing undeniable practical benefits, can also demand special effort in the pursuit of virtue throughout our lives. We now proceed to examine why this is so.

NOTES

1. US Department of Health and Human Services, "Poverty Guidelines."
2. Sheffield and Rector, "Air Conditioning."
3. US Conference of Catholic Bishops, "Economic Justice," 16–17.
4. E.g., health care tax credits under the US Affordable Care Act are available to families with incomes up to four times the federal poverty level. See HealthCare.gov, "Subsidized Coverage."
5. Mack, "Absolute and Overall Poverty."
6. Johnson and Smeeding, "Consumer's Guide."
7. See, e.g., Evans, Wolfe, and Adler, "SES and Health Gradient"; Ravallion, "Poverty Lines."
8. Bailey, Rethinking Poverty, 9.
9. Bailey, 15.

10. Balestra and Tonkin, "Inequalities," 69.

11. Asante-Muhammad et al., "Road to Zero Wealth," 29.

12. Sheffield and Rector, "Air Conditioning."

13. Cloutier, Vice, chap. 4.

14. Frank, Levine, and Dijk, "Expenditure Cascades."

15. Clark, Frijters, and Shields, "Relative Income."

16. Kahneman and Deaton, "High Income Improves Evaluation."

17. Luttmer, Neighbors, 29.

18. Increased income is not the only way to address the bandwidth tax among the poor. E.g., Mullainathan and Shafir also propose that reliable public provision of child care could help poor parents recapture bandwidth by eliminating a persistent source of worry; Mullainathan and Shafir, Scarcity, 177.

19. Kraus, Piff, and Keltner, "Social Class," 248–49.

20. See, e.g., Massaro, United States Welfare Policy, 154–55.

21. Gutiérrez, Theology, 288.

22. CELAM, "Medellín Document: Poverty."

23. Meghan J. Clark details this "already but not yet" quality of human dignity in both Catholic social thought and United Nations documents; Clark, "Development."

24. Paul VI, "Gaudium et spes," para. 26.

25. Oduyoye, "Poverty," 26.

26. United Nations Development Program, "Multidimensional Poverty Index."

27. Pieris, God's Reign, 4.

28. See, e.g., Goss, Queering Christ, 166.

29. US Department of Housing and Urban Development, "Measuring Housing"; US Department of Agriculture, "Definitions."

30. Margaret Mitchell quotes Peter Brown's insight that the early Christians invented "the poor" as a particular theological category, the people to whom Christians owned a duty of charitable assistance. Mainstream Greco-Roman communities did not see the poor this way. Mitchell, "Silver Chamber Pots," 100.

31. Barbour and Wickware, "Breaking the Chains," 49.

32. See, e.g., Gutiérrez, "Faith," 42–43; and Pieris, Asian Theology, 20–21.

33. Rodes, "On Professors," 527–28.

34. Chapp, "Precarity of Love."

35. Pope Francis notes that other groups of people are treated as disposable: "the poor, the elderly, children, the infirm, the unborn, the unemployed, the abandoned, those considered disposable because they are only considered as part of a statistic." Pope Francis, "Address."

36. Gutiérrez, "Liberation," 250.

37. Resource Generation, "Join Resource Generation!"

38. Wood, "Who Are the Millionaires?"

39. Rieger, "Ethics."

40. Reeves, "Classless America?"

41. Saez, "Striking It Richer"; Kenny, "We're All the 1 Percent." In the United States, people earning $34,000 make more than 59 percent of their fellow citizens, according to a Wall Street Journal calculator; Van Dam, "What Percent Are You?"

42. Certainly, many authors would point out that inherited advantage allows some to earn higher wages than others; see, e.g., Coates, "Case for Reparations." Regardless of these

debates, I do not regard the distinction between earned and inherited wealth as significant for wealth's virtue impact, as becomes clear in chapter 5 below.

43. Johnson, *American Dream*, 172–73.

44. Hobgood, *Dismantling Privilege*, 64–65. It is worth noting that Thomas Piketty recently
pointed out that many wealthier working people are in fact capitalists; they own wealth
in investments such as retirement accounts. Piketty, *Capital*, 395.

45. Hobgood, *Dismantling Privilege*, 65–66.

46. O'Neill, *Golden Ghetto*, xii.

47. Martin, *Primates*, 28, 49.

48. Allard, *Places*. This is not to undercut attempts to draw attention to the real, and ongoing,
practice of racial segregation in US suburbs.

49. Wheeler, *Wealth*, 136. On scriptural views of wealth, see also Barton, *Understanding Old
Testament Ethics*; Kinsler and Kinsler, *God's Economy*; Blount, *Then the Whisper Put on
Flesh*; and Moore, *Wealthwatch*.

50. Cloutier, *Vice*, 6.

51. De La Torre, *Doing Christian Ethics*, 178.

52. Aloysius Pieris warns of the danger for even vowed religious who voluntarily renounce
wealth to develop allegiances with mammon when they are supported in comfortable
lifestyles by wealthy people: "Instead of the victims being partnered by the renouncers,
we see the renouncers maintained by the rich." As an example, he cites his own Jesuit
community's control of wealth and land. Pieris, *God's Reign*, 61.

53. Wood, "Secret Fears."

54. Nussbaum, *Creating Capabilities*.

55. Nussbaum. Many theologians have drawn on the Capabilities Approach promoted by
Nussbaum and, in a slightly different form, by the economist and philosopher Amartya
Sen. For a few examples, see Claassens, "Woman"; Hicks, "Self-Interest"; and Kahiga
Kiruki, "Poverty," 215–27.

56. Paul VI, "Gaudium et spes," para. 26.

57. Political freedoms are an obvious example.

58. Iceland, *Poverty*, 48.

59. Cahill, "Catholic Feminists." As Cahill points out, a particular theologian, or indeed an
individual work, can in fact embody both "streams" of concern. The other streams Cahill
identifies are neo-Augustinian, which visualizes the Christian community against the
world, and Junian, a more radical stream personified by African, Asian, and Latin American feminists.

60. See Rubio, *Family Ethics*; Cloutier, *Vice*; McCarthy, *Becoming Nonviolent Peacemakers*;
and Grimes, *Christ Divided*.

61. Because I also evaluate the impact of unjust systems on persons and propose systemic solutions for change in chapter 7, I regard this work as both neo-Thomist and neo-Franciscan.

CHAPTER 5

WEALTH, VIRTUE, AND THE DANGERS OF HYPERAGENCY

In 2013, sixteen-year-old Ethan Couch—driving under the influence of alcohol, marijuana, and Valium—killed four people and injured more in a tragic multiple-car wreck near his Texas home. A psychologist who testified in his defense said Ethan suffered from "affluenza," meaning that his family's wealth had damaged his ability to understand right and wrong.[1] If we can deduce anything from the ensuing public excoriation of Couch's parents, many Americans agree that growing up in an environment of wealth can harm children's moral development. Yet as grown adults, Christians rarely give much thought to the impact of their own wealth on their lifelong virtue pursuit.

This chapter demonstrates how wealth can function as moral luck. As moral luck, wealth shapes, but does not unilaterally determine, the pursuit of virtue for those who have it. I focus on two significant ways wealth functions as moral luck. First, as theologians have long cautioned, wealth can become an *end in itself*, distracting our efforts from our true end. Second, wealth imparts *hyperagency*, giving persons abundant power, freedom, and choice beyond that enjoyed by other members of society. Wealth shapes communities by enabling segregation; increases access to practices of virtue and vice alike; and can inflate self-regard beyond reasonable humility. This chapter begins by making clear how wealthy people—those who have more than they need—experience hyperagency with respect to the poor who struggle to survive. I go on to detail the impact of wealth, understood as "having more than I need," on the virtues described in chapter 2: prudence, justice, solidarity, fidelity, humility, self-care, temperance, and fortitude.

In some instances, I consult sources whose definition of wealth differs significantly from my own, such as Paul Schervish and Jessie O'Neill, experts on the psychological impacts of multi-million-dollar fortunes. When I do this, it is because I believe their insights on wealth and virtue can function as a signpost to the moral impact of having more than we need. Throughout, I explicitly share my sources' own definition of wealth and make it clear when I believe their insights can fairly be applied to those with more than we need.

DEFINING HYPERAGENCY FOR CHRISTIAN ETHICS

The sociologist Paul Schervish uses the term *hyperagency* to call attention to the fact that wealthy people exert control in more areas of their lives, and the control they exert is more total, than is the case for people with more limited means. Schervish applies this term to people with fortunes of several million dollars, while I will argue that my theological account of hyperagency applies to everyone with more than they need. First, I will detail Schervish's account before moving on to show how people who are wealthy in the sense of having more than they need also experience hyperagency *in comparison with* and *over* people who must struggle to survive.

For Schervish, wealth gives persons power to exert control through time, by influencing the future, redressing any past mistakes, and enjoying unusual amounts of free time. Wealthy people also exert control through space, as when they travel freely without needing to worry about safety or resources, and when they are able to create spaces where they control the terms of interaction with others.[2] Hyperagency conveys psychological empowerment, the expectation that one's desires are legitimate and should be met.[3]

Although everyone exerts agency in at least some areas of their own lives, Schervish says, "What is different for wealth holders is that they can be more legitimately confident about actualizing their expectations and aspirations because they are able to directly effect the fulfillment of their desires."[4] This neatly explains the mechanism for wealth's impact on self-image and personal qualities like the virtues. The consistent ability to achieve one's goals through the resources of wealth influences perception of one's own importance and expectations of control over environments and other people.

Whereas many people construct their identity around how they fit within the established structures of the world, Schervish contends that wealthy people rather influence the world's structures to adapt them to their own views.[5] Though Schervish's philanthropists have broad scope in the structures they can shape, those who are wealthy in the sense of having more than they need also exercise social power in ways not available to the poor.

What hyperagency among those with more than they need has in common with Schervish's definition is its extension across time and space. Hyperagency is not limited to direct power over another individual, like the CEO who gives orders to employees or the middle-class homeowner who humiliates an hourly housekeeper.[6] Like Schervish's philanthropists, those with more than they need also shape environments, including markets, through their consumption, and through economic segregation, which is discussed further in chapter 7. They exercise hyperagency *in comparison* with the poor, who are denied access to the dizzying array of choices available to those with discretionary income under global capitalism, as well as to the much more fundamental power of basic survival security. Those with more than they need also exercise hyperagency *over* the poor, because discretionary income puts customers in a position to directly command low-wage workers in retail stores, restaurants, and nail salons, or to grant or withhold lifesaving measures to desperately poor persons around the globe.[7]

Those who have more than they need shape the structures where they exercise hyperagency through their use of discretionary income. The theologian Dan Finn draws on critical realist social theory to prove the existence of a power relation between consumers and those who produce, transport, and sell the goods consumed. Markets are an emergent reality—they emerge from, and do not exist apart from, relationships among millions of consumers and providers. These emergent structures exercise power over participants that can be constrictive, enticive, or constitutive—shaping participants' preferences before their decision-making.[8]

However, though all humans must consume to survive, those who exercise choice in their spending bear a greater responsibility for the types of harm (poverty wages, abusive working conditions, and environmental despoliation) that can arise within markets. "The fact that all consumers bear some moral responsibility . . . does not mean that all consumers are equally obligated," Finn writes. "While a man making minimum wage in Chicago and I may both be wearing shirts made in the same factory in Dhaka—thus we are both causally related to any injustices occurring there—my relative advantages create a stronger obligation for me."[9] Global supply chains link people struggling to survive, from sweatshop workers to gig economy delivery drivers, to many others who have more than they need and disburse that surplus through their discretionary income. People who have more than they need shape the markets where those struggling to survive make their living—or to put it another way, wealthy consumers exercise hyperagency over the global and local poor.

Discretionary income gives us hyperagency over those with whom we interact in markets, and an even more profound sort of power: the power to save lives or fail to do so. It is clear that amounts of money that are negligible from the point of view of many consumers in the United States,

Europe, and elsewhere can be decisive for the life and health of others living in global poverty.[10] Nor is this reality due to the imbalances of modern global capitalism—ancient Christian thinkers made the same observation. As Charles Camosy convincingly shows, the Catholic tradition consistently shares the view of the provocative philosopher Peter Singer that people in need have rights to the surplus of those with more than they need. Singer and the Catholic tradition agree that this right can be correctly interpreted to mean that refusing to commit financial surplus to saving the lives of the poor is morally equivalent to murder.[11]

As we saw in chapter 1, average global income is about $960 per month, meaning many working-class people in the United States and Europe are near the top of the global income hierarchy.[12] If these people have discretionary income remaining after meeting their basic needs, Singer and the Catholic tradition hold that the global poor have rights to that surplus. Perhaps we most often tend to think of this relationship, as Singer does, on utilitarian grounds; a small sacrifice from someone with more than she needs can literally mean life or death to someone poor. Christian ethical reflections on this insight often ask how much surplus is justified in a world where those surplus funds can save others' lives. They use such concepts as the order of love (special duties to those closest to us), hospitality and feasting, or environmental impact.[13] I urge us also to consider this power relationship through a virtue perspective. Someone who walks around every day, able to save precious human lives through her freely available surplus, and chooses not to do so, is deformed morally both by the system she inhabits, which distributes the basic goods of life so unequally, and by her own choices within that system. Those with more than they need do not habitually think about the life-or-death power they hold over other human beings who are poor; nor did they choose to inhabit such an unequal power relation. Yet they operate out of that power nonetheless, and it shapes their actions and who they become.

Hyperagency is a challenging label for acts so widely viewed as innocuous as moving to a certain neighborhood for the schools, or purchasing healthy foods for our family. It sounds implausible until we accept the profound aggregate impact that such choices have on the poor, and the extent to which people living in poverty view such acts as entirely out of reach. In her memoir of single motherhood, struggling to survive through housecleaning work and government benefits, Stephanie Land wrote movingly of her daughter's excitement at enjoying "as many berries as I wanted" at a friend's party.[14] Land explains that this simple, wholesome abundance was simply not within her power to offer her daughter.

Buying berries to share with children and guests is hard to characterize as an act of vice. It is much easier to interpret it as an act in pursuit of virtues like fidelity and hospitality (of course, we would need to know the motivation behind the act to assess it fully). But acts of virtue done through hyperagency are still enabled by, and reinforce, this disproportionate power. Although this act of virtue is out of reach for Land and many other poor parents, hyperagents live in a world where they can choose it, and could with equal ease choose to use their surplus viciously. Using disposable income to buy berries for the family is still an act of hyperagency, reinforcing the hyperagent's sense that she is in control, that her whims and desires are valid and deserve to be met, even that it is right and fitting that others should labor in difficult conditions to help meet her whims and desires. The hyperagent may not wish for farm workers' exploitation or grocery workers' low pay, but she has power over these workers regardless.

Suppose someone with more than she needs tried to do everything possible to limit her own hyperagency. The first step might be to eliminate all unnecessary consumption, donating her surplus to organizations helping the global poor live in dignity. In order to reduce her power over workers in the supply chain, she could grow her own food (with handmade tools?), eschew electronic devices, and generally avoid paying others for services she could do herself or do without. Such a lifestyle might seem romantic and appealing, or impossibly demanding. Regardless, it is still a choice (or a series of choices) made by someone with the power to choose otherwise. Compared with typical consumption, this restricted lifestyle obviously places fewer demands on the environment and on other people. But from a virtue perspective, its message to the hyperagent is the same. She chooses and determines her destiny; her choices are important and valid. There are many sound reasons to support the common good by avoiding unnecessary consumption and redirecting resources to the poor. Even though these may be virtuous choices, choosing not to consume when one could is still a choice made out of hyperagency.

I am arguing that any amount of money we control beyond what goes to satisfy our basic needs grants hyperagency over workers in supply chains and also represents hyperagency compared with those who are struggling to survive. I sought to estimate how many people in the United States experience hyperagency in this way through data on US discretionary income— the amount households have left to spend after paying for necessities such as housing, utilities, food prepared at home, taxes, and health care.[15] I calculated the average discretionary income for each decile of the US population using spending data for 2018 from the US Bureau of Labor Statistics (BLS). To do this, I added average expenditures on food, housing, transportation, apparel, health care, and personal care (hygiene items), and I subtracted this total from the average after-tax income for each decile. One caveat is that though each of these spending categories does represent basic needs, it is possible to spend beyond reasonable need in a basic needs category. Clothing is a basic need, but a closet stuffed with garments in the latest styles is not, and BLS data do not distinguish between basic needs spending and what we might call luxury purchases in the same category. If anything, then, the figures presented here slightly underestimate the number of people in the United States who experience hyperagency.[16]

In a sobering reminder of the scale of US inequality, I found that nearly a third of US households have negative discretionary income, meaning that their essential expenditures are more than their income. (This can occur when a household draws down savings or goes into debt to pay for basic needs.) Households in the third income decile, earning from roughly $21,000 to $31,000 yearly, report a negative discretionary income of $4,579 after taxes and basic needs spending.[17] Poorer households go even further into the red to pay for basic needs. The lowest-income households, with incomes up to $12,102 yearly, have an average deficit of $14,601 after paying for basic needs, and the second income decile posts a deficit of $5,910.[18]

Although many US households cannot afford to meet their basic needs, a majority control nontrivial amounts of discretionary income. Households in the fourth decile, whose income tops out at $41,489, post a positive average discretionary income of $1,613.[19] The fifth decile, whose yearly income ranges from just under $42,000 to over $54,400, has an average of $7,346 in yearly discretionary income, and the sixth income decile nearly doubles that, with those whose income tops out at slightly over $70,000 controlling $14,561 in average yearly discretionary income. The remaining third of US families, obviously, controls even more.

It is clear that many US households, including many who are far more likely to identify as middle class than rich, disburse at least tens of thousands of dollars yearly according to pure preference. The calculations given above, despite their limitations, suggest that 40 percent or more of US families fall into this group. (Recall that the BLS data do not allow us to identify spending beyond reasonable need in a basic needs category.) These thousands of discretionary dollars enable an untold number of small, everyday decisions that afford the spender freedom of choice and the ability to disburse her income according to her own preferences. Each one of these small, repeated acts shapes environments and shapes the agent, supporting the belief that her preferences are valid and important. This freedom is not experienced by those with no or negative discretionary income, whose spending decisions are made under the constraint of struggling to survive.

The witnesses of people living in poverty provide the most compelling evidence locating hyperagency in what might seem ordinary middle-class use of discretionary income. As the next chapter shows, people living in poverty clearly describe the wealthy, including those whose security is quite modest, as exercising power they themselves lack, including power over themselves.[20] My account of hyperagency is indebted more than anything to their insights. As Finn writes, "People who live within the penumbra of influence created by the power of others are far more likely to be aware of power and more able to articulate its shades of influence."[21] Poor people clearly see the hyperagency that is often invisible to those who wield it.

Schervish's sociological account of hyperagency is descriptive rather than normative. His primary objective is to present and understand how the wealthy describe their lives and motivations, though he does not rule out that "empowerment may become an ominous danger—to the fate of others as well as to the souls of the rich."[22] A theological perspective need not be so circumspect.

I argue that wealth, understood as having more than we need, grants hyperagency. Although hyperagency can be used either to help or to harm others, given the human tendency to sin, it is vulnerable to misuses that threaten the hyperagent's virtue.[23] In what follows, when I avoid qualifiers in statements like "wealth interferes with fortitude," that is what I mean—not that it does so in every act, but in the course of every life. I use "hyperagency" in the sense described above, to mean the hyperagency of those with more than they need.

For much of human history, the lines between rich and poor were starker and more obvious than they are in wealthy nations now. This may insulate us from the realization that the moral effects of wealth that have troubled Christian theologians for centuries fairly describe middle-class experience in the contemporary United States. Christians like Augustine, John Chrysostom, Francis of Assisi, and Thomas Aquinas charged that the rich see their wealth as self-made rather than as a gift from God; that they spend their surplus on their own pleasure, including on vice, instead of using it to help poor people survive; and that they use wealth to shield themselves from the struggle of the poor. We do not have to be members of the "1 percent" to fail in these precise ways even today. For much of Christian history, having enough surplus to insulate oneself from need and consume according to one's wishes was, in fact, reserved to a rare wealthy few. Today, it is common enough to pass as unremarkable.

If hyperagency tempts wealthy people to vice while poor people lack power to the extent that they must struggle to survive, and the categories "wealthy" and "poor" are mutually exclusive, does anyone in the world exercise appropriate or healthy moral agency? Christian believers are already well aware, in fact, that no one does. Everyone who acts does so in a world already tainted by sin and as human persons already susceptible to it. In this sense, my Christian ethical account of hyperagency does not point out anything new.

What I have tried to do is offer a precise language for warning the wealthy—those with more than they need, those with the leisure to read theological books and ponder the impact of their life circumstances on their virtue—against the particular ways their life circumstances can tempt them to misuse their moral agency in ways that harm their own virtue and the lives of others. Although poverty can impede the pursuit of virtue by denying the wherewithal to perform virtuous acts—as the next chapter shows—wealthy hyperagency enables the pursuit of vice. In her Christian ethical analysis of power, Christine Firer Hinze warns: "Experience confirms that power-holders face the constant temptation to exercise prerogatives over others in an irresponsible and self-serving fashion. . . . It is no wonder that Christians have frequently argued that to exercise power is to come into contact with, if not sin itself, at least with 'near occasions' of sin, corruption, and evil."[24] Both power and privation can pose "near occasions" of sin, and we who live in this fallen world should know what forms those might take, given our particular life circumstances.

PRUDENCE

Wealth has ambiguous effects on the pursuit of prudence, the virtue that helps us set ends in pursuing the good. Scarcity affects the brain in ways that can hamper long-range planning, and wealth protects against this. However, wealth interferes with understanding, a part of prudence, in several ways. It encourages us to maintain social taboos against discussing wealth and even to lie to ourselves and to others about the sources of our prosperity. Most importantly for an account of prudence, wealth interferes with the appointment of ends by becoming an end in itself.

The hyperagency of wealth wields conflicting results for prudence. Psychologists know that scarcity burdens cognitive capacity. Resource scarcity, and the mental energy it demands, burden self-control, focus, and long-range planning in ways with which wealthy people do not have to contend. This does not mean that wealthy people have inherently greater cognitive capacity than poor people; rather, poverty places burdens on minds under which, as Sendhil Mullainathan and Eldar Shafir say in their book *Scarcity*, "we all would have (and have!) failed."[25] So in one sense, wealth encourages our pursuit of the virtue of prudence by protecting the mental capacity to make long-range plans.[26]

Conversely, wealth affects understanding, a key part of prudence, in several detrimental ways.[27] In the United States, a strong cultural taboo against discussing wealth and its provenance erodes a correct understanding of wealth's impact on our lives. The sociologist Heather Beth Johnson found that Americans, whether they are wealthy or of modest backgrounds, tend to support the "American dream" narrative, which holds that one can become successful through hard work and merit, regardless of one's initial privileges or disadvantages. Paradoxically, she found that inheritors of significant generational wealth were able to espouse this narrative even while acknowledging their gratitude to the family members who had endowed them with wealth and other privileges.[28] Wealthy people were able to clearly articulate that inequality persists due in part to generational wealth transfer,[29] but most continued to insist that their own privileges were deserved by virtue of their own achievements.[30] And though they were proud to pass along advantages to their own children, wealthy people similarly insisted that any successes their children experienced in life would be due to their own hard work and merit.[31] When interviewers asked them to directly engage the tension between inherited privilege and the American dream of meritocracy, says Johnson, some wealthy interviewees became "frazzled." Yet it became clear that they genuinely believed in both these ideologies, which were complexly interwoven in their worldviews and the way they made sense of their own lives.[32] People who know they have inherited significant advantage along with their wealth should be in a unique position to challenge the "American dream" ideology of equal opportunity according to hard work, and yet their wealth seems to interfere with right understanding of the reality of access to opportunity.

Wealth's tendency to interfere with right understanding is not limited to very affluent heirs. The theologian Mary Elizabeth Hobgood speaks for professional and managerial workers when she writes: "We learn mostly to admire and identify with those above us in the class system and to blame those below us. In this way, the ideology protecting our privileges in the upper tiers of the working class conditions us to deny attention and feeling to those we have learned are unworthy."[33]

Hobgood's trenchant summary echoes the observations of the early economist Adam Smith (1723–90), who believed that humans naturally "sympathize" or identify with those who are better off than themselves, while "despising" those who are worse off out of a desire to avoid sharing their suffering.[34] Wealth's role in these perverse sympathies is clear: the wealthier we are, the greater the proportion of humanity we see as beneath our notice, and the fewer people who appear worthy of our care and concern.

This asymmetrical sympathy of wealth for greater wealth is grossly compounded by racism. As the journalist Ta-Nehisi Coates shows, white Americans enjoy significantly greater wealth, on average, than Black Americans, due to centuries of racist economic systems from slavery to real estate redlining. Yet middle-class white Americans fail to demonstrate an understanding of this situation when they continue to insist that the wealth they do have was earned under circumstances available to anyone.[35]

The fourth-century theologian John Chrysostom was aware of the double consciousness that can result when wealth discourages right understanding. Addressing his wealthy congregation, he announced that vast wealth was proof that injustice had been done to acquire it. Even those who had inherited their wealth should not regard themselves as exempt from complicity in injustice, he said, because they could not claim that they were exactly sure how the wealth had come about and that no one had been harmed in the process.[36]

Like Chrysostom, contemporary liberation theologians have remarked on the tendency of wealth to shape perspectives and inhibit understanding. For example, José Míguez Bonino writes, "The world simply looks differently when seen from an executive's office and from a shanty town. Perspectives hide certain things and make other things visible. Since poverty is the dominating reality in our world, a theologian who looks at the world from the social location of the rich will remain unavoidably blind to reality."[37]

Jon Sobrino has made a similar point, writing about how his mind was changed as a theologian by awakening to the reality of poverty in El Salvador. From the standpoint of the poor, he writes, a different perspective emerges on what it means to be human: the Western anthropology of individuality and power is revealed as seriously deficient.[38] More recently, Pope Francis has commented in the same vein: "We fail to see that some are mired in desperate and degrading poverty, with no way out, while others have not the faintest idea of what to do with their possessions, vainly showing off their supposed superiority."[39] The idea that wealth affects our perception of reality recurs throughout the Christian tradition and is corroborated by the findings of social science.

Along with obfuscating understanding, perhaps the primary way wealth can interfere with the development of prudence is by becoming an end in itself. For Christian thinkers, who constantly warn against this aspect of wealth, the right end for humans is, of course, union with God. Contemporary secular thinkers, informed by the therapeutic culture, often understand the human end to be subjective happiness. However, both perspectives agree that wealth can become a false goal that interferes with humans' ultimate end. For example, the psychologists Richard Ryan and Tim Kasser found that adolescents who aspired to attain wealth and fame exhibited higher rates of depression and low self-esteem than those who aspired to intrinsically rewarding goals, such as good relationships or connections to their communities.[40] Wealth and fame are examples of extrinsic goals whose pursuit can interfere with happiness.[41]

Christian thinkers almost universally insist that wealth can affect virtue by becoming an end in itself. This caution has ample support in the New Testament, where wealth is portrayed as an object of devotion that can compete with God and as a stumbling block to discipleship with Jesus.[42] Not all thinkers specify that wealth interferes with prudence—for example, Augustine repeatedly says just that wealth is "dangerous" to the Christian believer and implies that it is safer to divest.[43] But we can always count on Aquinas for a precise explication of particular virtues, and here he does not disappoint.

Aquinas insists that, despite what we imagine, wealth can never cause true happiness.[44] Rather, the pursuit of riches can interfere with the appointment of ends along our path to happiness. He says that we recognize happiness because it is self-sufficing—we know when we have achieved happiness because we cease to desire it.[45] Wealth, as an end in itself, is easily confused with happiness because it can seem to have this same self-sufficing quality. We imagine that if we had wealth, we would be able to purchase anything we might desire, and then we would cease to desire other things—Aquinas describes the tendency to act on this belief as the vice of covetousness.[46] Viewing wealth as an end in itself clearly disrupts the pursuit of prudence, the virtue that helps us appoint ends in pursuing the good.

It might seem that one does not have to be wealthy to run the risk of covetousness. Anyone can allow wealth to become an end in itself in her life, whether she actually has wealth or is just pursuing it. (I discuss this objection in chapter 6.) But Aquinas certainly sees a materialist aspect to the way wealth functions as moral luck.[47] He says over and over that wealth, once possessed, tends to become an end in itself. Although he does not give material ownership of wealth inevitable moral force, neither does he allow the wealthy to spiritualize what they have, so far as to disclaim any moral impact.[48] Arguing for voluntary poverty in religious life, he insists that though some argue that they can have wealth without remaining overly attached to it, "others congratulate themselves on neither owning nor loving it, for this is the safer course."[49] Indeed, once riches are possessed, they interfere with "the perfection of charity" by "enticing and distracting the mind."[50] Here Aquinas argues not that riches interfere with prudence, the appointment of ends, but that they interfere with charity by taking the place of God as the proper object of our love. Still, he clearly is warning specifically those who have wealth against the danger of its becoming an end. Again, he says that covetousness "exceeds in retaining," a vicious tendency only available to those who already have something to retain and who refuse to give to the needy out of mercy. (The other part of covetousness is to "exceed in receiving," a vicious immoderation possible for both those who have wealth and those who do not.)[51]

Although Aquinas always placed the final determination of the human moral journey in God's hands, it simply cannot be said that he saw wealth as morally neutral, or that he believed the wealthy and the poor face the same threats to their virtue. Yes, wealth can displace God as end for anyone—but Aquinas clearly insists that those who have wealth are at particular risk.

Theologians and social scientists alike agree that wealth can interfere with prudence. Wealth disrupts right understanding when owning it encourages us to think we earned it even when we know we did not. Wealth can lead us in the wrong direction when it takes the place of intrinsic goods. Most significantly, wealth can become an end in itself, distracting us from the pursuit of our proper end.

JUSTICE

Justice in Christian virtue thought is the virtue that encourages and enables us to give to others what is their due. To demonstrate this virtue, we need to understand what is due to others and be ready to share it with them without internal struggle. The hyperagency that wealth bestows can give wealthy people an overinflated sense of their own due, warping the view of what is due to others and interfering with the formation of justice. This phenomenon is well documented in social science and is recognized by theologians.

Jessie O'Neill, a therapist who works with inheritors of generational wealth, notes that the wealthy are often socialized to expect preferential treatment over others, at significant cost to their development of the virtue of justice. O'Neill says, "Embarrassing accounts of the rich and famous demonstrating the inability to tolerate frustration or delay gratification abound in the media and in our literature. To the disgust of the average-income person, who often waits long and patiently for the smallest reward, the affluent frequently demand instant and preferential treatment in restaurants, shops, hotels, and other public places."[52] Demanding that one's needs and desires will be gratified before those of others, even when it comes to relatively petty inconveniences like waiting in line, is a clear sign of a failure to exercise the virtue of justice.

O'Neill frames impatience as a trait of the extremely wealthy, as contrasted with those of "average income." But for the climate scientist Kevin Anderson, everyone who spends money on air travel indulges impatience at the cost of placing others in harm's way. Committed to avoiding flying, with its significant environmental impact, because of his position as a climate role model, Anderson notes that "slow forms of travel fundamentally change our perception of the essential."[53] Refusing to use airplanes requires travelers to revise their sense of their own importance, to re-weigh their own comfort and convenience against the common good of planetary security.

Many, many people with more than they need, myself included, fly in planes, contributing to climate destruction that will disproportionately harm the poor, when we would not trouble ourselves to take ground or water transportation the same distance. Our desire for our own convenience outweighs our sense of what is due to others. Our hyperagency allows us to develop practices that place our own convenience over others' well-being, at a cost to our virtue of justice. Anderson's perspective allows us to see that spending even ordinary amounts of discretionary income can be done in ways that distort our sense of what is due to us versus others. As another example, the entitled, even abusive customers experienced by big box retail and fast food employees are not likely to be O'Neill's inheritors, but among those with more than they need.[54]

I do believe that the thoughtless consumption of those with more than we need violates justice just as much as more egregious examples. And I would point out that it is only our wealth (our more than we need) that enables us to thoughtlessly consume in this way. Someone without the money for a plane flight may be tempted to other violations of justice, but they will not be able to travel in comfort at the cost of planetary destruction, whose impact disproportionately harms the poor. Those without discretionary income are not in a position to choose between, say, helping someone avoid malaria or buying themselves a fancy coffee. Even if our surplus requires us to weigh each purchase carefully, we are not protected from spending it in ways that violate what is due to others and hinder ourselves in the pursuit of justice.

A group of studies by psychologists in the United States and Canada suggests that "upper-class" people are more likely to engage in unethical behavior, such as cheating and lying, than "lower-class" people.[55] The researchers assessed class and unethical behavior in many different ways. For example, they observed traffic and found that drivers of newer, more expensive cars were more likely to "cut off" other drivers and pedestrians. Other studies asked participants to self-report their social class and to respond to case studies about ethical and unethical behavior. Participants who self-reported higher social class were more likely to say they would engage in the unethical behaviors depicted in the case studies. They were more likely to cheat at games, and—suggesting a causal factor for the unethical behavior—they reported more positive views toward greed.[56] The researchers theorized that "relative independence from others" and "resources to deal with the downstream costs of ethical behavior" are among the reasons upper-class people were more likely to act unethically.[57] Independence and resources enabling unethical behavior are another way of saying that wealthy people's hyperagency interferes with their pursuit of the virtue of justice.

For Thomas Aquinas, even keeping the wealth we already have can be a vicious practice: pursuing the virtue of justice may require giving away some of what we have. We exhibit the vice of covetousness, which is opposed to justice, when we act immoderately in getting and keeping wealth.[58] "Immoderately" here means beyond what we need to live "in keeping with [our] condition of life."[59]

The "condition of life" caveat, nearly identical to one proposed by Augustine, should not be misused to encourage wealthy people to continue their status quo of ownership and consumption. Aquinas notes that there is often considerable leeway in what we need to spend to obtain "the decencies of life in keeping with [our] own position," and he advises those able to do so to give alms from within this realm of leeway.[60] Aquinas says that almsgiving from within this leeway amount is not demanded by justice, although justice does demand that we give from our surplus, from what we do not truly need.[61] A contemporary understanding of the systemic inequalities behind our incomes only bolsters Aquinas's insistence that almsgiving is a virtuous practice ideally suited to help rectify our sense of what is due to others and to ourselves, recalibrating our own sense of what we and others need. A virtue perspective demonstrates that almsgiving has multiple positive effects. Most obviously, it benefits the recipient; less obviously, it helps the giver develop her virtue of justice.

Social scientists who study philanthropy have long known that wealthy people donate a lower percentage of their income on a yearly basis to charity than middle-class or even poor people do.[62] One potential driver of this trend is that because wealthy people are able to live in wealth-segregated areas (a symptom of hyperagency), they may encounter less need on a daily basis, experiencing fewer reminders to be generous.[63] Those who are not in the habit of giving to the degree of others with lower incomes should be challenged by Aquinas's view about the viciousness of immoderate keeping. The good news is that improved almsgiving is a relatively straightforward practice to resist the impact of wealth on virtue.[64]

Wealth interferes with the virtue of justice when hyperagency allows wealthy people to prioritize personal convenience over others' necessity. Such acts, when repeated, can lead us to develop a distorted sense of what is due us relative to others, a failing in the virtue of justice. For Aquinas, withholding wealth when another needs it is vicious, while almsgiving can help reconnect us with a proper sense of what is due to others. In the United States, wealthier people give to a lesser degree of personal sacrifice than poorer ones do, indicating a failure on their part to pursue the virtue of justice.

SOLIDARITY

Solidarity is the virtue that describes recognition of our interdependence with others and a firm commitment to work together for the common good. For people with wealth, this means recognizing interdependence and working together with the poor, while for poor people, solidarity means working together with others like them.[65] The most significant way wealth interferes with the practice and development of solidarity is through hyperagency, which enables people with wealth to live separated from the poor.[66]

A group of psychologists from the University of California, Berkeley, conducted a series of studies that showed poorer people are more compassionate than wealthier ones. Compared with wealthier people, lower-class individuals expressed more compassion for others in a self-report survey and in a face-to-face situation, a mock job interview. This distinction held even at the biological level, as self-described lower-class people were more likely to exhibit a slowed heart rate, a physiological marker of compassion, when watching a touching video.[67] The researchers interpreted these findings in light of previous research that shows lower-class people learn to be more attentive to threats in their environment. This enables them to more easily read and respond to the cues that show others are suffering, and then to extend compassion. When it comes to the interpretation of others' emotions, the stereotype of rich people as oblivious to others' needs has a basis in scientific findings.

Another psychological study found that people with lower class status were better at decoding others' emotions in facial expressions than people with higher class status. This was true when the class status was objective, using education as a proxy, and when experimenters induced relative class position by asking participants to think about a person with higher class status than them.[68] Interpreting others' emotions is an important component of empathy. It is easy to see how difficulty "reading" others could inhibit the pursuit of solidarity. Occupying a class position far above that of another person reduces the likelihood that you will sympathize with her, let alone commit to making her concerns your own.

One facet of the hyperagency that wealth bestows is the ability to control one's environment, including remaining separate from poor people. Jessie O'Neill feels so strongly about the power of wealth to divide the wealthy from others that she named her book *The Golden Ghetto*.[69] The authors of a book called *Affluenza* (2001/2014), an influential cultural critique of the pitfalls of the US consumerist lifestyle, say that affluenza causes us to "cocoon" with those like ourselves, as evidenced by the fact that more than 10 percent of US homes are in gated communities.[70] This figure makes it clear that self-segregation is not limited to the extremely wealthy. Sociologists confirm that as income inequality increases, middle- and upper-income families increase their segregation from the poorest families.[71] The ongoing persistence of "white flight" is another example of spatial hyperagency among those with more than they need, more common in middle-class neighborhoods than poorer ones, and a driver of both economic and racial segregation.[72]

Segregation can also be imposed on the poor by the wealthy. The United States has seen a rapid rise in laws designed to keep poor people out of sight, such as laws outlawing begging or sleeping on benches and even laws that criminalize assisting a person who is homeless.[73] In New York City, a management company that earned tax breaks by including low-income housing in a new apartment building forced the low-income residents to enter through a separate "poor door" and excluded them from the building gym and pool.[74] The freedom and power of wealth allows wealthy people to remain almost completely free from opportunities to encounter, let alone develop solidarity with, the poor.

Many reflections on solidarity for wealthy and poor people assert that it already exists in a certain sense, due to the reality of their interconnectedness in the global market. Joerg Rieger notes that the very fact of wealth's existence denotes a certain connection between the wealthy and the poor. "Neither wealth nor power or privilege are ever based on individual accomplishment alone," he explains, "wealth and power are always produced in close relation to others. More specifically, under the conditions of free market economics, wealth and power are often produced on the backs of others in various ways."[75] The poor are the ones who labored to create the majority of the goods wealthy people end up controlling, Rieger argues, which should make us conscious of the reality of the interconnection of the human family and predispose us to developing solidarity.

In a similar key, Mary Elizabeth Hobgood locates common cause between wealthy and poor workers in their shared occupation as workers. She writes: "To maintain the class system, elites especially are socialized into an 'I versus others' worldview that supports individualism and self-interest at the expense of others. . . . [This view] would have professionals and managers believe that they are fundamentally distinct from the lower working class and have no commonality with them."[76]

Although asserting the similarity of wealthy and poor workers, Hobgood intends to trouble the complacency of the wealthy: "It is difficult to fully enjoy what we have when we realize that so many others have much less, and further that what we have is related to their impoverishment. . . . For one thing, we can no longer thank God for 'blessings' we have actually stolen from others."[77] Ultimately, Hobgood identifies solidarity for wealthy working people as identifying with poorer workers and working together for justice.[78]

Rebecca Todd Peters takes a different and, in my view, more satisfactory approach to wealthy solidarity. For Peters, solidarity for privileged First World Christians begins with the recognition of their *own* privilege and power. She writes that "as First World Christians read the story of the Exodus, most of us are far more like the Egyptians than the Hebrew slaves. Like the Egyptians, we are the landowners, the task masters, the ones who benefit from the labor of the workers."[79] Contra Rieger, the indubitable interconnection of wealthy consumers and poor workers in global markets does not by itself generate solidarity. Rather, those with money to spend exercise hyperagency over those forced by poverty to labor to create consumer goods.

Peters's view is correct, particularly if we think about the powerful position of a Western consumer in the global economy, but even if we compare professional and low-wage workers in the same country. The idealized solidarity that Rieger and Hobgood propose neglects the real power that wealthy people in the United States have to separate from and control their poorer fellow community members. True solidarity for wealthy people in the United States and other wealthy countries cannot look like a naive assertion of common cause, but demands real interrogation of the relative circumstances of the wealthy and the poor.

Wealth can interfere with the development of the virtue of solidarity when it affords wealthy people the power to conduct their lives separately from poorer ones. This separateness insulates wealthy people from the encounters that lead to true solidarity and hinders the salutary process of confronting the ways wealthy people benefit from a system that divides. Wealth's self-distancing results in more difficulty interpreting others' emotions for wealthy people, another potential barrier to pursuing solidarity.

FIDELITY

Fidelity is the virtue we express when we form and maintain close, loving relationships with others. Wealth has complex effects on fidelity, supporting some acts of fidelity while tempting to others that violate it. In support of fidelity, wealth can provide free time to spend with others and enable the acts of physical provision so crucial in relationships with children or other dependents. Financial security appears to undergird long-term commitment, although that by itself does not demonstrate virtue. Conversely, wealth has the potential to encourage a false version of fidelity where we express love to others only through spending, or devote time to maintaining wealth instead of relationships. When wealth becomes an end in itself, placing its pursuit above our close relationships also indicates a failure of the virtue of fidelity.

We must proceed with caution when attempting to draw conclusions about the virtue of fidelity from the social-scientific literature on marriage and divorce. It is hardly necessary to observe that a couple can remain married even while their daily actions belie the values of a loving commitment, or that a never-married couple could pursue the virtue of fidelity in their lives together. This caveat stated, resources of money and time have the potential to enable acts of fidelity in partnerships. Clearly, working around the clock to support a dependent loved one can be an act of fidelity if family need makes it necessary, but those with hyperagency, with money and time to dispose of, can pursue fidelity by using their resources to connect with loved ones and to meet their needs. (Equally obviously, wealth does not guarantee right use; a wealthy person could violate fidelity by using her resources selfishly, ignoring her loved ones' needs.)

The potential of wealth to enable acts of fidelity may be one reason why middle- and upper-class people are more likely to marry, less likely to divorce, and more likely to say they are "very happy" in their marriage than those with fewer resources.[80] The political scientist Robert Putnam describes how patterns of family life began to diverge along class lines in the 1970s, the beginning of a significant gap in marriage and family practices today. College-educated people tend to form "neotraditional" families. They are less likely to divorce and more likely to have children only within marriage, with both parents involved in raising them. Poorer adults are more likely to have children outside marriage and with more than one partner, to divorce if they do marry, and to repartner multiple times or to raise children as single parents.[81] "Multi-partner fertility" results in further instability as poorer adults who have children with more than one partner struggle to meaningfully support each child. Poor parents are far less likely than wealthier ones to remain with their children's other parent long term: "The shared desire to have a child usually fails to provide enough of a bond to persist through the trials of raising an infant amidst precarious work, fragile families, and dangerous neighborhoods."[82]

The sociologist Kathryn Edin, with her colleagues, has shown that poor adults do indeed value marriage and co-parenting, but see those goals as out of reach given their financial instability.[83] The political scientist Putnam and the economists Doepke and Zilibotti concur that the material deprivations of poverty, rather than different views on marriage and family, appear to be the primary driver of differences in family formation.[84] They argue that social supports for families, such as childcare provision and an increased availability of family-supporting jobs, could help reduce the "marriage gap."[85]

Other findings relating marriage to income are harder to parse. What to make of the fact that "home ownership stabilizes marriage apart from whether homeowners have a strong normative commitment to marital permanence"?[86] It appears that though some marriages last due to the genuine pursuit of fidelity on the part of one or both partners—pursuit which financial resources may support—others continue almost despite the partners' values, because marriage affords them a lifestyle they could not achieve alone.[87] This illustrates the danger of extrapolating to virtue from studies of marital longevity. Still, with all due caution about generalizing cause and effect, wealth, rightly used, can enable the performance of acts of fidelity, and this may help promote relational stability.

Although cultural expectations of what is best for children may differ among groups and can change, wealthy hyperagency means that rich parents are more likely to succeed at following their culture's dictates as they see them. A poignant illustration of this follows a broad cultural shift in parenting since the 1970s, in which both wealthy and poor parents in many rich countries came to believe that children needed much more intensive time engagement with parents than had formerly been the norm. (At its extreme, this shift results in the derisively termed "helicopter parenting.") The economists Matthias Doepke and Fabrizio Zilibotti explain that, as economic inequality grew in the United States after the 1970s, many parents came to believe that children need educational interaction starting at an early age in order to have the best chances of success in life.[88] Less-educated as well as more-educated parents began to spend more time interacting with children than had been the case in past generations.[89] In fact, in the period from 2008 to 2013, parents with only a high school education spent more time in "developmental child care" than parents with college degrees or more education did as recently as 2001.[90] (Developmental care, familiarly called "Goodnight Moon time" after the popular children's book, describes deliberately engaging with children to improve their social, cognitive, or language skills, as distinct from ordinary physical care.)

Despite poorer parents' best efforts, however, wealthy hyperagency means that a class discrepancy in time spent with parents has actually widened over that period. Although parents at all levels of education have increased their time spent in developmental child care over the past four decades, "high-educated parents have increased their developmental child care activities at a faster rate than parents with the lowest educational attainment."[91] The class gap in "Goodnight Moon time," then, is not due to differential love or even different understandings of what children need. Rather, "because high-educated parents possess the necessary resources to shift their behavior patterns so that they are in line with contemporary parenting ideals, they are the ones who are able to follow the dominant childrearing advice of experts and make substantial financial and time investments in their children."[92] Both rich and poor parents want to make a habit of spending quality time with their children, but wealthy parents have an easier time achieving these acts of virtue.

If wealth rightly used can enable faithful acts, it is equally clear that wrongly prioritized wealth can interfere with the pursuit of fidelity. For example, O'Neill notes that inheritors of significant wealth can have difficulty trusting the motives of those who wish to partner with them, because they are unsure whether the potential partner is truly interested in their own qualities or only in their wealth.[93] Again, though O'Neill studies individuals who are so wealthy they do not need to work, those who earn a comfortable, though not lavish, living from work also take income into account in partnerships in ways that can seem rather unromantically practical. "Assortative mating," when people choose spouses of similar education and income level to themselves, has increased in recent decades and contributes significantly to the "marriage gap."[94] This suggests that distrust of potential partners from different income backgrounds extends far beyond O'Neill's extremely wealthy clients.

As we have seen, the hyperagency of wealth allows parents to bestow time and resources on children, giving them more power to prepare children for success in life.[95] This application of hyperagency has a profound downside when parents pressure children to strive and achieve in ways that damage the child's mental health and sense of self. As the psychologist Suniya Luthar has amply documented, affluent parents in the United States are particularly prone to this error, which treats children as objects to be burnished rather than as persons in relationship.[96] (Although poor parents can certainly push children to achieve, they do so with less of the free time and other resources that make wealthier parents so successful.) O'Neill discerns another potential error for parents with resources: based on her clinical experience, she argues that wealthy parents are prone to believing that goods and resources can replace time and support in relationships with their children. "It is little wonder that the children of financial giants often grow up with severe emotional and psychological problems," she writes. "They were raised in an environment that placed a higher value on material satisfaction than on emotional sustenance."[97]

Although O'Neill is describing the children of very wealthy families here, Luthar has discovered loneliness and a lack of connection to parents among children of the US upper middle class, more so than among families with fewer resources. In her research with youth from areas where the median family income ranged from $80,000 to $120,000 in the early 2000s, she found many signs of distress. Compared with national averages, such well-off youth use drugs at higher rates, and more troublingly still, use them in patterns consistent with self-medication rather than experimentation. Isolation from parents was as high as among an impoverished control group sample. Luthar writes: "Among upper-middle-class families, secondary school students are often left home alone for several hours each week, with many parents believing that this promotes self-sufficiency. Similarly, suburban children's needs for emotional closeness may often suffer as the demands of professional parents' careers erode relaxed 'family time' and youngsters are shuttled between various after-school activities."[98]

The psychologist Madeline Levine agrees with Luthar's assessment that economic privilege can lead to problems between parents and children. In addition to achievement pressure, "affluent youth . . . feel both physical and psychological isolation from adults—from their parents in particular."[99] If this seems counterintuitive, Levine points out that "we can be overinvolved in the wrong things and underinvolved in the right things both at the same time."[100] She criticizes the "culture of affluence" that values materialism and competition, squashes intrinsic motivation by focusing on outward achievements, and drives parents to work long hours to provide children with lavish opportunities.[101]

For parents who are wealthy, in my definition of having more than we need, though perhaps not, as O'Neill says, "financial giants," a major challenge in the pursuit of fidelity is discerning appropriate lines around providing children with resources. The abundant choice that wealth bestows makes these decisions more difficult, but Christian ethicists who write about consumerism and the family are hard at work discerning where these lines might lie. In *Following Christ in a Consumer Society*, John Kavanaugh warned that "the commodity form of life" atrophied Americans' ability to form meaningful, loving relationships as consumer practice trained them only to form relationships with things.[102] More optimistic when she assessed the lifestyles of middle-class US Catholic families almost forty years later, Julie Hanlon Rubio resisted the idea that their lives followed Kavanaugh's commodity form, but affirmed that while valuing family relationships, many Catholics still struggled for more time and deeper connections.[103] Pope Francis draws connections between abundance in wealthy societies, a "culture of instant gratification," and problems in the family: "Parents can be prone to impulsive and wasteful consumption, which then affects their children who find it increasingly difficult to acquire a home of their own and build a family."[104]

Certainly, discerning virtuous practice around resources of time and money is a major challenge in developing fidelity for parents. (The challenge is there in any close, faithful relationship, but particularly salient in the parent–child relationship because children depend on adults for the resources they need to live.) This highlights a salient characteristic of fidelity: it can conflict with other virtues in particularly painful ways.[105] For example, parents must at times choose between spending resources of time and money on children or on needy, more distant others. This can lead to tensions between developing the virtue of justice and the virtue of fidelity.[106] Fidelity itself may draw us in more than one direction, as Yiu Sing Lúcás Chan points out, as when adults must balance relationships of care for children and for their own elderly parents.[107]

Although wealth does not remove these tensions, it can make it possible for some to perform acts of both virtues. For example, people with the means can both care for children and assume the expenses of vulnerable elders, or pursue justice by donating to charitable causes without stinting their own children's needs. But the risk of letting expenditures substitute for genuine acts of fidelity remains ever present. Perhaps it is helpful to reflect on the distinction between "being" human and "having" goods that John Paul II makes in *Sollicitudo rei socialis*: "To 'have' objects and goods does not in itself perfect the human subject, unless it contributes to the maturing and enrichment of that subject's 'being,' that is to say unless it contributes to the realization of the human vocation as such."[108] It is also important to remember that spending time together is an expression of fidelity par excellence, so much so that James Keenan locates fidelity in the humble act of regularly "showing up."[109]

Despite great differences between his era's perspectives on family and partnership and those of our own, Aquinas seems to concur with the cautions of present-day thinkers like Kavanaugh and Rubio. He discussed the virtue we call fidelity under the name "particular justice."[110] He believed a person loves her spouse, parents, children, and friends out of charity, making these loving relationships an extension of the person's love for God, and God's love for her. And riches, he often said, interfered with charity: "The hope of gaining, or keeping, material wealth, is the poison of charity."[111] Wealth interferes with fidelity when it becomes an end in itself.

Wealth has complex implications for fidelity. Although it can enable acts of fidelity in close relationships, it can also interfere with trust and closeness. The types of relationships we tend through fidelity can conflict with one another or with our obligations to justice. Wealth, which poses the risk of allowing spending to substitute for true acts of fidelity, does not always mitigate these conflicts. To nurture fidelity, wealthy people should attend to spending time and to the universal destination of goods, whose purpose is to nurture human flourishing.

HUMILITY

Humility is the virtue that helps us form an accurate estimation of our own worth and goodness relative to God and to other people. Humble people respect others' worth as well as their own. When wealth becomes an end in itself, it interferes with humility by replacing a properly oriented self-image with a sense of worth focused on what we have, rather than who we are.

Thomas Aquinas notes that wealth places us at risk of the vice of pride, the vice opposed to humility.[112] For him, the wealthy are prone to wrongly identify themselves with God by regarding the gifts they have as issuing from themselves, rather than from their true divine source. So, Aquinas says, "those who wish to live virtuously need to avoid abundance of riches."[113] Augustine made a very similar point before Aquinas, preaching that "riches, more than anything else, engender pride," destroying humility by encouraging the wealthy to rely on their material possessions instead of depending on God.[114]

In a similar vein, a group of US and Canadian psychologists suggested, based on a review of the psychological literature, that "upper-class" people have self-concepts that are less communal and more focused on personal, individual agency. Compared with lower-class people, upper-class people express a heightened sense of personal control over situations—in other words, hyperagency.[115] A self-concept focused on individual agency can threaten the development of humility when our view of our own worth is contingent on what we can do, on our ability to earn money, or on our control over persons and situations.

Growing up in a milieu of privilege does more than mislead children about the genuine worth of others. It can also teach them to rely on externalities, not intrinsic goodness, even in establishing their own self-worth. O'Neill, the therapist who works with wealthy people, writes, "Many wealthy children grow up with a distorted sense of their importance in the world; they view themselves as special and deserving. . . . They tend to rely heavily on externals to tell them and others who they are."[116] O'Neill believes that children in wealthy families are often deprived of opportunities to feel needed because so much is done for them that they are not expected to contribute through even the simplest chores. Such children "are simply 'ornaments' on the family tree, and they know it."[117] Levine observes the same issues among children whose parents earn a comfortable living from professional work. She similarly warns that parenting focused on outward achievements and protecting children from challenge can damage "self-efficacy," the positive awareness of being able to act on one's own behalf.[118] O'Neill adds that inheritors of generational wealth may compare themselves unfavorably with the relative who first earned the family wealth, and feel like failures if they do not surpass that achievement.[119]

Although the experience of comparing oneself with the fortune-winning "family founder" may be unique to extremely wealthy families, the temptation to identify one's goodness solely with economic contribution to the family, and to feel worthless if that ability is taken away, exists at many income levels. Mary Elizabeth Hobgood argues that well-paid members of the managerial and professional working class do not escape the damage that comes from being "thingafied," her term for valuing oneself only in terms of what one's labor is worth.[120] Valuing oneself only as a revenue generator falls short of the rich Christian understanding of personhood.[121] And the Peruvian theologian Ricardo Antoncich, SJ, rightly notes that people who regard themselves as thingafied tend to see others in the same terms, as valuable only for what they possess: "Persons wrapped up in having are closed in upon themselves, unable to communicate *what they are* with other persons. Thereupon they tend to see in others, as well, not what they are, but what they have. And all of this occurs not only at the individual level, but at the level of society itself. A 'having society' becomes a dehumanizing, selfish, consumer society."[122]

As we will see in chapter 6, it is also possible for people struggling to survive to view themselves as valuable only on the basis of their income and to struggle if that source of personal dignity is lost. However, I argue that wealthy people are particularly in danger of developing this thingafied, reductive self-image, precisely because, based on this flawed value system, they might appear to be doing everything right. By inheriting wealth or securing well-paid work, they have succeeded in shaping themselves into the right kind of "thing." They have more to lose in questioning the reduction of personal dignity to one's net worth.[123] Views that value persons solely based on the wealth they have or might earn demonstrate a clear failure to develop humility.

When Jessie O'Neill says that wealth affects how we see ourselves, the insight sounds like a product of modern therapeutic culture, but Aquinas understood this well. He defined covetousness as a spiritual sin, rather than a sin of the flesh, even though the immoderate desire for wealth obviously deals with physical objects. Aquinas knew that what we really desire when we covet is the pleasure of "considering [ourselves] as a possessor of riches."[124] This is a spiritual (or we might say psychological) object, making covetousness a spiritual sin. Aquinas describes a phenomenon that modern marketers know well: we do not desire material goods for the goods in themselves but rather for how we think they will make us feel. It is a particular (however distorted) self-image that we desire when we desire wealth—a desire for which, as Aquinas reminds us, the wealthy are especially at risk.

Wealth interferes with humility by acting on our own self-image and the way we value others. It can tempt us to see ourselves and other people as "things" of only utilitarian value. This is to undervalue ourselves and others relative to true human worth.

SELF-CARE

Self-care is the virtue that encourages us to care for ourselves in body and mind and to look after our own moral development. As with prudence and fidelity, wealth has a complex relationship with the virtue of self-care. We need resources to practice self-care, and the abundant resources of wealth allow us to practice this virtue habitually, although plentiful choice can also enable self-harmful practices.

Jessie O'Neill illustrates how wealth can enable self-destructive behaviors as well as putting healing within reach. For example, wealth can exacerbate addiction by enabling the purchase of the addictive substance. She writes: "Money can cushion, or entirely prevent, the descent into the life-changing, spiritual, and physical 'bottoming out' that many addicts must experience in order to seek treatment. . . . [However,] unlike the poor, should the wealthy decide to seek appropriate help, they have the ability to buy the best available."[125] The hyperagency of wealth can translate into near-total freedom from correction or intervention by others. This isolating effect of wealth may undermine self-care for those engaged in self-harming practices.

The psychologist Suniya Luthar has found so many difficulties with self-care among wealthy young people that she describes them with intentional provocation as "at-risk youth." Luthar's findings bear out O'Neill's commentary: she found that young people in wealthy families use drugs and alcohol, including hard drugs, at higher rates than poor youth. Wealthy youth also experience higher rates of depression and anxiety, likely due to high pressure to achieve from parents.[126]

Drug and alcohol abuse may be extreme examples of situations where wealth can pose both a challenge and a resource to developing self-care. In general, it is self-evident that many ordinary self-caring behaviors are easier to pursue with the freedom and power that come with even modest amounts of wealth. Examples are eating a variety of healthy foods (and even eating regular meals), enjoying exercise and nature, remaining safe from crime and workplace injury, and seeing a doctor when one is sick.

Augustine and Aquinas both condone a certain degree of luxury in wealthy people's self-caring practices. We have already discussed how Aquinas allowed wealthy people to maintain a living standard "in keeping with [their] mode of life."[127] Augustine was less accommodating. In a sermon on almsgiving, he described how the rich claim that they are used to "costly" food and concluded "let the rich follow the custom induced through their debility, but let them regret that they are unable to do otherwise."[128] When Aquinas allows believers to maintain the mode of life to which they are accustomed, it sounds problematic, and in a sense it is—as if it is all right for poor people, but not rich ones, to eat bad food or to live in substandard housing, because, after all, they are used to it. But this is not what Aquinas meant. In his own life, he fought to join a mendicant order instead of one with a more comfortable lifestyle, and he repeatedly taught that voluntary poverty was the holiest path.[129] His allowance for maintaining one's familiar standard of living, like Augustine's, comes couched in a tone of judgment for the pampered rich person who cannot make do with the common lot.[130] The reservations Augustine and Aquinas express should remind us not to make too free with the standard of "custom" or "mode of life" in determining how we use resources to care for our selves. The pursuit of self-care must be balanced with other virtues, including justice.

A complicating factor is that because self-caring practices tend to be more readily available to wealthy people, we can be tempted to pursue self-care not for its own sake but as a marker of status. The sociologist Michèle Lamont observed that wealthy Americans treat self-improvement, with regard to both physical fitness and cultural sophistication, as an important moral value and a status signifier.[131] "The centrality of self-actualization in American upper-middle-class culture," she observes, "could be explained by the very fact that it can be taken to indirectly signal high ranking on the moral, cultural, and socioeconomic status hierarchies."[132] To truly foster virtue, right practices must be oriented toward a good end.

Wealth can provide access to the resources needed to practice and develop the virtue of self-care, although the Christian tradition urges scrutiny of our choices in this regard. Wealthy hyperagency can also interfere with self-care by enabling self-destructive practices. Wealth interferes with moral self-care when it functions as moral luck to disrupt the pursuit of virtue.

TEMPERANCE

Temperance is the virtue that helps us moderate our use of goods in ways consistent with our flourishing. A temperate person has reasonable desires, not immoderate desires that she must actively and painfully restrain. The most basic, commonsense understanding of this virtue makes clear how wealth can interfere with its pursuit. Wealth permits abundant choice, enabling us to consume intemperately in order to satisfy immoderate desires fostered by advertising and constant innovation. Finally, wealth is readily convertible to power. Virtue ethicists remind us that the desire for power is one we ought to moderate through temperance, and that power is one of the resources wealth can encourage us to use intemperately.[133]

Above, I explained how wealth bestows hyperagency, abundant power, freedom, and choice beyond that experienced by those struggling to survive. Wealth does this even when we understand it in the sense of having more than we need. Any margin of discretionary income represents power to control space, time, and other persons in ways denied to those struggling to survive. The hyperagency conveyed by wealth clearly opposes the development of temperance. Knowing that one can control a situation through purchasing power hardly encourages us to resist consuming goods, or even to develop more temperate desires for them.

Hyperagency might sound like a good thing to someone who has struggled with feeling powerless, as many of us do from time to time. However, abundant power does not translate into happiness. O'Neill writes: "Sometimes the feelings of power and control that come with having money are so strong that they overwhelm those who earn it or inherit it. . . . An endless continuum of choices breeds depression; the wealthy may perceive their lives as out of control."[134] O'Neill points out that the experience of constantly having one's desires met can lead to unreasonable expectations of control and extreme frustration when they are not met.[135] She writes, "The characteristics that most hinder and interfere with recovery from affluenza are the inability to delay gratification and tolerate frustration. The destructiveness of these two traits cannot be over-emphasized."[136] Nor is this limited to the extremely wealthy. The authors of *Affluenza* (2001/2014) argue that in contemporary global capitalism, anyone with discretionary income encounters endless choices, which do not increase happiness, as promised, but tend to breed dissatisfaction and overspending. The ability to delay gratification and accept limited control over situations is crucial for temperance and for the virtuous life more broadly.

The economic historian Avner Offer finds that our ability to exercise self-control bears a complex relationship to affluence. In general, poverty erodes self-control: it makes certain choices more difficult, placing a heavy load on our decision-making capacity.[137] Thus, in some cases, wealth protects our ability to make meaningful decisions, because small, everyday financial decisions—whether to buy lunch or pay for parking—are less demanding.[138] Wealthy people may find it easier to make choices that delay gratification because they expect greater rewards. For example, they might delay childbearing until later in life because a college degree is at stake.[139]

However, Offer found that as overall affluence increases in a society, the ability to exercise self-control does not increase accordingly. This is because a more affluent society offers consumers more choices. Living with many choices constantly available erodes self-control for both the rich and poor, even as increased consumption does not translate into greater happiness. Novelty encourages more purchasing, but harms the development of temperance: "Under affluence, novelty tends to produce a bias toward short-term rewards, toward individualism, hedonism, narcissism, and disorientation."[140] In virtue terms, increased societal wealth erodes the overall practice of temperance.[141] This is another reason why wealth's impact on virtue matters even beyond those who are wealthy. Increased wealth in a society affects everyone who is exposed to the greater array of tempting consumer choices.

Wealthy persons' hyperagency does not affect only their own flourishing. It has ramifications as well for the well-being of others in the community, and for environmental sustainability. The economist Robert H. Frank describes the "spending cascade" that characterizes the life of many middle-class Americans, who must spend more than earlier generations to achieve a similar quality of life. It happens when "top earners initiate a process that leads to increased expenditures down the line, even among those whose incomes have not yet risen," and increasing inequality tends to encourage this process.[142] Keeping up appearances as living standards change is one reason for this, but not the only one. Safety is another—for example, because many cars today are larger than they once were, a midsized car does not provide the same level of protection, in the case of an accident, that it once did. So when wealthy people purchase hyper-safe, extra-heavy family vehicles, they make the roads less safe for everybody else (and increase the toll on the natural environment through the consumption of fuel and other resources). Wealthy hyperagency is not only a problem of developing temperance for wealthy people; it threatens the common good as well. Nor is this a recent observation. Saint Basil, in the fourth century CE, criticized how the hyperagency of the wealthy in his own time allowed them to hoard food needed by others and to enslave, imprison, and threaten the lives of those who criticized their unjust practices.[143]

In Christian thought, it has always been the case that temperance is not merely about living simply but also about reducing one's overall control of wealth. To "live simply" while hoarding immense wealth is to miss the point.[144] The American theologian John A. Ryan (1869–1945) noted how the market economy encourages us to constantly develop new desires and to imagine that satisfying them will make us happy. We become reliant on new conveniences and lose our "power to do without." As Christine Firer Hinze explains, temperance for Ryan was about training one's desires for goods in ways that align our desires with the pursuit of heaven, resisting the distorted desire promoted by market economies. It was no less important that moderate use of goods allows us to distribute more resources to others who need them.[145]

It is far from the case that only extreme wealth can interfere with one's development of temperance. As David Cloutier points out in his argument for a return to a Christian critique of luxury, a surplus of $10 a week can either be spent on a few lattes—small "luxuries"—or used to upgrade one's customary purchases to those produced in conditions of more justice for workers.[146] As Cloutier makes clear, anyone who controls this amount of discretionary spending exercises an incremental amount of power over workers who produce the goods they buy. People who are wealthy, even in this limited but important sense, can choose to exercise this hyperagency in a temperate fashion, or fail to do so.

To Cloutier's concern about the potential of our small expenditures to do more good elsewhere, Aquinas would add that allowing oneself even small luxuries tends to increase our taste for those pleasures. Possessing goods causes us to "despise" the goods we have and pushes us to seek other goods to satisfy our disordered desires.[147] If the luxury is one that increases our status in the eyes of others—Aquinas's example is fancy attire—the indulgence can also encourage us to develop the vice of pride.[148] These potential pitfalls of possessing goods no doubt contribute to Aquinas's view that simply possessing wealth increases the risk of sin. Citing Augustine, he wrote, "The possession of worldly things draws a man's mind to the love of them. . . . According to [1 Timothy 6:9], 'They that will become rich, fall into temptation and into the snare of the devil.' This attachment is put away by those who embrace voluntary poverty, but it gathers strength in those who have wealth."[149] Aquinas concludes that exercising temperance in our use of goods frees up resources we can use in others' service, and it helps protect us from developing vice.

Wealth threatens the development of temperance by encouraging us to obey the dictates of consumer culture, and thus developing the habit of spending in pursuit of novelty or luxury rather than working to moderate our desires. Hyperagency—the power, freedom, and choice bestowed by wealth—can shape us into persons who wield power immoderately rather than temperately. Temperance is far from a concern only for personal morality, because it has to do with the use of resources. Our own use of resources always affects other persons who work to produce them, or who may have need of our surplus.

FORTITUDE

Wealth interferes with the development of fortitude, the virtue that helps us persevere and act bravely in pursuit of the good. We have already discussed how wealth can interfere with the ability to delay gratification, an aspect of temperance but also one needed for perseverance. Wealth bestows hyperagency, which can encourage us to become too easily frustrated when things do not come easily. It can also hinder commitment to goals by making it always possible for us to seek more appealing options.

Members of Resource Generation, an activist group for young people with wealth, warn that wealthy people who seek to join social movements can exhibit a negative behavior they call "the waffle effect," when a wealthy person used to having innumerable choices resists committing to a movement, cause, or responsibility.[150] This is a failure to develop fortitude in the sense of perseverance and commitment. Another threat to fortitude comes when a person evades the discomfort that comes when another tries to teach them something that may be challenging. Of course, nobody likes to feel uncomfortable, but wealthy people may be more likely to assume that they can always expect to feel comfortable.[151] Levine concurs, observing that many well-off parents strive to shield their children from even temporary discomfort or challenge, ironically leaving the young people with a diminished sense of their own ability to overcome obstacles.[152]

Wealth's deterrent effect on fortitude can begin early in life. The psychiatrist Robert Coles wrote sensitive, detailed profiles of American children from various walks of life beginning in the 1960s. In a book on privileged children, he reflected on wealth's power to insulate children from developing fortitude, in the sense of daring or bravery: "Well-to-do parents have more than occasionally tried to figure out why their children lack all ambition and even spirit. In the ghetto children learn to negotiate their ways through dark, broken-down buildings and incredibly dangerous streets. And in our well-to-do suburban communities parents worry because their children seem confused or bored or unwilling to take on or negotiate anything."[153]

Coles first wrote those words in 1971. Today, almost fifty years later, educators are still raising concerns about parents lavishing such abundant time and attention on their children that it interferes with young ones' healthy development of independence.[154] The sociologist Schervish, in his interviews of extremely wealthy parents, found that "many children of privilege take either too many risks, because they know the consequences of failure are minimal, or too few, because they feel assured in their financial well-being."[155] Both excessive risk-taking and avoidance of reasonable risk indicate failures of the virtue of fortitude.

For Aquinas, fear could be sinful when we fear things out of their proper order—for example, when we fear losing wealth when we should be worried about the good of our souls.[156] He wrote, "Riches engender many anxieties in their possessors. Hence our Lord speaks of them as 'thorns' which, by their care, choke the Word of God in the hearts of the hearers."[157] The fear of losing the wealth we have accumulated is a false fear not directed to our true end, and in responding to this fear we lose the opportunity to develop fortitude by facing well-ordered fears with bravery.

Fortitude is often discussed as a virtue developed through striving for justice, an opportunity that wealthy people may miss if they self-segregate and avoid solidarity. Yiu Sing Lúcás Chan notes that biblical exemplars of fortitude were persecuted because of their hunger and thirst for righteousness for the poor.[158] In a contemporary context, Barbara Hilkert Andolsen describes fortitude as the virtue necessary for white people to confront the sin of systemic racism. She finds that this virtue has been historically lacking in white people and white institutions (including the US Catholic Church) who did not see how racism was also "their problem." Andolsen notes that encounter with the true magnitude of racism often causes guilt in white people, but insists that "it is morally irresponsible to remain paralyzed by the guilt feelings; . . . a prolonged guilty paralysis is another way to ignore racism."[159] I think that the same can be said of confronting wealth and its effects on virtue, and Andolsen's words are applicable to the necessity of fortitude in working for greater economic justice. Fortitude, in the sense of courage, is necessary to emerge from guilty paralysis; and fortitude, in the sense of perseverance, is necessary to remain committed to pressing forward for the sake of righteousness.

Wealth interferes with fortitude when it allows us the freedom to remain aloof from committing to hard work, difficult challenges, and personal transformation. We miss the opportunity to develop true fortitude when we fear what will happen to our wealth instead of what will happen to our souls. By making things easy, wealth insulates us from opportunities to develop fortitude under its aspect of perseverance.

CONCLUSION

When presented with the idea that wealth can harm virtue, many people's first reaction is to assume that there must be a "safe" income level where one is neither in desperate poverty nor wealthy enough to have virtue damaged. David Cloutier has referred to this fallacy as the "middle-class exemption," and I agree that it is too easy a way out.[160] Wealth can function as moral luck to impede virtue through shaping practices, communities, and self-regard even at relatively modest levels of wealth, such as the tens of thousands of dollars in discretionary income that a plurality of US families spend each year. Hyperagency and wealth as an end interfere with virtue pursuit for people with more than they need, even if the "more" is not infinite.

It is worth restating that discussing the virtue effects of wealth and poverty does not deny that people in both groups retain moral freedom. Rather, it simply attempts to give an accurate picture of the environment where this freedom is exercised. If we envision the moral life as a journey, we might say that the poor person travels a rocky, uphill path, one that presents obstacles even as it helps the traveler grow strong. The wealthy person, conversely, walks a leisurely path lined with deceptively appealing diversions. Walls block her view of those in need, mirrors encourage her to focus on herself, and comfortable seating tempts her to cease the effort to continue at all. In both cases, whether the traveler completes her journey is not primarily determined by the character of the path. It requires her own moral effort and God's assistance.

The Christian tradition understands human moral freedom as conditioned by many factors, including life circumstances, though the emphasis on personal freedom is a relatively contemporary shift. Jean Porter insists that "we must acknowledge that on Aquinas's view, human freedom is limited and conditioned by the agent's beliefs and emotional dispositions."[161] For Aquinas, Porter continues, human freedom is limited by God's predestination. The initial movement of the human will toward God is always already initiated by God through grace.[162] Porter argues that though this doctrine appears "troubling, even repugnant" when we envision God arbitrarily predestining some and not other humans to salvation, it ought to inspire "humility and trust" when we consider our own radical dependence on God amid human motivations that can remain opaque even to ourselves.[163] It is in this vein that I hope to urge Christians to consider how wealth functions as moral luck with regard to virtue: not to inspire moral paralysis in those of us who possess wealth, but to urge humility, conversion, and persistence.

Discussing the many pitfalls to a virtuous life of wealth is not meant to make people give up. If wealth makes it hard to attain virtue, we could easily say that life makes it hard to attain virtue—think of the wide range of mortal sins that Aquinas lists in the *Summa*. Wealth is one type of moral luck that can affect persons' pursuit of virtue, one type among many. But glossing over the particular dangers and pitfalls of particular lives will not help anyone pursue virtue. Examining them in detail just might.

NOTES

1. The psychologist, Dick Miller, later said he regretted using the term "affluenza," because he believes the phenomenon of wealth affecting young people's choices for the worse is extremely common. Quoted by Mooney, "Worst Parents Ever."
2. Wealthy people also control space quite literally when they use their financial resources to build or change existing spaces. Schervish, "Introduction," 4–5.
3. Schervish, "Hyperagency," 10.
4. Schervish, 12.
5. Schervish, 9.
6. E.g., Ehrenreich, *Nickel and Dimed*, 83–84; and Land, *Maid*, 71–72.
7. The omnipresence of the $15 manicure is a striking example of how a small amount of discretionary income enables one to command a fellow worker in the performance of a skilled and physically intimate service. However, the growth of the nail industry in the

United States is also a story of the diligence and creativity of Black and immigrant entrepreneurs. See Sharma et al., "Nail Files"; and Adele Free Pham, *Nailed It*.

8. Constitutive power takes place when coercions and enticements succeed in shaping the
   constitution or personal makeup of those influenced. Finn, *Consumer Ethics*, 88–89.

9. Finn, 140. As Finn suggests, someone making minimum wage in Chicago, a high-cost-
   of-living city, would likely be struggling to survive and would qualify as poor by my
   definition.

10. E.g., in 2020, the nonprofit evaluator Givewell estimated that a treated mosquito net to
    prevent malaria cost about $5; deworming drugs, including the cost to administer them,
    cost less than $1. Both interventions can be lifesaving; see Givewell.

11. Camosy, *Peter Singer*, 143–45.

12. Piketty, *Capital*, 62.

13. See, e.g., Camosy, *Peter Singer*, chap. 4; Rubio, *Family Ethics*, chap. 7; and Hartman, *Chris-
    tian Consumer*.

14. Land, *Maid*, 130–31.

15. "Disposable income" is a common misnomer for discretionary income, but they are not
    the same thing. Economists define disposable income as the income left over after taxes,
    from which households pay for all their basic necessities—so reported amounts of dis-
    posable income always outstrip discretionary income.

16. Another caveat: Virtue is a quality of a person, but these data are calculated by house-
    hold. The fact that a household has X to spend does not mean any given member of
    the household has the same power. I occasionally also use "families" synonymously with
    "households," though the BLS definition of "consumer unit" is broader than either and
    can include, e.g., a single person living in a group facility.

17. The fourth income decile has an average of $1,613 left over after paying for basic needs.
    Comparing this with the income deficit of the third decile, I think it is a reasonable guess
    that fully a third of US households, or 33.34 percent, have negative discretionary income.

18. Bureau of Labor Statistics, "Table 1110"; also helpful was Bureau of Labor Statistics,
    "Consumer Expenditures." The figures are available upon request.

19. With this relatively low average discretionary income, it is probable that some house-
    holds in this decile still go into the red to pay for basic needs. It is also possible that
    expenditures needed for survival (notably, education) are not covered under the group of
    basic needs expenses I summarize here, and that many families whose income falls into
    this decile are among those struggling to survive.

20. See, e.g., Bragg, *All Over*, 121.

21. Finn, *Consumer Ethics*, 78.

22. Schervish, Coutsoukis, and Lewis, *Gospels*, 267.

23. See also Ward, "Wealthy Hyperagency," 77–90.

24. Hinze, *Comprehending Power*, 274.

25. Mullainathan and Shafir, *Scarcity*, 161.

26. Aquinas describes long-range planning, or "foresight," as one of the integral parts of pru-
    dence in *Summa Theologica* (hereafter *ST*), II-II 48.1.

27. Aquinas, *ST*, II-II 48.1.

28. Johnson, *American Dream*, 14.

29. Johnson, 118.

30. Johnson, 17. Johnson notes that at this portion of the interview, wealthy people often
    raised their voices and leaned in toward the tape recorder to emphasize their point—"they

spoke with fervor and conviction when crediting themselves with their own success" (p. 134).

31. Johnson, 113.

32. Johnson, 147; Schervish, "Introduction," 11. Schervish describes the life stories told by wealthy people similarly, as a "dialectic of fortune and virtue" that allows wealthy people to emphasize their own agency in their lives while acknowledging the advantages they had inherited.

33. Hobgood, *Dismantling Privilege*, 82.

34. As David Cloutier points out, Smith disapproved of this tendency; Cloutier, *Vice*, 73; I myself read Smith's morals as ultimately supporting the status quo, including such judgments. Ward, "Mere Poverty."

35. Coates, "Case for Reparations."

36. Mitchell, "Silver Chamber Pots," 92–94.

37. Míguez Bonino, "Doing Theology," 370–71.

38. Sobrino, "Awakening," 364–70.

39. Pope Francis, "Laudato si'," para. 90.

40. De Graaf, Wann, and Naylor, *Affluenza*, 99.

41. De Graaf, Wann, and Naylor.

42. Wheeler, *Wealth as Peril*, chap. 8.

43. See, e.g., Augustine, *Letters Vol. II*, sermon 104.

44. Aquinas, *ST*, I-II, 1.

45. True human happiness for Thomas is beholding God in God's essence. We can work toward true happiness in this life but only achieve it after death. Aquinas, I-II, 3.8.

46. Aquinas, *ST*, II-II, 118.3.

47. For materialist vs. spiritualized views of wealth in Christian thought, see Ward, "Wealth."

48. Augustine's views are similar; see Ward, "Porters to Heaven."

49. Aquinas, "Liber Contra Impugnantes Dei."

50. Aquinas, *ST*, II-II, 186, article 3, reply to ad. 4.

51. Aquinas, 118.8.

52. O'Neill, *Golden Ghetto*, 45.

53. Anderson; see also Le Quéré et al., "Towards a Culture of Low-Carbon Research."

54. See, e.g., Tirado, *Hand to Mouth*, chap. 4; and Guendelsberger, *On the Clock*, 277–78. I am basing this contention on Guendelsberger's testimony that each of her coworkers had experienced food throwing and other abuse by customers. There can only be so many O'Neill-style wealthy inheritors in a given city, and it beggars belief that they would all frequent the same McDonald's.

55. Piff et al., "Higher Social Class." In these studies, class takes into account both raw income and positionality with respect to others.

56. Piff et al., 4088.

57. Piff et al., 4089.

58. Aquinas, *ST*, II-II, 118.3. Thomas defines covetousness in two senses, one opposed to justice (immoderate getting and keeping) and one opposed to liberality (immoderate interior attachment to wealth). See the discussion of the virtue of prudence in this chapter.

59. Aquinas, II-II, 118.1.

60. Aquinas, II-II, 32.6.

61. Aquinas, II-II, 117.1; 32.5.

62. Stern, "Why the Rich Don't Give"; Gipple and Gose, "America's Generosity Divide."

63. Koenig, "Mismatch."
64. However, see chapter 7 below for a cautionary note: under certain circumstances, giving to charity can reinforce rather than combat wealthy hyperagency; chapter 7 discusses how to avoid this.
65. See chapter 2.
66. Wealth does, in fact, impart freedom, even if the wealthy person does not characterize it as such. The sociologist Michèle Lamont found that wealthy French people are more likely to speak of their wealth in ambiguous terms, while Americans much more uniformly characterize wealth as positive and associate it explicitly with providing freedom. Lamont, *Money*, 69.
67. Stellar et al., "Class and Compassion."
68. Kraus, Piff, and Keltner, "Social Class," 248–49.
69. O'Neill, *Golden Ghetto*, 140.
70. De Graaf, Wann, and Naylor, *Affluenza*, 57.
71. Reardon and Bischoff, "Income Inequality."
72. Kye, "Persistence."
73. National Law Center on Homelessness and Poverty, "No Safe Place."
74. Navarro, "'Poor Door.'"
75. Rieger, *No Rising Tide*, 20.
76. Hobgood, *Dismantling Privilege*, 81.
77. Hobgood, 102–3.
78. Hobgood, 105.
79. Peters, "Conflict," 72–73.
80. Wilcox and Wang, "Marriage Divide." In this study, middle- and upper-class people are defined as those with a college degree and/or income at the 50th percentile and above; poor families have incomes lower than the 20th percentile; and working class is defined as between the 20th and 50th percentiles. All incomes were adjusted for family size.
81. Putnam, *Our Kids*, 63. Putnam defines poorer parents as those with only a high school education.
82. Putnam, 68–69.
83. Edin and Kefalas, *Promises*; Edin and Nelson, *Doing the Best*.
84. Doepke and Zilibotti, *Love*, 146; Putnam, *Our Kids*.
85. Doepke and Zilibotti, *Love*, 154; Putnam, *Our Kids*, chap. 6.
86. Wilcox and Wang, "Marriage Divide," 9.
87. The psychologist Madeline Levine describes this as a common situation in her clinical practice; Levine, *Price*, 191.
88. Doepke and Zilibotti, *Love*.
89. Putnam, *Our Kids*, 126.
90. Putnam, 127. Putnam, 44–45, uses education as a reliable proxy for class because it can be more reliably tracked throughout a variety of studies; citing Altintas, "Widening Education Gap."
91. Altintas, "Widening Education Gap."
92. Altintas.
93. O'Neill, *Golden Ghetto*, 97.
94. Greenwood et al., *Marry Your Like*.
95. Doepke and Zilibotti, *Love*, 146.

96. Luthar and Becker, "Privileged but Pressured?" 1593; Luthar, "Culture"; Luthar and Latendresse, "Children"; Luthar, "Problem."

97. O'Neill, *Golden Ghetto*, 80.

98. Luthar and Latendresse, "Children," 50.

99. Levine, *Price*, 30.

100. Levine, 29.

101. Levine, 170–71.

102. Kavanaugh, *Following Christ*, chap. 1.

103. Rubio, *Family Ethics*, 191.

104. Pope Francis, "Laudato si'," 162.

105. See chapter 2 for a discussion of the potential for virtues to conflict.

106. For conflict between these two virtues, see Keenan, "Proposing." Keenan highlights the fact that justice and fidelity can make completing claims on persons, while I call attention to the ways fidelity and justice are similar—both involve the giving of what is due, either to all persons (justice) or to particular persons (fidelity). For Aquinas, the close relationships with those we love are governed by what he calls particular justice. He says that different things are due to different people based on their degree of closeness to us. Aquinas, *ST*, II-II, 58.7.

107. Chan, *Ten Commandments*, 77.

108. John Paul II, "Sollicitudo rei socialis."

109. Keenan, *Virtues*, 52–53.

110. Aquinas, *ST*, II-II, 58.7.

111. Aquinas, "Liber de Perfectione," chap. 6.

112. Aquinas, *ST*, II-II, 162.3.

113. Aquinas, III, 40.3.

114. Augustine, *Commentary*, sermon 11, "On the Beatitudes."

115. Kraus et al., "Social Class." These researchers examine class through different lenses, including self-reported real income and positionality relative to others, created in a laboratory exercise.

116. O'Neill, *Golden Ghetto*, 173.

117. O'Neill, 174.

118. Levine, *Price*, 74–75.

119. O'Neill, *Golden Ghetto*, 46; see also Martin, *Primates*, 187–92.

120. Hobgood, *Dismantling Privilege*, 99–100.

121. Catholic social thought teaches that the purpose of work is the flourishing of the human person who works, in contrast with the capitalist economic assumption that a person's purpose is to work and to produce. See, e.g., John Paul II, "Laborem exercens," para. 6.

122. Antoncich, "Sollicitudo rei socialis," 215–16.

123. Levine, *Price*, 171.

124. Aquinas, *ST*, II-II, 118.6.

125. O'Neill, *Golden Ghetto*, 53.

126. Luthar, "Culture"; Luthar and Latendresse, "Children," 49–53. In a reminder of the importance of practicing fidelity in the sense of "showing up," having at least one family dinner a week was a protective factor for wealthy and poor children alike, associated with lower rates of depression and anxiety and with higher grades in school.

127. Aquinas, *ST*, II-II, 118.1.

128. Augustine, *Commentary*, 285.

129. Weisheipl, *Friar Thomas*. See Aquinas, "Liber de Perfectione"; Aquinas, "Liber Contra Impugnantes," chap. 5; and Aquinas, *ST*, II-II, 186, article 3.

130. See Aquinas, *ST*, II-II, 32, article 10, reply to obj. 4.

131. Lamont, *Money*, 99–100.

132. Lamont, 100.

133. The philosophers Michael Walzer and Michael Sandel have reflected, in separate works, on wealth's near-universal influence. Both recommend that society should limit the spheres of life in which wealth can operate, in order to limit the reach of wealth's power and help to level the playing field between poor and wealthy people. Walzer, *Spheres*; and Sandel, *What Money Can't Buy*.

134. O'Neill, *Golden Ghetto*, 152.

135. O'Neill, 136–37.

136. O'Neill, 70.

137. See chapter 6.

138. Offer, *Challenge*, 74.

139. Offer, chap. 3.

140. Offer, 74.

141. Offer somewhat collapses the virtues of prudence and temperance as classically understood, describing "prudence" as both appointing ends in service of future goals and as moderating one's use of goods in the service of future goals. The first habit is traditionally associated with prudence and the second with temperance.

142. Frank, "How the Middle Class Is Injured," 140–41.

143. Siepierski, "Poverty," 323.

144. See, e.g., Pieris, *God's Reign*, 60, in which the author asserts that voluntary poverty must be oriented to God's liberation.

145. Hinze, "What Is Enough?"

146. Cloutier, "Problem," 16.

147. Aquinas, *ST*, I-II, 1, reply to obj. 3.

148. Aquinas, "Liber Contra Impugnantes," chap. 1, ad. 7.

149. Aquinas, *ST*, II-II, 183.3.

150. Pittelman and Resource Generation, *Classified*, 81.

151. Pittelman and Resource Generation, 85.

152. Levine, *Price*, 77.

153. Coles, *Children*, 462.

154. Lythcott-Haims, "Kids."

155. Wood, "Secret Fears."

156. Aquinas, *ST*, II-II, 125.3.

157. Aquinas, "Liber Contra Impugnantes," chap. 5.

158. Chan, "Ten Commandments," 189–191.

159. Andolsen, "Grace," 79.

160. Cloutier, *Vice*, 5–6. I also appreciate Alberto de Mingo Kaminouchi's commentary on spiritualizing biblical warnings about wealth: "This has all the earmarks of a subterfuge that would exempt someone from the essential commitments of the Gospel." Mingo Kaminouchi, *Introduction*.

161. Porter, "Recent Studies," 210.

162. Aquinas, *ST*, I-II, 109.6.

163. Porter, "Recent Studies," 213–14.

CHAPTER 6

POVERTY, VIRTUE, AND
THE IMPACT OF SCARCITY

This chapter examines the impact of poverty on the pursuit of the virtues described in chapter 2. Poverty functions as moral luck, impeding the pursuit of virtue, when stigma becomes internalized, harming self-regard. A lack of resources can inhibit access to virtuous practices, and poverty shapes communities in ways that can promote both virtue and vice. The full picture of poverty's work as moral luck is complex.

Some might worry that it is damaging or unfair to poor people even to ask whether poverty harms the pursuit of virtue. To begin, I show why it is vital to ask this question, and that it can be done with care and respect. Poor people reflecting on their own experience assert that poverty burdens their virtue, and social science helps drive home the point. I discuss the virtues in turn to demonstrate this. Not only does poverty impede the pursuit of virtue, but to use Lisa Tessman's term, it also burdens virtue for the poor, sometimes making virtue costly for the virtuous person's flourishing. Poverty burdens virtue especially when two virtues conflict.

POVERTY CAN IMPEDE THE PURSUIT
OF VIRTUE: A HARMFUL CLAIM?

Contemporary Christian thought on economic life presumes that poverty is not inevitable, but results from the greed of the wealthy. Human choice creates poverty and, given the will, could eliminate it.[1] In contrast to this view, a widespread belief that poverty is the poor person's fault has gained particular prominence in the United States, where belief in meritocracy reigns. The historian Stephen Pimpare has shown that Americans throughout history have tried to blame poverty on poor people, on their individual faults or a so-called "culture of poverty."[2] It might seem that a focus on virtue could appear to stigmatize poor persons as vicious, contributing to the tendency to blame those living in poverty for their own suffering.[3] Perhaps talking about the impact of virtue on poverty is no more than "kicking people when they're down."

Caution is wise, because it is true that well-intended attempts to describe the experience of poverty can be misused to stigmatize people living in it. For example, as an official in the US Department of Labor, Daniel Patrick Moynihan popularized the idea of a "culture of poverty" to describe how poor people in the United States pursued different sets of priorities than those who were better off. The well-known "Moynihan Report" aimed to advocate for increased social assistance to those living in poverty. Unfortunately, its "culture of poverty" notion was widely misinterpreted, and subsequently was consciously adopted to blame poor people, particularly poor Black people, for their own plight.[4] Anyone who wishes to avoid adding another negative association to the common stereotypes of people living in poverty had better proceed with great humility when discussing the moral formation of people living in poverty.

Yet if it is true, as I contend, that poverty makes it harder for persons to pursue virtue, refusing to talk about it is, once again, to treat poor people as nonpersons. Such a refusal says that a poor person's ability to pursue virtue does not matter. It amounts to exhorting poor people to "pull themselves up by their bootstraps," morally speaking, without asking whether they are realistically able to pursue virtue and what, if anything, wealthy people can do to help. The psychiatrist Robert Coles, who spent decades investigating the lives of poor children, notes how easy it can be for well-off people to absolve themselves of serious thought about the suffering of poor people by rationalizing that the poor develop unusual virtue thanks to their suffering. The antidote to this is for wealthy people to confront the realities of the lives of those living in poverty and the concrete, specific ways in which their dignity is denied.[5]

The Salvadoran liberation theologian Jon Sobrino incisively describes this attitude of genteel disregard toward poor people's lived reality:

> It is really an affront to continue to say to the many millions of the poor and the victimized that they are human beings "like everyone else," or to continue to exhort them to "hold out" because someday they will be like everyone else, complete with democracy and television sets. . . . We must realize that there are fundamental differences in the way people live. There are those who take life for granted and those who take anything but life for granted. To be a human being

today has much to do, for instance, with whether one has food to eat. . . . Whether one has dignity, self-respect and rights depends to a great degree on an accident of birth; it helps considerably to have been born in the United States or Germany rather than in El Salvador or Pakistan.[6]

"I am not poor," Sobrino owns, "but I try to reflect the voice of the poor."[7] When he notes that many poor people lack the virtue of self-respect, it is not because he blames them for the failure to develop it. Rather, he acknowledges that things as basic as access to food affect persons' pursuit of virtue, just as they affect their ability to live in a way befitting their God-given human dignity.

Several commitments of liberation theology endorse inquiry into poverty's impact on persons' ability to pursue virtue. First, liberation theology constantly insists that poor people must be "stewards of their own destiny," able to advocate for themselves in society.[8] Denied the chance to pursue virtue, they must struggle to steward their own physical and social well-being, let alone their moral destiny. Second, because theologians of liberation often work in close contact with poor people, they are among the first to caution against romanticizing poor people or poverty. Even as the poor provide the guiding light to liberation theology, which begins with acknowledgment of and reflection on their experience, liberation theologians frequently caution against divinizing the poor or regarding them as perfect. For example, Sobrino, speaking of the privileged place of the poor in liberation epistemology, notes that "though they are the way to learn what is true, what is good, what is bad, they can also make mistakes."[9] Speaking for themselves, poor people agree.[10] Yes, it furnishes a different context for the moral life than wealth, but poverty does not make one a saint.

The bishops of Latin America and the Caribbean, in the concluding document of their Aparecida Conference, agree with Sobrino's caution against romanticizing the virtue of poor people and explicitly acknowledge how poverty and wealth have a direct impact on the moral life: "The poor are far from being holy; they are sinners as much as the rich. The fact that they are forced to be poor does not automatically make them holy. . . . In fact they may sin precisely because of their poverty, just as the rich may sin because of their riches."[11] The framers of Aparecida agree that the lived experience of wealth or poverty affects the moral life in concrete, observable ways.

Liberation theologians from various contexts take for granted that the deprivations of poverty can shape persons morally, psychologically, and spiritually. Summarizing the insights of his fellow Latin American liberation theologians in 2009, Gustavo Gutiérrez writes: "Our perception of poverty is now deeper and more complex, and no longer limited to its economic dimension (as important as this may be.) Instead, we now understand that being poor means being rendered socially insignificant."[12]

Minjung liberation theology, from Korea, is a preeminent example of a movement focusing on the moral and psychological impacts of such social insignificance. Minjung refers to all persons who are oppressed or marginalized, such as poor, colonized peoples, and the "minjung of the minjung," women. A key topic in minjung theology is *han*. The Indian intercultural theologian Michael Amaladoss defines this nearly untranslatable concept as "the feeling of resentment, depression, repressed anger, helplessness, just indignation, etc., which is combined with the desire for a better future."[13] *Han*, as a key category for minjung liberation theology, implicitly acknowledges how poverty affects the pursuit of virtues like self-respect and hope.

Although liberation theologies date from the late twentieth century, the idea that wealth and poverty can impact virtue pursuit is nothing new in Christian ethics. We have already seen that Thomas Aquinas gives an account of moral luck.[14] He warns that both wealth and poverty pose "occasions of sin," that is, moments when we might be tempted to sin, and interfere with the pursuit of the virtuous life:

> Those who wish to live virtuously need to avoid abundance of riches and beggary, in as far as these are occasions of sin: since abundance of riches is an occasion for being proud; and beggary is an occasion of thieving and lying, or even of perjury. . . . Yet neither is every kind of beggary an occasion of theft and perjury, . . . but only that which is involuntary, in order to avoid which, a man is guilty of theft and perjury.[15]

Aquinas is careful to point out that even involuntary poverty does not inevitably lead to sins like theft and perjury, but that some involuntarily poor people are tempted to sin to alleviate their need. Neither wealth nor poverty removes moral agency, but both pose occasions of sin, inviting vigilance. To the obvious rejoinder that some wealthy people also engage in the sins of theft and perjury Aquinas would no doubt agree, but he believed that wealth per se did not pose a temptation to commit these types of sins. Wealth and poverty both threaten virtue, although in different ways. This is not a new idea in the Christian tradition, but one with deep historical roots.

A final objection might be that those concerned about the well-being of the poor should focus on helping them meet their basic material needs and leave virtue alone. To this I reply that helping poor people get basic economic security is a laudable goal, but it is not enough. It is worse than not enough—it is patronizing—to say that poor people do not need to be concerned about their virtues, or that any failings of virtue can be explained away by their poverty. Because to have virtue is to flourish, a lack of virtue, or a lack of opportunity to develop it, harms the person profoundly.[16] Can we possibly be content to say that it does not matter if a poor person develops virtue, because her failure to do so could be blamed on poverty? No, this is to display the type of callous thoughtlessness lampooned in the Letter of James, like saying to one with no food or clothing "Go in peace, keep warm and eat well" (James 2:16). Christians and all others who are concerned about human flourishing want everyone on earth to have the opportunity to develop to their full potential, and that includes pursuing virtue.[17]

The question is not simply whether poor people can pursue virtue. Virtuous people in, or formerly in, poverty show it with their lives. This does not change the fact that poverty presents serious challenges for the pursuit of virtue, and that this is another one of the many burdens poverty places on persons.[18] A particular way poverty threatens the development of virtue is when material scarcity forces tough choices between two or more genuine human goods.

Although Thomas Aquinas did not envision that different virtues could make competing claims on a moral agent, many contemporary virtue theorists agree with James Keenan that the vicissitudes of human life introduce conflict into our virtue pursuit.[19] Each of us encounters situations where two or more virtues cannot be pursued at the same time.[20] Everyone faces conflicts between virtues, but scarcity often forces those living in poverty to make difficult choices between good ends while wealth enables others to pursue multiple goods simultaneously. For example, poverty can force tough choices between caring for self and family, or between caring for self or family and pursuing justice for others. These tough choices cause lasting harm.[21]

The philosopher Lisa Tessman calls moral qualities developed under conditions of oppression or scarcity "burdened virtues."[22] Burdened virtues are formed under systemic oppression when pursuing virtue either demands heroic effort, or comes at significant cost to the moral agent's well-being. For example, bravery in defense of one's rights, typically considered a virtue, may become a burdened virtue if the broader society responds to such bravery with heightened oppression of the agent and her community. Virtues that must be pursued in conflict with other virtues are particularly likely to become burdened, exacting a cost on the person who pursues them. Because poverty increases the likelihood that virtues will conflict, it poses a particular risk of burdened virtue that harms moral selves. To be sure, in other cases poverty can encourage the development of certain virtues, as I show below. To truly understand poverty's impact on virtue, we must attend to its occasions of moral burden as well as the opportunities it affords for developing virtue.

Taking up the virtues one by one, we now examine the unique and particular ways poverty burdens their pursuit and may place them in conflict. Social scientists and liberation theologians speak about the poor, and more credibly still, currently or formerly poor people speak from their own experience.

PRUDENCE

Poverty has complex effects on the pursuit of prudence, the virtue that helps us appoint ends in pursuing the good. In many ways, poverty harms the ability to pursue prudence. As psychologists have found, the stress of poverty imposes neurological changes that can reduce appropriate tolerance for risk and the ability to plan for the future. Poverty burdens decision-making capacity, an important part of prudence. Conversely, some people living in poverty testify that it helps them see reality more clearly, clarifying discernment of the true good for humanity and aiding the choice of ends in the pursuit of the good.

Ample psychological research on poverty's effects on the brain helps us understand its impact on the virtue of prudence. Sendhil Mullainathan, an economist, and Eldar Shafir, a psychologist, study the impact of scarcity—shortage of money, time, and other important goods—on cognitive processing. Using a term for the volume of information computers can process over time, they refer to the ability to complete mental tasks as "bandwidth." In study after study, they show that poverty exerts a significant "bandwidth tax" on the ability to complete ordinary tasks with skill, reliability, and precision. When people living in poverty were merely asked to think about money concerns, their score on a test of fluid intelligence dropped by a factor greater than that caused by missing a night's worth of sleep.[23] Constant worry over making ends meet distracts significantly from the mental tasks of everyday life. As the authors poetically put it, "Thoughts such as, Should I risk being late again on my credit card? can be every bit as loud as a passing train."[24] Poverty's "bandwidth tax" affects poor people in widely different cultural contexts. Farmers in India performed better on tests of intelligence and self-control after the harvest, with cash at hand, than before the harvest, when they were struggling to make ends meet.[25] Mullainathan and Shafir write:

"Psychologists have spent decades documenting the impact of cognitive load on many aspects of behavior. . . . The size of these effects suggests a substantial influence of the bandwidth tax on a full array of behaviors, even those like patience, tolerance, attention and dedication that usually fall under the umbrella of 'personality' or 'talent.' So much of what we attribute to talent or personality is predicated on cognitive capacity and executive control."[26]

A taxed bandwidth seems like a sympathetic handicap. After all, who has not had a day when too many concerns made it hard to focus? But the sobering point that Mullainathan and Shafir make here is that few bother to distinguish taxed bandwidth from the stigmatized attributes it can simulate: poor education, a lack of motivation, or skill deficits.[27] Understanding bandwidth challenges the common misconception that individual shortfalls in skill, intelligence, or energy cause poverty. The researchers clarify: "We are emphatically not saying that poor people have less bandwidth. Quite the opposite. We are saying that all people, if they were poor, would have less effective bandwidth."[28]

Bandwidth research helps interpret poverty's impact on many virtues. Prudence, for example, demands skill in planning for the future, which Aquinas calls foresight.[29] Limited bandwidth due to the stresses and strains of poverty can impede long-range decision-making, such as saving for the future and avoiding ruinous loans. The authors write: "Like all the worthy goals that do not matter when you're speeding to the hospital, the long-term economics of the payday loan do not matter at that moment."[30] Making wise choices to pursue future goals is harder when present difficulty crowds the mind, as is the case in situations of scarcity.

The psychologists Johannes Haushofer and Ernst Fehr further elaborate how poverty can interfere with future planning. Due to neurological changes caused by stress, they report, poverty seems to "lower the willingness to take risks and to forgo current income in favor of higher future incomes."[31] That is, poverty affects the way people evaluate and appoint ends. Under the neurological load of poverty, poor people tend to "time-discount"; that is, they pursue short-term gains over longer-term investments of time and resources that could result in greater payoffs.[32]

Time-discounting is not caused by inherent deficits in people who are poor. Rather, the environment of poverty shapes the brains of those who are born into it in ways that could happen to anyone. Through controlled experiments, Haushofer and Fehr show that poverty does not simply *correlate* with preference for closer payoffs and less risk-taking, which could indicate that people with these maladaptive preferences tend to become poor. Rather, there is a *causal* relationship between poverty and shorter-term thinking.

When poor people received an unexpected windfall, their tolerance for risk and long-term investment increased.[33]

Significant prior research has found causal effects, not just correlations, between poverty and stress and between poverty and negative affect, or unpleasant feelings such as sadness and anger.[34] Haushofer and Fehr show that stress and negative affect can impose changes in risk tolerance and time-discounting. This suggests that it is not that poor people tolerate risk less because they know they cannot afford a loss; emotions as well as rational calculation play a role. Poverty changes the neurochemistry of the brain in ways that affect stress and happiness levels, which in their turn affect risk tolerance and planning for the future. Tragically, because long-term planning can be crucial for escaping poverty, a negative feedback loop results, which can keep people living in poverty stuck there.[35]

Poverty changes the way people evaluate and pursue ends. These changes appear to be neurologically based and to be caused by, not simply correlated with, poverty. In particular, the neurochemical burden of poverty seems to impede the aspects of prudence that Aquinas calls foresight and caution, envisioning the future and directing acts to it.[36]

I want to be clear that I am not equating cognitive function with prudence, which could imply the falsehood that those with more cognitive capacity are more virtuous.[37] Significant psychological research suggests that the constant mental juggling required by poverty simply occupies too much room in the brain to afford poor people the same good judgment as people who do not have to worry about daily expenses.[38] This effect is observed both among subsistence farmers in India—who are poor by any definition of the term—and poor people in the United States, who are relatively well off compared with the rest of the world but must devote significant mental effort to survival in their local context.[39] The issue is not that poverty reduces processing below a certain benchmark—implying that a high level of cognitive function is necessary for virtue. Rather, poverty diminishes a person's cognitive functioning relative to what it would otherwise be. In particular, it diminishes the cognitive functioning that helps us make choices, an important part of prudence.

Linda Tirado, a writer, received government assistance while working service-sector jobs and raising her family.[40] In a memoir reflecting on her experience of working poverty in the United States, she responds to the research on poverty's debilitating impact on the brain: "Poor people didn't need to wait for the science to know this. . . . We feel it."[41] She eloquently explains the consequences of diminished long-range planning ability in poor people's lives:

Poverty is bleak and cuts off your long-term brain. It's why you see people with four different babydaddies instead of one. You grab a bit of connection wherever you can to survive. You have no idea how strong the pull to feel worthwhile is. It's more basic than food. You go to these people who make you feel lovely for an hour that one time, and that's all you get. . . . We don't plan long term because if we do we'll just get our hearts broken. It's best not to hope. You just take what you can get as you spot it.[42]

Tirado comments on both poverty's neurochemical impact (it "cuts off your long-term brain") and on the conscious reasoning poor people engage in about their future prospects. As she argues, focusing on the short term is in some ways a rational response to the limited options many poor people have. This suggests that prudence, for poor people, is often a burdened virtue, allowing persons to appoint only a limited menu of ends toward the good. Tirado's account from experience validates the insights of psychological research with regard to poverty's impact on long-range planning. Again, we do not need to equate cognitive ability with virtue to identify a problem when poverty's cognitive load interferes with virtue pursuit.

Although poverty burdens foresight and the appointment of ends, it has positive effects on other aspects of prudence. Parts of prudence, as defined by Aquinas, include understanding, or good intuition about first principles, and shrewdness, the ability to see patterns quickly.[43] Economic research suggests that poverty encourages people to develop these aspects of prudence. Poverty promotes understanding of economic realities; for example, it makes people more conscious of price increases.[44] When a tax on cigarettes increased the sticker price, both poor and better off people smoked less—however, poor people also smoked less when the sales tax, which is not reflected in the sticker price, rose. Only the poor smokers were sensitive to the less obvious cost of a sales tax increase.[45] "The poor, in short, are expert in the value of a dollar," conclude the researchers.[46]

Again, contrary to the popular belief that wealthy people got that way through their superior understanding of finances, Mullainathan and Shafir found that poor people display innate understanding of opportunity cost. They asked people to imagine that they had bought a sports game ticket for $20 that was now worth $75. What did the study participants now feel the ticket was worth? Poor people were more likely than wealthy ones to say they felt the worth of the ticket was $75, reflecting an innate understanding of the economic concept of "opportunity cost"—if they kept the ticket rather than selling it, it would indeed be a loss of $75. Ironically, when a group of economists were surveyed, 78 percent answered this question wrong, even though they teach opportunity cost in their classrooms. This is powerful evidence that poor people may think more "rationally" about financial matters than wealthy ones, although this intense focus can come at a cost in other areas of life.[47]

In addition to poverty's contribution to economic intuition, it helps develop understanding in less quantifiable ways. Many people who write about their own experiences of poverty feel that poverty somehow gives them insight into the deep reality of the way things are, insight that wealth causes the wealthy to miss. For example, poverty encourages poor people to study the ways of the rich in the hope of bettering their lot, even if their attention is not always admiring. Jesmyn Ward, who grew up poor and Black on the US Gulf Coast, attended a private school where the students were mostly white and wealthy and writes of "studying the entitlement they wore like another piece of clothing."[48] Similarly, the writer and artist Leah Lakshmi Piepzna-Samarasinha describes how her mother, anxious to gain her daughter the economic and class security that had eluded herself, taught her to watch and learn the ways of wealthier people: "Not knowing upper-class people, not liking them, but studying them. . . . There is one accent for home and one for being out in the world. . . . But we hate the rich kids; they don't know anything real, anything about life."[49] And Linda Tirado addresses her well-off readers: "You guys don't really ever talk to us and have no idea what our daily lives are like. But we watch and notice what you do when you are politely ignoring us."[50] This aspect of prudence, encouraged by poverty, resembles what Aquinas calls circumspection, or assessing circumstances when contemplating an action.[51] Wealthy people do not need to be aware of the way poor people live, but poor people must assess the perspective of wealthy people if they are to survive.

Liberation theologians affirm the unique and valuable standpoint of those living in poverty when it comes to assessing reality. Sobrino writes: "Realities—or at least concepts or words like 'peace,' 'justice,' 'democracy,' 'elections'—mean different things if you look at them from the view of the poor instead of from the point of view of the oppressors."[52] And Míguez Bonino writes: "The poor are not purer or less corruptible or more generous [than others]. But they stand at a different place, and therefore they have a different perspective. They experience things which we do not experience, and therefore they can see things that we cannot see."[53] Again, this reflects a gift for assessing circumstances that poverty can encourage in the poor.

Poverty can both burden and encourage prudence in different ways. It hampers foresight through "bandwidth tax" and through the neurochemical changes fostered by the stress of poverty, which discourage healthy risk-taking and promote short-term thinking. However, poverty can encourage certain aspects of prudence by helping people be attuned to economic reality—understanding and shrewdness—and to the circumstances around them, or circumspection. Certainly, poor people can and do pursue prudence. But there are serious reasons to think that poverty makes this more difficult than it could be.

JUSTICE

Social science research suggests that in many ways, poor people are more inclined to develop the virtue of justice than wealthy people. Liberation theology tends to agree. However, cautions remain. Poverty can burden the virtue of justice, placing it in tension with other virtues and harming the person who pursues it. Unequal social structures can also exclude poor people from civic life, an important venue for practicing the virtue of justice.

In Christian virtue thought, sharing resources with those in need is often regarded as an act of justice, reflecting the belief that a share in the world's resources is every person's due.[54] Consistent with the Gospel story of the "widow's mite" (Mark 12:41–44), many studies show that poor people in the United States give more in charity, as an overall percentage of their income, than wealthy people do. A group of empirical psychological studies found that "relative to upper class people, lower class people exhibited more generosity, more support for charity, more trust behavior toward a stranger, and more helping behavior toward a person in distress. Despite their reduced resources and subordinate rank, lower-class individuals are more willing than their upper-class counterparts to increase another's welfare, even when doing so is costly to the self."[55]

The researchers found that lower-class individuals expressed "more concern for the welfare of others" than wealthier people, a motivating factor for their more generous behavior.[56] One reason for this may be that wealthy people tend to withdraw from extreme need; perhaps poorer people give more because their day-to-day lives expose them to more people in need of help.[57] Clearly, poor people can pursue and attain the virtue of justice despite limited resources.

That said, poverty can burden justice in various ways. It can encourage people to hold false ideas of justice. The Argentinian theologian Humberto Miguel Yáñez describes the way that the social marginalization of poverty leads to the creation of unique, insular cultural expressions among the poor, which can manifest in a false type of solidarity. When a culture forms on the basis of exclusion, it is one "often rooted in rebellion and resentment. . . . In the midst of perverse behavior there are reactions of solidarity, albeit a closed solidarity, often like that of the mafia."[58] Speaking about the Argentinean context, although with insight citizens of many nations would recognize, Yáñez sums up: "Poverty changes our national identity by fragmenting it."[59] He believes that when people identify more with the negative aspects of their life in poverty than with other, more positive aspects of identity, their sense of what is due to others cannot remain intact.

When poor communities must rely on outside aid to survive, their vision of what justice is due to them can also become distorted. The Tanzanian theologian Aquiline Tarimo exposes the way economic globalization, shaped by wealthy Western nations for their own benefit, deprives African nations of trading their resources at fair prices and locks them into depending on aid: "Dependence [on aid] limits choices available to the poor, and the alternatives set by external forces of domination become the only available option. Excessive control from outside leads to the breakdown of the domestic ability and willingness to do anything that could bring about radical change."[60]

In the US context, poor people might create insular groups that exclude others who are also poor. For example, the sociologist Jennifer Sherman found that in a poor, rural US town, relying on welfare to survive was widely viewed as shameful and immoral, even though many in the town did so and none were very well off. She proposes that promoting a view of welfare as immoral benefited those who did not need it at the expense of those members of the town who did.[61] Even those members of the town who did receive welfare saw it as shameful. As Yáñez observed in Argentina, poverty fragmented the sense of community the town might have had, turning citizens against one another.

Although most of us eventually must choose between nurturing relationships with close others and helping more distant others receive their due, leading to conflicts between justice and fidelity, these conflicts are likely to be especially frequent and burdensome in the lives of the poor. For example, someone from a family of modest means who has achieved a certain degree of financial success may feel torn between assisting older relatives who need her help, and investing resources in her children's future.[62] Such a conflict clearly places moral burdens on every party in the scenario. Those with the ability to give are burdened by the need to choose between loved ones who need their assistance, while older family members who need help may be burdened with the knowledge that their need draws resources away from their own grandchildren.[63] For their part, younger family members may feel torn between pursuing careers that foster justice in the world or supporting their family by pursuing financial stability.[64] There are often times when justice demands sharing material goods, which is difficult when you do not have enough for your own needs.

Poverty also burdens justice by taking away the wherewithal to practice it. Aquinas puts the practice of religious duties under justice, and he insists that poor people are bound to pay tithes—10 percent of any harvest or income contributed to the Church.[65] Although this might seem like "tying up heavy burdens" for poor people, Aquinas notes that "we pay God honor and reverence, not for His sake . . . but for our own sake, because by the very fact that we revere and honor God, our mind is subjected to Him."[66] He insists on the importance of external acts of religion to help believers unite their minds to God.[67] If a poor person cannot afford to tithe, Aquinas might say, she is denied an opportunity to form her virtue of justice through the practice of acts that orient her rightly to God.

Certainly tithing is not the only possible way a person can pursue justice. Even justice to God can be practiced through other acts, including devotion and prayer.[68] Yet this is a notable example of Aquinas acknowledging life circumstances as constitutive moral luck. He acknowledges that poverty can hinder one particular act of justice, but insists that poor Christians are bound to it anyway. One could also develop a burdened virtue of justice by fulfilling one's obligation to tithe at significant cost to the practice of other virtues, such as fidelity or self-care.

I hope this clarifies how exploring poverty's impact on virtue neither demonizes nor canonizes the poor, but helps the wealthy see the poor accurately, as moral agents navigating complex circumstances. This right understanding urges us to build a world where virtuous practices such as tithing are within reach for as many people as possible, without conflict with practices of other virtues such as fidelity.

Because working for the common good helps foster the virtue of justice, poverty can take away the wherewithal to practice justice when it inhibits involvement in civic life.[69] In the United States, poverty is often a barrier to acts of civic participation such as voting and volunteering. The political scientists Kay Schlozman, Sidney Verba, and Henry Brady note that even minor obstacles to civic engagement, such as producing identification for voter registration or finding the time to vote, demand resources many poor people do not have.[70] Even grassroots activism can demand more than someone living in poverty has to give: "Lacking a stake in the system, a sense that they can make a difference, and the skills and resources that facilitate political participation, the worst off in disadvantaged groups usually do not join social movements."[71] As Schlozman, Verba, and Brady point out, democratic representation suffers when poor people struggle to join in political life. And persons suffer when poverty bars them from civic participation and they are denied opportunities to practice the virtue of justice. As Humberto Miguel Yáñez succinctly notes, in societies marked by extreme inequality, "the poor are not really citizens."[72]

Linda Tirado affirms that poverty inhibits the pursuit of justice in civic life. She comments from her own experience: "Poor people are busy keeping a roof over their own heads, . . . and that's about all that many of us have got time to be concerned about. Environmental concerns, campaign financing, civic engagement writ large—these are luxury worries for people with time and influence."[73] Conversely, Tirado affirms from her own experience what studies of charitable giving suggest:

> Poor people are, as a rule, a bit more generous. We understand what it might be like to have to beg even if we have never done it ourselves. . . . If good citizenship consists of a well-ordered life, then we poor people make terrible citizens. But if it means being willing to help out your fellow human beings, I'd say we're right out in front waving a flag and waiting for everyone else to get on the bandwagon.[74]

Poor people demonstrate the virtue of justice when they share their resources with those in need. As Tirado points out, this in itself is "good citizenship."

As Tirado shows, poor people can and do pursue justice to a praiseworthy extent, despite limited resources. However, poverty can burden the virtue of justice in various ways: distorting the sense of what is due to others; burdening virtue by heightening conflicts between justice and other virtues; and removing the wherewithal to perform virtuous acts like voting and tithing.

SOLIDARITY

Chapter 2 explained that the rich display solidarity when they work with the poor for their justice, and that the poor display it when they work with other poor people for their mutual justice. As Gustavo Gutiérrez says, "The option for the poor is not something that should be made only by those who are not poor. The poor themselves are called to make an option that gives priority to the 'insignificant' and oppressed."[75] There is ample evidence that poor people can and do pursue solidarity. Jon Sobrino finds that "the poor of this world" demonstrate "active hope" in God's justice which is "marked by notable generosity and boundless, even heroic altruism."[76] Yet, poverty can burden the pursuit of solidarity. This is not because poor people do not feel solidarity with one another, but because lacking resources such as money, time, and political power can hinder the acts of solidarity that contribute to developing virtue. Poverty can also burden solidarity by placing it in conflict with other virtues.

Tirado unveils concrete expressions of solidarity among the working poor: "There's definitely mutual covering of asses going on in the lower classes. (Hey, why should the upper classes do all the ass covering?)"[77] Examples that Tirado mentions are covering work shifts and helping coworkers find and pay for childcare, acts which both benefit the one in need and keep things running smoothly for other coworkers. Solidarity is expressed through gifts of time and effort expended on behalf of one another.

The Aparecida Document notes that when poor people are able to find work, they are able to practice solidarity by sharing material goods: "The generous remittances sent from the United States, Canada, European countries and elsewhere by Latin American immigrants witness to their capacity for sacrifice and love in solidarity toward their own families and homelands. It is usually aid from the poor to the poor."[78] Unsaid but quite clear is the fact that the work which enables the practice of solidarity takes people far away from their families and communities, inhibiting daily acts of fidelity even as fidelity is expressed in the remitting of money. Solidarity is thus a burdened virtue for these working migrants.

Solidarity may be more prevalent among people living in poverty because they are better able to feel its necessity and impact on their daily lives. The sociologist Sudhir Venkatesh studied economic behavior in a low-income neighborhood in Chicago. His research reveals a strong practice of solidarity among many participants in the community, whether they were small business owners—among the most well-off people in the community—or "street hustlers," the poorest, frequently homeless group of off-the-books workers profiled in his study.

In the impoverished inner-city area Venkatesh studied, small business entrepreneurs pursued many types of business activity in order to stay rooted in the community. Their relationships within the community predicted their success better than wholesale investment in one particular business practice. Venkatesh writes that these entrepreneurs' business decisions "are mediated by the ability to ensure that their current relationships are not jeopardized. Their entrepreneurial spirit reverses the conventional 'bootstrap' thesis that is so often applied to inner-city Black Americans: namely, that the urban poor should learn to pull themselves up without others' help.... [Business owners] see their own chances of success as predicated on their capacity to bring others along with them."[79]

Even businesspeople whose income could have allowed them to leave the impoverished neighborhood and pursue success elsewhere preferred to remain in the community where their success could benefit their customers, whose interests and habits they knew. They did not expect banks to extend them credit or wealthy white customers to buy their services, but they trusted the poorer, familiar local community to keep their businesses afloat.[80]

Not all these people could be considered poor by my definition of lacking or having to struggle for the necessities of life. But as Venkatesh shows, all of them were in close community with people who do fit that definition. Out of necessity, or what they viewed as necessity, they displayed solidarity by remaining in the community they came from, accepting common cause with people living in poverty.

The "street hustlers" Venkatesh also profiled certainly do fit my definition of poverty. Their community relationships clearly demonstrate solidarity. Often homeless, hustlers did "off the books" work like foraging for scrap metal, prostitution, or guarding vacant buildings for $5 a night. Venkatesh describes the situation:

> Given these hustlers' desperation and outright poverty, it is easy to imagine them constantly fighting with each other, vying for resources and moneymaking schemes. . . . And yet, trust and cooperation generally trump strife. Even when there are visible, and at times violent, disputes, hustlers draw on shared codes of conduct that help resolve conflicts before they get out of hand. [One hustler said,] "Everyone is struggling, we don't go for the kill with one another. We try to be compassionate."[81]

Venkatesh quotes another hustler:

> Don't you think it's strange, that the ones who ain't got nothing, not even a roof over their head, we're the ones who are caring for each other. We are the social vulnerables, the ones who really understand, I mean really understand, that you can't live alone, you always need somebody. . . . If you're rich, you always can buy a hotel, a friend. But, lot of us have nothing in our pockets. We have to know how to live with each other or else we couldn't get by. See, this is what you must understand about the ghetto, about this community.[82]

These "street hustlers" clearly articulated that people with the fewest re-sources have the greatest need to support one another. They explained that they practice solidarity out of necessity, but that they also see it as a positive moral value, using words like "care" and "compassion" to describe their com-munity members' treatment of one another.

Although Venkatesh's research shows how poverty can encourage the virtue of solidarity, it also highlights how poverty can burden solidarity, bringing it into conflict with other virtues and causing harm to the person who pursues it. In a context where much income-generating activity is at best off the books and at worst illegal, working for community betterment burdens solidarity by placing it in conflict with virtues such as fidelity and self-care. For example, community organizers may decide that they can help keep children in the community by striking deals with gang leaders: gang activity stays away from schools, and community leaders turn a blind eye to it. But this places a burden on community activists. As Venkatesh writes: "Because they are implicated in the very dangerous and destabilizing activi-ties they are trying to address, . . . in the long run their success as mediators does little to help them advance personally. Their grinding labor does not create more productive relationships with those outside the borders of their community who have the resources, influence, and capacity to help turn things around."[83]

Everyday acts of solidarity can damage the well-being of the one who does them, as Lisa Tessman would remind us. Paradoxically, in a poor com-munity, the types of acts of solidarity that may be necessary can even hin-der long-term change. Organizations are affected as well as individuals: for formal organizations, time developing the social capital that matters in the underground economy is time not spent on the "transferable human capi-tal" that leads to helpful relationships outside the impoverished area.[84] Heads of households bear a similar burden when they accept money their family needs to survive even though they know the money comes from work that is at best off the books and at worst harmful to the worker or to others.[85]

Poor people can and do demonstrate solidarity with one another by shar-ing resources and working for the mutual betterment of their communities. Poverty often helps foster the pursuit of solidarity, as the poor person sees clearly the need to come together with others for their mutual good. How-ever, solidarity can be a burdened virtue for the poor. Pursuing it can harm persons, as when demonstrating solidarity requires sacrifices from the agent on behalf of her community. The strictures of poverty make such burden-ing of virtue more likely. When Lisa Tessman speaks of burdened virtues in social movements for liberation, she is thinking of traits that "apart from the circumstances [that necessitate resistance] would be thought to have no place in a flourishing life," such as habitual anger.[86] And yet virtues that truly contribute to flourishing, like solidarity, can also become burdened and harm the person who displays them when circumstances such as poverty force them into conflict with other virtues.

FIDELITY

Poverty can burden the pursuit of fidelity, the virtue that helps us nurture close relationships with others, when limited resources interfere with the ability to perform acts of fidelity that demand money and time. Poor people can and do pursue fidelity; for example, parents who support their children by working long hours at jobs that separate them are pursuing fidelity. But fidelity is burdened when people must pursue it in situations harmful to themselves, to others, or to the relationship they are trying to honor. This section discusses how poverty can cause or exacerbate painful conflicts between justice and fidelity or between fidelity and self-care.

Social scientists and theologians note the tragic reality that poverty can make it more difficult to practice the virtue of fidelity by fulfilling our responsibilities to close family members. José Míguez Bonino writes: "What is the meaning of being 'father' when you have no protection to offer, no food to provide, no wisdom to transmit because your brain and your heart are damaged and your eyes look without light or tears at the newborn baby lying on the floor?"[87] Consistent with Míguez Bonino's observation, the psychological "bandwidth tax" of poverty can harm persons' ability to care for others. The scarcity researchers Mullainathan and Shafir write quite bluntly:

> The poor are worse parents. They are harsher with their kids, they are less consistent, more disconnected, and thus appear less loving. They are more likely to take out their own anger on the child; one day they will admonish the child for one thing and the next day they will admonish her for the opposite; they fail to engage with their children in substantive ways; they assist less often with the homework; they will have the kid watch television rather than read to her. . . . In most of the developing world, the poor are less likely to send their children to school. . . . The poor are less likely to get their children vaccinated. The poorest in a village are the ones least likely to wash their hands or treat their water before drinking it. When they are pregnant, poor women are less likely to eat properly or engage in prenatal care.[88]

It is difficult to read this list of failings among the poor, which seems to echo the familiar stigma that such failures are due to some defect in poor people, such as a lack of ability or lack of caring. Mullainathan and Shafir suggest that to the contrary, "poverty—the scarcity mind-set—causes failure."[89] Children in families on food stamps encounter more discipline problems in school at the end of the month, when scarce funds were likely causing their parents extra stress. Air traffic controllers, who are usually not poor but whose job makes high demands on bandwidth, display worse parenting behavior after more stressful workdays.[90] As this example shows, even the wealthy can find that their parenting suffers in situations of scarcity. Poor parents have the great misfortune to be parenting under scarcity all the time.

In addition to the neurological demands of poverty's bandwidth tax, poor people may consciously choose to parent in ways that demonstrate a burdened virtue of fidelity. Poor parents may feel bound to confront their children with the harsh realities they themselves have experienced, believing that it is best for the children even though it causes them pain. When the psychologist Robert Coles interviewed poor Appalachian families in the 1960s, he asked, "How consciously does a migrant mother transmit her fears to her children, or her weariness, or her sense of exhaustion and defeat, or her raging disappointment that life somehow cannot be better?"[91] Some fifty years later, Tirado asserts, as if in response to his question, that poor parents pass their view of reality on to their children quite consciously, and do so as an act of love:

> I'm not preparing our kids for a gentle world, full of interesting and stimulating experiences. I'm getting them ready to keep their damn mouths shut while some idiot tells them what to do. I'm preparing them to keep a sense of self when they can't define themselves by their work because the likeliest scenario is that (unlike doctors and lawyers and bankers) they will not want to. . . . Learning and thinking is only a hobby for the working class, and I think it's best they're prepared.[92]

Teaching children about the world and their prospects in it is an act of genuine fidelity. Per Tirado, this fidelity becomes burdened when poor parents must teach their children that the world is harsh and does not welcome their creativity or intellect, but only their cheap labor.[93]

Bearing the burden of racism intensifies the pressure on virtue for poor parents who must teach their children about life's harsh realities. Jesmyn Ward describes how the twin, constant pressures of poverty and racism combined to erode fidelity in her hometown:

My entire community suffered from a lack of trust: we didn't trust society to provide the basics of a good education, safety, access to good jobs, fairness in the justice system. And even as we distrusted the society around us, the culture that cornered us and told us we were perpetually less, we distrusted each other. We did not trust our fathers to raise us, to provide for us. Because we trusted nothing, we endeavored to protect ourselves, boys becoming misogynistic and violent, girls turning duplicitous, all of it hopeless.[94]

Ward movingly attests that failure to develop virtue never occurs in isolation. The harmful, yet self-protecting, behaviors such a culture seems to demand wage war on virtues like humility and fidelity. In a similar key, Ward describes her community as one "where trust—between children and fathers, between lovers, between the people and their country—was in short supply."[95] Many testimonies relevant to fidelity describe the parent–child relationship, but Ward notes that fidelity in romantic partnerships is also burdened when poverty teaches people that the world is untrustworthy.

In $2.00 a Day, their book on extreme poverty in the United States, the sociologists Kathryn Edin and Luke Shaeffer describe a woman they call Jennifer, whose story movingly illustrates how poverty can burden fidelity. Jennifer, a single mother, had a job that covered her expenses, just barely. But the job required her to work upwards of 70 hours a week, and both Jennifer and her children felt their relationship suffered as a result.[96] When Jennifer left that job to spend more time with her children, she could no longer afford rent and she and her children moved in with a series of family members. Sadly, one relative with whom they stayed ended up abusing Jennifer's daughter. Jennifer immediately removed her family from the home, and fortunately, they were able to move into a shelter.[97]

Jennifer's story illustrates beyond a doubt that people living in poverty can and do possess virtue. Jennifer demonstrated perseverance, fidelity, and courage, among other virtues, in her active, loving care for her children. At the same time, her poverty placed her in tragic situations that laid severe burdens on her virtue of fidelity. If she had kept her job, her family could have lived independently, but at significant cost to her time with her children. When she moved in with the relative, she secured shelter for her family, and inadvertently exposed her daughter to abuse. In both scenarios, Jennifer's poverty limited her ability to keep her children safe.

In addition to curtailing the resources needed to perform acts of fidelity, poverty can burden the virtue of fidelity when fidelity and self-care conflict, a particular risk for poor mothers. The Indian theologian Astrid Lobo

Gajiwala writes of the pressure placed on poor mothers whose very bodies sacrifice when they bring children into the world:

> What of my undernourished sisters? Their bodies protest the repeated pregnancies that demand what they can no longer provide, and yet their spirits refuse to abandon their flesh. Little ones slung across their emaciated torsos, they continue their backbreaking work in the fields or at construction sites. Loads they cannot put down even as they walk miles in search of firewood or water. At home they set a Eucharistic meal drawing on their meager reserves, body and blood providing sustenance for hungry mouths.[98]

Burdens on fidelity can damage self-care even when the mothers in question are not, like Gajiwala's poorest countrywomen, literally starving. In the United States, a study of mothers living in poverty found that inadequate access to diapers for their children placed mothers at higher risk of mental health problems.[99] Inadequate access to diapers is inconvenient for parents, potentially unhealthy for babies, and, worse, can affect access to daycare, work, and government assistance programs. The added inconvenience and stress obviously threaten mothers' mental health, and perhaps also at stake is a mother's image of herself as capable and caring. Although it is a symptom of poverty, the inability to perform this basic act of care may harm one's respect for self as a mother.

The sociologist Sudhir Venkatesh shows how work in the underground economy, with its dangers and marginal status, burdens fidelity for impoverished mothers. For example, he interviewed women working as prostitutes who expressed that their work both helped sustain and endangered their families. Because of the work they felt they needed to do to support their children, they risked losing their children to social services or exposing them to criminal influences. They also feared that they would not live long enough to experience loving care from their children once grown. Although women engaged in illicit work felt this way most strongly, many women who worked off the books felt that the work they needed to survive threatened their families' safety. This was a painful catch-22 in which an act done out of fidelity also inhibits its practice.[100]

Tirado exposes yet another way fidelity can become a burdened virtue for people living in poverty. In the United States, with its culture of self-reliance, poor people are often criticized simply for pursuing relationships, including such elemental, human choices as having children.[101] Although having children young might not be "the wisest choice" for a poor young woman, at the same time, Tirado says, "It's not crazy. It's not even unrealistic. It's not like these girls have brilliant futures in the Ivy League that they're passing up to have babies; those are typically reserved for the children of brilliant Ivy Leaguers. They are deciding to have their toddlers while they themselves are young and have the energy. And plenty of people, no matter where they come from, simply have love to give."[102] Pursuing love and affiliation by having children is an understandable, human choice, stigmatized for people living in poverty in ways it never is for the wealthy.

Finally, poverty can burden friendships. As Tirado points out, friendships require some resources to nurture, even such minimal resources as time to spend together or the cash to reciprocate a gift.[103] The sociologists Edin and Kefalas report that the majority of poor mothers interviewed for their book did not have even one close friend. They say this is consistent with fifty years of sociological research in poor communities, where trust can be in short supply.[104]

Poor people can and do pursue and demonstrate the virtue of fidelity in their relationships with children, spouses, family members, and friends. But it is clear from their own testimonies that this pursuit can be severely burdened, and thus done at significant cost to self-care or to other virtues. Engaging in acts of fidelity often requires resources of time and money that may not be available to those living in poverty.

HUMILITY

Humility is the virtue of clearly seeing one's own actual goodness, worth, and limitations, and is not to be confused with self-abasement. Because nearly every societal and cultural setting values poor people less than others, poverty poses a major barrier to the pursuit of true humility. Loud and clear social messaging that poor people lack worth and human dignity clearly interferes with the development of the virtue of humility. To make a strong point about how society treats poor and marginalized people as worthless, liberation theology sometimes calls them "nonpersons." Of course, this does not mean that poor people are truly without inherent human dignity, but rather that they are so treated by society and may internalize that belief. Gustavo Gutiérrez says that Christian certitude in "a dehumanizing society" can be challenged by "the *nonperson*, that is to say, [the one] who is not recognized as such by the existing social order: the poor, the exploited, one who is systematically deprived of being a person, one who scarcely knows that he or she is a person."[105] To internalize one's own dehumanization to the extent that one "scarcely knows that he or she is a person" is certainly to fail to develop true humility, in the sense of understanding one's own worth as well as one's limits. Certainly the society that proclaims such a falsehood about human worth is as much to blame as the poor persons who come to believe such a lie about themselves.

The concern that poverty stigma can become internalized, leading the poor person to view herself as a nonperson, is found in both theological and secular perspectives from around the globe. Michael Amaladoss writes of the psychological damage to the Dalit people in India, who are economically poor and also excluded from social life because of caste discrimination, and who "interiorize" their despised status.[106] The Ghanaian feminist theologian Mercy Amba Oduyoye shows how the "multiple burdens" of poverty, colonialism, and economic neocolonialism shape the self-image of people in Africa: "These situations are the most alienating because people come to accept what is said of them. They become strangers to their own potential and cannot imagine any other way of organizing society or their personal lives."[107] From Latin America, Sobrino affirms that "poor people don't even have the chance of saying who they are, what they are, and what they are suffering."[108]

Writing about her peers attempting to resist the twin stigmas of poverty and racism, Jesmyn Ward remembers: "We tried to outpace the thing that chased us, that said: *You are nothing.* We tried to ignore it, but sometimes we caught ourselves repeating what history said, mumbling along, brainwashed: *I am nothing.* We drank too much, smoked too much, were abusive to ourselves, to each other. . . . There is a great darkness bearing down on our lives, and no one acknowledges it."[109] Ward painfully and eloquently accounts for the damage poverty does to humility. To accept oneself as worth nothing, even only reluctantly or only for a moment, demonstrates a lack of true humility.

Societal assaults on humility that teach poor people to see themselves as worthless take place in a thousand large and small ways. In the US context, the therapist Jessie O'Neill points out that the tradition of Christmas presents going only to "good" children can carry "tragic" moral consequences: "Rich kids are by definition 'good,' while poor kids bear the toxic shame of being labeled 'bad.'"[110] Tirado notes that in low-wage retail jobs, managers search workers' lockers and personal possessions, treating every worker as a potential thief: "To be poor is to be treated like a criminal, under constant suspicion of drug use and theft."[111]

The historian Stephen Pimpare traces how in the US context, aid to the poor has often carried the expectation of a demeaning performance of gratitude from aid recipients, coupled with aspersions on the character of those who accept aid at all. The ensuing stigmas are so severe and pervasive that studies show even recipients of government assistance endorse them.[112] Humility is burdened, placed in conflict with self-care and fidelity, when people who accept aid to ensure their own and their family's survival are stereotyped as "lazy" or "entitled."

Humility depends to a degree on the person's ability to meet her own self-imposed standards of human worth, in addition to the standards of society. For example, personhood in the dominant US culture is all but defined by autonomy. Whether we agree with this cultural value, we can recognize that people in the United States who are unable to achieve a high level of autonomy may come to regard themselves as less than human, with potential damage to their virtue of humility. Take the case of Royce, a laid-off Detroit autoworker interviewed by the sociologist Victor Tan Chen. Despite providing loving care to his five-year-old son, Royce struggled with problems in his marriage and felt that he was disappointing everyone he loved. "No one can depend on me," he told Chen. "I'm not able to make promises to my kids."[113] We might wish that Royce could understand his own human worth as less closely tied to the money he makes and come to value his important role in his family as a caregiver for his son. But we need to encounter and respect the fact that his view of human worth, like those of many other people in the United States, ties a man's human dignity to his ability to earn a good income. Royce's pursuit of the virtue of humility—his ability to appreciate his own true worth—is harmed when cultural expectations meet his poverty.

For Aquinas, humility helps us moderate hope. Humility "restrains presumptuous hope," encouraging us to restrain our hopes in line with our God-given limitations. Magnanimity, humility's twin virtue, encourages us to hope for everything of which we are capable.[114] Fullam and other contemporary virtue ethicists tend to combine the two opposed energies, saying that hope encourages us—but not too much.[115]

Poverty's tendency to beat down and destroy hope in persons is a serious threat to the formation of humility. Rick Bragg, a Pulitzer Prize–winning author who grew up, as he says, "poor white trash" in Alabama, wrote:

> The only thing poverty does is grind down your nerve endings to a point that you can work harder and stoop lower than most people are willing to. It chips away a person's dreams to the point that the hopelessness shows through, and the dreamer accepts that hard work and borrowed houses are all this life will ever be. While my mother will stare you dead in the eye and say she never thought of herself as poor, do not believe for one second that she did not see the rest of the world, the better world, spinning around her, out of reach.[116]

Tirado writes that many people living in poverty give up on the hope of beating the odds and leaving it: "You can hope for your one real shot, but you sure as hell don't plan for it. It hurts too much to plan and plan again and keep waiting for the magic day."[117]

Poverty's destruction of humility can be read in the body. The epidemiologists Wilkinson and Pickett explain how "inequality gets under the skin" through its effects on self-image. Psychologists studied stress in a variety of situations that threaten self-image and raise cortisol, a stress hormone. The most stressful situation "combined a social evaluative threat"—threat of judgment by others regarding one's social status—"with a task in which participants could not avoid failure."[118] We can readily see how being poor in a highly unequal society presents the constant threat of social judgment with no possibility of success. The constant stress of this tension harms physical health—increasing heart disease risk, for example—and divides a person from her community through shame and the constant fear of judgment.[119] Poverty's multiple assaults on humility have serious physical consequences.

Few things are clearer than poverty's impact on the pursuit of humility, understood as a clear view of one's own goodness, worth, and limitations. Poor people are treated as nonpersons and may come to internalize that belief. Cultural practices in the workplace and family confirm the false belief that full human dignity requires money. Poverty's assaults on humility place stress on the body and can destroy hope.

SELF-CARE

It is clear how poverty could interfere with the performance of acts of self-care, the virtue that governs our relationship with our self and through which we care for ourselves physically, mentally, spiritually, and in our moral life. Poverty deprives persons of the resources they need to care for themselves, such as healthy food and time for enough sleep. The stress of poverty can also promote self-destructive practices such as drug use as a short-term relief.

The pressure of poverty may encourage self-destructive choices, and even conscious, deliberate self-harm. For example, Tirado writes that even though she knows cigarette smoking is expensive and harms health, it helps her cope with working situations that can be physically punishing and mentally degrading. She admits that smoking "is not a good decision, but it is one that I have access to. It is the only thing I have found that keeps me from collapsing or exploding."[120] She recounts a conversation with a neighbor who knew that people in their neighborhood had lower life expectancies than wealthy people not far away. Instead of raging against this, he took it as a warrant to continue smoking. Tirado comments: "If you already figure you're going to die early, what's the motivation for giving up something that helps get you through the here and now?"[121] Jesmyn Ward corroborates the connection between self-hatred and drug use. In the face of systemic poverty and racism, "some of us turned sour from the pressure, let it erode our sense of self until we hated what we saw, without and within. And to blunt it all, some of us turned to drugs."[122] In a society that grants poor people, on average, fewer years of life than wealthier ones, pursuing self-care can acquire an air of futility.

The journalist Sarah Smarsh also observed that many members of her poor, rural US family turned to self-harming behaviors to cope with the constant pressures of poverty: "Dad's booze and gambling, Mom and Grandma's incessant smoking, and Chris's pills were just as much the result as they were the cause of difficult situations. . . . They suffered from weaknesses of character, yes—just like every other person, in every other income bracket. What really put the shame on us wasn't our moral deficit. It was our money deficit."[123] As she describes her family's experience with generational rural working poverty, she observes that though "weaknesses of character" are universal, poverty can encourage destructive choices but not more self-caring ones.

In addition to encouraging self-destructive practices, poverty discourages self-caring, self-preserving acts. As the sociologist Göran Therborn writes, "People who have little control of their basic life situation, of finding a job, of controlling their work context, of launching a life-course career, may be expected to be less prone to control the health of their bodies—to notice and to follow expert advice on tobacco, alcohol and other drugs, on diet and exercise—than people who have a sense of controlling their own lives."[124]

The stress-imposed "bandwidth tax" of poverty is one major culprit in this pattern. One life-threatening outcome of bandwidth scarcity is nonadherence to medication, which has long been known to be most common among the poor.[125] Sleep is another victim of low bandwidth. With major consequences for health and functioning, "thoughts of scarcity erode sleep. . . . These effects are quite strong for the poor. . . . Studies show that sleeping four to six hours a night for two weeks leads to a decay in performance comparable to going without sleep for two nights in a row. Insufficient sleep further compromises bandwidth."[126] As Tirado says, "Doctors are fans of telling you to sleep and eat properly, as though that were a thing one can simply do."[127] It is difficult to develop the virtue of self-care without the funds, time, leisure, and information that facilitate self-caring practices.

Obtaining medical care is a self-caring practice that is out of reach for many poor people in the United States and other nations.[128] Poverty burdens

self-care and can also place it in conflict with humility, in the sense of awareness of one's own dignity. Tirado writes of the humiliation of doctors assum-
ing poor people are unaware of the possibility of self-care simply because it
is unavailable to them. Although dealing with a chronic health problem, she
often had health care providers explain to her that it could be taken care of
relatively simply—"as if [surgery] were something I'd never heard of simply
because it was something I couldn't have"—but none would agree to provide
the surgery at a price she could afford.[129]

Another self-caring practice that can be more difficult for poor people is
keeping oneself safe from violence. For Mercy Amba Oduyoye, the feminiza-
tion of poverty helps explain violence against women to a certain degree: "In
Ghana, . . . some of the reasons given for staying in dysfunctional relationships are: I have nowhere to go. Where will I sleep? and What will I eat?"[130]
Although escaping abuse is difficult for anyone in any context, poverty makes
it harder for women, children, or any exploited person to practice self-care
and change their situation. Oduyoye also points out that desperate attempts
to leave poverty, such as backbreaking work and prostitution, can contribute to self-respect, however paradoxical this seems. Although such choices
harm the person, they demonstrate agency.[131] Self-care is a burdened virtue
for people living in poverty, because the only available actions to demonstrate self-care may also cause self-harm.

If poverty makes it difficult for women (especially, though not exclu-
sively) to escape relationship violence, poor young men face the inability to
protect themselves from violence by the state or other authorities. Rick Bragg,
a white American man who grew up poor in Alabama, was once interviewed
as a suspect in a murder, along with his brothers and other poor white and
Black young men from the area. "It is a point of fact that they did not question the rich kids who lived near," Bragg writes. His mother panicked and
buried an old pair of shoes that might have inaccurately seemed to link Bragg
to the crime scene. "She knew we had not done anything," Bragg writes, "but
for a woman who had grown up at the mercy of rich folks, that did not mean
a damn thing. It terrified her because she thought the police would hang the
crime on one of us purely because they could, purely because we were who
we were."[132] For Bragg, this experience "confirmed, fiercely, my notions of
class, and power. It was not so much having the power to do a thing as it was
having the power to stop things from being done to you."[133] Their poverty
left Bragg unable to protect himself from the threat of state-sanctioned violence, and his mother unable to protect her son. The experience of lacking
that power galvanized Bragg to enroll in a college course, the first step in his
successful career as a journalist.[134]

Jesmyn Ward's brother Joshua was not, like too many other young, poor, Black men, killed by state violence. But society's indifference to violence against men like him haunted his death all the same. The white drunk driver who killed Ward's brother was sentenced to just five years in jail for leaving the scene of an accident, and did not even serve that entire sentence. For Ward, the killer's relatively minor sentence made one thing clear: "By the numbers, by all the official records, here at the confluence of history, of racism, of poverty, and economic power, this is what our lives are worth: nothing. We inherit these things that breed despair and self-hatred, and tragedy multiplies."[135] Ward makes quite clear how much she and her loved ones internalized their society's racism and hatred for the poor, and how this led many people in her community to self-destructive behavior.

Poverty severely burdens the virtue of self-care. It deprives persons of resources needed for self-care—medical attention, food, even sleep. Internalizing negative societal views of the poor can also diminish one's subjective desire to care for oneself, making self-care difficult or impossible to pursue without conflict with other virtues.

TEMPERANCE

The usual context for temperance envisions a moral agent with access to plenty of useful goods; her temperance lies in choosing whether, when, and how to use them. An account of virtue that includes poor people as moral agents profoundly challenges this traditional portrayal. A poor person—with limited or unreliable access to goods such as money, food and drink, and power—would obviously experience challenges in developing and practicing temperance.

According to psychologists, the "bandwidth tax" imposed by scarcity can inhibit behavioral qualities often attributed to character or virtue, including "patience, tolerance, attention, and dedication."[136] Low bandwidth makes it harder to resist temptation. The mental energy consumed by worry about bills is not available for healthy food choices or patience with family members. (The researchers point out that dieting or chronic shortage of time also tax bandwidth, but they insist that these experiences are not comparable to poverty, in that one can relatively easily choose otherwise.[137]) "The *temptation tax* is regressive," they write, "it is levied more heavily on those who have less" (italics in the original).[138] Someone who is constantly thinking about her budget, taxing her bandwidth and self-control, is unlikely to be able to afford an impulse purchase and its potential consequences. Regrettably, the bandwidth tax makes it more likely that she will succumb.

Tirado notes that one needs access to goods in the first place to develop temperate practices for their use: "It is impossible to be good with money when you don't have any. . . . When I have a few extra dollars to spend, I can't afford to think about next month—my present-day situation is generally too tight to allow me that luxury."[139] Poor people usually don't have enough spare resources to practice the discipline of saving, Tirado says, and lack the mental and physical energy to shape their consumption practices in service of the greater good, for example, for the environment: "Overconsumption is a concern for people who've made it to regular consumption."[140] That said, Tirado argues that the way poor people must live by necessity is more respectful of resources and less harmful to the planet.[141]

Adrian Nicole LeBlanc is a journalist who spent ten years reporting *Random Family*, a 2004 account of a constellation of family and friends living in poverty in the Bronx. She indicates another way poverty can burden temperance with her account of Coco, a young woman living in a homeless shelter with her two children, working a job and trying to learn life skills like budgeting. "Budgeting didn't mitigate one of Coco's greatest problems," LeBlanc writes. "Everyone around her also needed, and Coco didn't know how to refuse. Sometimes Coco spent down her money just so she could be the one to use it, which allowed her to maintain her integrity."[142] In a way, "spending down her money" was a temperate practice for Coco; it helped her ensure that her scant resources went toward her own children's needs. But this temperance conflicted with fidelity, as Coco also felt strongly that she should help those she cared about when they were in need. If Coco had not been poor, she would have been better positioned to practice temperance by budgeting and also practice fidelity by helping out her extended family. Her poverty burdened her virtue.

Thomas Aquinas understood that poverty urges a focus on money that can crowd out other goods—similar to Mullainathan and Shafir's bandwidth tax. It is reasonable enough to focus on wealth when one lacks basic needs, but Aquinas believed the focus on wealth that poverty engenders easily spills over into avarice, making wealth an idol. He wrote that "spiritual danger ensues from poverty when the latter is not voluntary; because those who are unwillingly poor, through the desire of money-getting, fall into many sins."[143] Elsewhere, he wrote plainly that "involuntary poverty . . . causes covetousness."[144] This causal relationship shows that Aquinas did not believe that people became poor through moral failings, but rather that the pressures of poverty can shape the moral life.

Michael Amaladoss more or less agrees with Aquinas's assessment. He cautions that both rich and poor people can be hindered in their pursuit of virtue by desires for goods: "Egoism and the desire for more material goods, either for enjoyment or as a status symbol, is certainly at the root of the unjust distribution of the wealth produced and of the exploitation of the poor. The poor may be egoists, too. The poor may lack exterior freedom, while both the poor and the rich may lack interior freedom."[145]

It is difficult to pursue temperance, the virtue that helps moderate desires for temporal goods, when living in poverty. Low bandwidth may hamper the ability to perform acts of temperance, or they may not even appear possible in a context of scarce access to goods. As an extreme consequence, the constant need for money can develop into a vicious obsession.

FORTITUDE

Poor people reflecting on their own experiences, liberation theologians, and social scientists all agree that poverty encourages the development of fortitude, because it places persons in life situations where they have no choice but to persevere. This does not dismiss the possibility that the fortitude developed from living in poverty is a burdened virtue. The psychiatrist Robert Coles puts it well: "Of course people under stress can develop special strengths, while security tends to make one soft, though no one in his right mind can *recommend* hardship or suffering as a way of life, nor justify slavery, segregation, or poverty because they sometimes produce strong, stubborn people."[146] Forced hardship may develop fortitude, but certainly through a burdened process.

Adrian Nicole LeBlanc's account of the young woman Coco demonstrates how fortitude can be burdened for the poor. At the time of this account, Coco lived in a homeless shelter with her children and worked full-time, trying to save enough to move into an apartment of their own:

> [Coco's] caseworker, Sister Christine, worried about Coco's generosity. When you were poor, you had to have luck and do nearly everything absolutely right. In a life as vulnerable to outside forces as Coco's and her two little girls', the consequences of even the most mundane act of kindness could be severe. The $10 loan to the neighbor might mean no bus fare, which might mean a missed appointment, which might lead to a two-week loss of WIC [government food assistance]. Hungry children increased the tension of a stressed household. . . . But to Coco, nothing was more important than family. . . . Sister Christine wanted to tell Coco, *Get away from your family*. But she couldn't. Not everyone could clamber onto a lifeboat from a sinking raft. You either

made your way by hardening up, . . . or you stayed stuck. . . . The word that came to Sister Christine's mind whenever she thought of Coco was *enmeshed*. Coco would have said that she had heart.[147]

Of course, both rich and poor people need to evaluate competing claims, and must demonstrate fortitude in persevering through life's conflicts. But wealthy people do not need to make the heart-wrenching choices Coco did, between saving for her own modest independence and helping loved ones in truly desperate need. Mullainathan and Shafrir's research on bandwidth uses the term "temptation tax," an expression of the fact that lapses in self-control have worse consequences for those in a condition of scarcity. Obtaining enough surplus to move out of scarcity "does not merely require an occasional act of vigilance. It requires constant, everlasting vigilance; almost all temptations must be resisted almost all the time."[148] Surely this temptation tax contributed to Coco's difficulty saving for her children in the face of demands from other loved ones.

Jesmyn Ward writes that in the context of her growing up, the poor, rural US South, Black men "were devalued everywhere except in the home, and this is the place where they turned the paradigm on its head and devalued those in their thrall. The result of this, of course, was that the women who were so devalued had to be inhumanly strong and foster a sense of family alone."[149] "Inhuman strength" perfectly describes burdened fortitude, fortitude that harms the one who develops it. Developing the strength life demands requires people living in poverty to resist others' claims on them, becoming less vulnerable, less human.[150] Although virtue can be pursued in situations of privation like the one Ward describes, it comes at a cost.

Some argue that the grim endurance that contributes to fortitude for the poor conflicts with the virtue of hope. Tirado writes: "You have to understand that we know that we will never not feel tired. We will never feel hopeful. We will never get a vacation. Ever. We know that the very act of being poor guarantees that we will never not be poor."[151] And Bragg adds: "You can dream on welfare. You can hope as you take in ironing. It is just less painful if you don't."[152] One way poverty can burden the virtue of fortitude is by placing it in conflict with other virtues.

In contrast to these bleak views, others say hope does animate the forward-thinking choices made by those who persist despite poverty. Sudhir Venkatesh, the sociologist who studied underground economic life in a poor urban area, writes that "survival strategies" fails to adequately describe the committed, wise, deliberate choices people living in poverty make to maintain their lives and improve their situations. He said that none of the women he profiled believes that her life is driven by poverty and constraint, void of an imagined future. They make sense of their present conditions in terms of their potential for social mobility. They use the phrases "hustling," "getting by," "just taking it day by day," to describe their contemporary actions, but these clichéd renditions of la vie quotidienne in the ghetto do not fully describe who they are or how they live. [The women] plan, weigh options and envision alternate paths, entertain investment and accumulation strategies, opine on thrift and sacrifice. Mobility, for them, is organized around needs and visions, urgencies and dreams. Their decisions to attend to their present predicaments are wrapped up in their thirst for a future in which some of their present predicaments will disappear.[153]

Hopeful fortitude in poverty can look like this. Fortitude may be burdened for women working off the books; they may be able to pursue it only at cost to the self. Yet their endurance in pursuit of hope is certainly fortitude. Jesmyn Ward provides a beautiful reflection on fortitude enduring poverty: "We who still live do what we must. . . . We raise children and tell them other things about who they can be and what they are worth: to us, everything. We love each other fiercely, while we live and after we die. We survive; we are savages."[154]

Circumstances may force poor people to develop fortitude, but fortitude that does not contribute to one's flourishing can be a burdened virtue. Although some endure in the face of lost hope, others find a living hope that infuses their perseverance.

CONCLUSION

This chapter has relied on sources that amplify the voices of poor people. Some are written by people living in poverty themselves, others by those who take the voices of poor people as primary authorities. These sources are clear about the ways poverty can impede the pursuit of virtue through its impact on communities, practices, and self-regard. Yet neither these sources nor I support the view that poverty can ever give the final word on a person's virtue.[155] Poor people always retain moral agency and express it in many ways, from daily acts of endurance and loving service to others, to religious observance and faith-based action for justice.[156] These testimonies show how poor people do pursue and develop virtue, even when circumstances make it difficult. Still, we must acknowledge that developing virtue in poverty can demand heroic effort if we are to be honest with ourselves about the type of systems we inhabit and the type of community we are. If the path to virtue in wealth offers comforts that distract from a successful journey, the path to virtue in poverty is a rocky and difficult terrain.

This chapter has argued that poverty, understood as having less than one needs or meeting one's needs only through constant struggle, affects the ability to pursue virtue. Far from blaming those living in poverty, this argument stands on their own accounts of their lives. I have demonstrated that poverty affects the virtues in complex ways, encouraging some virtues while rendering the pursuit of others difficult to nearly impossible. Often, poor people can and do pursue a particular virtue, but they are more likely than wealthy people to find their virtues burdened when scarcity places two virtues in conflict. Exploring poverty's effects on the pursuit of virtue shows that moral luck and burdened virtue do useful work in Christian virtue ethics. More important, this work insists that conversations about poverty and inequality take poor persons' whole flourishing into account, and it enlightens Christian ethics with poor people's insights into their own lives.

NOTES

1. See, e.g., Francis, *Evangelii gaudium*. In a similar vein, the ethicist Larry Rasmussen and the biblical scholar Bruce Birch interpret Jesus's comment that "the poor are always with you" as a criticism of the failure of the Christian community to help the poor. Rasmussen and Birch, "Difficult Text."
2. Pimpare, *People's History*, 192–93.
3. Cohen, "Scholars Return."
4. Coates, "Black Family."
5. Coles, *Children*, 200.
6. Sobrino, "Awakening," 368.
7. Seneze, "Jon Sobrino."
8. Gutiérrez, "Option," 84.
9. Sobrino, "Death," 27.
10. See, e.g. Tirado, *Hand to Mouth*, 152.
11. CELAM, "Aparecida," 59.
12. Gutiérrez, "Option," 322.
13. Amaladoss, *Life*, 4; Kwang-Sun Suh, "Priesthood."
14. See chapter 3.
15. Thomas Aquinas, *Summa Theologica* (hereafter *ST*), part III, 40.3.
16. Aquinas, *ST*, I-II, 5.4. William Frankena points out that because virtue not only leads to flourishing but also may make the performance of morally right acts more enjoyable, the adage is true that virtue is its own reward. Frankena, *Ethics*, 94.
17. Notably, secular reflection on human development is moving toward a goal of holistic flourishing for those in poverty, quite in step with long-standing concerns of liberation

theology. See Nussbaum, "Poverty"; Nussbaum, *Creating Capabilities*; Sen, *Development*; and Krishna, *One Illness Away*.

18. Analogously, James Keenan and Enda McDonagh noted in a piece on HIV/AIDS that the public health activist Paul Farmer says that poverty means people are more likely to get sick, while the economist Jeffrey Sachs emphasizes that illness is a major factor driving people into poverty. Keenan and McDonagh, "Instability," 6. As my earlier comments suggest, the idea that personal failings of virtue can lead to poverty is well-established, indeed overestablished, in mainstream US society. In contrast, the reverse mechanism, how poverty can harm virtue, has not been systematically investigated.

19. Aquinas, *ST*, I-II, 65.1.

20. Keenan, "Proposing"; Ricoeur, "Love"; Spohn, "Return"; Hauerwas, *Community*. Among Keenan's students who take his view on conflicts between virtues are Daniel Daly, Lisa Fullam (with the reservations described in chapter 2), the late Lúcás Chan, and Monica Jalandoni.

21. As I have argued elsewhere, they can cause moral injury, when a person's sense of her own goodness is harmed because of something she has done. Ward, "Moral Injury."

22. Tessman, *Burdened Virtues*.

23. Mullainathan and Shafir, *Scarcity*, 50–51; Mani et al., "Poverty," 976–80; Shah, Mullainathan, and Shafir, "Some Consequences," 682–85.

24. Mullainathan and Shafir, *Scarcity*, 64–65. Linda Tirado vividly describes this from her own experience, writing about the cognitive load of being part of the working poor: "Regardless of our mood, we're never fully checked into work because our brains are taken up with at least one and sometimes all of the following: (1) calculating how much we'll make if we stay an extra hour; (2) worrying we'll be sent home early because it's slow and theorizing how much we will therefore lose; and (3) placing bets on whether we will be allowed to leave in time to make it to our other job or pick up our kids. Meanwhile, we spend massive amounts of energy holding down the urge to punch something after the last customer called us an idiot." Tirado, *Hand to Mouth*, 61.

25. Mullainathan and Shafir, *Scarcity*, 58–59.

26. Mullainathan and Shafir, 65.

27. Mullainathan and Shafir.

28. Mullainathan and Shafir, 66; see also Keenan and McDonagh, "Instability."

29. Aquinas, *ST*, II-II, 49.6.

30. Mullainathan and Shafir, *Scarcity*, 109.

31. Haushofer and Fehr, "On the Psychology," 862.

32. Haushofer and Fehr, 863.

33. Haushofer and Fehr.

34. Haushofer and Fehr, 864.

35. Haushofer and Fehr, 866.

36. Aquinas, *ST*, 49.6, 49.8.

37. Miguel Romero movingly and convincingly argues a Thomistic case for the virtue and happiness of those with profound mental disabilities. See Romero, "Profound Cognitive Impairment"; and Romero, "Happiness."

38. Mani et al., "Poverty Impedes."

39. Increased income is not the only way to address the bandwidth tax among the poor. E.g., Mullainathan and Shafir also propose that reliable public provision of child care could help poor parents recapture bandwidth by eliminating a persistent source of worry. Mullainathan and Shafir, *Scarcity*, 177.

40. Tirado identifies this experience as poverty, acknowledging that in the United States, a worker can be employed full-time and still struggle to survive. In sociological studies, low-wage workers with families similarly testify to the necessity of struggle, although not all would join Tirado and me in describing this experience as poverty. Halpern-Meekin et al., *It's Not like I'm Poor*; Edin and Lein, *Making Ends Meet*, chaps. 4–5, 8. In some US states, certain government benefits such as food assistance are offered to families making multiple amounts of the federal poverty income level. This is a tacit acknowledgment that the federal poverty level describes an income far below what is needed to achieve the necessities of life without struggle. Halpern-Meekin et al., *It's Not like I'm Poor*, 34–58.

41. Tirado, *Hand to Mouth*, 86–87.

42. Tirado, xvii.

43. Aquinas, *ST*, 49.2, 49.4.

44. Mullainathan and Shafir, *Scarcity*, 94. If not for the persistent and pernicious myth that people are poor because they are less skilled with money than the rich, this would sound, quite properly, self-evident.

45. Mullainathan and Shafir, 94.

46. Mullainathan and Shafir.

47. Mullainathan and Shafir, 102–3. "One would also be tempted to conclude that economists would be better at economics if they were paid less," quip the authors.

48. Ward, *Men We Reaped*, 5.

49. Piepzna-Samarasinha, "Scholarship Baby," 202.

50. Tirado, *Hand to Mouth*, 185.

51. Aquinas, *ST*, II-II, 49.7.

52. Sobrino, "Poverty," 268–69.

53. Míguez Bonino, "Poverty as Curse," 9.

54. An equally vivid strain of Christian thought views almsgiving as an act of charity rather than justice. Broadly speaking, there are those, like Thomas Aquinas, who view it as charity focus on the inner orientation of the one who imitates God's mercy by giving; Aquinas, *ST*, II-II 32.1. And there are those who view it as justice, like Augustine and other Church Fathers, who focus on the relative social positions of donor and giver and the potentially unjust ways the donor acquired wealth. Ward, "Porters," 235–36.

55. Piff et al., "Having Less," 780. The group of studies surveyed in this article includes some where class position was relative and artificially induced, e.g., by asking participants to compare themselves with those at the very bottom or top of the "economic ladder," and others which incorporated actual economic class via participant self-report.

56. Piff et al.

57. Stern, "Why the Rich Don't Give." As I argue in chapter 7, addressing self-segregation by the wealthy could help address both structural justice and virtue development.

58. Yáñez, "Opting for the Poor," 15.

59. Yáñez.

60. Tarimo, "Globalization," 36.

61. Sherman, *Those Who Work*.

62. Johnson, *American Dream*, 97. Johnson describes this tension as being particularly difficult for middle- and upper-class Black families in the United States, due to both cultural expectations of care and less average wealth.

63. Chiteji and Hamilton, "Family Connections."

64. The *Chronicle of Higher Education* interviewed several college students or graduates from low-income families who articulated this tension. Rhiana Gunn-Wright, a Yale graduate

and Rhodes scholar, expressed it this way: "You have these gifts, and you know that if you don't use them, people in leadership positions won't look like you, and they might not care about the people that you care about.... At the same time, you have real responsibilities to everyone else [in your own family]." Carlson, "Poor Kids."

65. Aquinas, *ST*, II-II, 87.4, II-II 87.1; Respondeo, II-II, 87.2.

66. Aquinas, II-II, 81.7.

67. Aquinas.

68. Aquinas, II-II, 82, 83.

69. Wadell, *Happiness*, 225–26; Porter, *Justice as a Virtue*, 252–54.

70. Schlozman, Verba, and Brady, *Unheavenly Chorus*, 567.

71. Schlozman, Verba, and Brady, 451.

72. Yáñez, "Opting for the Poor," 17.

73. Tirado, *Hand to Mouth*, 154.

74. Tirado, 166.

75. Gutiérrez, "Option," 325.

76. Sobrino, "Awakening," 367.

77. Tirado, *Hand to Mouth*, 24–25.

78. CELAM, "Aparecida," 416.

79. Venkatesh, *Off the Books*, 104.

80. Venkatesh, 145–46.

81. Venkatesh, 186–87.

82. Venkatesh, 187–88.

83. Venkatesh, 362.

84. Venkatesh, 385.

85. Venkatesh, 381.

86. Tessman, *Burdened Virtues*, 114.

87. Míguez Bonino, "Poverty as Curse," 6–7.

88. Mullainathan and Shafir, *Scarcity*, 152–53.

89. Mullainathan and Shafir, 155.

90. Mullainathan and Shafir, 156–57.

91. Coles, *Children*, 157.

92. Tirado, *Hand to Mouth*, 122–23.

93. This is resonant with a story recounted by Martin Luther King Jr. of the pain of explaining to his young daughter why he could not take her to a segregated amusement park. Fidelity is burdened for parents when a necessary lesson causes pain for their children and themselves. All parents encounter this to some extent, but the poor and excluded, like King, in disproportionate and burdensome ways. Haley, "Alex Haley Interviews."

94. Ward, *Men We Reaped*, 188.

95. Ward, 222.

96. Julia Mavity Maddalena notes that contemporary US welfare policy forces poor mothers of young children into the workplace, preaching a rhetoric of self-sufficiency. This is an ironic reversal from earlier in the twentieth century, when poor mothers who worked out of necessity were blamed for the misbehavior of youth because they were neglecting their "job" of caring for children at home. Maddalena, "Floodwaters."

97. Edin and Shaefer, *$2.00 A Day*.

98. Gajiwala, "Passion," 187–200.

99. Smith et al., "Diaper Need."

100. Venkatesh, *Off the Books*, 52–53. Another example of conflicts to fidelity presented by poverty is when a loved one who is engaged in illicit activity needs help or offers to contribute to the family income. Accepting money from someone engaged in crime, or offering him a place to stay, can jeopardize a family's security even though it might honor their values. Venkatesh, 48–49.

101. Pimpare, *People's History*, 120–26. The sociologist Sharon Hays traces the "family cap" prohibition on benefits to new children born to a mother on welfare to a punitive version of this stigma. "Welfare mothers have children for reasons other than the desire to get a few extra dollars in their welfare check," she insists in italics. "On this score, most welfare mothers are no different than most Americans." Hays, *Flat Broke*, 70.

102. Tirado, *Hand to Mouth*, 118; sociologists agree with Tirado's observation. A recent study observed "social stratification" in birth patterns of US millennials to the extent that "there is little commonality between the typical family formation patterns of the non-college-educated and the college-educated." Cherlin, Talbert, and Yasutake, "Changing Fertility Regimes."

103. Tirado, *Hand to Mouth*, 96; see also 101.

104. Edin and Kefalas, *Promises*, 34, 34n9.

105. Gutiérrez, "Faith as Freedom," 43.

106. Amaladoss, *Life*, 23.

107. Oduyoye, "Creation," 5.

108. Sobrino, "Poverty," 274.

109. Ward, *Men We Reaped*, 249.

110. O'Neill, *Golden Ghetto*, 157.

111. Tirado, *Hand to Mouth*, x–xi.

112. Pimpare, *People's History*, esp. chap. 6, "Respect: The Price of Relief"; Halpern-Meekin et al., *It's Not like I'm Poor*.

113. Chen, *Cut Loose*, 148.

114. Aquinas, *ST*, II-II, 161.2.

115. See chapter 2.

116. Bragg, *All Over*, 24–25.

117. Tirado, *Hand to Mouth*, 77–78.

118. Pickett and Wilkinson, *Spirit Level*, 38–39.

119. Pickett and Wilkinson, 84, 36–44.

120. Tirado, *Hand to Mouth*, xvii.

121. Tirado, 82–83.

122. Ward, *Men We Reaped*, 188.

123. Smarsh, *Heartland*, 162.

124. Therborn, *Killing Fields*, 82–83.

125. Mullainathan and Shafir, *Scarcity*, 151.

126. Mullainathan and Shafir, 160.

127. Tirado, *Hand to Mouth*, 50.

128. Globally, more than 400 million people do not have access to basic health services such as prenatal care and vaccinations; World Health Organization, "New Report." In the United States, 27.6 million people lacked health insurance in 2016. Of these, one in five went without care in the past year due to cost; Henry J. Kaiser Family Foundation, "Key Facts."

129. Tirado, *Hand to Mouth*, 48–49.

130. Oduyoye, "Poverty Renders African Women Vulnerable," 27.

131. Oduyoye, 28. Poverty also exacerbates the harm of intimate partner violence in the United States. Although intimate partner violence is not limited to any social class, it is more common in low-income households and incidents of violence increase when the male partner experiences unemployment. Echoing Oduyoye's observation, in the United States, "more than a third of [intimate partner violence] survivors report becoming homeless as a result of trying to end the abusive relationship." Renzetti, "Economic Stress," 5.

132. Bragg, *All Over*, 120.

133. Bragg, 121.

134. Bragg, 121–23.

135. Ward, *Men We Reaped*, 237.

136. Mullainathan and Shafir, *Scarcity*, 65.

137. Mullainathan and Shafir, 148–49.

138. Mullainathan and Shafir, 82. See also Banerjee, *Shape*.

139. Tirado, *Hand to Mouth*, 141.

140. Tirado, 153. In a similar vein, Paul Evans, an Appalachian former coal miner interviewed by Robert Coles, talked about how even though the natural beauty of the mountains was so important to his family, they sometimes responded to the difficulty of finding steady work and the pressure of extremely limited income by throwing their garbage into the creek, in a spirit of "what the hell difference does it make." Coles, *Children*, 290.

141. Tirado, *Hand to Mouth*, 153.

142. LeBlanc, *Random Family*, 146.

143. Aquinas, *ST*, II-II, 183.3.

144. Aquinas, "Liber Contra Impugnantes."

145. Amaladoss, *Life*, 137.

146. Coles, *Children*, 469.

147. LeBlanc, *Random Family*, 148.

148. Mullainathan and Shafir, *Scarcity*, 132.

149. Ward, *Men We Reaped*, 84.

150. See the discussion of Christian anthropology in chapter 2.

151. Tirado, *Hand to Mouth*, xvi.

152. Bragg, *All Over*, 153.

153. Venkatesh, *Off the Books*, 40.

154. Ward, *Men We Reaped*, 249–50.

155. Aquinas, *ST*, I-II, 5.4. Aquinas says that outward influences on our behavior can disturb our happiness by hindering many acts of virtue, but that we can hold on to virtue by bearing trials in a virtuous way: "Outward changes can indeed disturb such like happiness, in so far as they hinder many acts of virtue; but they cannot take it away altogether because there still remains an act of virtue, whereby man bears these trials in a praiseworthy manner." Respondeo. This strikes me as a good understanding of burdened virtue—it is still virtue, but does not contribute to the person's happiness to the degree it should. For Aquinas, circumstances can cause us to lose virtue only if they result in the will being changed from virtue to vice, and this does not happen automatically: "Man's will can be changed so as to fall to vice from the virtue, in whose act that happiness principally consists; . . . however, the virtue [may] remain unimpaired." *ST*, I-II, 5.4, Respondeo.

156. Míguez Bonino, "Doing Theology," 97.

CHAPTER 7

INEQUALITY AND VIRTUE

Thus far, I have argued that both wealth and poverty function as moral luck, affecting without fully determining how persons are able to pursue the virtues. Because this book has promised to give an account of the impact of wealth, poverty, and inequality on virtue, what remains to be shown is how economic inequality exacerbates the impact of both wealth and poverty on the virtues. This should be suggested by the work of the preceding chapters, but the present one explains it in more detail.

Some previous reflections on inequality's impact on the moral life are only addressed to hearers who are, in my definition, wealthy. For example, when Pope Francis diagnoses inequality as a symptom of exclusion, he is clearly speaking not to the poor whom inequality excludes but to those who have more than they need yet are indifferent to those who struggle.[1] Although deeply important, this messaging overlooks the fact that inequality also morally affects the poor.

With an understanding of moral luck, we can observe that inequality does indeed have moral effects, but these differ depending on whether we have more than we need or struggle to survive. I show here how inequality tends to exacerbate wealth's threats to virtue, particularly hyperagency and the danger of wealth becoming an end in itself. Inequality also threatens the virtue pursuit of poor persons when it heightens the impact of scarcity and sharpens societal disregard for the poor. After detailing how inequality exacerbates the impact of both poverty and wealth on the virtues, this chapter proposes solutions for action drawn from economic and theological understandings. Structural solutions can help by discouraging economic segregation and redistributing wealth to the poor, but spiritual solutions will remain necessary to address wealth and poverty's virtue effects. I conclude by reviewing the contributions of this work to Christian ethical thought on wealth, poverty, and inequality, and to Christian virtue ethics.

WEALTH AND VIRTUE IN UNEQUAL SOCIETIES

Chapter 5 argues that one major way wealth hinders the pursuit of virtue is that it grants hyperagency: wealthy people, those who have more than they need, wield disproportionate power, control, and choice compared with others. Hyperagency affects virtue in at least two ways. Wealth enables many practices: some that may help promote virtue, like practices of self-care; and others that may harm virtue, such as self-segregation from the poor. Hyperagency also shapes understanding of self and others, encouraging the wealthy person to view herself and her own concerns as more important than others and their concerns. Another threat to virtue is wealth being viewed as an end in itself. Although poor people can also fall into this error, social scientists and theologians suggest wealthy people are especially at risk.

Inequality clearly exacerbates the hyperagency of wealth. Wealth could not translate into hyperagency over other persons were it not for the fact that some have much more than enough and others must struggle for what they need to survive. Increased inequality can translate into increased hyperagency, as the example of CEO-to-worker-compensation ratio helps demonstrate. In 1965, the average CEO made 20 times the salary of the average worker in the same industry. By 2017, the average large-firm CEO earned more than 270 times the average worker in the same industry.[2] In both cases, the CEO clearly experiences hyperagency compared with the workers. But the wider gap between CEO and worker pay in 2017 afforded CEOs much greater ability to affect the world around them than an average employee, in matters ranging from their own personal health and safety to national politics. Thus an increase in inequality translates into an increase in hyperagency, with, we would expect, a concomitant impact on virtue.

Inequality also functions as moral luck when it enables segregation in communities, with serious implications for virtue pursuit. Sociologists found that as US inequality increased between 1970 and 2000, so did residential segregation by income. Most of this change was caused by people at the wealthier end of the spectrum withdrawing from middle-class and poorer families.[3] The researchers argue convincingly that inequality produces economic segregation, rather than the other way around. They raise concerns that the segregation of the affluent can harm poorer people, because rich people who have limited or no contact with poorer people may be less willing to invest in public programs to benefit the poor.[4] Economic segregation contributes to the impact of wealth on the virtue of justice, making it easier for the wealthy to ignore the poor.[5]

Another way wealth threatens virtue is by becoming an end in itself. Inequality exacerbates this risk in at least two ways: by heightening wealth's perceived importance; and by normalizing the view of wealth as an end rather than a means. First, an unequal society is one where a descent from wealth to poverty threatens many aspects of a dignified human life. When one risks losing not just money but also hyperagency, political voice, and other goods that disproportionately accrue to the wealthy in unequal societies, a focus on keeping and increasing wealth could easily gain outsize precedence. One risks not just a decline in living standards but also the loss of one's full humanity. One reaction to this reality could be to focus on wealth as an end in itself. In the highly unequal Roman Empire, Saint Augustine observed that the "fear of losing" seemed to trouble the wealthy more than the desire for sufficiency did the needy.[6] This remains a moral danger in unequal societies today.

The economist Thomas Piketty showed us that in today's unequal economies, wealth outearns the combined influence of all people's work. Self-perpetuating inequality can make it appear both natural and inevitable that wealthy people should receive more wealth, and should strive to maintain the status quo in which their wealth increases, instead of focusing on being grateful for what they have or giving away their surplus. When societies continue to allow inequality to not only persist but also grow, they implicitly approve of this state of affairs. The Gospel's insistence that "much will be required of the person entrusted with much" (Luke 12:48, NAB) is replaced with Billie Holiday's ironic insight "Them that's got shall have, them that's not shall lose."[7]

Inequality exacerbates the ways wealth threatens virtue through hyperagency and wealth becoming an end in itself. Inequality increases hyperagency by extending the resources available to wealthy people, which strengthens their ability to choose practices and can inflate self-regard. It shapes the communities where the wealthy pursue virtue by promoting self-segregation. Self-perpetuating inequality, which translates into inequality of many other human goods, affects the self-regard of the wealthy by conveying the message that wealthy people deserve preferential treatment and should preserve that as the status quo.

POVERTY AND VIRTUE IN UNEQUAL SOCIETIES

We have already examined the evidence that poverty—lacking the basic needs of life or meeting them only through constant and precarious struggle—affects virtue in two primary ways. Poverty can affect the pursuit of virtue

through scarcity, which affects the brain and can limit access to some virtuous practices. It can also harm the self-regard of the poor person as societal disregard can become internalized. Inequality exacerbates both these
processes.

One major feature of poverty's influence on virtue is diminished personal
self-regard, when poor people internalize society's disregard at cost to virtues
including humility, solidarity, and justice. It is clear how extreme inequality
makes this worse. The greater the gap between those with more than they
need who are treated as fully human and those who struggle for survival, the
greater the threat to the self-regard of the poor.

This book's introductory chapter described multiple studies that connect
inequality to poor health outcomes for people at all income levels, and to
shrinking life expectancies for poor women.[8] One researcher linked inequality to poor health outcomes via "dignity-denying events."[9] If one's status in an
unequal society measurably affects physical health and even life expectancy,
it should come as no surprise that it can also affect less quantifiable realities
such as self-regard, which play a role in virtue pursuit.

Today's pervasive global and local communication networks make it
effectively impossible for poor people in unequal societies to avoid comparing themselves with the rich. The dignity-denying gap in society's valuation
of the lives of the wealthy and the poor becomes inescapable. Describing her
impoverished upbringing on a reservation in the 1960s, the Native American activist Mary Crow Dog (Mary Brave Bird) wrote: "We kids did not
suffer from being poor, because we were not aware of it.... We were not
angry because we did not know that somewhere there was a better, more
comfortable life. To be angry, poverty has to rub shoulders with wealth....
TV has destroyed the innocence, broken through the wall that separates the
rich whites from the poor nonwhites."[10]

The conspicuous consumption of wealthy people harms the poor in
many ways, one of which is eliciting negative emotions like anger and jealousy. Conspicuous consumption also inspires competitive consumption,
which drives spending that does not contribute to well-being and has been
described as a cost that rich people impose on society.[11] Positional or status-
signaling consumption occupies more mental resources for people living in
areas with more inequality.[12] Here, it is worth noting, however, that despite
the temptation to positional consumption, poorer people stand to benefit from improved economic integration. Low-income people who moved
from neighborhoods of extreme poverty to ones of low poverty experienced
major increases in well-being, comparable to an increase in income of more
than 50 percent.[13]

Another major way poverty affects virtue is through scarcity. Under contemporary conditions, rising inequality increases scarcity for the poor by directing more of a finite pool of resources to the rich. Compounding this problem, markets in unequal economies may shift in ways that increase the pressures of scarcity on the poor—for example, cheaper versions of necessary goods may be harder to come by.[14] Scarcity of money and time burdens cognitive processing, impeding the development of prudence and a host of other virtues.[15] Scarcity can also inhibit the practice of virtues—such as fidelity, justice, and self-care—for which common practices demand material resources. The pressures of scarcity increase the likelihood that virtues will conflict and that the person will find herself in a situation where she cannot, for example, pursue justice and fidelity at the same time.

Inequality compounds the impact of scarcity and lowered self-regard for the poor as they strive to pursue virtue. Rising inequality shapes the range of practices available to persons—constraining those of the poor, broadening those of the rich. Inequality shapes self-regard by amplifying the message that the rich and the poor are two completely different types of people with different worth, gifts, and prospects. And inequality increases segregation in communities. Chapter 3 showed how life circumstances can function as moral luck when they affect practices, self-regard, and communities, those key components of virtue acquisition. Inequality evidently influences virtue pursuit, for poor and wealthy persons, in all three of these aspects.

INEQUALITY'S IMPACT ON VIRTUE: POTENTIAL SOLUTIONS

Inequality is a structural problem with profound effects on individual persons' pursuit of virtue. Because social structures emerge from relationships between persons, as Daniel Finn helpfully shows, structural changes have the potential to help persons in their pursuit of virtue.[16] Gustavo Gutiérrez has criticized Christians for endorsing the idea that "it is no use to change social structures, if the heart of man is not changed.'" This, he said, "is a half truth which ignores the fact that the 'heart' of man also changes when social and cultural structures change."[17] As one possible expression of this, Joerg Rieger suggests that a sense of solidarity on the part of the wealthy might increase in times of economic downturn: "Being increasingly pushed to the margins, more and more of us are endowed with an unexpected potential to see more clearly."[18] Benedict XVI, espousing a different order of events, wrote that just structures "neither arise nor function without a moral consensus in society on fundamental values, and on the need to live these values with the necessary sacrifices, even if this goes against personal interest."[19] These theologians agree that the mutual connection between social structures and virtue is clear: virtuous structures create virtuous people, and vice versa.

Chapter 1 described the research of the epidemiologists Kate Pickett and Richard Wilkinson, who found that societies with greater inequality evidenced higher rates of fear and distrust and reduced empathy. Pickett and Wilkinson believed this link was not just correlative but also causative, and could work in reverse: a shift toward greater equality in wealthy, unequal countries could lead to a concomitant increase in empathy among their citizens.[20] Their work endorses the views of Gutiérrez and Rieger: structural changes that promote economic equality can help remedy inequality's pernicious effects on virtue.

PRACTICAL ECONOMIC SOLUTIONS

Economists and political scientists have offered approaches to reducing economic inequality within the global community as well as individual nations. Different solutions may be called for in different contexts. Democratic deliberation, focused on the needs of the most vulnerable, can help societies choose the most appropriate responses in particular situations. There is good reason to think that reducing economic inequality by any of these means could help ameliorate its negative impact on virtue. What follows is a brisk rundown of several proposals.

Governments and other authoritative bodies can reduce inequality's practical and moral damages by building economically integrated communities, and individuals can help through their own personal choices. We have discussed how wealthy self-segregation is a major symptom of hyperagency, accelerated by rising inequality. Economic segregation harms the poor practically, decreasing their access to the goods associated with a dignified life, and harms the wealthy morally, decreasing the likelihood that they will encounter the poor and develop the virtues of solidarity and justice. Virtue pursuit in communities can benefit from practical proposals to decrease segregation. These could include mandating an integrated educational system through policies such as busing; building affordable housing in wealthy neighborhoods; refusing public investment to communities that are self-segregated by income; and including poverty among the aspects of diversity to be sought, for example, by colleges and universities.[21] These practical, effective measures for reducing economic segregation could diminish the material harm that such segregation imposes on the poor and could help reduce the virtue effects of wealth, poverty, and economic inequality.

Government regulation of markets can either promote or restrict inequality. The economists Brink Lindsey and Steven Teles propose "liberaltarian" reforms to regulation in the United States, reasoning that liberals (in the US sense) wish to reduce inequality while libertarians favor minimal government regulation and restriction. "Rent-seeking" occurs when participants in markets pursue artificial scarcity for the goods or services they offer in order to inflate profits. Regulatory capture due to rent-seeking drives scarcity in areas from income to medication pricing to housing availability, manifesting wealthy hyperagency and helping inequality self-perpetuate. Practical proposals to stave off rent-seeking include heightened federal and state oversight of new regulations and improving the policy staff assistance available to Congress to decrease reliance on lobbyists for information.[22] Acknowledging the irony, Lindsey and Teles also note that wealthy funders may produce "countervailing power" to oppose rent-seeking, whether out of personal interest or civic spirit.[23] Politically effective though it may be to have powerful donors engage with rent-seeking, as they have done for environmentalism and other causes, this model of change does nothing to discourage wealthy hyperagency.

Proposals to limit inequality often tackle the problem from one of two directions: improving the lot of the poor and constraining the gains of the most wealthy. Done correctly, taxation can combat inequality at both ends of the spectrum by curbing the amount of wealth the richest can accumulate and helping the poor through redistribution. Anthony Atkinson, one of the most influential economists studying inequality, offers a full slate of proposals. These include progressive tax structures, with the highest incomes taxed at 65 percent and an earned income discount for the lowest earners; avoiding the use of tax reductions as business incentives; a progressive tax on inheritances based on the amount an individual receives over her lifetime, which could encourage the spread of wealth across inheritors; and a progressive property tax.[24] Piketty agrees with progressive taxation within nations and believes that poorer workers in wealthy nations should be taxed especially lightly, because their economic position is harmed by globalization while their wealthy compatriots benefit from it most of all.[25]

With Piketty's call in *Capital in the 21st Century* for a global tax on capital, he showed that taxation's promise for addressing extreme inequality goes beyond the undeniable promise of redistribution. A global tax on capital would help slow the rate of gains on investment compared with economic growth, and, equally important, create transparency about global wealth accumulation where none currently exists. Piketty argues that the contemporary financial system is not capable of accurately reporting wealth capture due to investments, or of preventing wealthy individuals from hiding the extent of their true assets from government, which he denounces as "theft" from the common good.[26] In his view, a modest tax on capital of no more than a few percent "would promote the general interest over private interest while preserving economic openness and the forces of competition."[27] Such a tax could generate significant income for governments and provide transparency without confiscating all the returns on capital, leaving the incentive to invest in new projects intact.[28] Poorer countries, including many in Africa where corruption does significant damage, especially stand to gain from increased global transparency.[29] Atkinson agrees that this proposal is potentially feasible, and he suggests offering individuals the status of "global taxpayer" to enter into a global tax system and opt out of national and local tax laws.[30]

When it comes to redistributing tax revenues to address inequality, many economists favor government provision of services and income to the poor or even, in certain cases, to all members of society. Atkinson reports that no wealthy nation has been able to reduce inequality without considerable social spending.[31] He proposes a robust social safety net, including guaranteed minimum-wage public employment;[32] a cash Child Benefit given to all families, but taxed progressively;[33] and a guaranteed minimum wage set at a living wage.[34] Health care costs are a major factor keeping people in poverty in contexts as diverse as India and the United States, so the political scientist Anirudh Krishna recommends that societies work to provide health care to their members.[35] Any type of social safety net benefit that redistributes wealth to the poor stands, at minimum, to enable virtuous practice where it is constrained by scarcity or a lack of resources, and to help reduce wealthy hyperagency.

THE LOGIC OF PRACTICAL SOLUTIONS: HUMAN WORTH AND UNIVERSAL BASIC INCOME

Particularly if our concerns are animated by virtue, it is important to pay attention to the logic behind practical economic proposals, as well as to their anticipated results. Economic policies not only shape access to practices; they are also statements by communities about what they value and why. Economic policies encode community judgments about who matters, shaping the community and self-regard mechanisms where, as we have seen, wealth and poverty can function as moral luck to influence virtue pursuit.

Perhaps uniquely among distributive programs, the final practical proposal I discuss here stands out because its internal logic acknowledges the universal value of each human person that lies at the heart of Christian anthropology. Universal basic income (UBI) would provide a cash income to every adult in a society, regardless of income and without means testing.[36] UBI, also called guaranteed minimum income, is usually understood to provide a survival income; advocates propose about $1,000 a month in the United States.[37] By design, UBI goes to every member of society, but it can be taxed along with income to avoid subsidizing the very wealthy.

UBI promises to reduce poverty and eliminate many unintended consequences of means-tested programs, including expensive bureaucracy, stigma, and the "poverty trap" that results when means-tested benefits decline as recipients earn more. More appealing still from the perspective of Christian ethics is UBI's animating logic, which rejects the premise that people only deserve basic needs if they work for wages. I have argued that UBI encodes the logic of Christianity, whose "central mystery . . . is a gift to the undeserving."[38] Because it could afford people the time for caregiving, making art, volunteering, and other forms of useful work that go beyond wage labor, UBI reminds us that such activities indeed are work and contribute significantly to building up flourishing communities.[39] Pope Francis enthused about this logic of UBI in his 2020 book *Let Us Dream*, saying the policy would help us all "recogniz[e] the value to society of the work of nonearners."[40] As I said above, any redistributive policy stands to help address inequality's virtue effects by enabling virtuous practice for the poor and helping limit wealthy hyperagency. Certainly, UBI is not the only proposal with the potential to address inequality's practical harm and virtue effects. It stands out, however, because the practice of universal aid implicitly challenges one of inequality's most harmful messages: that the poor are somehow different than the wealthy, and less deserving of the basic needs of life. By creating a society-wide basic needs "floor" below which no one can fall, no matter what, UBI powerfully challenges the pervasive message that the poor are less worthy of human dignity.

With concrete proposals on the table for addressing inequality at national, international, and community levels, it is up to each nation's citizens to make sure that reducing economic inequality becomes and remains politically feasible. Any proposal that successfully reduces economic inequality has the potential to improve virtue by fostering trust and encounter, and by reducing the disparate social valuing of rich and poor persons that can corrode the self-regard of people in both groups.

THEOLOGICAL SOLUTIONS

This section focuses on theological approaches to address the impact of inequality on virtue, and the next one makes practical suggestions for how members of the Christian community can carry them out in practice. Many, though not all, of these recommendations are aimed at the wealthy, whom I expect to be the primary readers of this work. Theological tactics for addressing the impact of inequality on virtue include encounter, conversion, satisfaction with contentment, pursuing Kingdom reversal, and renewal of dependence on God.

Encounter

One of the primary ways wealth and poverty function as moral luck is by affecting the communities where persons pursue virtue. Inequality exacerbates this by enabling increased wealth segregation. Self-regard is affected for wealthy and poor people alike by persistent cultural messaging that only wealthy people deserve treatment that accords with full human dignity. As a solution to all the ways life circumstances, including wealth and poverty, can fracture communities, theologians have frequently proposed spiritual practices of encounter.

Pope Francis has made the call to encounter a theme of his papacy, and he lays it out clearly in his apostolic exhortation *Evangelii gaudium*. Whether it is the encounter with Jesus or with the neighbor in need, encounter describes a relationship where genuine self meets genuine self, a relationship that changes the person and her life. Francis's understanding of encounter reflects the virtue that James Keenan has called Jesuit hospitality, which is practiced out on the road, "journeying towards those for whom nobody is caring."[41] Phrases like "going forth" and "going out of ourselves" are repeated over and over in *Evangelii gaudium*, evoking Augustine's understanding of sin as being *incurvatus in se*, closed in on oneself.

Francis's view of encounter clearly draws from deep engagement with liberation theology, of which a few examples suffice. Gustavo Gutiérrez reminds us that the Christian call to love one's neighbor should not apply merely to "the person I meet on *my* road." Rather, Christians need to view our neighbor as "the 'distant' person to whom I draw near, . . . the one whom I go out to seek in the streets and marketplaces, in the factories and marginal neighborhoods, in the farms and mines."[42] This passage reminds us of how economic segregation is a symptom of inequality with particularly fatal potential for virtue formation. "My" local, limited understanding of the neighbor may not place me where I need to be to grow in virtue. Gutiérrez's solution is one frequently evoked by Pope Francis: going out, drawing near to the distant one.

Daily contacts between the rich and the poor do, of course, take place in today's unequal societies. Often, they take place around the retail cash register, or in the hundreds of other settings where the working poor serve those who are better off. Obviously, this is not true encounter in the sense that Francis has in mind.[43] Encounter takes place when we recognize the humanity of the other and allow our view of self and our view of truth to be changed. As Jon Sobrino notes, when wealthy people encounter poor people, their theological questions are changed to "Are we really human and if we are believers, is our faith human?"[44] Encounter describes both the physical meeting of embodied persons and the openness of the one in a position of power—the wealthy person—to being changed by that event.

Conversion

Both wealth and poverty affect self-regard, with implications for virtue. Cultural understandings of wealthy people as worthy of full human dignity, and of poor people as beneath human dignity, become internalized and affect the way persons see themselves and the world. This reality demands what Bernard Lonergan calls the process of intellectual conversion, asking all the possible questions to gain correct understanding, expanding our horizon beyond what we think we know.[45]

Jon Sobrino illustrates the need for conversion, suggesting that well-off people are deliberate in their ignorance of poverty: "The world of poverty truly is the great unknown. . . . It isn't that we simply do not know; we do not *want* to know because, at least subconsciously, we sense that we have all had something to do with bringing about such a crucified world. And as usually happens where scandal is involved, we have organized a vast cover-up before which the scandals of Watergate, Irangate, or Iraqgate pale in comparison."[46] Sobrino's analysis recalls Lonergan's description of bias, or the deliberate exclusion of information that we should have known. For Lonergan, bias calls for conversion to expand what we know and can see.[47]

Michael Amaladoss illustrates how joining in the struggle of the poor for liberation can invite conversion for the wealthy: "When one reads the parable of the Good Samaritan, for example, one normally thinks of the Samaritan. But one could also stop to think about the thieves: Why are there thieves? How can we have a world where thieving will not be necessary?"[48] Encounter and having one's mind changed about wealth and poverty can invite unpredicted questions, with disquieting answers.

That said, conversion can take place even without encounter. Wealthy people have created ways to encourage their fellow wealthy people to conversion about the issues of wealth, poverty, and inequality. David Cloutier writes about a practical process to encourage intellectual conversion among wealthy Christians (those who have more than they need). In a parish-based program called Lazarus at the Gate, families meet to learn about socioeconomic problems in a context of frank discussion about how they use their own wealth, even sharing family budgets.[49] A secular organization, Giving What We Can, encourages similar frankness about wealth by sharing information about effective charities and encouraging donors to publicly commit to giving a certain percentage of their income and to recruit friends to do the same.[50] The activist group Resource Generation, which organizes very wealthy young people, has a similar mission.[51] Although these groups of wealthy people do not necessarily practice encounter with the poor, any practice that encourages discussion of how wealth is used, countering the powerful taboos of that conversation in US culture, has the power to encourage conversion. Encounter's power to change us is a function of our human capacity for relationship; our ability to experience conversion without encounter is thanks to our capacity to reason.

The journalist Sarah Smarsh, who grew up in a rural working-poor family in the United States, provides an eloquent account of the power of intellectual conversion for poor persons. She describes how understanding the systemic reasons for inequality helped her see her family's poverty as caused, in part, by the policy choices of those in power, providing context for what could have appeared to be simply personal failings.[52] Coming to understand how inequality is created and how the wealthy choose to stereotype people like her and her family caused her to experience "double consciousness," a concept created by W. E. B. Du Bois to describe the sense of having two selves.[53] As Smarsh encountered the ignorance that so many wealthy people have about people like her family, she grew determined to tell stories like her family's, bridging the gap between their experience and the privileged, insular settings where decisions affecting the poor are made.[54] Conversion for the poor can encompass understanding the systemic factors shaping poverty and inequality and the ways they limit the choices available to the poor. Smarsh's work offers the reality of poverty to the wealthy as an opportunity for their own conversion. As she says, the poor are experts on their own situation whose insights are indispensable for a correct understanding of inequality.[55]

Satisfaction with Contentment

Lúcás Chan has proposed a particular virtue with the potential to help the wealthy resist their hyperagency: the virtue of satisfaction with contentment. Resisting the temptation to covet, as prohibited by the Tenth Commandment, we can practice the virtue of satisfaction with contentment by adjusting our desires—or by, as Elizabeth Hinson-Hasty depicts it, "having the moral courage to recognize when [we have] enough."[56] Chan's other recommendations for personal practice of this virtue include emulating those in voluntary poverty, such as Jesus and contemporary vowed religious; and meditation and prayer.[57] Importantly, Chan notes that the virtue of satisfaction with contentment does not relate only to personal practice but can also be used to evaluate society as a whole. Seeking the virtue of contentment at a societal level demands criticizing materialist cultural aspects of society; ending exploitative practices in the economy; and abandoning the culturally sanctioned individualism that teaches contempt for the poor.[58] Because the vice of coveting so often leads to practices that exploit the poor and workers, its opposite, the virtue of contentment, "challenges the rich and society itself to restore and respect the value and dignity of human beings."[59] In light of inequality's impact on virtue, wealthy Christians should pursue satisfaction with contentment as a metavirtue to help in the pursuit of many others.

Embracing Kingdom Reversal

The biblical depiction of the Kingdom of God is characterized by a total social upheaval that the biblical scholar Daniel Harrington has referred to as "the great reversal."[60] The theme of Kingdom reversal—found prominently in the Hebrew Bible's prophets, Mary's Magnificat (Luke 1:46–55), and Jesus's beatitudes and woes (Matthew 5:3–12 and Luke 6:20–26)—explains that when the fullness of God's plan for humanity comes to pass, those who are poor, sorrowing, and lonely will delight in abundance and joy while those who are rich, powerful, and widely admired will experience loss and abandonment.

Reversal is widely noted as one of the primary biblical descriptors of God's Kingdom. Without exhaustively reviewing a very broad literature, I believe it is fair to say that when theologians discuss this aspect of the Kingdom, they frequently portray it as good news for the poor, who can expect to finally enjoy peace and security after long suffering. It is much less common to hear extensive discussion about what God's promise of reversal means for the rich, secure, and powerful, for whom these promises of Scripture can fairly be regarded as "hard sayings." Can those of us who are rich—who have more than we need—bear to hear it when Scripture promises us hunger, mourning, being thrown down? Furthermore, can we live as if we believe and welcome these biblical promises?

Embracing Scripture's promises of Kingdom reversal is a primary theological and spiritual task for those of us who are rich. Kingdom reversal powerfully warns the rich against accepting a status quo of inequality. How can we say that people are rich because God favors them, when Scripture is clear that God's plan for the rich is to make them poor? If it is easy to see God's loving hand at work when the poor receive enough to eat, Scripture is equally clear that God loves the rich by unseating them from wealth and power. Divesting from wealth, giving up the ways we exercise hyperagency over others, enacts the values of the Kingdom just as much as working to make sure the hungry are fed.

Amaryah Shaye Armstrong analyzes the spiritual and economic implications of dispossession, a voluntary sort of Kingdom reversal. In the spiritual sense, Christians should allow the Spirit to dispossess them of themselves, incorporating them more fully into the divine life.[61] Practical forms of wealth redistribution or property sharing can allow Christians to pursue dispossession in the literal economic sense. An example of such "'risky' forms of being together in the world" is Community Land Trusts, which provide for human needs while disrupting reliance on the institution of private property as a path to the common good.[62] Armstrong expertly reminds us that God desires and enables those with economic power to let go of their mastery of wealth. This active dispossession enables the historically dispossessed—for Armstrong, Black and poor families shut out of economic development—to access the common good. What is more, it allows those possessed of economic privilege to open themselves up to God.

While Armstrong heralds the promise of spiritual and economic dispossession, Vincent Lloyd advises that the hope of becoming dispossessed is a "hope against hope" that invites the wealthy to despair. He outlines how liberation theology and Black theology locate hope in the hope to be among the ones to whom God is preferentially close—that is, in the hope to become poor or Black. These are correct expressions of theological hope because they are oriented toward objects that are good and in the image of God's design. At the same time, such hope is isolating. The privileged person can never fully join the communities favored by God because of "the residuum of privilege," even while her desire to draw near to the marginalized will threaten her place in her own, privileged community. As an apparently futile hope, the hope to become Black and poor invites despair, but together with this despair at the difficulty of renouncing privilege is the hope that the good might be pursued, that whites now may be able to participate in God as long as all idols are abandoned—a hope against hope. The hope to become poor, or Black, must be accompanied by despair so that this hope does not become fantasy, so that it does not become yet another idol. The hope to become poor, or Black, that is to say the proper hope of whites, is a despairing hope, a hope for hopelessness.[63]

Facing the reality of life circumstances such as wealth and race, and the way these life circumstances divide human beings from one another and from God, invites despair at the seeming futility of redressing these divisions. Lloyd reminds us how the theological virtue of hope is only truly present when it enables us to hope in the middle of despair. He points out that poor and oppressed persons are intimately familiar with hope amid despair, which is, perforce, directed away from this world, which has failed them so profoundly, and toward another world where God's plan of universal fulfillment will be realized.[64] For the wealthy, touching this despair—encountering the seemingly insuperable difficulty of becoming poor or Black—is a necessary first step to truly exercising the virtue of hope. To realize that God is close to the dispossessed and that we, ourselves, are not among that number frequently invites despair. But Lloyd insists that this despair is not to be lamented but to be gratefully accepted, because it means we have begun to understand God's self-disclosure.

I have described hyperagency as something that always shapes virtue pursuit for those with more than we need, whether we spend that surplus on ourselves or donate it to the poor. With Lloyd, I hope that confronting this inevitability invites the wealthy to move from despair to the hope of welcoming Kingdom reversal. As Lloyd suggests, "despair at the difficulty of renouncing privilege" can remind those with privilege of something the poor know intimately—the depth of human dependence on God.

Dependence on God

Confronting the necessity and difficulty of dispossession recalls the wealthy back to a fundamental truth: how profoundly we depend on God for our virtue. Theologies of liberation that describe God as poor and the poor as *imago Dei* are already powerful exemplars of helping the poor regain the self-regard they are often denied. Emulating this, Christians must develop contextual theologies for the rich to help counter the pernicious effects of wealth on virtue. Although I have refrained from addressing the connections between virtue and salvation in this work, Jean Porter has argued that Aquinas's view of predestination should inspire us to humility in contemplating our own radical dependence.[65] Reinhold Niebuhr's deep skepticism about groups and their power also holds considerable promise as a contextual theology to help wealthy Christians grapple with the impact of their wealth on their pursuit of virtue. Our pervasive complicity with sinful structures in the economy, which harms others and threatens our own pursuit of virtue, cannot help but inspire fear and trembling, an awareness of dependence on God's mercy, and a firm recommitment to pursuing the good.

For Kathryn Tanner, attempting to live in conformity with God's will teaches us how profoundly we depend not only on God but also on each other: "Recognition of dependence on God shapes how one relates to oneself as the moral subject of action. Because one depends on God rather than on oneself in this most fundamental of relations with oneself, one should be willing to recognize dependence on other people too."[66] For Tanner, this means that Christian belief and practice fundamentally oppose finance-dominated capitalism, which presumes an individualistic vision of society where individuals compete for gains and are personally responsible for individual failures. In contrast, those who follow God cooperate noncompetitively, sometimes despite their own best efforts. In the Christian life, Tanner says, I am as likely to encourage others to persevere when I (inevitably) fail as when I succeed, and the prize we all seek—achieving God's will for us in life and union with the divine after death—is available equally to all.[67]

Encounter, conversion, satisfaction with contentment, embrace of Kingdom reversal, and radical dependence on God all hold promise as Christian theological resources for addressing the impact of wealth, poverty, and inequality on virtue. Now I discuss how Christian communities can embody these theological responses through concrete practices.

PRACTICES FOR THE CHRISTIAN COMMUNITY

It is not enough to simply suggest theological approaches to construing a problem. Christian theology can and should make distinctive contributions to a virtue ethic for wealth, poverty, and inequality by suggesting particular virtuous practices. Practical approaches to remedying inequality's harm to virtue include acting in the political sphere for change; a renewed look at tithing and aid; and fostering encounter in parishes and education settings.

Political Action

Although concern about inequality has only recently gained prominence in Christian ethics, the Christian tradition has long viewed a society's goodness as tied to its equitable distribution of goods. Aquinas taught that goods have a universal destination: "Whatever particular goods are procured by man's agency—whether wealth, profits, health, eloquence, or learning—are ordained to the good life of the multitude."[68] And although Aquinas was no democrat—he argued that the most perfect form of government is rule by a virtuous king—he denounced as "oligarchy" a power structure where a few are able to oppress others by means of their wealth.[69] Aquinas insists that the end of human society is to live virtuously, not to acquire wealth, and that the most important role of rulers is to help all members of society achieve virtue.[70] The body of Catholic social thought similarly challenges extreme inequality and paints the political realm as one appropriate arena in which believers can respond. Kenneth Himes writes, "In the contemporary situation of the United States, the existence of vast inequality between the rich and the rest of the population serves as a clear contradiction to the vision of Catholic social teaching."[71] Christians fulfill the vision of their theological tradition when they act in the political realm to reduce wealthy people's dominance over common life and to create a more equitable society free from the obstacles that wealth and poverty can create for the pursuit of virtue.

We have already discussed Pope Francis's call to encounter. With statements like "it is essential to draw near to new forms of poverty and vulnerability," Francis appears to address people with some degree of power within global inequality, those I have called "rich" in this book.[72] It should be clear how crucial it is for people who have more than they need to go out to those who struggle for what they need, not only to help them, but also so each person can be formed by the encounter. Creating sites for encounter where poor and wealthy people can interact on an equal footing, with neither serving the other, is a key task for Christian institutions. It may also be necessary to pursue the virtue of Jesuit hospitality in "going out" to those wealthy few who wield disproportionate power in our unequal economy, working to persuade them to give up their own power and privilege for the sake of their own virtue and the common good. Some of the people I have called rich in this book, but who might prefer to self-define as middle class, may be in a unique position to perform such acts of encounter in service of reducing inequality and in service of the virtue of all. Certainly, action in the political sphere can be one way of pursuing encounter with the wealthy who retain power within the system of global inequality.

Rethinking Tithing and Aid

In the recent revival of virtue ethics, Julie Hanlon Rubio has offered very helpful and specific contributions for using our wealth to promote our virtue. Rubio examines spending within a family context, asking how parents can form their children in virtuous practice with respect to money. She concludes that families should tithe an amount that will be felt in the family living standard, even though this may feel difficult, in order to train all the members of the family in the virtue of temperance.[73] She recognizes that Christians should look at aid given to the poor in two ways: its usefulness to the one who needs it, and the effect of giving on the one who gives.

In light of wealthy hyperagency, Christians need to look at aid with Rubio's dual perspective, which amply challenges conventional wisdom about relationships between the wealthy and the poor. For much of modern history, it has been viewed as perfectly acceptable for aid from the wealthy to the poor to come completely on the terms of the wealthy, according to what the wealthy think the poor need, and through methods that help wealthy people feel good about themselves.[74] A recent movement to provide aid to the poor based on research into where funds can alleviate the most suffering, rather than based on what the wealthy would like to do, is viewed as so novel that it has its own name: "effective altruism."[75] Despite effective altruism's undeniable appeal, both these approaches to giving reinscribe wealthy hyperagency. Both assume that the wealthy donor will choose what to do with her economic power; effective altruism simply aims to encourage donors to give based on social science, rather than their own whims. Approaches to aid couched in market transactions, such as "fair trade," also reinscribe hyperagency for the wealthy by encouraging practices of consumer choice. If we want to limit hyperagency's impact on virtue, we need to explore what giving would look like if wealthy people gave in ways that voluntarily *limited* their own power and choice.

We can envision approaches to aid that both prioritize effective assistance to those in need and limit opportunities for the wealthy to exercise their hyperagency. Approaches to social change should truly place the surplus of the wealthy at the disposal of the poor. For example, donors should fund community organizations where all the decision-makers are poor or otherwise marginalized, even if those organizations are not formally tax-exempt.[76] Supporting crowdfunding appeals by those in poverty, where help is requested and given on the poor person's terms, is another way for wealthy people to share power with the poor without reinscribing their own hyperagency. Paying living wages and advocating for higher taxes at one's own income level, to be used to benefit the poor, are others. Such acts of concrete solidarity can inculcate virtue against hyperagency, and some also provide opportunities for true encounter.

Sites of Encounter

Christian communities should engage in concrete practices to foster encounter. Drawing on Dalit liberation theology, Michael Amaladoss makes suggestions for Christian responses to caste and economic inequality, both within Christian communities and in the broader society. He urges Christians to promote "inter-dining and intermarrying," bringing inclusion to cultural sites of caste discrimination.[77]

The Eucharist should be a preeminent site of interdining among wealthy and poor, but given wealth's tendency to segregate itself, it often is not. Responding to the racial self-segregation of white people in the United States, Katie Grimes has suggested that dioceses organize parish Masses so that white Catholics will have to travel to parishes where Black Catholics predominate in order to participate in the Eucharist.[78] This suggestion of deliberate, challenging integration has promise as a tool against economic inequality as well.

As Grimes's insight about parish segregation shows, Catholic institutions too often are not, in their ordinary practices, sites of encounter and resistance to inequality. Jacquineau Azetsop notes that due to the cost of education and health care in Africa, "the mission schools or hospitals built for the neediest become accessible only to the upper class. Sons and daughters of those who have destroyed the education, health care, economy, and social services are often the first beneficiary of Catholic education."[79] In the United States, too, Catholic hospitals, colleges, and universities are complicit in economic inequality.[80] Catholic institutions court wealthy donors and compete to serve the wealthy as patients and students. One way Catholic universities can serve the virtue of their wealthy constituent base is to educate them about the impact of wealth on the virtues. However, if their donors take hyperagency seriously, they might contribute their dollars to community organizations led by the poor, rather than endowing a new institutional building.

There is much more that institutions of Catholic higher education can do to foster a culture of encounter between rich and poor. How powerful the impact could be if mission trips designed to expose wealthy students to poverty introduced them to the poor from whose poverty they themselves benefit, be it maquiladora workers in Mexico's Apple factories or, better yet, the US working poor who staff the coffee shops and retail palaces of student leisure time. In addition, Catholic institutions of higher education should organize sites of encounter for employees at all income levels—janitorial, food service, and adjunct faculty workers talking (and ideally eating) with tenured faculty and administrators. This is a practical way for mission and ministry departments to make their theological charisms visible and imme- diate to university staff.

Christian individuals, families, and institutions may be complicit in eco- nomic inequality, but there is much they can do to resist it. We can rethink tithing and aid to consider both the need of the donee and the virtue of the donor, encouraging wealthy Christians (and people of other or no faith) to choose giving practices that resist hyperagency. We can take political action together against extreme economic inequality. And in a thousand creative, challenging ways, we can pursue encounter in our parishes and Catholic institutions.

CONTRIBUTIONS OF THIS WORK

This book has sought to accomplish two goals. It uses resources from the Christian tradition to make the case that wealth, poverty, and inequality affect virtue, and it provides a language for this process—moral luck—and an example of its use. As such, it contributes to the literature on Christian economic ethics and to research on ethical methods, particularly virtue ethics.

As chapter 1 demonstrated, previous theological work on inequality often focuses on its consequences in the political realm. For example, Doug- las Hicks argues that Christians should be concerned about inequality when it translates into inequality of basic functioning.[81] This book highlights another reason to be concerned about inequality: the way it functions as moral luck to shape virtue pursuit. Similarly, too much Christian theological work on wealth and poverty focuses on the practical impact of poverty on poor people, addressing wealthy people only insofar as they are expected to help the poor. Although there is ample warrant in the Christian tradition for attending to the virtue impact of wealth and poverty, as this book has shown, contempo- rary theological ethical works that explore it this way are few. Julie Hanlon Rubio's *Family Ethics* and David Cloutier's *The Vice of Luxury* come to mind as standout exceptions.[82] My work on the virtue impact of wealth, poverty, and inequality adds to this growing field.

My primary goal in writing about the impact of wealth, poverty, and inequality on virtue has been, simply, to reflect something real. Hearing the voices of poor writers, and how they say their poverty affects their virtue, readers gain a more complete understanding of the virtuous life. For wealthy people, I hope this work will encourage them to reflect on how their wealth affects their virtue in ways they may not have considered. I locate this work within two of the strands of Catholic feminism delineated by Lisa Sowle Cahill.[83] In its exhortation to consider the personal spiritual life and daily practices, this work is neo-Franciscan; in its conviction that we can learn from the social sciences and work within public life to build a better world, it is neo-Thomist.

In addition to drawing from the long Christian tradition on wealth, this work "talks back" to it. A virtue approach to wealth, poverty, and inequality should help rout the excessively spiritualized view of wealth that has long lurked in the Christian tradition. If I am right about wealth's impact on virtue, Christians can no longer claim that the proper attitude to wealth can make its possession morally neutral—or, in Augustine's phrasing, that it is possible to "have wealth as not having it." Wealthy people need to face and acknowledge the ways that our wealth affects our virtue and recommit to practices that cultivate virtue in spite of this.

Practical solutions can reduce inequality by redistributing wealth to the poor and can provide the space for theological approaches to work. For example, reducing economic segregation in communities can improve the possibility of encounter, the meeting of genuine selves that changes our view of the world and our own place in it. Structural economic solutions are vital for improving the situation of poor people in unequal economies and for reducing practical burdens on their virtue pursuit, such as bandwidth scarcity. Ultimately, virtue pursuit needs dispositions such as conversion and recognition of our own dependence, spiritual solutions that no structural change can guarantee.

NOTES

1. Francis, *Evangelii gaudium*, 53.
2. Mishel and Schieder, "CEO Pay Remains High."
3. Reardon and Bischoff, "Income Inequality," 1139–40.
4. Reardon and Bischoff, 1140.
5. See chapter 5.
6. Ward, "Porters," 218–19.
7. Hobart, "Life."
8. Potts, "What's Killing Poor White Women?"; Mann, "Medicine."
9. Mann, "Medicine."
10. Crow Dog, *Lakota Woman*, 26.
11. Pickett and Wilkinson, *Spirit Level*, 222–23.
12. Walasek, Bhatia, and Brown, "Positional Goods."

13. Ludwig et al., "Neighborhood Effects."
14. Atkinson, *Inequality*, 126–27.
15. See chapter 6.
16. Finn, *Consumer Ethics.*
17. Gutiérrez, "Faith," 35.
18. Rieger, *No Rising Tide*, 30–31. Of course, if Rieger is right, the troubling corollary is that we can expect to see *less* solidarity from wealthy people in times of economic recovery.
19. Benedict XVI, "Address," paragraph 4.
20. Pickett and Wilkinson, *Spirit Level*, 231.
21. Jargowsky, "Architecture."
22. Lindsey and Teles, *Captured Economy*, chap. 6.
23. Lindsey and Teles, 154–59.
24. Atkinson, *Inequality*, 179–200.
25. Piketty, *Capital*, 497.
26. Piketty, 522.
27. Piketty, 471.
28. Piketty, 528.
29. Piketty, 539. The preceding paragraph is largely taken from my blog post: Ward, "Capital."
30. Atkinson, *Inequality*, 202–4.
31. Atkinson, 205.
32. Atkinson, 140.
33. Atkinson, 206–18.
34. Atkinson, 147–53.
35. Krishna, *One Illness Away*, 157–59.
36. Parijs, "Basic Income Capitalism"; Parijs, "Basic Income for All"; Parijs, "Universal Basic Income."
37. Ward, "Universal Basic Income," 1271.
38. Ward, "Does Catholic Social Teaching Support a Universal Basic Income?" Atkinson's proposal of a "participation income" fails this test, in my view, because it still projects that someone's right to basic needs depends on their contributions to society (to say nothing of the major difficulties in verifying "participation"). Atkinson, *Inequality*, 218–23.
39. Ward, "Universal Basic Income."
40. Francis and Ivereigh, *Let Us Dream*, 131–32.
41. Keenan, "Jesuit Hospitality?" 237; see also Ward, "Jesuit and Feminist Hospitality," 71.
42. Gutiérrez, "Faith," 32.
43. Is it a coincidence that with rising inequality we see an emphasis on "emotional labor" in the retail context, as the employer expects to control not just the bodies and schedules of retail employees but their emotional affect as well? See, e.g., Noah, "Labor."
44. Sobrino, "Awakening," 365.
45. Doran, "What Does Bernard Lonergan Mean?" 5.
46. Sobrino, "Awakening," 366–67.
47. Copeland, *Enfleshing Freedom*, 220–23.
48. Amaladoss, *Life*, 17.
49. Cloutier, *Vice*, 19.
50. "Giving What We Can: About Us," www.givingwhatwecan.org/about-us/.
51. "Resource Generation, "Mission."
52. Smarsh, *Heartland*, 261.

53. Smarsh, "Poor Teeth."
54. Smarsh, *Heartland*, 263.
55. Wick, "Interview."
56. Chan, *Ten Commandments*, 137; Hinson-Hasty, *Problem*, 128.
57. Chan, *Ten Commandments*, 137–38.
58. Chan, 139.
59. Chan.
60. Harrington, *Meeting St. Luke*, 73–74, 85.
61. Armstrong, "Spirit," 64.
62. Armstrong, 68, 67.
63. Lloyd, "For What Are Whites to Hope?" 179.
64. Lloyd, 176.
65. Porter, "Recent Studies," 213–14.
66. Tanner, *Christianity*, 210.
67. Tanner, chap. 6.
68. Aquinas, "De Regno," 114.
69. Aquinas, 11.
70. Aquinas, 106.
71. Himes, "Catholic Social Teaching," 306.
72. Francis, *Evangelii gaudium*, 210.
73. Rubio, *Family Ethics*, chap. 7.
74. Pimpare, *People's History*.
75. Singer, "Logic"; Banerjee and Duflo, *Poor Economics*.
76. This is the approach encouraged by Resource Generation, the group that organizes wealthy young people to combat inequality. See "Resource Generation, "Guidance."
77. Amaladoss, *Life*, 30–31.
78. Grimes, *Christ Divided*.
79. Azetsop, *Structural Violence*, 283–84.
80. Carlson, "Poor Kids"; Supiano, "College"; Keenan, *University Ethics*.
81. Hicks, *Inequality*.
82. Rubio, *Family Ethics*; Cloutier, *Vice*.
83. Cahill, "Catholic Feminists," 27–51. The other two strands are neo-Augustinian, which promotes a view of Church as countercultural amid the sin of the world, and Junian, a multivalent strand embodying the prophetic views of feminists from Africa, Asia, and Latin America.

BIBLIOGRAPHY

Adams, Robert Merrihew. "Self-Love and the Vices of Self-Preference." *Faith and Philosophy* 15, no. 4 (October 1, 1998): 500–513.

Adewale, Olubiyi Adeniyi. "An Afro-Sociological Application of the Parable of the Rich Man and Lazarus (Luke 16:19–31)." *Black Theology* 4, no. 1 (January 2006): 27–43.

Alison, James. *The Joy of Being Wrong: Original Sin through Easter Eyes.* New York: Crossroad, 1998.

Allard, Scott W. *Places in Need: The Changing Geography of Poverty.* New York: Russell Sage Foundation, 2017.

Altintas, Evrim. "The Widening Education Gap in Developmental Child Care Activities in the United States, 1965–2013." *Journal of Marriage and Family* 78, no. 1 (February 1, 2016): 26–42. https://doi.org/10.1111/jomf.12254.

Amaladoss, Michael. *Life in Freedom: Liberation Theologies from Asia.* Maryknoll, NY: Orbis Books, 1997.

American Academy of Religion, Moral Injury and Recovery in Religion, Society, and Culture Group. "Call for Papers (Comments)." No date. https://papers.aarweb.org/content/moral-injury-and-recovery-religion-society-and-culture-group.

Anderson, Gary A. *Charity: The Place of the Poor in the Biblical Tradition.* New Haven, CT: Yale University Press, 2013.

Anderson, Kevin. "Hypocrites in the Air: Should Climate Change Academics Lead by Example?" *KevinAnderson.Info* (blog), April 12, 2013. http://kevinanderson.info/blog/hypocrites-in-the-air-should-climate-change-academics-lead-by-example/.

Andolsen, Barbara Hilkert. "The Grace and Fortitude Not to Turn Our Backs." In *The Church Women Want: Catholic Women in Dialogue,* edited by Elizabeth A. Johnson, 73–82. New York: Crossroad, 2002.

Antoncich, Ricardo, SJ. "Sollicitudo rei socialis: A Latin American Perspective." In *The Logic of Solidarity: Commentaries on Pope John Paul II's Encyclical "On Social Concern,"* edited by Gregory Baum and Robert Ellsberg, 211–26. Maryknoll, NY: Orbis Books, 1989.

Aquinas, Thomas. "De Regno Ad Regem Cypri (On Kingship)." Ed. Joseph Kenny, OP. Trans. Gerald B. Phelan and I. Th. Eschmann, 1949. http://dhspriory.org/thomas/DeRegno.htm.

———. *Disputed Questions on the Virtues.* Edited by E. M. Atkins and Thomas Williams. Cambridge Texts in the History of Philosophy. New York: Cambridge University Press, 2005.

———. *Disputed Questions on the Virtues.* Trans. Ralph McInerny. South Bend, IN: St. Augustine's Press, 1999. http://dhspriory.org/thomas/english/QDdeVirtutibus.htm.

———. "Liber Contra Impugnantes Dei Cultum et Religionem." Ed. Joseph Kenny, OP. Trans. John Procter, OP. DHS Priory, 1902. http://dhspriory.org/thomas/ContraImpugnantes.htm#25.

———. "Liber de Perfectione Spiritualis Vitae [The Perfection of the Spiritual Life]." Trans. John Procter, OP. DHS Priory, 1950. http://dhspriory.org/thomas/PerfectVitaeSpir.htm.

———. *The Summa Theologica of St. Thomas Aquinas.* Trans. Dominican Fathers of the English Province. London: Burns Oates & Washbourne, 1921.

Armstrong, Amaryah. "The Spirit and the Subprime: Race, Risk, and Our Common Dispossession." *Anglican Theological Review* 98, no. 1 (Winter 2016): 51–69.

Asante-Muhammad, Dedrick, Chuck Collins, Josh Hoxie, and Emanuel Nieves. "The Road to Zero Wealth." Institute for Policy Studies, 2017. http://www.ips-dc.org/wp-content/uploads/2017/09/The-Road-to-Zero-Wealth_FINAL.pdf.

Astorga, Christina A. *Catholic Moral Theology and Social Ethics: A New Method.* Maryknoll, NY: Orbis Books, 2014.

Atkinson, Anthony B. *Inequality: What Can Be Done?* Cambridge, MA: Harvard University Press, 2015.

Augustine. *Commentary on the Lord's Sermon on the Mount, with Seventeen Related Sermons.* Trans. Denis J. Kavanaugh. New York: Fathers of the Church, 1951.

———. *Letters Vol. II.* Trans. Sister Wilfrid Parsons. Fathers of the Church. Washington, DC: Catholic University of America Press, 1953.

———. *The Trinity.* Brooklyn: New City Press, 1991.

Austin, Nicholas Owen. "Thomas Aquinas on the Four Causes of Temperance." PhD diss., Boston College, 2010.

Azetsop, Jacquineau. *Structural Violence, Population Health and Health Equity.* Riga: VDM, 2010.

Bader-Saye, Scott. "Closing the Gap: A Social Imaginary for the Common Good." *Anglican Theological Review* 98, no. 1 (2016): 91–109.

Bailey, James P. *Rethinking Poverty: Income, Assets, and the Catholic Social Justice Tradition.* Notre Dame, IN: University of Notre Dame Press, 2010.

Baker, David, and Natacha Keramidas. "The Psychology of Hunger." *Monitor On Psychology* 44, no. 9 (October 2013): 66.

Baker, Dean. "Rising Inequality: It's Not the Market." *Journal of Catholic Social Thought* 12, no. 1 (January 2015): 5.

Balestra, Carlotta, and Richard Tonkin. "Inequalities in Household Wealth across OECD Countries: Evidence from the OECD Wealth Distribution Database." OECD Statistics Working Paper 88, June 20, 2018.

Bane, Mary Jo. "Catholic Social Teachings, American Politics and Inequality." *Journal of Catholic Social Thought* 11, no. 2 (July 2014): 391–404.

Banerjee, Abhijit. *The Shape of Temptation: Implications for the Economic Lives of the Poor.* NBER Working Paper 15973. Cambridge, MA: National Bureau of Economic Research, 2010.

Banerjee, Abhijit V., and Esther Duflo. *Poor Economics: A Radical Rethinking of the Way to Fight Global Poverty.* New York: PublicAffairs, 2011.

Barbour, Amy R., and Marvin E. Wickware Jr. "Breaking the Chains of Chattel Teamwork: The Future of Black Liberation Theology." *Union Seminary Quarterly Review* 64, nos. 2–3 (2013): 44–51.

Barrera, Albino. *God and the Evil of Scarcity: Moral Foundations of Economic Agency.* Notre Dame, IN: University of Notre Dame Press, 2005.

Barton, John. *Understanding Old Testament Ethics: Approaches and Explorations.* Louisville: Westminster John Knox Press, 2003.

Beed, Clive S. (Clive Saunders), and Cara Beed. "Recent Christian Interpretations of Material Poverty and Inequality in the Developed World." *Journal of Markets & Morality* 16, no. 2 (2013): 407–27.

Benedict XVI. "Address of His Holiness Benedict XVI to the Fifth General Conference of the Bishops of Latin America and the Caribbean," May 13, 2007. http://w2.vatican.va /content/benedict-xvi/en/speeches/2007/may/documents/hf_ben-xvi_spe_20070513 _conference-aparecida.html.

———. "Caritas in Veritate (Charity in Truth)," June 29, 2009. www.vatican.va/holy_father /benedict_xvi/encyclicals/documents/hf_ben-xvi_enc_20090629_caritas-in-veritate _en.html.

Berg, Andrew G., and Jonathan D. Ostry. "Inequality and Unsustainable Growth: Two Sides of the Same Coin?" International Monetary Fund, April 8, 2011. www.imf.org/external /pubs/ft/sdn/2011/sdn1108.pdf.

Berkman, John. "Are Persons with Profound Intellectual Disabilities Sacramental Icons of Heavenly Life? Aquinas on Impairment." *Studies in Christian Ethics* 26, no. 1 (2013): 83–96.

Blount, Brian K. *Then the Whisper Put on Flesh: New Testament Ethics in an African American Context*. Nashville: Abingdon Press, 2001.

Bonner, Raymond. "The Diplomat and the Killer." *Atlantic*, February 11, 2016. www.theatlantic .com/international/archive/2016/02/el-salvador-churchwomen-murders/460320/.

Bounds, Elizabeth Margaret. "Way Down in the Hole: Imprisonment and Moral Injury." Paper presented at Moral Injury and Recovery section at American Academy of Religion 2014 annual meeting.

Bourg, Florence Caffrey. *Where Two or Three Are Gathered: Christian Families as Domestic Churches*. Notre Dame, IN: University of Notre Dame Press, 2004.

Bowlin, John R. *Contingency and Fortune in Aquinas's Ethics*. New York: Cambridge University Press, 1999.

Boyd, Craig A. "Pride and Humility: Tempering the Desire for Excellence." In *Virtues and Their Vices*, edited by Kevin Timpe and Craig A. Boyd, 245–66. Oxford: Oxford University Press, 2014.

Bragg, Rick. *All Over but the Shoutin'*. New York: Pantheon Books, 1997.

———. "All She Has, $150,000, Is Going to a University." *New York Times*, August 13, 1995. www.nytimes.com/1995/08/13/us/all-she-has-150000-is-going-to-a-university.html.

———. "She Opened World to Others; Her World Has Opened, Too." *New York Times*, November 12, 1996. www.nytimes.com/1996/11/12/us/she-opened-world-to-others -her-world-has-opened-too.html.

Breslow, Jason M. "Dolores Huerta: An 'Epidemic in the Fields.'" *Frontline*, June 25, 2013. www.pbs.org/wgbh/frontline/article/dolores-huerta-an-epidemic-in-the-fields/.

Bretherton, Luke. "Soteriology, Debt, and Faithful Witness: Four Theses for a Political Theology of Economic Democracy." *Anglican Theological Review* 98, no. 1 (Winter 2016): 71–89.

Bretzke, James T. "Human Rights or Human Rites? A Cross-Cultural Ethical Perspective." *East Asian Pastoral Review* 41 (2004): 44–67.

Brock, Rita Nakashima, and Gabriella Lettini. *Soul Repair: Recovering from Moral Injury after War*. Boston: Beacon Press, 2012.

Bureau of Labor Statistics. "Consumer Expenditures Surveys Glossary." 2015. www.bls.gov /cex/csxgloss.htm#inc.

———. "Table 1110: Deciles of Income before Taxes—Annual Expenditure Means, Shares, Standard Errors, and Coefficients of Variation, Consumer Expenditure Survey, 2018." www.bls.gov/cex/2018/combined/decile.pdf.

Cahill, Lisa Sowle. "Catholic Feminists and Traditions: Renewal, Reinvention, Replacement." *Journal of the Society of Christian Ethics* 34, no. 2 (2014): 27–51.

———. "Community Versus Universals: A Misplaced Debate in Christian Ethics." *Annual of the Society of Christian Ethics* 18 (January 1, 1998): 3–12.

———. *Global Justice, Christology, and Christian Ethics.* New York: Cambridge University Press, 2013.

———. "Justice for Women: Martha Nussbaum and Catholic Social Teaching." In *Transforming Unjust Structures: The Capability Approach*, edited by Séverine Deneulin, Mathias Nebel, and Nicholas Sagovsky, 83–104. Dordrecht: Springer Netherlands, 2006.

Camosy, Charles Christopher. *Peter Singer and Christian Ethics: Beyond Polarization.* EBSCO Academic Collection Ebooks. New York: Cambridge University Press, 2012.

Campos, Clement. "Doing Christian Ethics in India's World of Cultural Complexity and Social Inequality." In *Catholic Theological Ethics in the World Church*, 82–90. New York; London: Continuum, 2007.

Cannon, Katie G. *Black Womanist Ethics.* American Academy of Religion Academy Series 60. Atlanta: Scholars Press, 1988.

Card, Claudia. "Gender and Moral Luck [1990]." In *Justice and Care: Essential Readings in Feminist Ethics*, edited by Virginia Held, 79–99. Boulder, CO: Westview Press, 1995.

———. *The Unnatural Lottery: Character and Moral Luck.* Philadelphia: Temple University Press, 1996.

Carlson, Scott. "Poor Kids, Limited Horizons." *Chronicle of Higher Education*, January 17, 2016. http://chronicle.com/article/Poor-Kids-Limited-Horizons/234950/?key=9aQrcr1j VCDk-wUQmLeqjMpffH8pnCUIm-zGpxhVihJfMTl5SHdEVlJLbmtQWi1mMjlqN2 FUNWNlSURqbE9VQjE1Wk5kak4zQlFv.

Carroll, M. Daniel. *Christians at the Border: Immigration, the Church, and the Bible.* Grand Rapids: Baker Academic, 2008.

Cates, Diana Fritz. "The Virtue of Temperance (IIa IIae, Qq. 141–170)." In *Ethics of Aquinas*, 321–39. Washington, DC: Georgetown University Press, 2002.

Cavanaugh, William T. *Being Consumed: Economics and Christian Desire.* Grand Rapids: William B. Eerdmans, 2008.

CELAM (Consejo Episcopal Latinoamericano; General Conference of the Bishops of Latin America and the Caribbean). "Aparecida Concluding Document." May 13, 2007.

———. "Medellín Document: Peace." September 6, 1968. www.shc.edu/theolibrary/resources /medpeace.htm.

———. "Medellín Document: Poverty of the Church." September 6, 1968. www.shc.edu /theolibrary/resources/medpeace.htm.

Chan, Yiu Sing Lúcás. "The Hebrew Bible and the Discourse on Migration: A Reflection on the Virtue of Hospitality in the Book of Ruth." *Asian Horizons* 8, no. 4 (December 2014): 665–79.

———. *The Ten Commandments and the Beatitudes: Biblical Studies and Ethics for Real Life.* Lanham, MD: Rowman & Littlefield, 2012.

Chapp, Larry S. "The Precarity of Love: Dorothy Day on Poverty." *Communio* 42, no. 3 (2015): 381–93.

Chen, Victor Tan. *Cut Loose: Jobless and Hopeless in an Unfair Economy.* Berkeley: University of California Press, 2015.

Cherlin, Andrew J., Elizabeth Talbert, and Suzumi Yasutake. "Changing Fertility Regimes and the Transition to Adulthood: Evidence from a Recent Cohort." Paper presented at

Population Association of America Annual Meeting, Boston, May 3, 2014. http://krieger
.jhu.edu/sociology/wp-content/uploads/sites/28/2012/02/Read-Online.pdf.

Chetty, Raj, Michael Stepner, Sarah Abraham, Shelby Lin, Benjamin Scuderi, Nicholas
Turner, Augustin Bergeron, and David Cutler. "The Association Between Income and
Life Expectancy in the United States, 2001–2014." *JAMA* 315, no. 16 (April 26, 2016):
1750–66. https://doi.org/10.1001/jama.2016.4226.

Chiteji, N. S., and Darrick Hamilton. "Family Connections and the Black/White Wealth Gap
among Middle-Class Families." *Review of Black Political Economy* 30, no. 1 (June 2002):
9–28. https://doi.org/10.1007/BF02808169.

Christiansen, Drew. "On Relative Equality: Catholic Egalitarianism after Vatican II." *Theological Studies* 45, no. 4 (1984): 651–75.

Chuhan-Pole, Punam, Luc Christiaensen, Allen Dennis, Gerard Kambou, Manka Angwafo,
Mapi Buitano, Vijdan Korman, Camila Galindo Pardo, Aly Sanoh, Francisco H. G. Ferreira,
Delfin Go, Maryla Maliszewska, and Israel Osorio-Rodarte. "Africa's Pulse: An Analysis of
Issues Shaping Africa's Economic Future." World Bank Office of the Chief Economist
for the Africa Region, October 2013. www.worldbank.org/content/dam/Worldbank
/document/Africa/Report/Africas-Pulse-brochure_Vol8.pdf.

Claassens, L. Juliana. "The Woman of Substance and Human Flourishing: Proverbs 31:10–31
and Martha Nussbaum's Capabilities Approach." *Journal of Feminist Studies in Religion* 32,
no. 1 (2016): 5–19. https://doi.org/10.2979/jfemistudreli.32.1.02.

Clark, Andrew E., Paul Frijters, and Michael A. Shields. "Relative Income, Happiness, and
Utility: An Explanation for the Easterlin Paradox and Other Puzzles." *Journal of Economic
Literature* 46, no. 1 (March 2008): 95–144. https://doi.org/10.1257/jel.46.1.95.

Clark, Charles M. A. "Wealth as Abundance and Scarcity: Perspectives from Catholic Social
Thought and Economic Theory." In *Rediscovering Abundance: Interdisciplinary Essays on
Wealth, Income, and Their Distribution in the Catholic Social Tradition*, edited by Helen
Alford, Charles M. A. Clark, S. A. Cortright, and Michael J. Naughton, 28–56. Notre
Dame, IN: University of Notre Dame Press, 2006.

Clark, Meghan J. "Development as Freedom Together: Human Dignity & Human Rights in
Catholic Social Teaching & Capabilities Approaches." In *Integral Human Development:
Catholic Social Teaching and the Capabilities Approach*, edited by Severine Deneulin and
Clemens Sedmak. Forthcoming from University of Notre Dame Press.

———. *The Vision of Catholic Social Thought: The Virtue of Solidarity and the Praxis of Human
Rights*. Minneapolis: Fortress Press, 2014.

Clarke, Kevin. "Sister Helen Prejean's 'Happy Day' as Pope Francis Revises Teaching on the
Death Penalty." *America Magazine*, August 3, 2018. www.americamagazine.org/faith/2018
/08/03/sister-helen-prejeans-happy-day-pope-francis-revises-teaching-death-penalty.

Cloutier, David M. "Exclusion, Fragmentation, and Theft: A Survey and Synthesis of Moral
Approaches to Economic Inequality." *Journal of Moral Theology* 7, no. 1 (January 2018):
141–72.

———. "The Problem of Luxury in the Christian Life." *Journal of the Society of Christian
Ethics*, March 1, 2012.

———. *The Vice of Luxury: Economic Excess in a Consumer Age*. Washington, DC: Georgetown University Press, 2015.

Coates, Ta-Nehisi. "The Black Family in the Age of Mass Incarceration." *Atlantic*, October
2015. www.theatlantic.com/magazine/archive/2015/10/the-black-family-in-the-age-of
-mass-incarceration/403246/.

———. "The Case for Reparations." *Atlantic*, June 2014. www.theatlantic.com/features/archive /2014/05/the-case-for-reparations/361631/.

Cohen, Patricia. "Scholars Return to 'Culture of Poverty' Ideas." *New York Times*, October 17, 2010. www.nytimes.com/2010/10/18/us/18poverty.html.

Coles, Robert. *Children of Crisis: Selections from the Pulitzer Prize–Winning Five-Volume Children of Crisis Series*. Boston: Little, Brown, 2003.

Cone, James H. *Martin & Malcolm & America: A Dream or a Nightmare*. Maryknoll, NY: Orbis Books, 1991.

Copeland, M. Shawn. *Enfleshing Freedom: Body, Race, and Being*. Minneapolis: Fortress Press, 2010.

———. "Presidential Address: Political Theology as Interruptive." *Proceedings of the Catholic Theological Society of America* 59 (2004): 71–82.

———. "Toward a Critical Christian Feminist Theology of Solidarity." In *Women and Theology*, edited by Mary Ann Hinsdale and Phyllis H. Kaminski, 3–38. Annual Publication of the College Theology Society, Annual Volume 40 (1994). Maryknoll, NY: Orbis Books, 1995.

———. "'Wading Through Many Sorrows': Toward a Theology of Suffering in Womanist Perspective." In *Feminist Ethics and the Catholic Moral Tradition*, edited by Charles E. Curran, Margaret A Farley, and Richard A. McCormick, 136–63. New York: Paulist Press, 1996.

Cowen, Tyler. "Income Inequality Is Not Rising Globally. It's Falling." *New York Times*, July 19, 2014. www.nytimes.com/2014/07/20/upshot/income-inequality-is-not-rising-globally -its-falling-.html.

Crow Dog, Mary. (Mary Brave Bird). *Lakota Woman*. First edition. New York: G. Weidenfeld, 1990.

Curran, Charles E. *Directions in Fundamental Moral Theology*. Notre Dame, IN: University of Notre Dame Press, 1985.

Curzer, Howard. "Aristotle's Account of the Virtue of Temperance in Nicomachean Ethics III.10–11." *Journal of the History of Philosophy* 35, no. 1 (1997): 5–25.

Daley, Suzanne. "Hunger on the Rise in Spain." *New York Times*, September 24, 2012. www .nytimes.com/2012/09/25/world/europe/hunger-on-the-rise-in-spain.html.

Daly, Daniel J. "Structures of Virtue and Vice." *New Blackfriars* 92 (2011): 341–57.

Davidson, Paul. "Does a $70,000 Minimum Wage Work?" *USA Today*, May 26, 2016. www.usatoday.com/story/money/2016/05/26/does-70000-minimum-wage-work /84913242/.

Day, Dorothy. "Foreword to *House of Hospitality*." New York: Sheed & Ward, 1939. www .catholicworker.org/dorothyday/articles/435.html.

———. "Room for Christ." *The Catholic Worker*, December 1945. https://www.catholic worker.org/dorothyday/articles/416.html.

———. *The Long Loneliness: The Autobiography of the Legendary Catholic Social Activist*. San Francisco: HarperOne, 2009.

———. "The Mystery of the Poor." *Catholic Worker*, April 1964. www.catholicworker.org /dorothyday/articles/189.html.

De Graaf, John, David Wann, and Thomas H. Naylor. *Affluenza: How Overconsumption Is Killing Us—And How We Can Fight Back*. 3rd ed. San Francisco: Berret-Koehler, 2014.

De La Torre, Miguel A. *Doing Christian Ethics from the Margins*. 2nd rev. ed. Maryknoll, NY: Orbis Books, 2014.

———. *Latina/o Social Ethics: Moving beyond Eurocentric Moral Thinking*. New Perspectives in Latina/o Religion. Waco, TX: Baylor University Press, 2010.

Decosimo, David. *Ethics as a Work of Charity: Thomas Aquinas and Pagan Virtue*. Stanford, CA: Stanford University Press, 2014.

Doak, Mary. *Divine Harmony: Seeking Community in a Broken World*. New York: Paulist Press, 2017.

Doepke, Matthias, and Fabrizio Zilibotti. *Love, Money, and Parenting: How Economics Explains the Way We Raise Our Kids*. Princeton, NJ: Princeton University Press, 2019.

Doran, Robert. "What Does Bernard Lonergan Mean by Conversion?" St. Michael's, Toronto, 2011. www.lonerganresource.com/pdf/lectures/What%20Does%20Bernard%20Lonergan %20Mean%20by%20Conversion.pdf.

Duncan, Greg J., Kjetil Telle, Kathleen M. Ziol-Guest, and Ariel Kalil. "Economic Deprivation in Early Childhood and Adult Attainment: Comparative Evidence from Norwegian Registry Data and the US Panel Study of Income Dynamics." In *Persistence, Privilege, and Parenting: The Comparative Study of Intergenerational Mobility*, edited by Timothy M. Smeeding, Markus Jäntti, and Robert Erikson, 209–34. New York: Russell Sage Foundation, 2011.

Dwyer-Lindgren, Laura, Amelia Bertozzi-Villa, Rebecca W. Stubbs, Chloe Morozoff, Johan P. Mackenbach, Frank J. van Lenthe, Ali H. Mokdad, and Christopher J. L. Murray. "Inequalities in Life Expectancy Among US Counties, 1980 to 2014: Temporal Trends and Key Drivers." *JAMA Internal Medicine* 177, no. 7 (July 1, 2017): 1003–11. https://doi.org/10 .1001/jamainternmed.2017.0918.

Edin, Kathryn, and Maria Kefalas. *Promises I Can Keep: Why Poor Women Put Motherhood before Marriage*. Berkeley: University of California Press, 2005.

Edin, Kathryn, and Laura Lein. *Making Ends Meet: How Single Mothers Survive Welfare and Low-Wage Work*. New York: Russell Sage Foundation, 1997.

Edin, Kathryn, and H. Luke Shaefer. *$2.00 A Day: Living on Almost Nothing in America*. Boston: Houghton Mifflin Harcourt, 2015.

Edin, Kathryn, and Timothy Jon Nelson. *Doing the Best I Can: Fatherhood in the Inner City*. Berkeley: University of California Press, 2013.

Ehrenreich, Barbara. *Nickel and Dimed: On (Not) Getting By in America*. New York: Metropolitan Books, 2001.

Elliott, Larry. "World's 26 Richest People Own as Much as Poorest 50%, Says Oxfam." *Guardian*, January 21, 2019. www.theguardian.com/business/2019/jan/21/world-26-richest -people-own-as-much-as-poorest-50-per-cent-oxfam-report.

Evans, William, Barbara Wolfe, and Nancy Adler. "The SES and Health Gradient: A Brief Review of the Literature." In *The Biological Consequences of Socioeconomic Inequalities*, edited by Barbara Wolfe, William Evans, and Teresa E. Seeman, 1–37. New York: Russell Sage Foundation, 2012.

Farley, Margaret. *Personal Commitments: Beginning, Keeping, Changing*. New York: Harper & Row, 1986.

Finn, Daniel K. *Christian Economic Ethics: History and Implications*. Minneapolis: Fortress Press, 2013.

———. *Consumer Ethics in a Global Economy: How Buying Here Causes Injustice There*. Washington, DC: Georgetown University Press, 2019.

———. *The Moral Ecology of Markets: Assessing Claims about Markets and Justice*. New York: Cambridge University Press, 2006.

Flescher, Andrew Michael. *Heroes, Saints & Ordinary Morality*. Moral Traditions Series. Washington, DC: Georgetown University Press, 2003.

Francis. "Address of the Holy Father: Meeting with the Members of the General Assembly of the United Nations Organization," September 25, 2015. http://w2.vatican.va/content/francesco/en/speeches/2015/september/documents/papa-francesco_20150925_onu-visita.html.

———. "Evangelii gaudium (The Joy of the Gospel)," apostolic exhortation, November 24, 2013. http://w2.vatican.va/content/francesco/en/apost_exhortations/documents/papa-francesco_esortazione-ap_20131124_evangelii-gaudium.html.

———. "Laudato si': On Care for Our Common Home." May 24, 2015. http://w2.vatican.va/content/francesco/en/encyclicals/documents/papa-francesco_20150524_enciclica-laudato-si.html.

Francis and Austen Ivereigh. *Let Us Dream: The Path to a Better Future*. New York: Simon & Schuster, 2020.

Frank, Robert H. "How the Middle Class Is Injured by Gains at the Top." In *Inequality Matters: The Growing Economic Divide in America and Its Poisonous Consequences*, edited by James Lardner and David A. Smith, 138–49. New York: New Press, 2005.

Frank, Robert H., Adam Seth Levine, and Oege Dijk. "Expenditure Cascades." *Review of Behavioral Economics* 1, nos. 1–2 (January 15, 2014): 55–73. https://doi.org/10.1561/105.00000003.

Frankena, William K. *Ethics*. 2nd ed. Foundations of Philosophy Series. Englewood Cliffs, NJ: Prentice Hall, 1973.

Fullam, Lisa. "From Discord to Virtues: Reframing Sexual Ethics." In *Transformative Theological Ethics: East Asian Contexts*, edited by Agnes M. Brazal, Aloysius Lopez Cartagenas, Eric Marcelo O. Genilo, and James F. Keenan, 98–115. Quezon City: Ateneo de Manila University Press, 2010.

———. "Humility and Its Moral Epistemological Implications." In *Virtue*, edited by Charles E. Curran and Lisa Fullam, 250–74. Readings in Moral Theology 16. Mahwah, NJ: Paulist Press, 2011.

———. "Joan of Arc, Holy Resistance, and Conscience Formation." In *Conscience and Catholicism: Rights, Responsibilities, and Institutional Responses*, edited by David E. DeCosse and Kristin E. Heyer, 69–82. Maryknoll, NY: Orbis Books, 2015.

Gajiwala, Astrid Lobo. "The Passion of the Womb: Women Re-Living the Eucharist." In *Body and Sexuality: Theological-Pastoral Perspectives of Women in Asia*, edited by Agnes M. Brazal and Andrea Lizares Si, 187–200. Theology and Religious Studies Series. Quezon City: Ateneo de Manila University Press, 2007.

Gamoran, Adam. "What Will Decrease Educational Inequality?" Wisconsin Center for Educational Research, June 2003. www.wcer.wisc.edu/news/coverstories/decrease_ed_inequity.php.

Garcia, Emma, and Elaine Weiss. "Education Inequalities at the School Starting Gate: Gaps, Trends, and Strategies to Address Them." Economic Policy Institute blog, September 27, 2017. www.epi.org/publication/education-inequalities-at-the-school-starting-gate/.

Garcia, Richard A. "Dolores Huerta: Woman, Organizer, and Symbol." *California History* 72, no. 1 (1993): 56–71. https://doi.org/10.2307/25177326.

Garry, Patrick M. "Conservatism and the Real Problems of Income Inequality." *Modern Age* 58, Winter 2016. https://home.isi.org/conservatism-and-real-problems-income-inequality.

Gilkes, Cheryl Townsend. "The 'Loves' and 'Troubles' of African-American Women's Bodies." In *Womanist Theological Ethics: A Reader*, edited by Katie Geneva Cannon, Angela D. Sims, and Emilie M. Townes, 81–97. Louisville: Westminster John Knox Press, 2011.

Gipple, Emily, and Ben Gose. "America's Generosity Divide." *Chronicle of Philanthropy*, August 19, 2012. www.philanthropy.com/article/America-s-Generosity-Divide/156175/.

Givewell. http://Givewell.org/charities/top-charities. No date, consulted July 30, 2020.

"Giving What We Can: About Us." Accessed February 28, 2016. www.givingwhatwecan.org/about-us/.

Goss, Robert E. *Queering Christ: Beyond Jesus Acted Up*. Cleveland: Pilgrim Press, 2003.

Greenwood, Jeremy, Nezih Guner, Georgi Kocharkov, and Cezar Santos. *Marry Your Like: Assortative Mating and Income Inequality*. NBER Working Paper 19829. Cambridge, MA: National Bureau of Economic Research, 2014. www.nber.org/papers/w19829.

Grimes, Katie Walker. *Christ Divided: Antiblackness as Corporate Vice*. Minneapolis: Fortress Press, 2017.

Gudrais, Elizabeth. "Loaded Perceptions: What We Know about Wealth." *Harvard Magazine*, December 2011. http://harvardmagazine.com/2011/11/what-we-know-about-wealth.

Guendelsberger, Emily. *On the Clock: What Low-Wage Work Did to Me and How It Drives America Insane*. New York: Little, Brown, 2019.

Gutiérrez, Gustavo. "Faith as Freedom: Solidarity with the Alienated and Confidence in the Future." *Horizons* 2 (1975): 25–60.

———. "Liberation and Development." *Cross Currents*, Summer 1971, 243–56.

———. "The Option for the Poor Arises from Faith in Christ." *Theological Studies* 70 (2009): 317–26.

———. *The Power of the Poor in History: Selected Writings*. Eugene, OR: Wipf & Stock, 2004.

———. *A Theology of Liberation: History, Politics, and Salvation*. Trans. Caridad Inda and John Eagleson. Maryknoll, NY: Orbis Books, 1988.

Haley, Alex. "Alex Haley Interviews Martin Luther King Jr., Former Civil Rights Leader and Activist." *Playboy*, January 1965. www.alex-haley.com/alex_haley_martin_luther_king_interview.htm.

Halpern-Meekin, Sarah, Kathryn Edin, Laura Tach, and Jennifer Sykes. *It's Not like I'm Poor: How Working Families Make Ends Meet in a Post-Welfare World*. Berkeley: University of California Press, 2015.

Harrington, Daniel J. *Meeting St. Luke Today: Understanding the Man, His Mission, and His Message*. Chicago: Loyola Press, 2010.

———. "Old Testament Approaches to Suffering." In *Suffering and the Christian Life*, edited by Richard W. Miller, 3–18. Maryknoll, NY: Orbis Books, 2013. www.orbisbooks.com/chapters/978-1-62698-013-6.pdf.

Harris, Melanie L. *Gifts of Virtue, Alice Walker, and Womanist Ethics*. Basingstoke, UK: Palgrave Macmillan, 2010.

Hartman, Laura M. *The Christian Consumer: Living Faithfully in a Fragile World*. New York: Oxford University Press, 2011.

@HasBezosDecided. Twitter bio. *Twitter*, accessed 12/1/2020.

Hauerwas, Stanley. *A Community of Character: Toward a Constructive Christian Social Ethic*. Notre Dame, IN: University of Notre Dame Press, 1991.

Hauerwas, Stanley, and Charles R. Pinches. *Christians Among the Virtues: Theological Conversations in Modern Ethics*. Notre Dame, IN: University of Notre Dame Press, 1997.

———. "Practicing Patience: How Christians Should Be Sick." In *Christians Among the Virtues: Theological Conversations in Modern Ethics*, 166–78. Notre Dame, IN: University of Notre Dame Press, 1997.

Haushofer, J., and E. Fehr. "On the Psychology of Poverty." *Science* 344, no. 6186 (May 23, 2014): 862–67. https://doi.org/10.1126/science.1232491.

Hays, Sharon. *Flat Broke with Children: Women in the Age of Welfare Reform*. Oxford: Oxford University Press, 2003.

HealthCare.gov. "Subsidized Coverage." www.healthcare.gov/glossary/subsidized-coverage/.

Heckman, James. "Lifelines for Poor Children." *New York Times*, September 14, 2013. http://opinionator.blogs.nytimes.com/2013/09/14/lifelines-for-poor-children/.

Henry J. Kaiser Family Foundation. "Key Facts about the Uninsured Population." Blog, November 29, 2017. www.kff.org/uninsured/fact-sheet/key-facts-about-the-uninsured-population/.

Heyer, Kristin E. *Kinship across Borders: A Christian Ethic of Immigration*. Moral Traditions Series. Washington, DC: Georgetown University Press, 2012.

———. "Social Sin and Immigration: Good Fences Make Bad Neighbors." *Theological Studies* 71, no. 2 (June 1, 2010): 410–36.

Hicks, Douglas A. "How Economic Inequality Is a Theological and Moral Issue." *Interpretation* 69, no. 4 (October 2015): 432–46.

———. *Inequality and Christian Ethics*. New York: Cambridge University Press, 2000.

———. "Inequality, Justice, and the Myth of Unsituated Market Exchange." *Journal of Religious Ethics* 47, no. 2 (June 2019): 337–54. https://doi.org/10.1111/jore.12267.

———. "Self-Interest, Deprivation, and Agency: Expanding the Capabilities Approach." *Journal of the Society of Christian Ethics* 25, no. 1 (2005): 147–67.

Himes, Kenneth R. "Catholic Social Teaching on Building a Just Society: The Need for a Ceiling and a Floor." *Religions* 8, no. 4 (April 2017): 49. https://doi.org/10.3390/rel8040049.

———. "Catholic Social Teaching, Economic Inequality, and American Society." *Journal of Religious Ethics* 47, no. 2 (June 2019): 283–310. https://doi.org/10.1111/jore.12268.

———. "Consumerism and Christian Ethics." *Theological Studies* 68, no. 1 (March 2007): 132–53.

Hinson-Hasty, Elizabeth L. *The Problem of Wealth: A Christian Response to a Culture of Affluence*. Maryknoll, NY: Orbis Books, 2017.

Hinze, Christine Firer. *Comprehending Power in Christian Social Ethics*. Atlanta: Scholars Press, 1995.

———. *Glass Ceilings and Dirt Floors: Women, Work, and the Global Economy*. 2014 Madeleva Lecture in Spirituality. Mahwah, NJ: Paulist Press, 2015.

———. "What Is Enough? Catholic Social Thought, Consumption, and Material Sufficiency." In *Having: Property and Possession in Religious and Social Life*, edited by William Schweiker and Charles T. Mathewes, 162–88. Grand Rapids: William B. Eerdmans, 2004.

Hirschfeld, Mary L. "Rethinking Economic Inequality: A Theological Perspective." *Journal of Religious Ethics* 47, no. 2 (June 2019): 259–82. https://doi.org/10.1111/jore.12269.

Hobart, Mike. "The Life of a Song: 'God Bless the Child.'" *Financial Times*, August 29, 2016. www.ft.com/content/8526207e-6ae5-11e6-a0b1-d87a9fea034f.

Hobgood, Mary E. *Dismantling Privilege: An Ethics of Accountability*. Cleveland: Pilgrim Press, 2000.

———. "White Economic and Erotic Disempowerment: A Theological Exploration in the Struggle against Racism." In *Interrupting White Privilege: Catholic Theologians Break the*

Silence, edited by Laurie M. Cassidy and Alexander Mikulich, 40–55. Maryknoll, NY: Orbis Books, 2007.

hooks, bell. *Where We Stand: Class Matters*. New York: Routledge, 2000.

Huerta, Dolores. "Reflections on the UFW Experience," August 1985. https://libraries.ucsd .edu/farmworkermovement/essays/essays/MillerArchive/063AReflectionsonUFW Experience.pdf.

Huerta, Dolores, and Rachel Rosenbloom. "Ask a Feminist: Dolores Huerta and Rachel Rosenbloom Discuss Gender and Immigrant Rights." *Signs: Journal of Women in Culture and Society* 44, no. 2 (January 2019): 515–25. https://doi.org/10.1086/699486.

Hughes, Cheryl D. *Katharine Drexel: The Riches-to-Rags Life Story of an American Catholic Saint*. Grand Rapids: William B. Eerdmans, 2014.

Iceland, John. *Poverty in America: A Handbook*. 3rd ed. Berkeley: University of California Press, 2013.

Ignatius of Loyola, John C. Olin, and Joseph F. O'Callaghan. *The Autobiography of St. Ignatius Loyola, with Related Documents*. New York: Fordham University Press, 1992.

Jalandoni, Monica. "Fortitude in the Philippines: Impact on Women." In *Transformative Theological Ethics: East Asian Contexts*, edited by Agnes M. Brazal, Aloysius Lopez Cartagenas, Eric Marcelo O. Genilo, and James F. Keenan, 201–18. Quezon City: Ateneo de Manila University Press, 2010.

Jargowsky, Paul A. "Architecture of Segregation: Civil Unrest, the Concentration of Poverty, and Public Policy." Century Foundation, August 7, 2015. https://tcf.org/content/report /architecture-of-segregation/.

Jenkins, Willis. "Biodiversity and Salvation: Thomistic Roots for Environmental Ethics." *Journal of Religion* 83, no. 3 (July 2003): 401–20.

———. "Is Plutocracy Sinful?" *Anglican Theological Review* 98, no. 1 (Winter 2016): 33–50.

John Paul II. "Laborem exercens: On Human Work," September 14, 1981. www.vatican.va /holy_father/john_paul_ii/encyclicals/documents/hf_jp-ii_enc_14091981_laborem -exercens_en.html.

———. "Sollicitudo rei socialis (On Social Concern)," December 30, 1987. www.vatican.va /holy_father/john_paul_ii/encyclicals/documents/hf_jp-ii_enc_30121987_sollicitudo -rei-socialis_en.html.

Johnson, David S., and Timothy M. Smeeding. "A Consumer's Guide to Interpreting Various US Poverty Measures." University of Wisconsin–Madison Institute for Research on Poverty, May 2012. www.irp.wisc.edu/publications/fastfocus/pdfs/FF14-2012.pdf.

Johnson, Heather Beth. *The American Dream and the Power of Wealth: Choosing Schools and Inheriting Inequality in the Land of Opportunity*. New York: Routledge, 2006.

Kahneman, Daniel, and Angus Deaton. "High Income Improves Evaluation of Life but Not Emotional Well-Being." *Proceedings of the National Academy of Sciences* 107, no. 38 (September 21, 2010): 16489–93. https://doi.org/10.1073/pnas.1011492107.

Kavanaugh, John F. *Following Christ in a Consumer Society: The Spirituality of Cultural Resistance*. 25th anniversary ed. Maryknoll, NY: Orbis Books, 2006.

Kay, Judith W. "Getting Egypt Out of the People: Aquinas' Contributions to Empowerment." In *Aquinas and Empowerment: Classical Ethics for Ordinary Lives*, edited by G. Simon Harak, 1–46. Moral Traditions & Moral Arguments. Washington, DC: Georgetown University Press, 1996.

Kearney, Melissa S., and Phillip P. Levine. "Income Inequality and the Decision to Drop Out of High School." *Communities & Banking* (Federal Reserve Bank of Boston), Winter 2017.

www.bostonfed.org/publications/communities-and-banking/2017/winter/income
-inequality-and-the-decision-to-drop-out-of-high-school.aspx.

Keenan, James F. "Fundamental Moral Theology at the Beginning of the Twenty-First Century." *Theological Studies* 67, no. 1 (March 1, 2006): 99–119.

———. *A History of Catholic Moral Theology in the Twentieth Century: From Confessing Sins to Liberating Consciences.* New York: Continuum, 2010.

———. "Jesuit Hospitality?" In *Promise Renewed: Jesuit Higher Education for a New Millennium*, edited by Martin R. Tripole, 230–44. Chicago: Jesuit Way, 1999.

———. "Proposing Cardinal Virtues." *Theological Studies* 56, no. 4 (1995): 709–29.

———. "Seven Reasons for Doing Virtue Ethics Today." In *Virtue and the Moral Life: Theological and Philosophical Perspectives*, edited by William Werpehowski and Kathryn Getek Soltis, 3–18. Lanham, MD: Lexington Books, 2014.

———. *University Ethics: How Colleges Can Build and Benefit From a Culture of Ethics.* New York: Rowman & Littlefield, 2015.

———. "Virtue Ethics and Sexual Ethics." In *Virtue*, edited by Charles E. Curran and Lisa Fullam, 117–36. Mahwah, NJ: Paulist Press, 2011.

———. *Virtues for Ordinary Christians.* Kansas City: Sheed & Ward, 1996.

———. "The Virtue of Prudence (IIa IIae, Qq. 47–56)." In *Ethics of Aquinas*, 259–71. Washington, DC: Georgetown University Press, 2002.

Keenan, James F., and Joseph J. Kotva, eds. *Practice What You Preach: Virtues, Ethics, and Power in the Lives of Pastoral Ministers and Their Congregations.* Franklin, WI: Sheed & Ward, 1999.

Keenan, James F., and Enda McDonagh. "Instability, Structural Violence, and Vulnerability: A Catholic Theological Response to the HIV/AIDS Pandemic." *Progressio*, 2009. www.progressio.org.uk/sites/default/files/HIV+instability_2009_0.pdf.

Kendi, Ibram X. *Stamped from the Beginning: The Definitive History of Racist Ideas in America.* Reprint ed. New York: Nation Books, 2017.

Kenny, Charles. "We're All the 1 Percent." *Foreign Policy* (blog), February 27, 2012. https://foreignpolicy.com/2012/02/27/were-all-the-1-percent/.

Kim, Andrew. "Progress in the Good: A Defense of the Thomistic Unity Thesis." *Journal of Moral Theology* 3, no. 1 (January 2014): 147–74.

Kim, Sebastian. "Editorial." *International Journal of Public Theology* 7 (2013): 1–4.

King, Martin Luther, Jr. "Letter from a Birmingham Jail." Martin Luther King Jr. Research and Education Institute, April 16, 1963. https://kinginstitute.stanford.edu/king-papers/documents/letter-birmingham-jail.

Kinghorn, Warren. "Combat Trauma and Moral Fragmentation: A Theological Account of Moral Injury." *Journal of the Society of Christian Ethics* 32, no. 2 (2012): 57–74.

Kinsler, Ross, and Gloria Kinsler, eds. *God's Economy: Biblical Studies from Latin America.* Maryknoll, NY: Orbis Books, 2005.

Kiruki, Joseph Kahiga. "Poverty and Unemployment: Deprivations of Capabilities." *AFER* 46, no. 3 (September 2004): 215–27.

Klubertanz, George Peter. *Habits and Virtues.* New York: Appleton-Century-Crofts, 1965.

Kochuthara, Shaji George. "Economic Inequality: An Ethical Response." *Religions* 8, no. 8 (August 4, 2017): 141. https://doi.org/10.3390/rel8080141.

Koenig, Rebecca. "A Mismatch Between Need and Affluence." *Chronicle of Philanthropy*, July 8, 2015. https://philanthropy.com/interactives/how-america-gives-opportunity-index.

Konigsburg, Joyce Ann. "The Economic and Ethical Implications of Living Wages." *Religions* 8, no. 4 (April 2017): 74. https://doi.org/10.3390/rel8040074.

Kotva, Joseph. *The Christian Case for Virtue Ethics*. Washington, DC: Georgetown University Press, 1996.

Kraus, Michael W., Paul K. Piff, and Dacher Keltner. "Social Class as Culture: The Convergence of Resources and Rank in the Social Realm." *Current Directions in Psychological Science* 20, no. 4 (August 1, 2011): 246–50. https://doi.org/10.1177/0963721411414654.

Kraus, Michael W., Paul K. Piff, Rodolfo Mendoza-Denton, Michelle L. Rheinschmidt, and Dacher Keltner. "Social Class, Solipsism, and Contextualism: How the Rich Are Different from the Poor." *Psychological Review* 119, no. 3 (July 2012): 546–72. http://dx.doi.org.proxy.bc.edu/10.1037/a0028756.

Krishna, Anirudh. *One Illness Away: Why People Become Poor and How They Escape Poverty*. Oxford: Oxford University Press, 2011.

Kwang-Sun Suh, David. "The Priesthood of 'Han': 'Called to Witness to the Gospel Today.'" *Reformed World* 39, no. 4 (December 1986): 597–607.

Kye, Samuel H. "The Persistence of White Flight in Middle-Class Suburbia." *Social Science Research* 72 (May 1, 2018): 38–52. https://doi.org/10.1016/j.ssresearch.2018.02.005.

Laborde, David, Livia Bizikova, Tess Lallemant, and Carin Smaller. "Ending Hunger: What Would It Cost?" International Institute for Sustainable Development and International Food Policy Research Institute, 2016.

Lamont, Michèle. *Money, Morals, and Manners: The Culture of the French and American Upper-Middle Class*. Chicago: University of Chicago Press, 1992.

Land, Stephanie. *Maid: Hard Work, Low Pay, and a Mother's Will to Survive*. New York: Hachette Books, 2019.

Latus, Andrew. "Moral Luck." *Internet Encyclopedia of Philosophy*. Accessed March 8, 2018. www.iep.utm.edu/moralluc/.

Le Quéré, Corinne, Stuart Capstick, Adam Corner, David Cutting, Martin Johnson, Asher Minns, Heike Schroeder, Kate Walker-Springett, Lorraine Whitmarsh, and Ruth Wood. "Towards a Culture of Low-Carbon Research for the 21st Century: Tyndall Working Paper 161." Tyndall Centre for Climate Change Research, March 2015.

Lebacqz, Karen, and Shirley Macemon. "Vicious Virtue? Patience, Justice, and Salaries in the Church." In *Practice What You Preach: Virtues, Ethics, and Power in the Lives of Pastoral Ministers and Their Congregations*, edited by James F. Keenan and Joseph J. Kotva, 280–92. Franklin, WI: Sheed & Ward, 1999.

LeBlanc, Adrian Nicole. *Random Family: Love, Drugs, Trouble, and Coming of Age in the Bronx*. New York: Scribner, 2004.

Lee, Elizabeth. "The Virtues of Humility and Magnanimity and the Church's Response to the Health Care and Gay Marriage Debates." In *Religion, Economics, and Culture in Conflict and Conversation*, edited by Laurie M. Cassidy and Maureen H. O'Connell, 32–48. College Theology Society, Annual Volume 56. Maryknoll, NY: Orbis Books, 2011.

Leo XIII. "Rerum novarum: On Capital and Labor." May 15, 1891. http://www.vatican.va/holy_father/leo_xiii/encyclicals/documents/hf_l-xiii_enc_15051891_rerum-novarum_en.html.

Levine, Madeline. *The Price of Privilege: How Parental Pressure and Material Advantage Are Creating a Generation of Disconnected and Unhappy Kids*. New York: HarperCollins, 2006.

Lindsey, Brink, and Steven Michael Teles. *The Captured Economy: How the Powerful Enrich Themselves, Slow Down Growth, and Increase Inequality*. New York: Oxford University Press, 2017.

Litz, Brett T., Nathan Stein, Eileen Delaney, Leslie Lebowitz, William P. Nash, Caroline Silva, and Shira Maguen. "Moral Injury and Moral Repair in War Veterans: A Preliminary

Model and Intervention Strategy." *Clinical Psychology Review* 29, no. 8 (December 2009): 695–706. https://doi.org/10.1016/j.cpr.2009.07.003.

Lloyd, Vincent. "For What Are Whites to Hope?" *Political Theology* 17, no. 2 (March 3, 2016): 168–81. https://doi.org/10.1080/1462317X.2016.1161302.

Lohfink, Gerhard. *Jesus of Nazareth: What He Wanted, Who He Was*. Trans. Linda M. Maloney. Collegeville, MN: Liturgical Press, 2012.

Lonergan, Bernard J. F. *Insight: A Study of Human Understanding*. London: Longmans, 1958.

Lott, Bernice. "The Social Psychology of Class and Classism." *American Psychologist* 67, no. 8 (November 2012): 650–58. http://dx.doi.org.proxy.bc.edu/10.1037/a0029369.

Ludema, Jim, and Amber Johnson. "Gravity Payment's Dan Price on How He Measures Success After His $70k Experiment." *Forbes*, August 28, 2018. https://www.forbes.com/sites/amberjohnson-jimludema/2018/08/28/gravity-payments-dan-price-on-how-he-measures-success-after-his-70k-experiment/.

Ludwig, Jens, Greg Duncan, Lisa A. Gennetian, Lawrence F. Katz, Ronald C. Kessler, Jeffrey R. Kling, and Lisa Sanbonmatsu. "Neighborhood Effects on the Long-Term Well-Being of Low-Income Adults." *Science* 337, no. 6101 (September 21, 2012): 1505–10. https://doi.org/10.1126/science.1224648.

Luthar, Suniya S. "The Culture of Affluence: Psychological Costs of Material Wealth." *Child Development* 74, no. 6 (2003): 1581–1593.

———. "The Problem with Rich Kids." *Psychology Today*, November 5, 2013. www.psychologytoday.com/articles/201310/the-problem-rich-kids.

Luthar, Suniya S., and Bronwyn E. Becker. "Privileged but Pressured? A Study of Affluent Youth." *Child Development* 73, no. 5 (2002): 1593.

Luthar, Suniya S., and Shawn J. Latendresse. "Children of the Affluent: Challenges to Well-Being." *Current Directions in Psychological Science* 14, no. 1 (2005): 49–53.

Luttmer, Erzo F. P. *Neighbors as Negatives: Relative Earnings and Well-Being*. NBER Working Paper 10667. Cambridge, MA: National Bureau of Economic Research, 2004. https://doi.org/10.3386/w10667.

Lythcott-Haims, Julie. "Kids of Helicopter Parents Are Sputtering Out." *Slate*, July 5, 2015. www.slate.com/articles/double_x/doublex/2015/07/helicopter_parenting_is_increasingly_correlated_with_college_age_depression.html.

MacIntyre, Alasdair C. *After Virtue: A Study in Moral Theory*. 3rd ed. Notre Dame, IN: University of Notre Dame Press, 2007.

Mack, Joanna. "Absolute and Overall Poverty." *Poverty and Social Exclusion*, October 27, 2016. www.poverty.ac.uk/definitions-poverty/absolute-and-overall-poverty.

Maddalena, Julie A. Mavity. "Floodwaters and the Ticking Clock: The Systematic Oppression and Stigmatization of Poor, Single Mothers in America and Christian Theological Responses." *Cross Currents* 63, no. 2 (June 2013): 148–73.

Madrigal, Alexis C. "Kim Kardashian's Private Firefighters Expose America's Fault Lines." *Atlantic*, November 14, 2018. www.theatlantic.com/technology/archive/2018/11/kim-kardashian-kanye-west-history-private-firefighting/575887/.

Magesa, Laurenti. "African Indigenous Spirituality, Ecology, and the Human Right to Integral Development." In *The World Market and Interreligious Dialogue*, edited by Catherine Cornille and Glenn Willis, 164–89. Eugene, OR: Cascade Books, 2011.

Mani, Anandi, Sendhil Mullainathan, Eldar Shafir, and Jiaying Zhao. "Poverty Impedes Cognitive Function." *Science* 341, no. 6149 (August 30, 2013): 976–80. https://doi.org/10.1126/science.1238041.

Mann, Jonathan M. "Medicine and Public Health, Ethics and Human Rights." *Hastings Center Report* 27, no. 3 (May 6, 1997): 6–13. https://doi.org/10.2307/3528660.

Marable, Manning. *Malcolm X: A Life of Reinvention*. New York: Viking, 2011.

Markey, Eileen. *A Radical Faith: The Assassination of Sister Maura*. New York: Nation Books, 2016.

Martin, Emmanuel, Nicolas Lecaussin, and Jean-Philippe Delsol, eds. *Anti-Piketty: Capital for the 21st Century*. Washington, DC: Cato Institute, 2017.

Martin, Wednesday. *Primates of Park Avenue: A Memoir*. New York: Simon & Schuster, 2015.

Massaro, Thomas. *United States Welfare Policy: A Catholic Response*. Moral Traditions Series. Washington, DC: Georgetown University Press, 2007.

Massingale, Bryan N. "An Ethical Reflection upon 'Environmental Racism': In the Light of Catholic Social Teaching." In *The Challenge of Global Stewardship: Roman Catholic Responses*, edited by Maura A. Ryan and Todd Whitmore, 234–50. Notre Dame, IN: University of Notre Dame Press, 1997.

———. *Racial Justice and the Catholic Church*. Maryknoll, NY: Orbis Books, 2010.

Mathews, Rosita deAnn. "Using Power from the Periphery." In *A Troubling in My Soul: Womanist Perspectives on Evil and Suffering*, edited by Emilie Maureen Townes, 92–106. Maryknoll, NY: Orbis Books, 1993.

McCann, Dennis P. "Inequality in Income and Wealth: When Does It Become Immoral, and Why?" In *Rediscovering Abundance: Interdisciplinary Essays on Wealth, Income, and Their Distribution in the Catholic Social Tradition*, edited by Helen Alford, Charles M. A. Clark, S. A. Cortright, and Michael J. Naughton, 189–208. Notre Dame, IN: University of Notre Dame Press, 2006.

McCarthy, Eli Sasaran. *Becoming Nonviolent Peacemakers: A Virtue Ethic for Catholic Social Teaching and US Policy*. Eugene, OR: Wipf & Stock, 2012.

McCluskey, Colleen. *Thomas Aquinas on Moral Wrongdoing*. New York: Cambridge University Press, 2016.

McRorie, Christina. "Heterodox Economics, Social Ethics, and Inequalities: New Tools for Thinking Critically about Markets and Economic Injustices." *Journal of Religious Ethics* 47, no. 2 (June 2019): 232–58. https://doi.org/10.1111/jore.12263.

Mifsud, Tony. "Moral Reflection in Latin America: Challenges and Proposals within the Chilean Reality." In *Catholic Theological Ethics in the World Church: The Plenary Papers from the First Cross-Cultural Conference on Catholic Theological Ethics*, edited by James F. Keenan, 131–37. New York: Continuum, 2007.

Míguez Bonino, José. "Doing Theology in the Context of the Struggles of the Poor." *Mid-Stream*, no. 20 (October 1981): 369–73.

———. "Poverty as Curse, Blessing and Challenge." *Iliff Review* 34, no. 3 (September 1, 1977): 3–13.

Mikulich, Alex. "Where Y'At Race, Whiteness, and Economic Justice? A Map of White Complicity in the Economic Oppression of People of Color." In *The Almighty and the Dollar: Reflections on Economic Justice for All*, edited by Mark J. Allman, 189–211. Winona, MN: Anselm Academic, 2012.

Mingo Kaminouchi, Alberto de. *An Introduction to Christian Ethics: A New Testament Perspective*. Collegeville, MN: Liturgical Press, 2020.

Miron, Jeffrey. "The Role of Government in Creating Inequality." In *Anti-Piketty: Capital for the 21st Century*, edited by Jean-Philippe Delsol and Emmanuel Martin. Washington, DC: Cato Institute, 2017. https://eds.a.ebscohost.com/eds/ebookviewer/ebook

/ZTAwMHhuYV9fMTUxMjQ3M19fQU41?sid=de262def-3012-47b5-b4a0-d7180
bab65f6@sdc-v-sessmgr03&vid=0&format=EK&rid=1.

Mishel, Lawrence, and Jessica Schieder. "CEO Pay Remains High Relative to the Pay of Typical Workers and High-Wage Earners." Economic Policy Institute, July 20, 2017. www.epi.org/files/pdf/130354.pdf.

Mitchell, Margaret M. "Silver Chamber Pots and Other Goods Which Are Not Good: John Chrysostom's Discourse Against Wealth and Possessions." In *Having: Property and Possession in Religious and Social Life,* edited by William Schweiker and Charles T. Mathewes, 88–121. Grand Rapids: William B. Eerdmans, 2004.

Mooney, Michael J. "The Worst Parents Ever." *D Magazine,* May 2015. www.dmagazine.com /publications/d-magazine/2015/may/affluenza-the-worst-parents-ever-ethan-couch ?single=1&src=longreads.

Moore, Michael S. *Wealthwatch: A Study of Socioeconomic Conflict in the Bible.* Eugene, OR: Pickwick, 2011.

Morcroft, Greg. "Global Income Inequality: The Story in Charts." *International Business Times,* December 24, 2013. www.ibtimes.com/global-income-inequality-story-charts -1519376.

Morrison, Toni. *Beloved.* New York: Random House, 1987.

Mullainathan, Sendhil, and Eldar Shafir. *Scarcity: Why Having Too Little Means So Much.* New York: Times Books, Henry Holt and Company, 2013.

Murphy, William F., Jr. "Revisiting Contraception: An Integrated Approach in Light of the Renewal of Thomistic Virtue Ethics." *Theological Studies* 72, no. 4 (December 2011): 812–47.

Nagel, Thomas. "Moral Luck." In *Moral Luck,* edited by Daniel Statman, 57–71. Albany: State University of New York Press, 1993.

National Law Center on Homelessness and Poverty. "No Safe Place: The Criminalization of Homelessness in US Cities." 2014. www.nlchp.org/documents/No_Safe_Place.

Naudé, Piet, and Stan du Plessis. "Economic Inequality: Economics and Theology in Dialogue." *International Journal of Public Theology* 12, no. 1 (2018): 73–101. https://doi.org /10.1163/15697320-12341524.

Navarro, Mireya. "'Poor Door' in a New York Tower Opens a Fight Over Affordable Housing." *New York Times,* August 26, 2014. www.nytimes.com/2014/08/27/nyregion/separate -entryways-for-new-york-condo-buyers-and-renters-create-an-affordable-housing -dilemma.html.

Noah, Timothy. *The Great Divergence: America's Growing Inequality Crisis and What We Can Do about It.* New York: Bloomsbury, 2012.

———. "Labor of Love: The Enforced Happiness of Pret-à-Manger." *New Republic,* February 1, 2013. https://newrepublic.com/article/112204/pret-manger-when-corporations -enforce-happiness.

Norton, Michael I., and Dan Ariely. "Building a Better America—One Wealth Quintile at a Time." *Perspectives on Psychological Science* 6, no. 1 (2011): 9–12.

Nuechterlein, James A. "Living with Inequality." *First Things* 212 (April 2011): 3–4.

Nussbaum, Martha C. *Creating Capabilities: The Human Development Approach.* Cambridge, MA: Belknap Press, 2013.

———. *The Fragility of Goodness: Luck and Ethics in Greek Tragedy and Philosophy.* New York: Cambridge University Press, 2001.

———. "Non-Relative Virtues: An Aristotelian Approach." *Midwest Studies in Philosophy* 13, no. 1 (September 1, 1988): 32–53.

———. "Poverty and Human Functioning: Capabilities as Fundamental Entitlements." In *Poverty and Inequality*, edited by David B. Grusky and S. M. Ravi Kanbur, 47–75. Stanford, CA: Stanford University Press, 2006.

O'Connell, Maureen H. *Compassion: Loving Our Neighbor in an Age of Globalization.* Maryknoll, NY: Orbis Books, 2009.

———. "Viability of Virtue Ethics for Racial Justice." In *Journal of Moral Theology*, edited by David M. Cloutier and William C. Mattison, 3:83–104. Eugene, OR: Wipf & Stock, 2014.

Odozor, Paulinus Ikechukwu. "Truly Africa, and Wealthy! What Africa Can Learn from Catholic Social Teaching about Sustainable Economic Prosperity." In *The True Wealth of Nations: Catholic Social Thought and Economic Life*, edited by Daniel K. Finn, 267–87. New York: Oxford University Press, 2010.

———. *Moral Theology in an Age of Renewal: A Study of the Catholic Tradition since Vatican II.* Notre Dame, IN: University of Notre Dame Press, 2003.

Oduyoye, Mercy Amba. "Creation, Exodus and Redemption—an African Woman's Perspective on the Biblical Narrative." *Journal of African Christian Thought* 6, no. 1 (June 2003): 3–9.

Oduyoye, Mercy Amba. "Poverty Renders African Women Vulnerable to Violence." *Insights* 121, no. 2 (2006): 25–28.

OECD (Organization for Economic Cooperation and Development). *A Broken Social Elevator? How to Promote Social Mobility.* Paris: OECD Publishing, 2018. https://doi.org/10.1787/9789264301085-en.

———. "Crisis Squeezes Income and Puts Pressure on Inequality and Poverty." 2013. www.oecd.org/els/soc/OECD2013-Inequality-and-Poverty-8p.pdf.

———. *In It Together: Why Less Inequality Benefits All.* Paris: OECD Publishing, 2015. www.oecd-ilibrary.org/employment/in-it-together-why-less-inequality-benefits-all_9789264235120-en.

Offer, Avner. *The Challenge of Affluence: Self-Control and Well-Being in the United States and Britain since 1950.* Oxford: Oxford University Press, 2006.

Ohlheiser, Abby. "San Francisco Cathedral Will Stop Dousing Sleeping Homeless People with Water." *Washington Post*, March 18, 2015. www.washingtonpost.com/news/acts-of-faith/wp/2015/03/18/san-francisco-cathedral-douses-homeless/.

Olinto, Pedro, and Jaime Saavedra. "An Overview of Global Income Inequality Trends." *World Bank—Inequality in Focus* 1, no. 1 (2012): 1–4.

O'Neill, Jessie H. *The Golden Ghetto: The Psychology of Affluence.* Center City, MN: Hazelden, 1997.

Orobator, A. E. (Agbonkhianmeghe Emmanuel). "Caritas in Veritate and Africa's Burden of (under)Development." *Theological Studies* 71, no. 2 (June 2010): 320–34.

O'Sullivan, James P. "Twenty-First-Century Global Goal-Setting Addressing Global Inequality: An Interdisciplinary Ethical Analysis." *Religions* 8, no. 4 (April 2017): 1–10.

Oxfam International. "Just 8 Men Own Same Wealth as Half the World." January 16, 2017. www.oxfam.org/en/pressroom/pressreleases/2017-01-16/just-8-men-own-same-wealth-half-world.

Padberg, John, SJ, ed. *The Constitutions of the Society of Jesus and Their Complementary Norms.* Saint Louis: Institute of Jesuit Sources, 1996. https://jesuitas.lat/uploads/the

-constitutions-of-the-society-of-jesus-and-their-complementary-norms/Constitutions
%20and%20Norms%20SJ%20ingls.pdf.

Parijs, Philippe Van. "A Basic Income for All." *Boston Review*, November 2000. http://new
.bostonreview.net/BR25.5/vanparijs.html.

———. "Basic Income Capitalism." *Ethics* 102, no. 3 (April 1, 1992): 465–84.

———. "The Universal Basic Income." *Politics & Society* 41(2) (2013): 171–82.

Patel, Vimal. "To Make Do, These PhD Students Share Bills and a Bank Account." *Chronicle
of Higher Education*, June 2, 2014. www.chronicle.com/article/To-Make-Do-These-PhD
/146851.

Paul VI. "Gaudium et spes (Pastoral Constitution on the Church in the Modern World),"
December 7, 1965. www.vatican.va/archive/hist_councils/ii_vatican_council/documents
/vat-ii_const_19651207_gaudium-et-spes_en.html.

Pellegrino, Edmund, and David Thomasma. *The Christian Virtues in Medical Practice*. Washington, DC: Georgetown University Press, 1996.

Pelton, Robert S., ed. *Aparecida: Quo Vadis?* Scranton, PA: University of Scranton Press, 2008.

Peters, Rebecca Todd. "Conflict and Solidarity Ethics: Difficult Conversations on Economics,
Religion and Culture." In *Religion, Economics, and Culture in Conflict and Conversation*,
edited by Laurie M. Cassidy and Maureen H. O'Connell, 70–79. College Theology Society, Annual Volume 56. Maryknoll, NY: Orbis Books, 2011.

Pham, Adele Free. *Nailed It*. A coproduction of Center for Asian American Media and
WORLD Channel. https://worldchannel.org/episode/arf-nailed-it/.

Phelps, Jamie, OP. "Joy Came in the Morning: Risking Death for Resurrection." In *A Troubling
in My Soul: Womanist Perspectives on Evil and Suffering*, edited by Emilie Maureen Townes,
92–106. Maryknoll, NY: Orbis Books, 1993.

Pickett, Kate, and Richard Wilkinson. *The Spirit Level: Why Greater Equality Makes Societies
Stronger*. New York: Bloomsbury, 2011.

Pieper, Josef. *A Brief Reader on the Virtues of the Human Heart*. San Francisco: Ignatius Press,
1991.

———. *Fortitude and Temperance*. Translated by Daniel F. Coogan. New York: Pantheon
Books, 1954.

———. *Prudence*. London: Faber & Faber, 1960.

Piepzna-Samarasinha, Leah Lakshmi. "Scholarship Baby." In *Without a Net: The Female Experience of Growing Up Working Class*, edited by Michelle Tea, 199–206. Emeryville, CA:
Seal Press, 2003.

Pieris, Aloysius. *Asian Theology of Liberation*. Bloomsbury, 1988.

———. *God's Reign for God's Poor: A Return to the Jesus Formula*. 2nd rev. ed. Gonawala, Sri
Lanka: Tulana Research Centre, 2000.

Piff, Paul K., Michael W. Kraus, Stéphane Côté, Bonnie Hayden Cheng, and Dacher Keltner.
"Having Less, Giving More: The Influence of Social Class on Prosocial Behavior." *Journal
of Personality and Social Psychology* 99, no. 5 (November 2010): 771–84. https://doi.org
/10.1037/a0020092.

Piff, Paul K., Daniel M. Stancato, Stephane Cote, Rodolfo Mendoza-Denton, and Dacher
Keltner. "Higher Social Class Predicts Increased Unethical Behavior." *Proceedings of the
National Academy of Sciences of the United States of America* 109, no. 11 (March 13, 2012):
4086–91. https://doi.org/10.1073/pnas.1118373109.

Piketty, Thomas. *Capital in the Twenty-First Century*. Trans. Arthur Goldhammer. Cambridge,
MA: Belknap Press of Harvard University Press, 2014.

Pimpare, Stephen. *A People's History of Poverty in America*. New York: New Press, 2008.

Pittelman, Karen, and Resource Generation. *Classified: How to Stop Hiding Your Privilege and Use It for Social Change!* Brooklyn: Soft Skull Press, 2006.

Pius XI. "Quadrigesimo anno: On Reconstruction of the Social Order," May 15, 1931. www.vatican.va/holy_father/pius_xi/encyclicals/documents/hf_p-xi_enc_19310515 _quadragesimo-anno_en.html.

Pope, Stephen J. "Virtue in Theology." In *Virtues and Their Vices*, edited by Kevin Timpe and Craig A. Boyd, 393–414. Oxford: Oxford University Press, 2014.

Porter, Jean. "Chastity as a Virtue." *Scottish Journal of Theology* 58, no. 3 (January 1, 2005): 285–301.

———. *Justice as a Virtue: A Thomistic Perspective*. Grand Rapids: William B. Eerdmans, 2016.

———. "Recent Studies in Aquinas' Virtue Ethic: A Review Essay." *Journal of Religious Ethics* 26, no. 1 (1998): 191–215.

———. "Virtue Ethics." In *The Cambridge Companion to Christian Ethics*, edited by Robin Gill, 96–111. Cambridge: Cambridge University Press, 2000.

Potts, Monica. "What's Killing Poor White Women?" *American Prospect*, September 3, 2013. http://prospect.org/article/whats-killing-poor-white-women.

Powers, Brian S. "Moral Injury and Original Sin: The Applicability of Augustinian Moral Psychology in Light of Combat Trauma." *Theology Today* 73, no. 4 (2017): 325–37. https:// doi.org/10.1177/0040573616674852.

Prejean, Helen. *Dead Man Walking: An Eyewitness Account of the Death Penalty in the United States*. New York: Vintage, 1994.

———. *The Death of Innocents: An Eyewitness Account of Wrongful Executions*. New York: Random House, 2005.

———. "Regarding the Evolution of Catholic Teaching on the Death Penalty." August 2, 2018. www.sisterhelen.org/regarding-the-evolution-of-catholic-teaching-on-the-death -penalty/.

Putnam, Robert D. *Our Kids: The American Dream in Crisis*. New York: Simon & Schuster, 2015.

Quinn, Ben. "Anti-Homeless Spikes Are Part of a Wider Phenomenon of 'Hostile Architecture.'" *Guardian*, June 13, 2014. www.theguardian.com/artanddesign/2014/jun/13/anti -homeless-spikes-hostile-architecture.

Quinn, Joseph F., and Kevin E. Cahill. "The Relative Effectiveness of the Minimum Wage and the Earned Income Tax Credit as Anti-Poverty Tools." *Religions* 8, no. 4 (April 2017): 69. https://doi.org/10.3390/rel8040069.

Rashid, Hussein. "Where Am I From? Bullying, The Immigrant Muslim Experience, and Moral Injury." Paper presented at Moral Injury and Recovery section at American Academy of Religion 2014 annual meeting.

Rasmussen, Larry L., and Bruce C. Birch. "A Difficult Text: 'For You Always Have the Poor with You.'" In *Poverty: Responding Like Jesus*, edited by Kenneth Himes and Conor M. Kelly, 29–34. Brewster, MA: Paraclete Press, 2018.

Ravallion, Martin. "Poverty Lines Across the World." In *The Oxford Handbook of the Economics of Poverty*, edited by Philip N. Jefferson. Oxford: Oxford University Press, 2012. 10.1093/ oxfordhb/9780195393781.013.0004.

Razu, John Mohan. "India Unleashed or India Leashed: Perspectives on Globalization and Inequality." *Bangalore Theological Forum* 37, no. 2 (December 1, 2005): 61–88.

Reardon, Sean. "Income Inequality Affects Our Children's Educational Opportunities." Washington Center for Equitable Growth, September 1, 2014. https://equitablegrowth.org/income-inequality-affects-our-childrens-educational-opportunities/.

Reardon, Sean F., and Kendra Bischoff. "Income Inequality and Income Segregation." *American Journal of Sociology* 116, no. 4 (2011): 1092–1153. https://doi.org/10.1086/657114.

Reeves, Richard V. "Classless America, Still?" Brookings Institution blog, August 27, 2014. www.brookings.edu/blog/social-mobility-memos/2014/08/27/classless-america-still/.

Reich, Robert B. "Secession of the Successful: How the New US Emphasis on 'Community' Legitimizes Economic Inequality." *Other Side* 31, no. 4 (July 1, 1995): 20–26.

Reimer-Barry, Emily. "In Sickness and in Health: Toward a Renewed Roman Catholic Theology of Marriage in Light of the Experiences of Married Women Living with HIV/AIDS." PhD diss., Loyola University Chicago, 2008.

Renaud, Myriam. "A Call for a Theology of Theologies to Address Increasing Income Inequality in Mainline Protestant Congregations." *Anglican Theological Review* 99, no. 1 (2017): 31–43.

Renzetti, Claire M. "Economic Stress and Domestic Violence." VAWnet.org: National Online Resource Center on Violence Against Women, September 2009. https://vawnet.org/sites/default/files/materials/files/2016-09/AR_EconomicStress.pdf.

Resource Generation. "Guidance for Giving to Black-Led Organizing for Black Liberation." Accessed February 29, 2016. http://resourcegeneration.org/what-we-do/supporting-black-led-black-liberation/guidance-for-giving-to-black-led-organizing-for-black-liberation-2/.

———. "Join Resource Generation!" November 19, 2017. https://resourcegeneration.org/new-members/.

———. "Mission, Vision, Values." Accessed June 4, 2015. http://resourcegeneration.org/about-us/misson-vision-values/.

Ricoeur, Paul. "Love and Justice." In *Radical Pluralism and Truth: David Tracy and the Hermeneutics of Religion,* edited by Werner G. Jeanrond and Jennifer L. Rike, 187–202. New York: Crossroad, 1991.

Rieger, Joerg. *No Rising Tide: Theology, Economics, and the Future.* Minneapolis: Fortress Press, 2009.

———. "The Ethics of Wealth in a World of Economic Inequality: A Christian Perspective in a Buddhist-Christian Dialogue." *Buddhist-Christian Studies,* January 1, 2013.

Rieger, Joerg, and Rosemarie Henkel-Rieger. *Unified We Are a Force: How Faith and Labor Can Overcome America's Inequalities.* Saint Louis: Chalice, 2016.

Roberts, Michelle Voss. "Retrieving Humility: Rhetoric, Authority and Divinization in Mechthild of Magdeburg." *Feminist Theology,* September 1, 2009.

Roberts, Robert C. "Temperance." In *Virtues and Their Vices,* edited by Kevin Timpe and Craig A. Boyd, 92–111. Oxford: Oxford University Press, 2014.

Roberts, Samuel K. "Virtue Ethics and the Problem of African American Clergy Ethics in the Culture of Deference." In *Practice What You Preach: Virtues, Ethics, and Power in the Lives of Pastoral Ministers and Their Congregations,* edited by James F. Keenan and Joseph J. Kotva, 128–39. Franklin, WI: Sheed & Ward, 1999.

Roccasalvo, Sr. Joan, CSJ. "Remembering the American Churchwomen Martyred in El Salvador." Catholic News Agency, December 2, 2015. www.catholicnewsagency.com/column/remembering-the-american-churchwomen-martyred-in-el-salvador-3393.

Roche, Mary M. Doyle. "Children, Virtue Ethics, and Consumer Culture." In *Virtue and the Moral Life: Theological and Philosophical Perspectives*, edited by William Werpehowski and Kathryn Getek Soltis, 77–93. Lanham, MD: Lexington Books, 2014.

Rodes, Robert E. "On Professors and Poor People: A Jurisprudential Memoir." *Journal of Law and Religion* 22, no. 2 (2007): 527–43. https://doi.org/10.1017/S0748081400004033.

Romero, Miguel J. "The Happiness of 'Those Who Lack the Use of Reason.'" *The Thomist* 80, no. 1 (January 2016): 49–96.

———. "Profound Cognitive Impairment, Moral Virtue, and Our Life In Christ: Can My Brother Lead a Happy and Holy Life?" *Church Life* 3, no. 4 (2014): 80–94.

Rubio, Julie Hanlon. *Family Ethics: Practices for Christians*. Moral Traditions Series. Washington, DC: Georgetown University Press, 2010.

———. "Passing on the Faith in an Era of Rising 'Nones': Practicing Courage and Humility." In *Virtue and the Moral Life: Theological and Philosophical Perspectives*, edited by William Werpehowski and Kathryn Getek Soltis, 95–111. Lanham, MD: Lexington Books, 2014.

Ruddick, Sara. "Virtues and Age." In *Mother Time: Women, Aging, and Ethics*, edited by Margaret Urban Walker, 45–60. Lanham, MD: Rowman & Littlefield, 1999.

Ruddy, Deborah Wallace. "The Humble God: Healer, Mediator, and Sacrifice." *Logos: A Journal of Catholic Thought and Culture* 7, no. 3 (2004): 87–108. https://doi.org/10.1353/log.2004.0030.

Ruether, Rosemary Radford. *Sexism and God-Talk: Toward a Feminist Theology*. Boston: Beacon Press, 1983.

Saez, Emmanuel. "Striking It Richer: The Evolution of Top Incomes in the United States (Updated with 2015 Preliminary Estimates)," June 30, 2016. https://eml.berkeley.edu/~saez/saez-UStopincomes-2015.pdf.

Sandel, Michael J. *What Money Can't Buy: The Moral Limits of Markets*. New York: Farrar, Straus & Giroux, 2012.

Schervish, Paul G. "Hyperagency and High-Tech Donors: A New Theory of the New Philanthropists." Paper presented at Social Welfare Research Institute, Boston College, Boston, November 14, 2003. www.bc.edu/content/dam/files/research_sites/cwp/pdf/haf.pdf.

———. "Introduction: The Wealthy and the World of Wealth." In *Gospels of Wealth: How the Rich Portray Their Lives*, by Paul G. Schervish, Platon E. Coutsoukis, and Ethan Lewis, 1–17. Westport, CT: Praeger, 1994.

Schervish, Paul G., Platon E. Coutsoukis, and Ethan Lewis. *Gospels of Wealth: How the Rich Portray Their Lives*. Westport, CT: Praeger, 1994.

Schiff, Karenna Gore. *Lighting the Way: Nine Women Who Changed Modern America*. New York: Hyperion, 2005.

Schlozman, Kay Lehman, Sidney Verba, and Henry E. Brady. *The Unheavenly Chorus: Unequal Political Voice and the Broken Promise of American Democracy*. Princeton, NJ: Princeton University Press, 2012.

Schmidtz, David, and John Thrasher. "The Virtues of Justice." In *Virtues and Their Vices*, edited by Kevin Timpe and Craig A. Boyd, 59–74. Oxford: Oxford University Press, 2014.

Schor, Juliet. "What Can We Do about Economic Inequality?" *Anglican Theological Review* 98, no. 1 (2016): 23–31.

Sen, Amartya. "Conceptualizing and Measuring Poverty." In *Poverty and Inequality*, edited by David B. Grusky and S. M. Ravi Kanbur, 30–46. Stanford, CA: Stanford University Press, 2006.

———. *Development as Freedom*. New York: Anchor Books, 1999.

Seneze, Nicolas. "Jon Sobrino, Theologian of the Cry of the Poor." La Croix International, March 24, 2015. https://international.la-croix.com/news/jon-sobrino-theologian-of-the-cry-of-the-poor/979.

Shah, Anuj K., Sendhil Mullainathan, and Eldar Shafir. "Some Consequences of Having Too Little." *Science* 338, no. 6107 (November 2, 2012): 682–85. https://doi.org/10.1126/science.1222426.

Sharma, Preeti, Saba Waheed, Vina Nguyen, Lina Stepick, Reyna Orellana, Liana Katz, Sabrina Kim, and Katrina Lapira. "Nail Files: A Study of Nail Salon Workers and Industry in the United States." UCLA Labor Center and California Healthy Nail Salon Collaborative. www.labor.ucla.edu/wp-content/uploads/2018/11/NAILFILES_FINAL.pdf.

Sheffield, Rachel, and Robert Rector. "Air Conditioning, Cable TV, and an Xbox: What Is Poverty in the United States Today?" Heritage Foundation, July 19, 2011. http://poverty-and-inequality/report/air-conditioning-cable-tv-and-xbox-what-poverty-the-united-states.

Sherman, Jennifer. *Those Who Work, Those Who Don't: Poverty, Morality, and Family in Rural America*. Minneapolis: University of Minnesota Press, 2009.

Siepierski, Paulo. "Poverty and Spirituality: Saint Basil and Liberation Theology." *Greek Orthodox Theological Review* 31, no. 3 (1988): 313–26.

Singer, Peter. "The Logic of Effective Altruism." *Boston Review*, July 6, 2015. https://bostonreview.net/forum/peter-singer-logic-effective-altruism.

Smarsh, Sarah. *Heartland: A Memoir of Working Hard and Being Broke in the Richest Country on Earth*. New York: Scribner, 2018.

———. "Poor Teeth." *Aeon*, October 23, 2014. https://aeon.co/essays/there-is-no-shame-worse-than-poor-teeth-in-a-rich-world.

Smeeding, Timothy M., Markus Jäntti, and Robert Erikson. "Introduction." In *Persistence, Privilege, and Parenting: The Comparative Study of Intergenerational Mobility*, 1–26. New York: Russell Sage Foundation, 2011.

Smith, Megan V., Anna Kruse, Alison Weir, and Joanne Goldblum. "Diaper Need and Its Impact on Child Health." *Pediatrics* 132, no. 2 (August 2013): 253–59. https://doi.org/10.1542/peds.2013-0597.

Snarr, C. Melissa. "Elaborating Faith: Labor and Interfaith Resistance to Economic Inequality." *Journal of Religious Ethics* 45, no. 2 (June 2017): 255–77.

Sniegocki, John. *Catholic Social Teaching and Economic Globalization: The Quest for Alternatives*. Milwaukee: Marquette University Press, 2009.

Sobrino, Jon. "Awakening from the Sleep of Inhumanity." *Christian Century*, April 3, 1991, 364–70.

———. "Death and the Hope for Life." *Church and Society*, November–December 1981, 24–30.

———. "Poverty Means Death to the Poor." *Cross Currents*, Fall 1986, 267–76.

Spohn, William C. "The Return of Virtue Ethics." *Theological Studies* 53, no. 1 (March 1992): 60–75.

Statman, Daniel, ed. *Moral Luck*. Albany: State University of New York Press, 1993.

Stellar, Jennifer E., Vida M. Manzo, Michael W. Kraus, and Dacher Keltner. "Class and Compassion: Socioeconomic Factors Predict Responses to Suffering." *Emotion* 12, no. 3 (June 2012): 449–59. https://doi.org/10.1037/a0026508.

Stern, Ken. "Why the Rich Don't Give to Charity." *Atlantic*, April 2013. www.theatlantic.com/magazine/archive/2013/04/why-the-rich-dont-give/309254/.

Student Union of Michigan. "Graduate Student Workers of the World, Collectivize Your Stipends!" Blog, April 4, 2014. https://studentunionofmichigan.wordpress.com/2014/04/04/graduate-student-workers-of-the-world-collectivize-your-stipends/.

Supiano, Beckie. "College and Class: 2 Researchers Study Inequality, Starting with One Freshman Floor." *Chronicle of Higher Education*, April 1, 2013. http://chronicle.com/article/CollegeClass/138223/.

Tanner, Kathryn. *Christianity and the New Spirit of Capitalism*. New Haven, CT: Yale University Press, 2019.

———. "Inequality and Finance-Dominated Capitalism: Recommendations for Further Reading." *Anglican Theological Review* 98, no. 1 (2016): 157–73.

———. *The Politics of God: Christian Theologies and Social Justice*. Minneapolis: Fortress Press, 1992.

Tarimo, Aquiline. "Globalization and African Economic Reforms." In *Applied Ethics in a World Church: The Padua Conference*, edited by Linda Hogan, 32–38. Maryknoll, NY: Orbis Books, 2008.

Tessman, Lisa. *Burdened Virtues: Virtue Ethics for Liberatory Struggles*. New York: Oxford University Press, 2005.

———. *Moral Failure: On the Impossible Demands of Morality*. New York: Oxford University Press, 2015.

Therborn, Göran. *The Killing Fields of Inequality*. Cambridge: Polity, 2013.

Tirado, Linda. *Hand to Mouth: Living in Bootstrap America*. New York: Putnam Adult, 2014.

Tirimanna, Vimal, C.Ss.R. "Globalization Needs to Count Human Persons." In *Catholic Theological Ethics in the World Church: The Plenary Papers from the First Cross-Cultural Conference on Catholic Theological Ethics*, edited by James F. Keenan, 245–52. New York: Continuum, 2007.

Townes, Emilie M. "To Be Called Beloved: Womanist Ontology in Postmodern Refraction." In *Womanist Theological Ethics: A Reader*, edited by Katie Cannon, Emilie Maureen Townes, and Angela D. Sims, 183–202. Louisville: Westminster John Knox Press, 2011.

United Nations Development Program. "Multidimensional Poverty Index (MPI)." In *Human Development Report*, various years. http://hdr.undp.org/en/content/multidimensional-poverty-index-mpi.

US Bureau of Labor Statistics. "Consumer Expenditures Surveys Glossary." February 13, 2015. https://www.bls.gov/cex/csxgloss.htm#inc.

US Conference of Catholic Bishops. "Economic Justice for All: Pastoral Letter on Catholic Social Teaching and the US Economy," 1986. www.usccb.org/upload/economic_justice_for_all.pdf.

US Department of Agriculture, Economic Research Service. "Definitions of Food Security," September 4, 2019. www.ers.usda.gov/topics/food-nutrition-assistance/food-security-in-the-us/definitions-of-food-security.aspx.

US Department of Health and Human Services, Office of the Assistant Secretary for Planning and Evaluation. "Poverty Guidelines." January 15, 2020. https://aspe.hhs.gov/poverty-guidelines.

US Department of Housing and Urban Development, Office of Policy Development and Research. "Measuring Housing Insecurity in the American Housing Survey." No date. www.huduser.gov/portal/pdredge/pdr-edge-frm-asst-sec-111918.html.

Van Dam, Andrew. "What Percent Are You?" *Wall Street Journal*, March 2, 2016. http://graphics.wsj.com/what-percent/.

van der Hoeven, Rolph. "Income Distribution." In *Handbook of Economics and Ethics*, edited by Jan Peil and Irene van Staveren, 252–60. Northampton, MA: Edward Elgar, 2009.

Vazquez-Torres, Jessica. "Does Moral Injury Have A Race? On Moral Injury and the Experience of Racialization in the United States." Paper presented at Moral Injury and Recovery section at American Academy of Religion 2014 annual meeting.

Venkatesh, Sudhir Alladi. *Off the Books: The Underground Economy of the Urban Poor*. Cambridge, MA: Harvard University Press, 2006.

Vogt, Christopher P. "Fostering a Catholic Commitment to the Common Good: An Approach Rooted in Virtue Ethics." *Theological Studies* 68, no. 2 (June 2007): 394–417.

———. *Patience, Compassion, Hope, and the Christian Art of Dying Well*. Lanham, MD: Rowman & Littlefield, 2004.

Vries, J. P. de (Jurjen Pieter). "Moral Considerations Concerning Income Inequality." *In Die Skriflig* 49, no. 1 (2015): 170–78. https://doi.org/10.4102/ids.v49i1.1846.

Wadell, Paul J. *Happiness and the Christian Moral Life: An Introduction to Christian Ethics*. Lanham, MD: Rowman & Littlefield, 2007.

Walasek, Lukasz, Sudeep Bhatia, and Gordon D. A. Brown. "Positional Goods and the Social Rank Hypothesis: Income Inequality Affects Online Chatter about High- and Low-Status Brands on Twitter." *Journal of Consumer Psychology* 28, no. 1 (January 1, 2018): 138–48. https://doi.org/10.1002/jcpy.1012.

Waliggo, John Mary. "A Call for Prophetic Action." In *Catholic Theological Ethics in the World Church: The Plenary Papers from the First Cross-Cultural Conference on Catholic Theological Ethics*, edited by James F. Keenan, 252–61. New York: Continuum, 2007.

Walker, Margaret Urban. "Moral Luck and the Virtues of Impure Agency." In *Moral Contexts*, 21–34. Lanham, MD: Rowman & Littlefield, 2003.

Walzer, Michael. *Spheres of Justice: A Defense of Pluralism and Equality*. New York: Basic Books, 1983.

Ward, Jesmyn. *Men We Reaped: A Memoir*. New York: Bloomsbury, 2013.

Ward, Kate. "Capital in the 21st Century 2/2: Piketty and CST." Political Theology Today blog, August 18, 2014. www.politicaltheology.com/blog/capital-in-the-twenty-first-century-22 -piketty-and-cst-kate-ward/.

———. "Does Catholic Social Teaching Support a Universal Basic Income?" *US Catholic Magazine*—Faith in Real Life blog, April 13, 2020. https://uscatholic.org/articles /202004/does-catholic-social-teaching-support-a-universal-basic-income/.

———. "Ethics as a Work of Charity: Thomas Aquinas and Pagan Virtue [Book Review]." *Political Theology* 17, no. 2 (March 2016): 219–21. https://doi.org/10.1080/1462317X .2016.1161318.

———. "Jesuit and Feminist Hospitality: Pope Francis' Virtue Response to Inequality." *Religions* 8, no. 4 (April 19, 2017): 71. https://doi.org/10.3390/rel8040071.

———. "'Mere Poverty Excites Little Compassion': Adam Smith, Moral Judgment and the Poor." *Heythrop Journal* 61, no. 1 (n.d.): 97–114. https://doi.org/10.1111/heyj.12260.

———. "Moral Injury and Virtue Ethics: Understanding the Moral Impact of Poverty." Paper presented at American Academy of Religion meeting, Atlanta, November 21, 2015.

———. "Porters to Heaven: Wealth, The Poor, and Moral Agency in Augustine." *Journal of Religious Ethics* 42, no. 2 (June 1, 2014): 216–42.

———. "Toward a Christian Virtue Account of Moral Luck." *Journal of the Society of Christian Ethics* 38, no. 1 (2018): 131–45.

———. "Universal Basic Income and Work in Catholic Social Thought." *American Journal of Economics & Sociology* 79, no. 4 (September 2020): 1271–1306.

———. "Wealthy Hyperagency in the Throwaway Culture: Inequality and Environmental Death." In *Integral Ecology for a More Sustainable World: Dialogues with Laudato si',* edited by Dennis O'Hara, Matthew Eaton, Michael T. Ross, and Peter Turkson, 77–90. Lanham, MD: Lexington Books, 2019.

———. "Wealth, Poverty, and Personal Holiness." In *The T&T Clark Handbook of Christian Ethics,* edited by Tobias Winright, 373–82. London: T&T Clark, 2021.

Ward, Kate, and Kenneth R. Himes, eds. *Growing Apart: Religious Reflection on the Rise of Economic Inequality.* Basel: MDPI, 2019.

Waterman, A. M. C. "Inequality and Social Evil: Wilkinson and Pickett on the Spirit Level." *Faith & Economics* 63 (2014): 38–49.

Waterman, Anthony Michael C., and Geoffrey Brennan. "Christian Theology and Economics: Convergence and Clashes." In *Christian Theology and Market Economics,* edited by Ian R. Harper and Samuel Gregg, 77–93. Northampton, MA: Edward Elgar, 2008.

Weaver, Darlene Fozard. *Self Love and Christian Ethics.* New York: Cambridge University Press, 2002.

Weisheipl, James A. *Friar Thomas D'Aquino: His Life, Thought, and Works: With Corrigenda and Addenda.* Washington, DC: Catholic University of America Press, 1983.

Weithman, Paul. "Religious Ethics and Economic Inequality." *Journal of Religious Ethics* 47, no. 2 (June 2019): 223–31. https://doi.org/10.1111/jore.12265.

Welby, Justin. "Does Inequality Really Matter?" *Anglican Theological Review* 98, no. 1 (2016): 7–13.

West, Traci. "A Response to Rebecca Todd Peters." In *Religion, Economics, and Culture in Conflict and Conversation,* edited by Laurie M. Cassidy and Maureen H. O'Connell, 80–81. College Theology Society, Annual Volume 56. Maryknoll, NY: Orbis Books, 2011.

Wheeler, Sondra Ely. *Wealth as Peril and Obligation: The New Testament on Possessions.* Grand Rapids: William B. Eerdmans, 1995.

Wick, Julia. "Interview: 'Poor Teeth' Writer Sarah Smarsh on Class and Journalism." Longreads blog, November 7, 2014. https://longreads.com/2014/11/07/interview-poor-teeth-writer -sarah-smarsh-on-class-and-journalism/.

Wiinikka-Lydon, Joseph. "Moral Injury as Inherent Political Critique: The Prophetic Possibilities of a New Term." *Political Theology* 18, no. 3 (2017): 219–32. https://doi.org/10 .1080/1462317X.2012.1104205.

Wilcox, W. Bradford, and Wendy Wang. "The Marriage Divide: How and Why Working-Class Families Are More Fragile Today." Opportunity America–AEI–Brookings, September 2017. www.aei.org/wp-content/uploads/2017/09/The-Marriage-Divide.pdf.

Williams, Bernard. "Moral Luck." In *Moral Luck,* edited by Daniel Statman, 35–55. Albany: State University of New York Press, 1993.

Williams, Delores S. "A Womanist Perspective on Sin." In *Womanist Theological Ethics: A Reader,* edited by Katie Cannon, Emilie Maureen Townes, and Angela D. Sims, 130–47. Louisville: Westminster John Knox Press, 2011.

Wilson, Mark A. "Moral Grief and Reflective Virtue." In *Virtue and the Moral Life: Theological and Philosophical Perspectives,* edited by William Werpehowski and Kathryn Getek Soltis, 57–73. Lanham, MD: Lexington Books, 2014.

Wood, Graeme. "Secret Fears of the Super-Rich." *Atlantic*, April 2011. www.theatlantic.com /magazine/archive/2011/04/secret-fears-of-the-super-rich/308419/.

———. "Who Are the Millionaires?" *National Review* blog, December 19, 2012. www .nationalreview.com/magazine/2012/12/31/who-are-millionaires/.

World Health Organization. "New Report Shows That 400 Million Do Not Have Access to Essential Health Services." June 12, 2015. www.who.int/mediacentre/news/releases/2015 /uhc-report/en/.

Yáñez, Humberto Miguel. "Opting for the Poor in the Face of Growing Poverty." In *Applied Ethics in a World Church: The Padua Conference*, edited by Linda Hogan, 13–20. Maryknoll, NY: Orbis Books, 2008.

Yohe, Katherine M. "Dorothy Day: Love for One's Daughter and Love for the Poor." *Horizons* 31, no. 2 (Fall 2004): 272–301.

Yuengert, Andrew M. "What Is 'Sustainable Prosperity for All' in the Catholic Social Tradition?" In *The True Wealth of Nations: Catholic Social Thought and Economic Life*, edited by Daniel K. Finn, 37–62. New York: Oxford University Press, 2010.

Zamagni, Stefano. "Catholic Social Thought, Civil Economy, and the Spirit of Capitalism." In *The True Wealth of Nations: Catholic Social Thought and Economic Life*, edited by Daniel K. Finn, 64–93. New York: Oxford University Press, 2010.

Zinsmeister, Karl. "Oseola McCarty." Philanthropy Roundtable, n.d. www.philanthropy roundtable.org/almanac/hall_of_fame/oseola_mccarty.

INDEX

ABOUT THE AUTHOR

KATE WARD, who received her PhD from Boston College in 2016, is an assistant professor of theology at Marquette University. Her research engages topics including wealth and poverty, work, virtue, and ethical method, and has appeared in journals including *Theological Studies*, the *Journal of Religious Ethics, American Journal of Economics and Sociology,* and the *Journal of the Society of Christian Ethics.* Ward holds a bachelor's degree in psychology and an M.Div. from Catholic Theological Union. She worked in the labor movement before earning her PhD.